INNOVATION
AND
CREATIVITY
AT WORK

. . . there is no more delicate matter to take in hand, nor more dangerous to conduct, nor more doubtful in its success, than to set up as a leader in the introduction of changes. For he who innovates will have for his enemies all those who are well off under the existing order of things and only lukewarm supporters in those who might be better off under the new. This lukewarm temper arises partly from the fear of adversaries who have the laws on their side, and partly from the incredulity of mankind who will never admit the merit of anything new, until they have seen it proved by the event.

Niccolò Machiavelli, *The Prince*

INNOVATION AND CREATIVITY AT WORK

PSYCHOLOGICAL AND ORGANIZATIONAL STRATEGIES

Edited by

MICHAEL A. WEST
University of Sheffield, UK

and

JAMES L. FARR
Pennsylvania State University, USA

JOHN WILEY & SONS
CHICHESTER · NEW YORK · BRISBANE · TORONTO · SINGAPORE

Other Wiley Editorial Offices

John Wiley & Sons, Inc., 605 Third Avenue,
New York, NY 10158-0012, USA

Jacaranda Wiley Ltd, G.P.O. Box 859, Brisbane,
Queensland 4001, Australia

John Wiley & Sons (Canada) Ltd, 22 Worcester Road,
Rexdale, Ontario M9W 1L1, Canada

John Wiley & Sons (SEA) Pte Ltd, 37 Jalan Pemimpin 05-04,
Block B, Union Industrial Building, Singapore 2057

Library of Congress Cataloging-in-Publication Data:
Innovation and creativity at work : psychological and organizational
strategies / edited by Michael A. West and James L. Farr.
p. cm.
Includes bibliographical references.
ISBN 0 471 92655 8
1. Organizational change. 2. Creative ability in business.
I. West, Michael A. II. Farr, James L.
HD58.8.I56 1990
658.4′063—dc20   89—21460
                                                        CIP

British Library Cataloguing in Publication Data:
Innovation and creativity at work.
1. Organization development
I. West, Michael A. II. Farr, James L.
658.406

ISBN 0 471 92655 8 (ppc)
ISBN 0 477 93187 x (pbk)

Typeset by Photo-graphics, Honiton, Devon
Printed and bound in Great Britain by Courier International Ltd., East Kilbride

Contents

Contributors

Dr Neil Anderson
MRC/ESRC Social and Applied Psychology Unit, Department of Psychology, University of Sheffield, Sheffield S10 2TN, UK

Robert M. Burnside
Center for Creative Leadership, 5000 Laurinda Drive, P O Box P-1, North Carolina 27402-1660, USA

Professor Fariborz Damanpour
Graduate School of Management, Rutgers University, 92 New Street, Newark, New Jersey 07102, USA

Professor James L. Farr
Department of Psychology, Pennsylvania State University, University Park, Pennsylvania 16802, USA

Professor Cameron M. Ford
Graduate School of Management, Rutgers University, 92 New Street, Newark, New Jersey 07102, USA

Professor Dr Siegfried Greif
Fachbereich Psychologie, Universität Osnabrück, Postfach 4469, D-4500 Osnabrück, West Germany

Alan L. Hillman
Department of Management, The Wharton School of the University of Pennsylvania, 2000 Steinberg Hall-Dietrich Hall, Philadelphia, Pennsylvania 19104-6370, USA

Professor Dr Heidi Keller
Fachbereich Psychologie, Universität Osnabrück, Postfach 4469, D-4500 Osnabrück, West Germany

Professor John R. Kimberley
Department of Management, The Wharton School of the University of Pennsylvania, 2000 Steinberg Hall-Dietrich Hall, Philadelphia, Pennsylvania 19104-6370, USA

Dr Nigel King
Centre for Primary Care Research, The Department of General Practice, University of Manchester, Rusholme Health Centre, Walmer Street, Manchester, M14 5NP, UK

Dr Nigel Nicholson
MRC/ESRC Social and Applied Psychology Unit, Department of Psychology, University of Sheffield, Sheffield S10 2TN, UK

Professor Harry Nyström
Department of Marketing, Institute for Economics, Box 7013, S-750 07, Uppsala, Sweden

Mark V. Pauly
Department of Management, The Wharton School of the University of Pennsylvania, 2000 Steinberg Hall-Dietrich Hall, Philadelphia, Pennsylvania 19104-6370, USA

Professor Roy Payne
Manchester Business School, Booth Street West, Manchester M15 6PB, UK

Laura R. Renshaw
Department of Management, The Wharton School of the University of Pennsylvania, 2000 Steinberg Hall-Dietrich Hall, Philadelphia, Pennsylvania 19104-6370, USA

Robert Rosenfeld
Idea Connection Systems Inc., 2065 Highland Avenue, Rochester, New York 14620, USA

J. Sanford Schwartz
Department of Management, The Wharton School of the University of Pennsylvania, 2000 Steinberg Hall-Dietrich Hall, Philadelphia, Pennsylvania 19104-6370, USA

Dr Jenny C. Servo
Dawnbreaker Inc., 3999 Buffalo Road, Rochester, New York 14620, USA

Jill D. Teplensky
Department of Management, The Wharton School of the University of Pennsylvania, 2000 Steinberg Hall-Dietrich Hall, Philadelphia, Pennsylvania 19104-6370, USA

Professor Barry M. Staw
School of Business Administration, University of California, Berkeley, California 94720, USA

Dr Michael A. West
MRC/ESRC Social and Applied Psychology Unit, Department of Psychology, University of Sheffield, Sheffield S10 2TN, UK

Preface

Judging by the volume of literature dedicated to this subject, innovation in work organizations has long been of great concern to social scientists and as research funds are increasingly directed towards subjects which are thought to be practically relevant, the area is attracting even more attention. However, the enormous volume of research and writing on innovation has failed to produce the advances in understanding for practitioners or researchers which might reasonably be expected from such an investment of intelligence and energy. In this volume the topic of innovation is discussed generally and terms used are carefully described. The research is reviewed and suggestions for alternative theoretical and research directions are put forward. It is argued that significant advances in understanding innovation at work can come from combining psychological approaches to the subject with the dominant organizational orientation in the existing research literature.

The book is divided into five parts. The first provides a discussion of *definitional issues and literature review*. In the introductory chapter conceptual overlaps with topics such as creativity in the existing psychological literature are explored. Different types of innovation at work are briefly described and a typology is suggested which distinguishes between innovations at the individual, group and organizational levels of analysis. In the literature review this distinction is maintained to clarify the literature and come to clearer understandings about innovation at each of these levels.

In Part II research on *individual and group innovation* is described. In particular Farr and Ford (Chapter 3) focus on the individual level of analysis and offer a new model for understanding individual innovation. King and Anderson (Chapter 4) describe studies which explore processes and correlates of innovation in elderly care institutions. They empirically compare existing process models of group innovation before proposing new strategies for research. Payne (Chapter 5) examines important and previously neglected research on effectiveness, innovation and creativity among research and development teams which points up important methodological issues in the area.

The third part of the book is dedicated to an exploration of *organizational level innovation* and four differing orientations are proposed. Each promises to advance theorizing by alerting us to the complexity of this topic. Damanpour urges a consideration of the different types of innovation (Chapter

xi

6); Nyström integrates structure, strategy and environment into a model of innovation (Chapter 7) and Kimberly *et al.* (Chapter 8) focus on consequences of innovation and alert us to the pro-innovation bias (innovation is good for the organization and good for all within it). Finally, Nicholson (Chapter 9) presents a careful and incisive analysis of the meaning of innovation and how the hidden assumptions of researchers, theoreticians and practitioners act as invisible rudders determining the directions and outcomes of their work.

The fourth part of the book focuses on *interventions* to facilitate innovation and creativity in work settings. Farr (Chapter 10) critically assesses the methods described in the existing literature for facilitating individual innovation. His chapter describes how individual approaches can be developed which utilize existing knowledge in the areas of attitude change and communication and argues that a research based approach is particularly effective for facilitating individual innovation at work. Greif and Keller (Chapter 11), in a boundary spanning chapter, show how work on exploratory behaviour in developmental psychology can be used to promote innovation in work settings. Rosenfeld and Servo (Chapter 12) describe the process by which internal change agencies can facilitate organizational innovation while in Chapter 13, Burnside describes a management method for answering important questions regarding creativity in organizations. All four chapters combine to offer very practical strategies for facilitating innovation.

In the final section the theme is *integration*. Staw (Chapter 14) produces a model of individual creativity and organizational innovation, blending psychological and organizational approaches. West in the final chapter focuses upon group level innovation and draws upon the research literature to generate a new theory of group innovation. He also integrates facilitator and process approaches for modelling innovation at work.

This then describes the structure of the book which has been collectively and carefully sculpted by the contributors. We as editors hoped to achieve a number of aims with the production of this book: to define what is meant by innovation and creativity at work and to provide cases as examples; to illustrate interventions to facilitate innovation at work; to present an accessible overview of existing research in the area; to present models of innovation and creativity at work; to integrate the ideas and experiences of researchers and practitioners; and finally to combine the ideas of academics and practitioners from America and Europe in one volume. By this we hope, in some measure, to have advanced understanding of what we believe to be an important aspect of change constantly impacting upon the lives of people in the world of work.

Michael A. West and James L. Farr
September 1989

Acknowledgements

We would like to thank a number of individuals and organizations whose support has enabled the production of this book. Our two institutions—the MRC/ESRC Social and Applied Psychology Unit, University of Sheffield, and the Department of Psychology, Pennsylvania State University—provided the support for James Farr's sabbatical trip to Sheffield which began our association. In particular Peter Warr and Nigel Nicholson were especially helpful in making James' transition an easy one. Frank Landy and John Mathieu of Pennsylvania State University gave helpful comments on earlier versions of chapters and the general concept of the volume as a whole. Kathryn Hewitt carefully prepared the manuscript and took on the administration load associated with producing an edited volume. Wendy Hudlass at Wiley has been both patient and supportive. Finally, we would like to thank the contributors for their co-operation with us and their commitment to the idea of the volume.

James L. Farr and Michael A. West
September 1989

Part I
Definitions and Previous Research

1 Innovation at work

Michael A. West and James L. Farr

University of Sheffield, UK, and Pennsylvania State University, USA

INTRODUCTION

Two major challenges which face us now more than ever are how to adapt successfully to change and how to bring about change in environments which are not conducive to our well-being and effectiveness. Work environments in particular are often directly damaging to health and well-being with stressors causing both physical and psychological damage to people (Cooper, 1986). Research among managers also indicates that their self-concepts at work are significantly less positive than their self-concepts outside work (Nicholson and West, 1988). The study of innovation and creativity at work promises strategies for meeting the challenge of how to bring about change in work environments. There is evidence that those who have opportunities to manipulate their work environments and to be creative at work are more satisfied and better adjusted than those with fewer opportunities (Broadbent, 1987; Nicholson and West, 1988).

But there are broader reasons beyond those concerned with immediately psychological issues for studying creativity and innovation at work. Innovation and creativity are often associated not only with economic prosperity but with specific advances in knowledge which improve the health and welfare of many in the population—ethically guided advances in medicine, education, science and psychology are examples. Moreover many of the most pressing human problems are institutionalized and it is only by bringing about innovative change that many of these problems can be overcome. For example, social systems and structures which institutionalize inequalities in resource and opportunity distribution within communities can promote alienation and inter-group hostility. Effective responses to these problems require changes

Innovation and Creativity at Work   Edited by M.A. West and J.L. Farr
© 1990 John Wiley & Sons Ltd

not only in individual behaviour but innovative change in the organizations and institutions which perpetuate them. As Zaltman *et al.* (1973) have argued: 'The importance of new ideas cannot be overstated. Ideas and their manifestations as practices or products are at the core of social change.'

Recently, research on innovation has spread from the administrative sciences, communications, and anthropology to psychology and sociology. This spread has been slow, partly perhaps because the study of innovation has been considered the domain of business management rather than human behaviour. Yet, as this volume will suggest, it is precisely within the discipline of psychology that the study of innovation most appropriately fits.

The interest of psychologists in creativity, in contrast, has a history almost as long as the history of contemporary psychology itself. It has occupied a central part in theorizing about individual differences and cognitive processes. Much of this work on creativity has examined individual differences in creativity as a personality trait or has focused on the creative products such as works of art, music and scientific discoveries. The concept of creativity as something expressed in a variety of ways in people's working lives, whether they be administrators, managers or artists, is new. However, in this volume it is suggested that an understanding of creativity may be considerably deepened by considering it in the context of work. It is suggested that far from being an isolated indication of genius, creative expression in the world of work is manifested by almost everyone, given the appropriate facilitating environmental conditions.

In this chapter we will give examples of innovation drawn from different literatures and highlight important components of the concept. The value, both theoretical and applied, of studying the psychology of innovation will be discussed, and innovation will be defined and distinguished from creativity and change. Finally, we will pose what we see as the major questions to be answered in a book dedicated to an understanding of the psychology of creativity and innovation at work.

INNOVATION

Examples of innovations which have been the subject of study abound in the literature. For example, Carlson (1976) studied the introduction of a Dial-a-Ride public transport system in Santa Clara County, California (an innovation that failed). Pelto (1973) examined the introduction of the snowmobile among the Skolt Lapps, a reindeer herding people who live in northern Finland. Rogers (1983) describes the spread of solar homes in one neighbourhood of California; the introduction of water boiling in a Peruvian village; the control of scurvy in the British Navy and the non-diffusion of the Dvorak keyboard. Kimberly (1981) has provided a first review of literature concerning managerial (as opposed to product) innovations. Gross *et al.* (1971) illustrate the introduction of a new role model for teachers, and Shaw (1985) describes the development of a neo-natal oxygen monitoring system. King and West (1987), in studies of less dramatic innovations at work, describe the introduction of cassette recorders by school inspectors to record the details of their visits, and West (1989) describes innovations introduced by health visitors (public health nurses) in Britain in the course of their day-to-day work. In Chapter 2, King will discuss the value of categorizing research in this area by level of analysis (e.g. individual, work group and organization). Here we will adopt this categorization to give examples of innovation and creativity at work at each level.

Individual

In a study of a sample of 92 health visitors (public health nurses) constituting 90% of those in one English city, West (1989) elicited 145 examples of innovations introduced in the previous year. The health visitors were asked to indicate whether they had initiated changes in each of four job areas: changed your work objectives or introduced new work objectives; changed your working methods; changed whom you deal with or how you deal with people; learned new skills. Innovations were rated on impact upon jobs, clients and colleagues, and supervisors were asked to rate each health visitor's innovativeness in the previous year.

Thirty eight per cent of respondents reported making changes in objectives, for example 'making ante-natal visits a priority'; 'introducing new developmental assessment sessions for four year olds'; 'increasing visits to infants at risk of cot death (sudden infant death syndrome)'. Many (31%) reported changing their working methods: 'setting up new office systems for stationery, restocking and filing'; 'taking action within 24 hours of a visit to a client and writing up notes immediately after the visit'; 'carrying out all developmental assessments on infants in the home rather than the clinic'. Seventeen per cent reported changing relationships: 'introducing regular case discussions with the social worker'; 'giving better support to student health visitors by organizing visiting and planning days out with them'; 'making contact with community workers within ethnic minority groups'. Some reported new skills as innovations at work, e.g. 'I have taken family planning training and now discuss this with each new mother'; 'I have started to learn Bengali and can now work with clients who speak only a little or no English'.

While it might be argued that some of these innovations are trivial in comparison with say, the development of neo-natal monitoring systems, this begs the question of how the significance of an innovation is to be judged. For the new mother who speaks no English, the visit of a nurse with some ability to communicate in her native language may represent a release from an enormous burden of uncertainty and anxiety. For the person innovating too some changes, which might seem unremarkable or commonplace to an outsider, may have a major impact upon her work. Setting up liaison meetings to discuss cases with other professionals is clearly not new in the helping professions but may represent a major new step forward for the individual initiating such liaison for the first time.

Work group

West and Wallace (1988) studied examples of work group innovation in eight primary health care teams consisting of doctors, nurses, social workers and health visitors. Statements about innovations introduced by the team within the previous two years were gathered from all members of the team. The list of innovations for each team was then rated by outside experts on the innovativeness of the practice and a high degree of concordance was obtained.

The teams varied in the quality and quantity of innovation introduced. In one the emphasis was on identifying and supporting particular at-risk groups: diabetic clinic set up; cervical smear clinic set up; weight support group set up; recall system for cervical cytology; increased use of age/sex register to identify at-risk groups. In another team the concern was with innovations in work group processes: seminar/discussion sessions at team meetings; collective decision-making and management; involvement of non-doctors in 'clinical' decision-making; equal pay structure; collective working. A third team described innovations largely involving the use of computers: 'computerisation of patient records; computerised recall of at-risk groups; computerised repeat prescribing'. Another team was emphasizing the type of health care provided: 'more emphasis placed on counselling as a form of treatment rather than medical drugs; holistic approach to patient care; patient access to medical records; regular relaxation classes set up; patients encouraged to take part in decision-making processes during consultations about treatment and options, enabling them to see some pattern of health and illness emerging'.

Clearly then, innovations vary widely in content even within groups which have similar structures and objectives. Consequently, it is important to note that judging innovativeness cannot always be accomplished by comparing a group's performance with a pre-determined list of what constitutes innovation as has sometimes been done (see, for example, Kimberly et al., Chapter 8 in this volume). Moreover, it can be seen that what one group may regard as innovative, another may see as folly. Innovation does not spell success. Some innovations fail while others prove disastrous. Kimberly (1981) has referred to the pro-innovation bias in the literature and counsels reseachers to pay attention to exnovation—the process by which a failing innovation is rejected or an innovation whose life course is complete is terminated.

Organization

The consideration of innovation at the organizational level leads to very difficult issues of definition and differentiation as will become clear in subsequent chapters. Zaltman *et al.* (1973) have suggested a number of dimensions for differentiating between innovations, and one of the most used and clearly most important is that of *routine–radical*.

The distinction between *routine* and *radical* innovation has been suggested to illustrate how organizations may need to deal with various innovations in importantly different ways (Nord and Tucker, 1987). A routine innovation is the introduction of something similar to previous organizational practice, although its specifics are new to the organization. A radical innovation, again new in its specifics for the organization, is also very different from what the organization has done before, thus is more disruptive and requires more change within the organization.

Nord and Tucker (1987) investigated the factors that facilitated the implementation of routine and radical innovations within 12 US financial organizations. The various organizations were each instituting on the same day a new financial product, a Negotiated Order of Withdrawal (NOW) account, which is an interest-bearing cheque (checking) account. One-half of the organizations were commercial banks which had offered cheque accounts for many years. The other six organizations studied were savings and loan associations which previously had not been allowed to offer this type of product. For the banks the NOW account was a routine innovation; for the savings and loan associations it was a radical innovation. It should be noted that the NOW accounts were tightly regulated by law and thus the 12 organizations were introducing virtually identical products in terms of operating characteristics.

Results of the Nord and Tucker study indicated that successful routine innovation was facilitated by achieving consistency with existing organizational policies and procedures. Those organizations that were competent in the conduct of previously offered similar products best implemented the NOW accounts by doing things in the same general way. For radical innovations, however, changing the past ways of thinking and acting were often required in order to be successful in the implementation. Other factors of importance seem to be open communication channels, upward and lateral as well as downward, and the creation of an organizational structure that was focused toward task accomplishment.

Thus, we see that at all three levels, individual, group, and organization, innovations can range from the (relatively) simple to the complex. A common thread seems to be the relation of the 'objective' characteristics of the change (innovation) to the previous experience of the adopting entity with it or similar characteristics. The *novelty* for the individual, group, or organization may be a more salient feature of a proposed innovation rather than its *newness* in relation to some larger constituency. The definition of innovation is explored in more detail below.

Defining innovation

The term innovation is used in many different ways which appear to vary systematically with the level of analysis employed. The more macro the approach (e.g. societal and cultural) the more varied and amorphous does the usage of the term become. However, some useful distinctions have been drawn such as that between *technical, administrative* and *ancillary* innovations (Damanpour, 1987 and Chapter 6 in this book). Technical innovations are defined as those:

> . . . . *that occur in the technical systems of an organization and are directly related to the primary work activity of the organization. A technical innovation can be the implementation of an idea for a new product or a new service, or the introduction of new elements in an organization's production or service operations . . . administrative innovations are defined as those that occur in the social system of an organization . . . the implementation of a new way to recruit personnel, allocate resources and structure tasks, authority and rewards. It comprises innovations in organizational structure and in the management of people. (Damanpour, 1987)*

Ancillary innovations are organization–environment boundary innovations (see p. 127).

Following Schein (1971), Nicholson (1984) defines *role innovation* as the initiating of 'changes in task objectives, methods, materials, scheduling and in the interpersonal relationships integral to task performance'. Those moving into *newly created jobs* are also implicitly innovative in their task performance and given that, among British managers, between a third and a half of all job moves are into newly created jobs (West *et al.*, 1987) this category of innovation is of some importance. West (1987b) has distinguished between those innovations which represent new departures for the individual initiating them (*development*) and those which are carried over by the individual from one work role to another (*conversion*). We might also analyse innovations in terms of their consequences of *success* or *failure* as rated by both those initiating them and those affected by them. Such distinctions are by no means exhaustive but by considering the variation which can occcur within the class of innovations we may become more sensitive to the phenomenon we are attempting to understand.

Existing definitions of innovation range from highly specific foci on technical innovations to very broad generalizations, too imprecise to enable operationalization. Myers and Marquis (1969) define innovation as '. . . a complex activity which proceeds from the conceptualisation of a new idea to a solution of the problem and then to the actual utilisation of economic or social value. (Alternatively) innovation is not just the conception of a new idea, nor the invention of a new device, nor the development of a new market. The process is all of those things acting together in an integrated fashion.' Zaltman *et al.* (1973) define innovation as '. . . any idea, practice, or material artifact perceived to be new by the relevant unit of adoption' (p. 10). Kanter (1983) defines innovation as '. . . the process of bringing any new problem-solving idea into use. Ideas for reorganizing, cutting costs, putting in new budgetting systems, improving communication or assembling products in teams are also innovations. Innovation is the generation, acceptance, and implementation of new ideas, processes, products or services' (p. 20). Drucker (1985) argues that successful entrepreneurs must use 'systematic innovation' which 'consists in the purposeful and organized search for changes, and in the systematic analysis of the opportunities such changes might offer for economic and social innovation' (p. 31).

A number of existing definitions suggest that the value of innovations lies in their contributions to profits. This represents both a value assumption (that the seeking of profits is in the best interests of all those affected by the innovation) and a mistake, since innovation may not always be economically valuable for an organization (Kimberly, 1981). Analysis of definitions also reveals wide disparity between them but some common themes do emerge such as novelty (either absolute or novelty simply to the unit of adoption of the innovation); an application component (i.e. not just ideas but the application of ideas); intentionality of benefit (which distinguishes innovations from serendipitous change or deliberate sabotage), and some reference to the process of innovation.

We define innovation as *the intentional introduction and application within a role, group or organization of ideas, processes, products or procedures, new to the relevant unit of adoption, designed to significantly benefit the individual, the group, organization or wider society.* Several aspects of this definition may be highlighted. First, innovation is restricted to intentional attempts to derive anticipated benefits from change. Second, a broad perspective on the anticipated benefits is adopted, rather than using a sole criterion of economic benefit. Thus, possible benefits might be personal growth, increased satisfaction, improved group cohesiveness, better interpersonal communication, as well as those productivity and economic measures more usually invoked. The definition also allows for the introduction of a new idea designed not to benefit the role, group or organization, but to benefit the wider society. The introduction of community members onto the management boards of nuclear processing plants is an example of an innovation which might not benefit the organization though benefiting the wider society. Further, the definition is not restricted to technological change but subsumes new ideas or processes in administration or human resource management. Indeed it has been claimed that innovation occurs frequently in management methods and organizational practices as well as in technological domains, and that administrative innovation has a facilitating effect on technological innovation (Damanpour and Evan, 1984). The definition also requires an application component, thus encompassing what many would regard as the crucial social element of the process of innovation. Finally, the definition does not require absolute novelty of an idea, simply (following Zaltman *et al.*, 1973) that the idea be new to the relevant unit of adoption. So if an individual brings new ideas to an organization from his or her previous job, this would be considered an innovation within the terms of the definition.

INNOVATION, CREATIVITY AND CHANGE

How are the overlapping concepts of innovation, creativity and change to be distinguished? Rogers (1954) defined creativity as '. . . the emergence in action of a novel relational product, growing out of the uniqueness of the individual on the one hand, and the materials, events, people or circumstances of his life on the other'. He gave examples such as painting a picture, composing a symphony, devising new instruments of killing, developing a scientific theory, discovering new procedures in human relationships, or creating new formings of one's own personality in psychotherapy. Amabile (1983) defines creativity as 'the production of novel and appropriate ideas by one individual or a small group working together'. Amabile introduces the notion of appropriateness to distinguish the creative from the merely chaotic. The *Oxford English Dictionary* defines 'create' as 'bring into existence, give rise to'. To innovate is to 'bring in novelties, make changes'. The distinction is one of emphasis perhaps rather than category but creativity appears to be understood more as absolute novelty (bring into existence) rather than the relative novelty of innovation (bring in novelties). The concept of innovation is also concerned with broader processes of change in this definition. Another useful way of distinguishing the concepts is to see creativity as the ideation component of innovation and innovation as encompassing both the proposal and applications of the new ideas (see discussion of this idea by Rosenfeld and Servo in Chapter 12).

According to most definitions referred to above, innovation may involve creativity, as in the discovery and development of a new process for refining oil, but not all innovations will be creative. Setting up autonomous work groups for the first time in one factory may not be creative since their use is already widespread, but would be innovative since the innovation is new to the relevant unit of adoption (cf. Damanpour, 1987).

Innovation according to our definition also involves intentionality of benefit. Such intentionality may not exist, for example, in the case of a poet who writes creatively without expectation of benefit other than the reward of simply doing the writing. Innovation also has a clear social and applied component since it impacts directly or indirectly upon others affected by the role, or others in the work group, organization or wider society. This necessary applied social component perhaps most sharply distinguishes it from creativity. There is an interaction between those who innovate and those who are affected by the innovation and recognition that one's action will affect others will influence that action. Innovation is a social process with the elements of the process being events that occur between people whereas creativity is an individual cognitive process in which events occur within the person.

How is innovation at work to be distinguished from organizational change more generally? Certainly all innovation in organizational terms is change. But not all change is innovation. Thus unintended or undesired change, such as the necessity of cutting work time in a factory during a particularly hot summer, would not constitute innovation. Neither would change involving nothing new be considered as innovation—an example would be the routine laying-off of hotel staff in winter when bookings fall. Finally, many organizational changes occur without intentionality of direct benefit but are simple adjustments in response to routine changes in internal or external environmental conditions. Thus, the routine hiring of new staff on the retirement of others, or promotion based on strict criteria of length of service, would not be considered innovation.

These then are the main distinctions which can be drawn between innovation, creativity and change, and which, together with the definitional issues and case examples which have been described, paint a picture of the subject of this volume. But what is the purpose of this volume? It is to advance understanding of innovation and creativity at work by answering some major questions.

One of the first questions to be answered is how common is innovation at work? Studies of individuals, groups and organizations can provide indications of how frequently innovation occurs and the extent of its success, significance and predictability. Equally important is identifying the antecedents of innovations at the different levels. What factors prompt or are associated with the occurrence of innovation at work? Which of these have most influence and under what circumstances? Many researchers have focused on the facilitators and inhibitors (or drivers and barriers) of innovation (see, for example, West and Frei, 1989). Others have chosen to concentrate more on the processes of innovation, often viewing them as temporally based (e.g. Zaltman *et al.*, 1973). Perhaps one of the most neglected areas of study is the consequences of innovation. Kimberly (1981) has noted that researchers have given much attention to the initiation, adoption and diffusion of innovation but less to the outcomes of innovation and to the process of 'exnovation' (ending the innovation) in organizations.

These are primarily research based questions and practitioners will ask to what extent knowledge gained from research can be applied in work settings. Are we in a position as organizational scientists to offer prescriptions about strategies for innovation and predictions about the likely reactions of others to innovations? The literature on the management of innovation is growing but much of it is based on impressionistic and 'best guess' views of practitioners.

But perhaps most important is to ask to what extent theorizing in this area has enabled us to understand, predict and control innovation. Which theories of innovation aid us most in these tasks? Which are richest in generating testable hypotheses? And to what extent is it possible to generate psychological theories of innovation which apply across different work settings and at different levels of analysis (individual, work group and organizational)? It is the aim of this volume to provide answers to some at least of these important questions.

The helplessness of individuals and small groups in the face of large organizations and powerful social forces is a common theme in modern sociological and psychological literature. The study of innovation presents an optimistic picture of people's involvement in their social and organizational contexts, and promises to advance our understanding of how they can be effective in transforming and shaping organizations.

Correspondence addresses:
Dr Michael A. West, MRC/ESRC Social and Applied Psychology Unit, Department of Psychology, University of Sheffield, Sheffield S10 2TN, UK.
Professor James L. Farr, Department of Psychology, Pennsylvania State University, University Park, Pennsylvania 16802, USA.

REFERENCES

Amabile, T.M. (1983). *The Social Psychology of Creativity*. New York: Springer-Verlag.
Broadbent, D. (1987). Is autonomy always a good thing? *The Occupational Psychologist*, 1, 7–15.
Carlson, C. (1976). Anatomy of a systems failure: Dial-A-Ride in Santa Clara County, California. *Transportation*, 5, 3–16.
Cooper, C.L. (1986). Job distress: recent research and the emerging role of the clinical occupational psychologist. *Bulletin of the British Psychological Society*, 39, 325–331.
Damanpour, F. (1987). The adoption of technological, administrative and ancillary innovations: impact of organizational factors. *Journal of Management*, 13, 675–688.

Damanpour, F. and Evan, W.M. (1984). Organizational innovation and performance: the problem of 'organizational lag'. *Administrative Science Quarterly, 29*, 392–409.

Drucker, P.F. (1985). *Innovation and Entrepreneurship: Practice and Principles.* London: Heinemann.

Gross, N., Giacquinta, J.B. and Bernstein, M. (1971). *Implementing Organizational Innovations: A Sociological Analysis of Planned Educational Change.* New York: Basic Books.

Kanter, R.M. (1983). *The Change Masters.* New York: Simon and Schuster.

Kimberly, J.R. (1981). Managerial innovation. In P.C. Nystrom and W.H. Starbuck (Eds.), *Handbook of Organizational Design.* Oxford: Oxford University Press.

King, N. and West, M.A. (1987). Experiences of innovation at work. *Journal of Managerial Psychology, 2*, 6–7.

Myers, S. and Marquis, D.G. (1969). *Successful Industrial Innovations.* National Science Foundation, NSF, 69–17.

Nicholson, N. (1984). A theory of work role transitions. *Administrative Science Quarterly, 29*, 172–191.

Nicholson, N. and West, M.A. (1988). *Managerial Job Change: Men and Women in Transition.* Cambridge: Cambridge University Press.

Nord, W.R. and Tucker, S. (1987). *Implementing Routine and Radical Innovations,* Lexington, MA: Lexington Books.

Pelto, P.J. (1973). *The Snowmobile Revolution: Technology and Social Change in the Arctic.* Mento Park, California: Cummings.

Rogers, C. (1954). Toward a theory of creativity. *A Review of General Semantics,* 11, 249–262.

Rogers, E.M. (1983). *Diffusion of Innovations.* New York: The Free Press.

Schein, E.H. (1971). Occupational socialization in the professions: the case of the role innovator. *Journal of Psychiatric Research, 7*, 401–426.

Shaw, B. (1985). The role of the interaction between the user and the manufacturer in medical equipment innovation. *Research and Development Management, 15*, 283–92.

West, M.A. (1987a). A measure of role innovation at work. *British Journal of Social Psychology, 26*, 83–85.

West, M.A. (1987b). Role innovation in the world of work. *British Journal of Social Psychology, 26*, 305–315.

West, M.A. (1989). Innovation amongst health care professionals. *Social Behaviour,* 4, 173–184.

West, M.A. and Frei, W. (1989). Innovation in der Arbeit. In S. Greif, H. Holling and N. Nicholson (Eds.), *Arbeits- und Organisationspsychologie.* Munich: Psychologie Verlags Union.

West, M.A., Nicholson, N. and Rees, A. (1987). Transitions into newly created jobs. *Journal of Occupational Psychology, 60*, 97–113.

West, M.A. and Wallace, M. (1988). Innovation in primary health care teams: the effects of roles and climates. Paper presented at the British Psychological Society Occupational Psychology Annual Conference, University of Manchester. Abstract in *Bulletin of the British Psychological Society,* Abstracts p. 23.

Zaltman, G., Duncan, R. and Holbek, J. (1973). *Innovations and Organizations.* London: John Wiley and Sons.

2 Innovation at work: the research literature

Nigel King

University of Manchester, UK

INTRODUCTION

For the researcher making first contact with the literature on innovation, the most daunting feature of it is not its size—though it is undoubtedly very large—but its sheer diversity. Work by social and occupational psychologists, personality theorists, sociologists, management scientists, and organizational behaviourists can all be found under the banner 'innovation'.

Given this, it is necessary to set boundaries to the scope of the present review. Firstly, the review is concerned mainly with work of a psychological nature. In particular it excludes sociological and systems-based work and also the large literature on the diffusion of innovations between organizations (see Rogers, 1983), except where it is of direct relevance to psychological approaches. Secondly, the literature on creativity and creative problem solving will only be covered where it is needed to understand the background to innovation research. Finally, the review concentrates on innovation as a phenomenon of the work environment.

Staw (1984) divides the innovation literature into three levels of analysis—individual, group and organizational—according to which of these is the main unit of adoption or production of innovations focused on in a particular study. This is an accurate representation of the major divisions in the literature; most empirical studies can readily be identified as being at one or other of these levels. The distinction is not always so clear in theoretical work; for instance, Zaltman *et al.* (1973) talk about 'multi-member adoption units' rather than groups or organizations, but it is clear from their discussion that it is with organizations that they are chiefly concerned.

Innovation and Creativity at Work   Edited by M.A. West and J.L. Farr
© 1990 John Wiley & Sons Ltd

Of the three levels of analysis, that of the group has received by far the least attention. The small body of literature that does exist on work group innovation is covered in Chapter 4 of this book; the present chapter will therefore concentrate on individual and organizational level innovation. Within these a further distinction will be made, between *antecedent* and *process* research. The former is much more common, and tends to follow a variance approach and be cross-sectional in design. It is concerned with identifying facilitators and inhibitors of innovation. Process research is either historical or longitudinal, and uses more qualitative, case-study methods to study the sequence of events that constitute the process of innovation (Schroeder *et al.*, 1986).

INDIVIDUAL LEVEL INNOVATION

At the individual level, the concepts of innovation and creativity are often confused. It is not the intention here to discuss the distinction between the two at length, as the issue is covered elsewhere in this volume. Put briefly, the distinguishing features of innovation are generally held to be that it need not involve absolute novelty—it may be the introduction of something familiar from one context into another context where it is unfamiliar (e.g. Damanpour and Evan, 1984)—and it is essentially a social activity; it must involve some attempt to have an influence wider than on just the individual him- or herself (e.g. King and West, 1987). However, as many writers continue to use the terms creativity and innovation interchangeably, and as much of the innovation literature draws upon the long-established creativity research tradition in psychology, some examination of work on creativity is unavoidable. Following the division of the literature proposed above, *antecedent* and *process* approaches to individual innovation will be examined in turn.

ANTECEDENT RESEARCH ON INDIVIDUAL INNOVATION

The discussion of antecedent factors will commence with a brief look at trait approaches, before turning to variables of a more situational or social nature such as discretion, positive affect, and feedback/recognition. The final part of this section will focus on attempts to place facilitators/inhibitors of individual innovation within a theoretical framework.

Trait approaches

Trait approaches in the creativity literature

In the mainstream literature on creativity, personality-based research has dominated. This has either involved attempts to identify and measure a 'creativity' trait (e.g. Guilford, 1959), or to isolate personality traits related to creative production (e.g. MacKinnon, 1962). Nicholls (1972) has argued persuasively that the former approach has not been successful and that '. . . approaches anchored to achievement criteria seem preferable'. Some of the traits frequently held to be associated with creative achievement are: a desire for *autonomy* (McCarrey and Edwards, 1973) and *social independence* or lack of concern for social norms—highly creative people are often labelled 'oddballs' by superiors (Kaplan, 1963; Coopey, 1987); *high tolerance of ambiguity* (Child, 1973); a *propensity for risk-taking* (Michael, 1979; Glassman 1986); and *anxiety* (Wallach and Kogan, 1965; Nicholson and West, 1988), though probably only at moderate rather than high levels.

These are only a few of the variables that have emerged in numerous studies. While this body of work does provide a relatively consistent picture of the creative individual, it has the major drawback of being almost entirely cross-sectional. To take an example from MacKinnon's (1962) classic study of architects, we have no way of knowing whether they are creative because of their independence, or whether their independence is a product of their creativity. Similarly, creativity may emerge as a means of coping with anxiety, or anxiety may result from the difficulties inherent in creative production. Even more important for applications to innovation, the study of characteristics associated with creativity cannot by itself tell us how creative performance in work settings can be stimulated or blocked—other than by selective hiring and firing.

Kirton's 'adaption–innovation' dimension

Before moving on to look at approaches other than personality, attention should be drawn to Kirton's (1976) attempt to define innovation in trait terms. He claims that: 'Adaption–innovation is a basic dimension of personality relevant to the analysis of organizational change, in that some people characteristically adapt while some characteristically innovate' (p.622). Put briefly, adaption is 'doing things better' (within the existing structure) while innovation is 'doing things differently' (outside the existing structure). Kirton has developed an inventory measuring people's position on this dimension, which has been used extensively (Kirton, 1978; Hayward and Everett, 1983; Goldsmith, 1984). He claims that the difference between adaptors and innovators is one of style not level of creativity—in other words, that they may be equally creative. This has been questioned conceptually (Payne, 1987), and indeed empirical evidence has shown that high innovativeness is related to high creativity on some standard tests (Torrance and Horng, 1980; Goldsmith and Matherly, 1987). In addition, his work has all the problems of the creativity trait tradition identified by Nicholls (1972; see above) and most importantly, it completely disregards social and organizational factors; this may be justifiable in discussing creativity, but not innovation.

Situational influences

A substantial body of work exists on variables of a more situational nature. This tends to focus on creativity and creative problem-solving in the work setting more often than the personality-based work does, and it is generally more directly relevant to innovation. A group of variables which might be labelled social/organizational can be included here. While work on factors such as organizational structure is principally concerned with the effects on organizational level innovation, a minority of studies examine their impact on individual creative or innovative performance. Some of the most commonly appearing situational factors are described below.

Discretion

Discretion or freedom of choice is frequently cited as a positive antecedent of creative or innovative performance (Amabile, 1984; Peters and Waterman, 1982; West, 1987). Freedom of time use appears to be particularly important (Lovelace, 1986), though Glassman (1986) states that findings such as those of Farris (1973) and Pelz and Andrews (1976) suggest that '. . . complete freedom of choice of how to spend one's time is not as effective as moderate freedom involving supportive consultations with supervisors or managers' (Glassman, 1986; p.176).

Positive affect

Isen *et al.* (1987) have examined the effects of *positive affect* on creative problem-solving. In a series of experiments they found that subjects in whom they induced positive feelings—in one case by watching an extract of a comedy film, in another by a small gift—performed better at tasks requiring creative solutions than the control groups. Simple arousal, produced by exercise, and induced negative affect had no influence on the level of creative performance. How this finding might be applied to individual performance in work organizations remains to be examined.

Leadership

Questions concerning leadership have received considerable attention, as researchers have sought to provide practical advice on how to manage creative people effectively. Many writers have stressed the need for participative and collaborative leadership (e.g Peters and Waterman 1982; Kanter, 1983), though Glassman (1986) has argued that no single style can be universally prescribed. Referring to work on 'Leadership Interaction Theory' (Fiedler *et al.*, 1976; Hersey and Blanchard, 1982), he suggests that leadership style should be modified according to the degree of self-direction exhibited by subordinates.

Feedback/recognition

Feedback and recognition from supervisors have been found to play an important role; Amabile (1984) found appropriate feedback to be an important facilitator of creativity amongst research and development (R & D) managers, while one of the obstacles to creativity mentioned by many of Glassman's (1986) participants—also from R & D—is 'lack of appreciation of creative accomplishment'. West (1989) found social support from superiors to be a predictor of innovation amongst community nurses.

Organizational structure

Consideration of organizational structure in relation to creative performance at work has focused on hierarchy. The consensual view is illustrated by Kanter (1983), who points out the deleterious effect on creativity of the 'elevator mentality' of organizations dominated by rigid vertical relationships and 'top down dictate'. Reviewing the literature, Lovelace (1986) concludes that 'an organic, matrix and decentralized structure will provide the creative individual with freedom sufficient to be creative' (p.165). The implication here is that organizational structure is important for individual creativity because it is a determinant of many of the variables discussed above, such as discretion.

Theoretical approaches to antecedent research on individual innovation

As can be seen, there is no lack of variables which have been proposed as influences on individual creativity or innovation, and in many cases there is considerable empirical support to back them up. However, there have been relatively few attempts to place facilitators and/or inhibitors within a theoretical framework which would help us to understand why particular factors have a particular effect. There are exceptions to this, and three of them will be discussed here: the work of Jones (1987), Lovelace (1986), and Amabile (1983).

Jones' information-processing model

Jones (1987) is concerned specifically with blocks or barriers to creativity. He collected data from managers, and from this proposed an information-processing model (based on Atkinson and Shiffrin, 1971) of blocks to creativity. The four types of block are 'strategic', 'values', 'perceptual' and 'self-image'. Of these, only strategic blocks—in effect, lack of appropriate creativity skills—can be dealt with by traditional creative problem-solving training. In all the other cases, the problem is not inadequate strategies for creativity, but that information-processing barriers exist which prevent access to the full range of strategies; what is required is training appropriate to the particular type of block. The three types of non-strategic block are summarized below.

(1) *Values blocks.* These occur where an individual's values prevent him or her from acting creatively. An example is the so-called 'Theory X' management belief that 'there's only one thing workers understand—and that's discipline'.

(2) *Perceptual blocks.* Here the manager may be consistently overlooking opportunities, or failing to anticipate threats as early as possible.

(3) *Self-image blocks.* These will be found when the individual does not have the self-confidence to resist anti-innovation social pressures, perhaps because of lack of assertiveness.

Jones' model is at an early stage of development, but there is much in it that is promising. The major criticism of it is that it ignores social and organizational influences; training might be able to remove blocks to creativity from individuals, but this could be to no avail if the groups or organizations within which creative ideas have to be implemented remain strongly anti-innovative.

Lovelace's motivational framework for stimulating creativity

Lovelace is concerned with how R & D managers can stimulate creativity in basic scientists. Citing Smeltz and Cross (1984) he maintains that creative performance is a function of both ability and motivation, and that it is therefore the responsibility of the R & D manager to manipulate the environment in such a way as to motivate scientists. As a theoretical foundation upon which recommendations for interventions can be based,

Lovelace suggests Maslow's (1943) need hierarchy theory of motivation. He claims that: 'In potentially creative individuals such as scientists, self-actualization needs will motivate the scientist to express fully his creativity' (p.166). The manager's goal should be to ensure that lower order needs are fulfilled (i.e. safety, social and esteem needs), allowing self-actualization to stimulate the scientist. Lovelace proposes three managerial activities by which this might be achieved: acting as a 'linking pin' between scientists and the rest of the organization; defining roles and setting objectives; and acquiring resources.

The major problem for Lovelace's work is its foundation upon Maslow's theory. Extensive research has found it very difficult to apply the need hierarchy in real organizational settings (Wahba and Bridwell, 1976). Lovelace should be given credit, though, for taking more account of factors outside the individual than Jones (1987) does, and for detailing how particular managerial interventions will satisfy particular needs of scientists.

Amabile's social psychological model

Amabile (1983) proposes a componential model of the social psychology of creativity, the three necessary components being *task motivation, domain-relevant skills*, and *creativity-relevant* skills. Although she does discuss the nature of the skill components, the main focus of her work—theoretical and empirical—is the part played by motivation. She proposes an 'intrinsic motivation hypothesis of creativity' which predicts that '. . . the intrinsically motivated state is conducive to creativity, whereas the extrinsically motivated state is detrimental' (p.91). Her early empirical work was all experimental and clearly supported this hypothesis, showing the inhibiting effects of extrinsic motivators such as rewards on creative performance. In her first field study testing the theory, using as subjects R & D managers (Amabile, 1984), she found that the overall pattern was largely as expected—extrinsic factors inhibited and intrinsic factors facilitated creativity. However, she did find some extrinsic motivators were described as facilitators; 24% of her subjects mentioned 'challenge' as a stimulus to creativity, 17% mentioned 'pressure' and 15% mentioned 'recognition'. Amabile does not offer an explanation of these findings, and states the need for further applied work. It seems likely that in real-world settings a simplistic intrinsic–extrinsic dichotomy is inadequate.

Summary: antecedent approaches to individual level innovation

There exists a large literature on antecedents of individual creative performance, much of which could be applied to the work setting—some indeed is concerned with the creativity of particular occupational groups (e.g.

MacKinnon, 1962; Glassman, 1986). However, a large proportion of this is concerned with the personality traits of creative people; such an approach is entirely asocial, and at best can only indicate which individuals are most likely to come up with creative new ideas. It tells us nothing about the likelihood of those ideas being implemented as actual innovations.

A substantial amount of work has been carried out on factors of a more situational kind, including social and organizational variables. As with the research dealing with individual characteristics, very little is explicitly focused on innovation, but quite frequently the terms 'creativity' and 'creative problem solving' are used synonymously with innovation. Work on some of these variables is quite extensive, particularly discretion, leadership styles, and feedback and recognition, where there is an emergent consensus on their effects on individual innovation. For instance, it is widely recognized that high discretion facilitates innovation (Amabile, 1984; Lovelace, 1986; West, 1987), except perhaps at very high levels (Farris, 1973; Pelz and Andrews, 1976). The major problem of the existing research into situational antecedents of individual innovation is that mostly it is not set in any theoretical framework. Quite recently, attempts have been made to address this problem (Jones, 1987; Lovelace, 1986; Amabile, 1983, 1984), but much remains to be done.

It will be seen in the next section, examining process approaches to individual innovation, that some of the problems noted here are found again; notably confusion of the terms 'creativity' and 'innovation', and inadequate attention to social factors. These points are discussed further in the conclusion to the review of individual level innovation literature.

PROCESS RESEARCH

Schroeder *et al.* (1986) describe the innovation process as '. . . the temporal sequence of activities that occur in developing and implementing new ideas' (p.1). There are not many models of this process at the individual level of analysis, even when process models of creativity and creative problem solving are included; this is in contrast to the organizational level, where there is an abundance. In this section, four models of theoretical or historical importance will be examined. The first, that of Wallas (1926), is the classic description of the creative process, which has had a continuing influence on models of creativity, creative problem solving, and individual innovation. The other models discussed are all quite recent and although only Rogers' (1983) is specifically concerned with innovation, the remaining two—Basadur *et al.* (1982), and Amabile (1983, 1986)— treat creativity in a way which is clearly analogous to individual innovation.

Wallas' model of creative thinking

The model of the creative thought process suggested by Wallas (1926) in his book *The Art of Thought* has had a lasting influence on research into creativity, and latterly innovation. Wallas identified four stages of creative thinking, based largely on introspective accounts such as Poincaré's (1924) descriptions of his own mathematical creativity. These are: *preparation* where the individual addresses the problem and clarifies his or her goal; *incubation*, where fully conscious work on the problem is suspended; *illumination*, the 'Eureka!' moment when the core (or even the whole) of the solution to the problem suddenly springs into awareness; and *verification* where the individual uses logical and rational thought processes to turn the sudden insight of illumination into a correct or appropriate solution, apparent as such to other people.

There is little disagreement that Wallas' model is too rigid in its stages (Vernon, 1970); they have been found in reality to overlap considerably (Eindhoven and Vinacke, 1952). Debate continues over the existence and influence of the incubation stage. Fulgosi and Guilford (1968) and Dreistadt (1969) found at least partial evidence for the facilitating effect of unconscious incubation, while studies by Olton and Johnson (1976) and Read and Bruce (1982) failed to support it. Weisberg (1986) strongly rejects the notion of unconscious incubation in creative thinking: 'It is simply a story that many people believe without consideration of its merits; in the face of contradictory resuts, however, it is a story that should be put aside' (p.34). He suggests that some of the apparent effects of incubation might be due to brief episodes of mulling over a problem, apparent in studies such as those of Patrick (1935, 1937)—what Olton (1979) called 'creative worrying'. However, he and other critics appear to have neglected the fact that the model does not insist that incubation always occurs entirely unconsciously. Wallas actually says that it may:

... take place (with 'risings' or 'fallings' of consciousness as success seems to approach or retire), in that periphery or "fringe" of consciousness which surrounds our "focal" consciousness as the sun's corona surrounds the disk of full luminosity. (Wallas, 1926; p.95)

Wallas' model is of little direct relevance to innovation as it is purely cognitive; its importance lies in the influence it has had on other models both in the creativity and innovation fields. Its continued prominence after more than sixty years may be attributed to the fact that it still 'rings true' to many people's experiences of creativity.

Basadur *et al.*'s model of creative problem solving

The next model to be considered differs considerably from Wallas'; it is Basadur *et al.*'s (1982) model of the 'complete process of creative problem solving'. Because of the authors' concern with creativity training in organizations, it is applicable to the work environment. There are three stages to the model: *problem finding, problem solving* and *solution implementation.* At each stage, a two-step process of *ideation–evaluation* occurs; ideation is the uncritical generation of ideas, while evaluation is the application of judgement to select the best of the generated ideas.

The authors use the model to derive hypotheses about creativity training which they tested in a field experiment, with qualified success. One unpredicted finding was that while creativity training did lead to increased practice of, and performance at ideation, preference for ideation in problem-finding did not increase as expected. By way of explanation, Basadur *et al.* suggest: 'It may be that one is able to get participants to do problem finding (cognitive and behavioural) yet still not to like problem finding (attitudinal)' (p.67).

Basadur *et al.*'s model is more sophisticated than Wallas' in that it distinguishes between the behaviours that occur in creative problem solving (problem finding, problem solving, solution implementation) and the thought processes involved (ideation and evaluation); Wallas' model is only concerned with thought processes. The partial support found by the authors for their model suggests that it requires further empirical testing and development.

Amabile's social psychological model of creativity

In her 'social psychology of creativity', Amabile (1983) presents not only the three components influencing innovation (see above) but also a five-stage description of the innovation process. The roles of the three components vary at each of the stages. Amabile's process model has more in common with that of Wallas (1926) than with Basadur *et al.*'s (1982), although as it is grounded in social rather than cognitive psychology, it does not contain an equivalent of the incubation stage. Her five stages, and the parts played by the three components at each of them, are described below.

(1) *Task presentation.* This is where the task to be undertaken or the problem to be solved is presented to the individual, either by another person ('external source') or by the person him- or herself ('internal source'). The individual is more likely to attempt to solve the problem creatively if intrinsic motivation is high, which in turn is generally more likely if the problem is from an 'internal source'.

(2) *Preparation.* At this stage, prior to the generation of responses or solutions, the individual, in Amabile's words, 'builds up or reactivates

a store of information relevant to the problem or task'. Skills in the task domain therefore play a major role here.

(3) *Idea generation.* Here, the individual produces possible responses in the search for solutions or ideas appropriate to the task in hand. The individual's skills in creative thinking will determine both the quality and quantity of ideas generated. Intrinsic, rather than extrinsic, task motivation will also facilitate idea generation.

(4) *Idea validation.* Each idea generated at stage 3 is checked for its appropriateness or correctness for the task at hand, by reference to the 'knowledge and assessment criteria included within domain-relevant skills'.

(5) *Outcome assessment.* As a result of the check against task criteria carried out in stage 4, a decision is made about the potential task solution. If it is accepted ('success') or rejected ('failure'), the process ends here. If, however, the response is not wholly appropriate but does constitute significant progress towards solution, the process returns to stage 1, and the 'information gained from the trial will be added to the existing repertoire of domain-relevant skills'.

There is much to recommend in Amabile's model, in particular in the way it suggests how—and where—the skills and motivation of the individual affect the progress of the process. It should be noted that in her recent work (1986), she applies this model to small group as well as individual creativity, and also includes it as part of a wider model of organizational innovation. However, although Amabile's is a social psychological model, social factors have only an indirect effect on the process described. That is, they have an effect on the three 'components' (motivation, task-domain skills and skills in creative thinking) which in turn influence the progress of the process. For instance, rewards and penalties for performance at a task will lead to the person being extrinsically motivated and thus to less likelihood of a creative response to the task and a reduction in the quantity and quality of ideas generated. A truly social psychological model of individual creativity or innovation would need to incorporate social influences and interactions within its description of the sequence of events which constitutes the process.

Rogers' model of the innovation-decision process

Within the diffusion research tradition, Rogers (1983) proposes a five-stage model of 'the innovation-decision process', the stages being *knowledge, persuasion, decision, implementation* and *confirmation*. The model is mostly concerned with the diffusion of policies, such as birth control in the Third World, or technological products, such as drugs or agricultural chemicals. However, it could be readily modified to apply to individual innovation at work, especially in its emphasis on inter-personal communications. As with the other three models discussed here, Rogers' is more concerned with mental events than actions in a social context. Factors outside the individual do appear though: 'norms of the social system' and 'socio-economic characteristics' of the individual are included as influences on his or her propensity to obtain knowledge about the innovation (the start of the process), and Rogers stresses that 'implementation involves overt behavioural change'. One serious limitation of the model as it stands is that it is not applicable to cases where an individual invents an innovation rather than adopts one from outside.

Rogers addresses the issue of whether there is evidence to support the notion that the innovation process has distinct stages—a seriously neglected point in the whole innovation literature. Examining existing case study evidence, he concludes that there is some support for it (Beal and Rogers, 1960; Coleman *et al.*, 1966), the strongest being for the knowledge and decision stages, and the weakest for the persuasion stage.

Summary: process research into individual innovation

Process-based studies of individual innovation are greatly outnumbered by those taking an antecedent approach. What work that has been done has mostly remained closely tied to the creativity tradition, typified by Wallas' (1926) model, and has therefore been highly cognitive in nature. Factors outside the individual appear as influences on motivation (Amabile, 1983), awareness of innovations (Rogers, 1983), or not at all (Basadur *et al.*, 1982).

There are strong similarities between the models examined in many of the actual stages proposed; all but Rogers' start with the identification of a task or problem, and all but Basadur *et al.*'s end with confirmation or verification. However, there remains a lack of empirical investigation of the sequence of stages in the process.

INDIVIDUAL LEVEL RESEARCH: CONCLUSIONS

The literature on individual level innovation at work suffers from an identity problem; it has yet to establish a clear sense of what its aim and concerns are. This is seen most clearly in the confusion surrounding the usage of the terms 'creativity', 'creative problem solving' and 'innovation'. If individual level innovation is to develop as a research area, progress in three areas is required:

(1) *Integrative theory*—little progress will be made simply by adding to the list of factors found to be predictors of individual innovative performance; rather, theoretical integrations of the effects of, and inter-

relationships between, predictor variables should be produced and tested.

(2) *Process*—antecedent research taking a variance approach is on its own inadequate. To take one example, the facilitating effect of discretion on individual creative production might be established beyond doubt, yet that same discretion might be an inhibitor of the implementation of innovations by the individual—perhaps because it is associated with low feedback and recognition. These kinds of relationship can only be tested by examining innovations over time, as the process unfolds. Empirical work is also needed to test the hypothesized sequences of stages in the process.

(3) *Social emphasis*—a fuller understanding of innovation demands that the individual is always seen in his or her social context. Research which ignores social factors influencing individual innovations will inevitably be of limited applicability. There is a need to examine how social psychological processes, such as conformity (Asch, 1956) and cognitive dissonance (Festinger, 1957) might affect individual innovation.

ORGANIZATIONAL LEVEL INNOVATION

Innovation at the level of the organization has been the main focus of the majority of theoretical and empirical studies of innovation. As with the individual level, two main research traditions exist, *antecedent* and *process* approaches. Again there is a preponderance of antecedent research, although the process at the organizational level has not been neglected to the same extent as that at the individual level. A third category of research may be distinguished here; that which attempts to identify and understand differences between *types of innovation*. This cuts across the antecedent–process distinction, and so is dealt with in a separate section at the end of this part of the review.

ANTECEDENT RESEARCH

Antecedents to organizational level innovation have received more attention than any of the other research areas dealt with in this review of the literature, and a very large number of facilitating and inhibiting factors have been suggested. Three main types of factor can be identified: *characteristics or behaviour of organizational members*, *characteristics of the organization*, and *extra-organizational factors*. These will be examined in turn.

Characteristics and behaviour of organizational members

The influence of member characteristics on organizations' innovativeness has been one of the longest standing research areas within the innovation field. The bulk of the work has concentrated on those controlling innovations—principally leaders and change agents. The influence of others within the organization has generally been referred to only in terms of resistance to change.

Leaders and decision-makers

Early work on organizational innovation was dominated by a focus on characteristics of leaders and/or decision-makers. In many cases, data for an organization was only collected from one individual. In Mohr's (1969) classic study of innovation in American and Canadian public health organizations, data for each department involved came only from the interview responses of the local health officer (see also Ettlie, 1983; Ackermann and Harrop, 1985). Although this approach does make it relatively easy to study a large number of organizations at once, it results in '. . . a picture of organizational innovativeness only as seen from the top' (Rogers and Agarwala-Rogers, 1976; p.172). An innovation attempt can involve any number of people within the organization, up to its entire membership, and all their viewpoints must be incorporated if we are to gain a full understanding of what is happening. Nevertheless, leadership variables remain important because almost all organizations are to some degree hierarchical and as a result decision-making power tends to be concentrated in the hands of leading individuals.

In the study mentioned above, Mohr (1969) found a significant relationship between *leader motivation*, conceptualized in terms of 'ideology-activism', and frequency of innovation. Where local health officers had more liberal ideologies and a more interactive view of their role, a higher level of innovation was found. There was, however, a strong interaction between leader motivation and resources: 'When resources are high . . . a unit increase in health officer motivation, as measured, has about $4\frac{1}{2}$ times the effect upon innovation as when resources are low' (p.124).

Kimberly and Evanisko (1981) also looked at leader characteristics in American health organizations. They examined separately the relationships between levels of innovation and characteristics of hospital administrators and chiefs of medicine, along with organizational and contextual factors. Overall, leader characteristics proved to be poorer predictors of innovation than organizational factors. Of the leader characteristics included, the *tenure*, *educational level* and *involvement in medical activities* of administrators positively predicted technological innovation, while time spent in committees was a negative predictor. Their *cosmopolitanism*, along with *educational level*, positively predicted administrative innovation. For chiefs of medicine the only significant relationship with innovation was a positive one between *involvement in administrative affairs* and technological innovation.

Pierce and Delbecq (1977) and Patti (1974) have stressed that pro-change *values* on the part of strategic decision-makers will facilitate organizational innovation. Hage and Dewar (1973) found that 'elite values' were responsible for more of the variance in innovation than any single structural variable.

Moving away from the effects of relatively stable characteristics such as values, educational level, tenure and so on, there is a considerable amount of work which looks at or makes prescriptions for the appropriate *management style* and actions to encourage innovation. Van de Ven (1986) proposes three principles for developing '. . . an infrastructure that is conducive to innovation and organizational learning' (p.605). First, critical limits for organizational innovation must be defined with a clear set of values and standards. Second, the organization needs to develop the capacity for 'double-loop learning'— that is, it must be able not only to detect and correct deviations from the standards it has set, but also to detect and correct errors in the standards themselves. Third, the organization must preserve rather than reduce uncertainty and diversity.

Much of the work on managing individual innovation can and has been applied to the organizational level. There is a consensus that a *democratic, participative leadership style* is conducive to innovation (Kanter, 1983; Nyström, 1979). Bouwen and Fry (1988) refer to studies carried out in several Belgian companies examining the management of innovation, and make the point that in managing novelty effectively it is not enough simply to avoid those practices and procedures that inhibit it; there is a need to *actively attend to the management of ideas.*

Idea champions and change agents

As stated earlier, a 'top-down' only view gives an incomplete picture of organizational innovation, yet it is taken in a large proportion of research. Of the work discussed so far, only Patti's (1974) addresses the issue of how decision-makers react to innovations proposed by subordinates. In the studies carried out by Bouwen and Fry (1988) and their colleagues, it was commonly observed that innovation required the extraordinary effort of an individual *idea champion*, and they argue that: 'Part of managing novelty is therefore concerned with how the enterprise allows and rewards such courageous persons to emerge and attract others' attention' (p.13).

Bouwen and Fry are chiefly concerned with individuals who informally adopt the 'idea champion' role, but often an individual (frequently an outsider) is formally appointed to the task of overseeing the innovation process. Such an individual is commonly called a 'change agent', and there exists a large body of research concerning the appropriate actions and characteristics of change agents. Findings in this area are summarized by Rogers (1983), who proposes from the available evidence that change agent success in securing clients' adoption of innovations is positively related to the following factors:

> ... *(1) the extent of change agent effort in contacting clients, (2) a client-orientation, rather than a change-agency orientation, (3) the degree to which the diffusion program is compatible with clients' needs, (4) the change agent's empathy with clients, (5) his or her homophily with clients, (6) credibility in the clients' eyes, (7) the extent to which he or she works through opinion leaders, and (8) increasing clients' ability to evaluate innovations.* (p.343)

Resistance to change

In looking at the characteristics and behaviour of organizational members, innovation researchers have, as mentioned earlier, tended to concentrate on leaders and/or decision-makers, with a separate strand of work looking at change agents. Where other members of the organization have been considered it is usually in the context of *resistance*. Watson (1971, 1973) discusses forces of resistance as they operate 'in personality' and 'in the social system', and a similar division will be used here.

A number of *individual psychological factors* have been studied in relation to resistance to organizational innovation. *Selective perception* is mentioned by both Watson (1973) and Zaltman and Duncan (1977); it is argued that having formed an attitude, people tend to respond to subsequent suggestions for change within their established outlook. There are clear parallels here with Jones' (1987) 'perceptual blocks' to creativity. Other factors associated with resistance include such things as conformity to norms, habit, low tolerance for change, dogmatism, low tolerance for ambiguity, and low risk-taking propensity. Some of these have already appeared as inhibitors to individual level innovation, which raises the question of how individual innovativeness is related to attitudes to organizational innovation—this appears to be an area that researchers have not addressed.

Five *social system factors* are commonly identified in the literature as sources of resistance to innovation (Bedeian, 1980); (i) *vested interests* of organizational members; (ii) *rejection of outsiders*, where an innovation is introduced by an external change agent; (iii) *misunderstandings due to lack of clarity*, especially between higher management and those on whom an innovation is imposed; (iv) an *organizational structure incompatible with the innovation*; (v) *lack of top-level support and commitment.* The last three of these factors were all major contributors to the relative failure of the new teaching system examined in Gross *et al.*'s (1971) case study of educational innovation.

Researchers have been over-ready to explain innovation failure in terms of resistance to change; few have examined how attitudes and behaviours of organizational members can facilitate innovation. Also, it is often accepted unquestioningly that innovation is a 'good thing' and resistance therefore a 'bad thing'. Because of this, Rogers (1983) argues that innovation research is marred by two pervasive biases: an 'individual-blame bias', with the implication that '. . . if the shoe doesn't fit, there's something wrong with your foot', and a 'pro-innovation bias', which sees innovation as an unqualified good, whatever the situation. There has been little attention paid to the positive role resistance can play for the organization—for instance, by highlighting unanticipated negative consequences of planned changes—though exceptions can be found (e.g. Zaltman and Duncan, 1977; Klein, 1967). The whole approach to the involvement in innovation of organizational members other than top decision-makers needs revising; the very term 'resistance to change' has deprecatory connotations, as if it were some kind of personality flaw endemic amongst those subordinate to the innovation planners. People may have very good reasons for resisting an innovation, not the least of which being that '. . . the advocated innovation is simply not functional enough; that is, it does not do what it purports to do' (Zaltman *et al.*, 1973; p.85).

Characteristics of the organization

A wide range of organizational characteristics have been studied as possible antecedents of innovation, including size, structure, resources, knowledge of innovations, and age. Recently, an increasing emphasis has been placed on strategy, climate and culture, though the last two in particular have not really developed beyond the level of speculation.

Organizational size

Kimberly and Evanisko (1981) found organizational size to be the best predictor of both technological and administrative innovation in American hospitals; the larger the hospital, the more innovations were adopted. Similar findings in hospitals and health departments have been obtained by Kaluzny *et al.* (1974), Mohr (1969), Mytinger (1968) and others. The evidence is not all one way though; Rogers (1983), for instance, cites a 1981 report from the US General Accounting Office which found the opposite relationship, while Utterback (1974) concludes in a review of innovation in industry that firm size does not appear to influence speed of adoption of innovations.

There are two major problems with the use of organizational size as a predictor variable for innovation. First, there is considerable variation in what is meant by organizational size and consequently in how it is operationalized (Kimberly, 1976). Second, size may not be a variable of theoretical interest or importance in itself, but rather 'a surrogate measure of several dimensions that lead to innovation' (Rogers, 1983; see also Aiken and Hage, 1971; Baldridge and Burnham, 1975). In Mohr's (1969) study, for instance it was found that size predicted innovation 'because it connoted a summary of factors that included motivation, obstacles, and resources in a highly conducive combination' (p.120).

Organizational structure

Structural variables have probably received the most attention of any in the organizational innovation literature. Three which are frequently examined together are centralization, formalization and complexity. *Centralization* refers to the extent to which authority and decision-making is concentrated at the top of the organizational hierarchy. *Formalization* is the degree of emphasis placed on following rules and procedures in role performance. *Complexity* refers to the amount of occupational specialization and task differentiation in the organization. Zaltman *et al.* (1973) argue that these variables have contrasting effects at the initiation and implementation stages of the innovation process (the so-called 'innovation dilemma'): initiation is facilitated by low levels of centralization and formalization and high levels of complexity, while implementation is facilitated by high centralization and formalization and low complexity. The evidence regarding each of these variables is examined below.

Centralization There is clear empirical evidence for Zaltman *et al.*'s proposition that high centralization inhibits initiation of innovations because it restricts channels of communication and reduces available information (e.g. Hage and Aiken, 1967; Burns and Stalker, 1961; Shepard, 1967). The greater participation that results from a decentralized structure allows more viewpoints to be brought into consideration and is likely to produce a greater diversity of ideas. The evidence is less clear for the facilitating effect of centralization on implementation of innovations, though Kimberly and Evanisko (1981) found a significant negative relationship between it and the adoption of technological innovations by hospitals. Zaltman *et al.* state that centralization helps organizational members to know what is expected of them, and thus reduces the ambiguity and role conflict which can be caused by implementing changes. However, they themselves admit that participation (a feature of decentralized structures) can 'increase organizational members' commitment to working through the sometimes difficult implementation stage' (p.144). Pierce and Delbecq (1977) argue that for this reason, centralization will inhibit implementation as well as initiation, though the effect will not be as strong.

Formalization Zaltman *et al.* (1973) hold that formalization is an inhibitor of innovation initiation, because 'rigid rules and procedures may prohibit organizational decision makers from seeking new sources of information' (p.138). Rogers (1983) and Pierce and Delbecq (1977) agree, though the latter raise the possibility that a formal mandate to innovate and experiment may actually stimulate innovation. The evidence for the reverse effect in the implementation stage is better than for centralization; for instance, a study by Neal and Radnor (1971) found a strong positive relationship between the establishment of procedural guidelines and the successful implementation of new operation research activities in large firms.

Complexity Organizational complexity is held by Zaltman *et al.* to be positively related to innovation initiation and negatively related to implementation. This is because at the initiation stage 'diversity in occupational backgrounds can . . . bring a variety of sources of information to bear, which can facilitate awareness or knowledge of innovations' (p.135), but at the implementation stage greater diversity provides more opportunities for conflict, making a consensus harder to reach. Studies by Sapolsky (1967) in department stores and Carroll (1967) in medical schools show this pattern of results, but Hage and Aiken (1967) found reasonably strong correlations between complexity and the adoption of innovations by social welfare organizations. Kimberly and Evanisko (1981) found specialization and functional differentiation (measured separately) to be significant predictors of hospital adoption of technological innovations. It may be that the facilitative effects on initiation outweigh the inhibitive effects on implementation; in other words, 'complex organizations may actually implement a greater number of innovations simply as a result of more being initiated' (Zaltman *et al.*, 1973; p.137).

To sum up, the evidence regarding the 'innovation dilemma' does offer some support but it is not full and unambiguous. For the proposition to be adequately tested, it is necessary for longitudinal studies to be carried out which can effectively monitor the influences of centralization, formalization and complexity on the different stages of the innovation process. Although this need has been recognized for some time (see Rogers and Agarwala-Rogers, 1976), such studies remain rare, in part because of the practical difficulties involved.

Of the other organizational structure variables which have been studied, probably the most important is *stratification*, that is, the number of status layers or levels within an organization. The consensus view is that high stratification inhibits innovation, because it leads to too much preoccupation with status and insufficient freedom for creative thinking. As mentioned earlier, Kanter (1983) found that an 'elevator mentality' in organizations led to a lack of creativity and innovation.

Resources

In examining the influence of resources on innovation, some studies (e.g. Mohr, 1969) have used a general resource measure such as expenditure. More frequently researchers have concentrated on the availability of *slack* resources; that is, 'the degree to which uncommitted resources are available to the organization' (Rogers, 1983). Not surprisingly, measures of available resources are consistently found to be positively related to innovation; this was so in Mohr's (1969) study where, as we have seen, resources also mediated the effects of leader motivation. Rogers and Agarwala-Rogers (1976) sugggest that very high levels of slack may actually create a need for innovation—they give as an example the technological innovations adopted by some Arab nations in order to make use of their oil wealth.

As with organizational size, there are problems with the measurement of slack. Rogers and Agarwala-Rogers (1976) make the criticism that much of the research operationalizes the variable in shallow or imprecise ways, such as by equating it with profit alone. They point out that the concept of slack '. . . is as much psychological as financial'; it is not just a matter of what resources exist but whether organizational decision-makers believe resources to be available specifically for innovation. Support for this contention comes from Meyer (1982), who looked at factors determining the responses of a group of hospitals to a severe 'environmental jolt' (a doctors' strike). He found that slack acted as a cushion against the impact of the strike; hospitals with high slack resources could avoid the need to innovate in response to the 'jolt', while some with lower slack used the strike as an opportunity for learning and subsequent innovation.

Patti (1974) gives another set of circumstances in which there may be a negative relationship between resources and innovation—when resources are in the form of 'sunk costs'. His argument parallels Teger's (1980) individual and group level work on escalation—the 'too much invested to quit' phenomenon. The more resources an organization has previously invested in an existing arrangement or pattern of behaviour the less likely it is to be willing to change it. Kimberly (1981) makes a similar point when he says that an organization may fail to 'exnovate' (i.e. choose to rid itself of) a non-effective innovation despite resultant costs because it is concerned with 'maintenance of prestige or . . . face saving'. The relationship between innovation and resources is clearly more complex than many writers have allowed for, and this needs to be recognized in future research.

Organizational knowledge of innovations

This variable refers to the organization's ability to identify potentially useful innovations in the environment. In part this will be determined by characteristics of key personnel—attributes such as professionalism and cosmopolitanism (Rogers and Agarwala-Rogers, 1976), but of at least equal importance is the extent to which the organization encourages and engages in active innovation-seeking behaviour (Kimberly, 1978; Tushman, 1977). Support for the facilitative effect upon innovation of this variable is not entirely consistent; Kimberly and Evanisko (1981) found that 'external integration' was not related to adoption of either technological or administrative innovations.

The use of the 'knowledge of innovations' variable presupposes that the organization will react to a performance gap by seeking to import an innovation from the external environment, rather than invent a solution of its own. Little effort has been made to determine the relative frequencies of internally generated and imported innovations, though a recent study by this author (King, 1989) in a psycho-geriatric ward found that of 17 innovations initiated over a seven-month period, 12 originated from ward members, and only two came from outside the hospital altogether. This bias towards imported innovation is probably a legacy of the early dominance of diffusion research in the field, but it is one which should no longer be sustained if we wish to gain a fuller understanding of organizational innovation.

Organizational age

Pierce and Delbecq (1977) propose that the relationship between organizational age and innovativeness will be a negative one; citing Aiken and Alford (1970) they state that 'the older the organization, the more bureaucratic the system and the less receptive the system is to policy innovations' (p.32). In contrast, Kimberly and Evanisko (1981) argue that older hospitals 'might be expected to adopt innovations as a way of insuring their status in the community' (p.699); they found positive relationships between age and both technological and administrative innovation, though only significant in the former case. As with organizational size, and slack, there are difficulties in operationalizing age. Taking the above examples, Pierce and Delbecq define it in terms of 'the length of tenure of strategic organizational members'; Kimberly and Evanisko do not state how they have operationalized age, but from their discussion it seems that they have used the absolute age of the organization—

that is, the length of time it has been in existence. There is a need for greater clarity in future research.

Organizational strategy, climate and culture

These factors are increasingly attracting attention in relation to organizational innovation, though as yet little empirical work on climate and culture has been carried out. A common approach to *strategy* has been to identify 'strategic types', and a number of studies have been carried out relating these to innovation. In Meyer's (1982) study of American hospitals (discussed above in relation to resources), he found that hospital responses to the crisis of a doctors' strike, including whether or not it was perceived as an opportunity for innovation, were determined more by strategy and ideology than by resources and structure: '. . . whereas ideologies and strategies exert strong forces guiding organizations' adaptations, structures and slack resources impose weak constraints' (p.534). Brooks-Rooney et al. (1987), using a modification of the strategic typology employed by Meyer (i.e. Miles and Snow, 1978), also found that strategy was an important determinant of the level and type of innovation observed, though they stress that there is no one ideal strategy for innovation. Cooper (1984) found strategy to be a significant predictor of firms' product innovation; the most innovative showed 'a union of technological prowess and aggressiveness with a strong market orientation' (p.256); they also placed more emphasis than less innovative firms on R & D.

Organizational *climate* and *culture* are identified as important antecedents of innovation by many writers, especially in more recent work in the field (e.g. Fischer and Farr, 1985; Kanter, 1983). There is considerable overlap and a lack of consistency in the usage of the terms; while recognizing this, it is generally the case that climate is a more limited concept than culture, to a large extent concerned with 'atmosphere' or 'mood', whereas culture comprises those symbols and structures which enable shared meaning, understanding and sense-making to be arrived at and maintained (Morgan, 1986).

The need for an organizational climate supportive of innovation is stressed quite frequently in the literature; less common are precise prescriptions as to what might constitute such a climate. Bower (1965) describes a 'working atmosphere' favourable to innovation as requiring participation and freedom of expression, but also demanding performance standards. It should be noted that his recommendations are not based on empirical work but on his thirty years of practical experience as a change agent in industry. In a study of police departments, Duncan (1972) identified three important dimensions of climate for organizational change: need for change, openness to change and potential for change. He found a significant positive correlation between openness to and potential for change, but significant negative correlations between need for change and the other two variables. Thus the greater the perceived need for change, the less the perceived openness to and potential for change. Zaltman and Duncan (1977) explain this somewhat counter-intuitive finding by suggesting that high perceived need for change creates anxiety which leads to the organizational personnel feeling that they cannot make the necessary changes. Fischer and Farr (1985) found 'surprising similarities' between the climates for innovation amongst R & D managers in China and the West.

The shift of interest from climate to culture in the study of organizations generally may be discerned in recent work on innovation, with recommendations for a 'pro-innovation culture' (West and Farr, 1989; Kanter, 1983). Handy (1985) suggests that a 'task culture' is most favourable to innovation— that is, a culture which emphasizes performance, minimizes style and status differences within teams, is flexible, adaptable and sensitive to its environment. However, he stresses that such a culture is not appropriate for all functions of an organization and argues for intra-organizational diversity of cultures.

At present, organizational culture is an area of speculation rather than empirical investigation in the innovation literature, though the growing recognition of its importance makes it very likely that this will change in the near future. There is a need for future research not only to examine which types of culture facilitate or inhibit innovation, but also the extent to which innovation necessitates changes in organizational culture. As Morgan (1986) says:

Attitudes and values that provide a recipe for success in one situation can prove a positive hindrance in another. Hence change programs must give attention to the kind of corporate ethos required in the new situation ... effective organizational change implies cultural change. (p.138)

Extra-organizational factors

Antecedents of innovation can be found outside of the organization as well as within it. These factors are generally called 'environmental' though the term is used in various ways: it may refer to the market or sector within which the organization operates, or it may be used in a political, cultural or simply geographical way, or some combination of these. Within the innovation literature, understanding of the effects of organizational environment is at a similar stage to that of the role played by culture; 'Studies of the influence of organizational environment on adoption of innovation are rare, although assertions that the environment makes a difference are not' (Kimberly, 1981; p.90). Extra-organizational variables which have been discussed include city or community size, competition, and environmental complexity and turbulence.

City or community size

In their study of hospital innovation, Kimberly and Evanisko (1981) found that size of city was the best contextual predictor of technological innovation, though the relationship was not significant independent of the effects of individual and organizational variables. A similar finding emerged from Mohr's (1969) study of the relationship between community size and public health department innovation: 'community size was important ... because it connoted a summary of factors that included motivation, obstacles, and resources in a highly conducive combination' (p.120). Thus, like organizational size, city or community size may not be of influence in itself, but rather may imply the presence of other antecedent factors.

Competition

It is frequently argued that competition will stimulate innovation; indeed, meeting competition is generally presented as the prime purpose of innovation in texts aimed at practitioners, as reflected in titles such as *Innovating to Compete* (Walton, 1987) and *Innovation: the Attacker's Advantage* (Foster, 1986). Some empirical support has emerged (Cooper, 1984; Milo, 1971), but what needs to be examined is the relative importance of competition compared to other factors. It should not be assumed that innovation is always the best response to competition; a cautionary example is Coca-Cola's development of 'New Coke' in response to the growing threat from Pepsi; the innovative product was rejected in many markets, resulting in the re-introduction of the original.

Kimberly (1981) suggests that competition between organizations may occur not simply for economic advantage but also for status and prestige. Organizations seek to increase their prestige in comparison to other similar organizations—what Caplow (1964) calls their 'organization set'. We may therefore predict that innovations adopted by higher status members of the set will tend to be copied by lower status members.

Environmental turbulence and complexity

Aiken and Alford (1970) state that a high degree of turbulence in the environment (i.e. instability and unpredictability) will stimulate innovation by making the organization more aware of 'cues' to innovate. Kimberly (1981) proposes an interaction between environment and structure in their effects on the adoption of innovation:

> *Where environments are relatively stable and predictable, formalization and centralization may facilitate adoption, whereas in cases of instability and environmental turbulence, these same characteristics may impede adoption by uncertainty. (p.89)*

Most writers who have considered the effects on organizational innovation of environmental complexity conclude that it will have a positive impact (Baldridge and Burnham, 1975; Kimberly, 1981). However, there is little agreement about precisely what it means and how it should be measured. As Brooks-Rooney *et al.* (1987) say: 'The first step to effective management of the environment is to perceive it. But there are many different possible ways of viewing one's environment' (p.54).

There is a danger of reductionism in the way in which the influence of the environment on innovation is treated; particular environmental factors have an effect because they imply the presence of organizational antecedents, as city size implied resources in Kimberly and Evanisko's study (1981). A more sophisticated approach to the nature of the organization's relationship with its environment is required, drawing perhaps on work such as Morgan's. (1986) conceptualization of 'organization as flux and change'.

Summary: antecedent factors research into organizational innovation

Antecedents of organizational level innovation which have been studied fall into three broad categories. First, there are *characteristics and behaviour of organizational members*. Here, research has concentrated on leaders and decision-makers, looking at variables such as educational level, values, and most commonly, management style. Change agents, and recently 'ideas champions' (Bouwen and Fry, 1988) have also received a substantial amount of attention, though most work on the former is in the diffusion tradition. Study of the influence on innovation of other members of the organization has mostly been confined to examination of resistance to change, a narrow and limiting approach which Rogers (1983) labels as an 'individual blame bias'.

There is a large literature on the influence of *characteristics of the organization* upon innovation. Aspects of organizational structure appear very frequently, and the notion of the 'innovation dilemma' (Zaltman *et al.*, 1973) is often referred to; the proposal that the structural variables of centralization, formalization and complexity have opposite effects on innovations before and after the point of adoption. Support for this prediction is not conclusive, though in parts quite strong. Other organizational characteristics studied include size, resources, knowledge of innovations, and age. Problems in operationalization are common amongst these variables; either due to lack of clarity about what has been measured (e.g. in what is meant by 'organizational age'), or to the use of inadequate or inappropriate measures (e.g. profit as the sole measure of resources). Recently, interest in another set of organizational characteristics has grown: strategy, climate and culture. As yet, only strategy has received much empirical investigation.

The third category of antecedents is *extra-organizational factors*. Variables studied include city or community size, competition and environmental turbulence and complexity. Although the influence upon innovation of the organizational environment is referred to quite frequently, like climate and culture the area has seen little empirical study, though this may be expected to change in the near future.

PROCESS RESEARCH

Considerably more attention has been paid to the process of innovation at the organizational level than at any other level, and there are numerous models proposing the stages or sequence of events comprising the process. As the stages suggested are mostly quite similar, a detailed description of one fairly recent model (Rogers, 1983) will suffice to indicate the general approach taken. This will help clarify the subsequent examination of how existing models differ on features such as the relative emphasis placed on pre- and post-adoption stages, the way in which the process starts, and how it finishes. The final part of this section looks briefly at how research into the process of organizational innovation might develop in the future.

Rogers's (1983) model of the organizational innovation process

There are two parts to the innovation process in Rogers's (1983) model: initiation and implementation. These in turn are divided into two and three stages respectively, described below (see also Table 1).

(1) Agenda setting This stage involves the definition of general organizational problems, which may create a perceived need for innovation, and the search in the environment for innovations which may be useful to the organization. Agenda setting is a continuous activity of the organization, and is thus not part of the innovation process proper; however, its inclusion in the model does help us to understand the process, in particular instances of innovation as 'it is here that the initial motivation is generated to impel the later steps' (Rogers, 1983; p.362).

Agenda setting can stimulate innovation in two ways. Firstly, a performance gap may be noted; that is, a gap between the organization's expected and actual performance, leading to a search for an appropriate innovation. Alternatively, whilst scanning the environment the organization may discover an innovation which can be matched to an existing problem. As organizations generally have many more problems than innovative solutions, this order of events is likely to be quite common. Rogers calls these two ways of stimulating the process 'problem-initiated' and 'innovation-initated'.

(2) Matching Here the organization attempts to predict how well the innovation will perform in regard to the problem to hand. Decision-makers try to anticipate the difficulties that might lie ahead for the innovation and weigh these against the likely benefits. The innovation is then either terminated or the decision is made to adopt it. This decision marks the end of the *initiation* phase of the model.

(3) Redefining/restructuring In the first *implementation* stage, the innovation starts to be used in the organization. It may be modified (or 're-invented') to fit the requirements of the organization, and similarly the organizational structure may be modified to accommodate the innovation.

(4) Clarifying The innovation is gradually put into wider use, and its meaning becomes clearer to organizational members. There may be misunderstandings or unwanted side-effects, against which corrective action will be needed if the innovation is to be used successfully.

(5) Routinizing This is where the innovation becomes incorporated into the daily life of the organization—in other words, it ceases to be considered innovative. Nevertheless, it may still be discontinued if circumstances and attitudes change.

Rogers does not consider his model to be absolutely rigid; the process may on occasions back-track or skip one or more stages. He insists though that 'Later stages . . . cannot be undertaken until earlier stages have been settled, either explicitly or implicitly' (p.362). The model has not as yet been formally tested—as is true of virtually all existing models of the process. However, Rogers does make use of earlier research to show how the model might be applied (Havelock *et al.*, 1974; Rogers *et al.*, 1979). Indirect support for the model comes from Pelz (1981), who studied the time-order of innovation process stages similar to the ones Rogers proposes; interestingly, Pelz found clear evidence for the expected time-order of stages when the innovation was imported from the outside, but the evidence was much more ambiguous in cases of internally generated innovation. Potentially the most problematic area of the model is the implementation phase, where (pending further research) doubts must remain as to whether boundaries between redefining/

Table 1 Models of the organizational level innovation process

Wilson (1966)	Harvey and Mills (1970)	Hage and Aiken (1970)	Zaltman et al. (1973)	Kimberly (1981) 'Innovation life cycle'	Rogers (1983)
1 Conception of change	1 Issue perception	1 Evaluation	1 Initiation stage (i) Knowledge–awareness substage		1 Initiation (i) Agenda setting
	2 Formation of goals		(ii) Formation of attitudes substage		
2 Proposing change	3 Search 4 Choice of solution	2 Initiation	(iii) Decision substage		(ii) Matching
3 Adoption and implementation	5 Redefinition	3 Implementation	2 Implementation stage (i) Initial implementation substage	1 Adoption	2 Implementation Redefining–re-structuring
		4 Routinization	(ii) Continued-sustained implementation sub-stage	2 Utilization 3 Exnovation	(ii) Clarifying (iii) Routinizing

restructuring, clarifying and routinizing will be identifiable in the majority of real-world cases.

A comparison of innovation process models

In the next section, Rogers' (1983) model and five earlier, influential models are compared. The models are from Wilson (1966), Harvey and Mills (1970), Hage and Aiken (1970), Zaltman *et al.* (1973), and Kimberly (1981). They are summarized in Table 1, with equivalent stages presented as far as possible in parallel; for example, the stage of 'proposing change' in Wilson's (1966) model is equivalent to the 'decision substage' in Zaltman *et al.*'s (1973) model, but precedes 'choice of solution' in Harvey and Mills (1970). Naturally such parallels can only be approximate. It must be pointed out here that Kimberly (1981) does not consider innovation to be a process, but rather the product of a 'life cycle' of adoption, utilization and exnovation processes. In effect though this is only a difference in the usage of terms and what he has to say about the innovation life cycle is entirely relevant to the discussion here. The comparison of the models will focus on three areas: the relative emphasis on pre- and post-adoption stages, the initiation of the process, and where the process ends.

Relative emphasis on pre- and post-adoption stages

The models vary quite considerably in the extent to which they focus on the process before and after the adoption of an innovation—what might be called the 'initiation–implementation balance'. Wilson (1966) and Harvey and Mills (1970) are mainly concerned with the process leading up to adoption, and to a lesser extent the same is true for Zaltman *et al.* (1973), who only distinguish between 'initial' and 'continued-sustained' implementation. Hage and Aiken (1970) and Rogers (1983) are more balanced in their attention to the pre- and post-adoption parts, while Kimberly's (1981) innovation 'life cycle' is at the opposite extreme to the first two, as it subsumes all that happens before an innovation is utilized under the heading 'adoption'.

The overall pattern in the literature is for most work, empirical and theoretical, to concentrate on the events in the process leading up to the innovation's adoption. In part this may be because implementation has tended to attract the interest of scholars of planned change and intervention (e.g. Schein, 1969; Beyer and Trice, 1978), who have a rather different orientation to the subject than organizational innovation researchers (see Zaltman *et al.*, 1973; pp.66–70). Neglecting the implementation part of the process can only lead to an incomplete picture of innovation; in particular it encourages a tendency to see the innovation process purely in terms of problem solving and decision-making, and thus to focus excessively on the actions of key decision-makers. When it is recognized that implementation is an integral part of the process, we cannot escape recognizing the fact that innovation is a social process; for it is during implementation that the innovation impacts directly upon the social system of the organization, and vice versa. Recommendations for practice which ignore this fact must be of questionable value.

The start of the process

How and why the process starts is a vital question for all attempts to describe innovation. A popular explanation is that it is the result of detecting a *performance gap*—the organization becomes aware that it is not performing as well as it should or could, and initiates an innovation attempt to deal with this (e.g. Rogers 1983; Zaltman *et al.*, 1973; Hage and Aiken, 1970). The concept is a useful one, and can be applied successfully in many cases; nevertheless, there remain situations where it is not applicable, unless the term is used so broadly that it is taken to refer to any perceived opportunity to improve some aspect of organizational performance. Rogers (1983), as noted earlier, believes that opportunistic scanning of the environment is responsible for at least as many innovations as the detection of specific performance gaps. Other circumstances where innovation may occur without the existence of a performance gap include legislative dictate, such as the banning of inflammable foam in household furniture, forcing manufacturers to use new materials, and invention, in which someone within the organization devises a new procedure or product where the possibility of change had previously not been recognized.

A significant point which becomes apparent when innovation process models are reviewed is that their focus is mostly on innovations imported from outside the organization rather than internally generated innovations. The same observation was made earlier regarding antecedent research. This tendency, which will be termed *diffusion bias*, might obscure important differences in the process between internally generated and imported innovations, as is suggested by Pelz's (1981) finding, referred to above, that the stages of the process were much more clearly identifiable in imported innovations than internal innovations.

The end of the process

Within the literature, most models present some form of routinization as the last stage in the innovation process; that is, after a sustained period of use, the innovation becomes absorbed into the routine life of the organization and ceases to be perceived as innovative (Hage and Aiken, 1970; Zaltman *et al.*, 1973; Rogers, 1983). Kimberly (1981) goes a step further than this,

and proposes 'exnovation' as the final point in the innovation 'life cycle'—
the process by which an organization consciously divests itself of an existing,
fully implemented innovation, generally to be replaced by a fresh innovation.
Because failure to exnovate will inhibit future innovation, this is a subject of
great importance to organizations, but as yet little research has been carried
out on it.

Future developments in process research into organizational innovation

Overall the quite high level of theoretical interest in the process of
organizational innovation has not been matched by a similar frequency of
empirical studies. Any empirical work in this area is therefore to be welcomed.
Two especially important areas for future development may be identified:
the integration of the process and antecedent approaches to organizational
level innovation, and the testing in the field of sequences of stages proposed
in process models.

Integration of process and antecedent factors research

The long-term aim of specifying the stages, or sequence of events, in the
innovation process must be to make it possible to identify and understand
influences on the process throughout its development. In effect this means
an integration of the antecedent and process approaches; the overall research
question would be: 'What factors influence the progress of innovation at
which points in its development and in what manner?' Work on the
'innovation dilemma' (Zaltman *et al.*, 1973; Wilson, 1966), discussed earlier
in this chapter, is relevant here, as it predicts that key antecedent factors
have a different effect at different points in the process.

Empirical testing of proposed sequences of stages

If integration of antecedent and process approaches is the direction towards
which organizational innovation research should be heading, a crucial
requirement is that we can be confident of the accuracy of the process models
used. The models discussed above do not claim that the stage sequences they
propose are true in all cases; on the contrary, they generally stress their
flexibility. Nevertheless, if the stages are not found as described, and in the
order proposed, in a substantial proportion of cases of innovation, their
utility for anything beyond provoking debate must be considered limited. In
a recent longitudinal study of innovations in a psycho-geriatric ward, the
present author (King, 1989) tested the accuracy of one of the process models
discussed earlier (Zaltman *et al.*, 1973). It was found that although the

overall sequence of events corresponded quite closely to the model, there was considerable overlap between sub-stages in the middle part of the process (i.e. between 'decision' and 'initial implementation' (see Table 1) with activities associated with several sub-stages all occurring at much the same time.

Schroeder *et al.* (1986) criticize the unquestioning acceptance of discrete developmental stages in existing models, which for the most part have been constructed with little or no validating empirical evidence. Such models, they warn, can 'quite easily become self-fulfilling prophecies'. In the light of this, Schroeder *et al.* have set out to study seven major and varied innovations in depth over time, using regular questionnaires and interviews, observations of relevant meetings, and so on. This work is still in progress, though they have already proposed a provisional model, based on common features of the innovations studied, which does not attempt to order these into a simple linear sequence. It is research of this kind, along with empirical testing of the stage-based models, that offers hope for real progress in increasing our understanding of the innovation process.

Summary: process research into organizational level innovation

The bulk of process research into innovation has been at the organizational level, and unlike other levels, models describing the sequence of the process proliferate here. Rogers' (1983) model has been described in detail as representative of the conventional approach, portraying the process as an ordered series of steps or stages. A comparison of six influential models of the process, including Rogers' (Table 1) has shown that there are considerable similarities between them, though differences in three main areas can be identified:

(1) *Initiation–implementation balance.* Some models emphasize the pre-adoption stages more than the post-adoption (e.g. Wilson, 1966; Harvey and Mills, 1970) while in others the situation is reversed (e.g. Kimberly 1981). Bias towards initiation is the dominant trend in the literature. This has the danger of leading to a neglect of social and other factors influencing the development and outcome of innovation after adoption.

(2) *Start of the process.* Several of the models describe the start of the process in terms of perception of a *performance gap*—a difference between potential and actual performance. There is a tendency to imply or assume that organizations will respond to a performance gap by searching for appropriate innovations in their environment; only Wilson (1966) explicitly refers to new ideas coming from within the organization.

(3) *End of the process.* Mostly, models describe the process as ending with the 'routinization' of the innovation. Only Kimberly (1981) of the six looked at here goes beyond this, to what he calls 'exnovation'—the conscious divestment of an existing innovation by an organization.

Schroeder *et al.* (1986) have challenged the assumption of discrete developmental stages in the process. They criticize existing models for not being grounded in observation of actual innovations, and propose an alternative, more fluid model, based on their study of seven ongoing innovations. Schroeder *et al.*'s model is an important development, though at present there are some problems regarding clarity and questions about generalizability to be addressed.

TYPES OF INNOVATION

Although different innovation types are frequently identified in the literature, discussion rarely goes beyond quite general, speculative comments. One exception is the distinction between *technical* and *administrative* innovation, upon which a considerable amount of work has been carried out. This will be looked at first, followed by a brief examination of the three-dimensional typology produced by Zaltman *et al.* (1973). Finally, other ways in which innovations have been categorized will be summarized.

The technical–administrative distinction

Damanpour and Evan (1984) define *technical innovations* as those 'directly related to the primary work activity of the organization' (p.394); this includes such things as new products and services, and new elements in the processes or operations producing these. In contrast, *administrative innovations* are concerned with relationships between people interacting to accomplish work tasks and goals, and 'those rules, roles, procedures, and structures that are related to the communication and exchange between people and between the environment and people' (p.394).

In a study of US libraries, Damanpour and Evan (1984) found support for Evan's (1966) concept of 'organizational lag' (i.e. the adoption of administrative innovations by organizations tends to lag behind the adoption of technical innovations) and showed that organizational lag was negatively related to performance. Also, adoption of administrative innovations tended to trigger technical innovation, but the reverse was not the case. Kimberly and Evanisko (1981) found different antecedents for technological and administrative innovations, in a study of American hospitals discussed earlier in this review. Daft (1978) found that administrative innovations in US High School Districts tended to originate from the 'administrative core'—school principals and superintendents—while technical innovations mostly came from the 'technical core'—i.e. the teachers. Furthermore, the higher the level of professionalism within a core, the more likely were its members to initiate innovation in the other core. Kimberly (1981) has criticized Daft for dichotomizing the life of an organization 'in a way which does not correspond with the realities of role interdependencies, work-flow patterns, and the distribution of authority' (p.91).

Zaltman *et al.*'s (1973) typology of innovation

Zaltman *et al.* (1973) propose that innovations be categorized along three dimensions. The first is *programmed–non-programmed*. Programmed innovations are scheduled in advance, for instance the extension of a production line, or the appointment of a permanent staff member to take over work previously carried out by consultants. Non-programmed innovations are not scheduled in advance and may be of two types: *slack*, where innovation is stimulated by the availability of resources, and *distress*, where innovation occurs in response to a pressing problem. The present author has proposed that a third type of non-programmed innovation be recognized, termed *proactive* (King, 1989). These characteristically involved an individual or group seeking to draw the organization's attention to an area where the need for change was not previously recognized. In the psycho-geriatric ward study, eight out of 17 innovations observed were of this type. Zaltman *et al.*'s second dimension is *instrumental–ultimate*, a distinction made by Grossman (1970). Put simply, ultimate innovations are those which can be considered ends in themselves, while instrumental innovations are those introduced in order to facilitate the subsequent introduction of ultimate innovations. The final dimension is *radicalness*. This can be seen as a combination of an innovation's *novelty* and *riskiness*; the most radical innovation is one which is both entirely novel and highly risky.

Having described the three dimensions, Zaltman *et al.* discuss how they might be combined in real-life cases. They contend that while 'the various types are not mutually exclusive . . . certain combinations are much more likely to come about than others' (p.32). Thus they consider that programmed innovations are likely to be routine (i.e. low radicalness) while non-programmed—and particularly distress—innovations will often be radical. However, empirical investigations of these dimensions remain scant (Normann, 1971; Miller, 1971; King, 1989).

Other innovation types

Many other types of innovation can be found described in the literature. Treatment of them varies from extensive reviews to little more than a passing mention. Often distinctions are made according to the area in which the innovation occurs; thus we have managerial innovation (Kimberly, 1981), educational innovation (Carlson, 1968), medical innovation (Coleman *et al.*, 1966), corporate innovation (Ackermann and Harrop, 1985), and so on. Whether these represent truly different phenomena or are just distinctions of convenience is not clear, though in the main, research under these different headings examines the same antecedents and process elements, using very similar methodologies. A more distinct category is *product innovation*. This is concerned with the development and marketing of new manufactured products (e.g. Normann, 1971; Cooper, 1984), and is the focus of much of the R & D management literature on innovation. There is a strong emphasis on invention and creativity, and how managers can enhance these qualities in their staff (Geschka, 1983; Glassman, 1986; Lovelace, 1986).

This does not claim to be an exhaustive list of innovation types, but it does indicate the range that can be found. In the light of the many and varied ways in which innovations may be categorized, the dearth of empirical work examining systematic differences between types is lamentable, especially as such a strategy was recognized more than a decade ago as a way of overcoming the inconsistencies in organizational innovation research findings (Downs and Mohr, 1976).

Summary: types of innovation

Many different types of innovation have been identified in the literature, but empirical studies comparing them—in antecedents, process or outcomes—are uncommon. The one exception is the technical–administrative dimension, which has received a considerable amount of attention. The concept of 'organizational lag' (Evan, 1966) utilizes this distinction, positing that administrative innovation tends to 'lag behind' technical. Evidence supporting this, and showing its negative consequences for organizational performance, has emerged (Damanpour and Evan, 1984). Zaltman *et al.* (1973) offer a useful three-dimensional typology of innovations, also suggesting likely combinations of types, but although work exists on individual types from it, it has not been studied empirically as a whole.

ORGANIZATIONAL LEVEL INNOVATION: CONCLUSIONS

Organizational level research into innovation has progressed further towards the formation of a coherent body of knowledge than has the individual level, yet a number of significant weaknesses exist in the literature which hamper a wider understanding of the subject. Six main criticisms can be made, each with implications for future research.

(1) More clarity and sophistication is required in the use of some variables, in particular *organizational size, age* and *resources*. It is vital that researchers make it clear precisely how they operationalized these variables, in order to make valid comparisons between the findings of different studies possible. Equally, in many cases, simplistic one-dimensional measures should be regarded as inappropriate; the measurement of slack resources purely in terms of profit, for instance.

(2) *Diffusion bias*—the tendency to assume that organizations will respond to problems by importing innovations from outside, ignoring the possibility of internally generated innovation—should be avoided. The relative frequencies of internal and external innovations, and the differences between them, are matters for empirical investigation.

(3) Empirical work on the influences of *organizational climate* and *culture*, and *extra-organizational factors* is needed, as they have up to now largely been treated in a speculative manner. Research should avoid reductionist approaches, which merely break down these concepts into clusters of familiar, well-tested organizational factors.

(4) As with the individual level, there is a strong need for a shift of emphasis towards the *process* of innovation. Existing process models should be tested against innovation case history data, and where found inadequate, modified or replaced by new empirically grounded models.

(5) The *individual blame bias* (Rogers, 1983) should be challenged, by seeking to examine perceptions of innovation from the perspectives of all those involved, not just those initiating and managing the process. Researchers should always consider the possibility that resistance to any innovation might be rational and justified from the viewpoint of the resisters, and could even be of benefit to the organization as a whole. Again, this calls for the use of case-study methods and in-depth interviews.

(6) Although various *types of organizational innovation* have been identified, and differences between them suggested, little empirical work has been carried out in the area. This should be rectified. Too much research in the past has regarded innovation as a unitary phenomenon, in effect treating a new shift system in a large factory as being in no significant way different from the introduction of word processors into a small office.

SUMMARY OF THE CHAPTER

This chapter has reviewed the literature on innovation at the *individual* and *organizational* levels of analysis. At both levels, it has been seen that research can be divided into two main approaches, *antecedent factors* and *process*, with the former dominating in quantity.

Individual level research

Antecedent factors research

The individual-level innovation literature has retained close links with the creativity research tradition, with the terms often used interchangeably. Within the antecedent factors approach, this is clearest in personality-based work, where *traits related to creative and/or innovative work performance* have been identified (e.g. MacKinnon, 1962; McCarrey and Edwards, 1973; Kirton, 1976). Turning to more situational factors, *discretion* is frequently held to facilitate innovation (Amabile, 1984; Lovelace, 1986; Peters and Waterman, 1982), though several studies have found that moderate freedom with some managerial support and control is more effective than complete freedom (e.g. Farris, 1973). Other situational variables found to have a positive influence on individual innovation include *positive affect* (Isen *et al.*, 1987), *participative leadership style* (Kanter, 1983), *feedback and recognition* (Glassman, 1986), and *non-hierarchical organizational structure* (Lovelace, 1986; Kanter, 1983).

Although a large number of possible antecedents to individual innovation have been studied, there have not been many attempts to place them within a theoretical framework. This review has looked at three exceptions to this: the work of Jones (1983) who has proposed an *information-processing model of blocks to creativity*; Lovelace (1986), who makes recommendations for stimulating creativity based on Maslow's (1943) *need hierarchy theory of motivation*; and Amabile (1983), who presents a *social psychological model of creativity*. Regardless of their differing individual merits and drawbacks, all these frameworks suffer from a lack of attention to social factors—even Amabile's theory only includes them explicitly as inhibitors of creative performance through extrinsic motivation.

Process research

There are few models of the process of individual innovation, even when relevant examples from the creativity and creative problem solving literature are included. The review examined four important models. Wallas's (1926) description of the *creative thought process* has had a lasting influence, though it is entirely mentalistic. Basadur *et al.*'s (1982) *model of creative problem solving* includes behavioural as well as cognitive elements, proposing a three step process in which at each stage the individual uncritically generates ideas (ideation) and critically examines them (evaluation). Amabile's (1983) *social psychological model* describes the process in five stages, progress through which is determined by motivation, domain-relevant skills, and task-relevant skills. Rogers' (1983) *model of the innovation-decision process* suggests stages of *knowledge, persuasion, decision, implementation* and *confirmation*, and emphasizes the role of inter-personal communications.

Future research directions

Three areas were identified in this review on which future individual level innovation research needs to concentrate if it is to progress. First, there is a need for more *integrative theory*, providing theoretical frameworks for the relationships between antecedent factors and innovation. Second, a much greater emphasis on studying the *process* of innovation is required. Third, greater attention should be given to the influence of *social factors* in determining levels of individual innovative performance.

Organizational level research

The bulk of innovation research (outside of the diffusion field) has focused on organizational level innovation, taking an antecedent factors approach. However, a quite substantial amount of theoretical work has been carried out on the process of innovation at this level. There also exists a smaller body of work which focuses on differences between types of organizational innovation.

Antecedent factors research

Antecedent approaches have concentrated on three main sets of variables, the first of which are *characteristics and behaviour of organizational members*. A great deal of attention has been paid to *leader characteristics* (Mohr, 1969; Kimberly and Evanisko, 1981; Ettlie, 1983), and *management style* (Van de Ven, 1986; Bouwen and Fry, 1988). Factors such as *educational level, cosmopolitanism, pro-change values*, and *participative management styles* have been found to be positively related to levels of organizational innovation. Some studies have focused on individuals other than leaders who attempt to introduce innovations, in particular *ideas champions* (Bouwen and Fry, 1988) and *change agents* (Rogers, 1983). The involvement of other organizational members has in the main been examined only in the context of *resistance to change* (Watson, 1973; Bedeian, 1980). This reflects an 'individual blame bias' (Rogers, 1983) in the literature, which should be challenged in future research.

The second set of factors to frequently appear are *characteristics of the organization. Organizational size* has been related to innovativeness, though the evidence suggests that size serves as a proxy for other factors, such as availability of resources. Probably the most commonly studied organizational characteristic has been *structure*. Zaltman *et al*. (1973) argue that high *centralization* and *formalization*, and low *complexity*, inhibit innovation at the initiation stage but facilitate it at the implementation stage (the so-called 'innovation dilemma'). There is some support for this proposition, though it is as yet not conclusive. Another structural variable which appears quite often in the literature is *stratification*, which is generally held to be negatively related to organizational innovativeness (Kanter 1983). Of the other characteristics of organizations appearing as antecedents to innovation, *resources* especially *slack* resources (Meyer, 1982), *knowledge of innovations* (Rogers and Agarwala-Rogers, 1976; Tushman, 1977) and *organizational age* (Aiken and Alford, 1977; Kimberly and Evanisko, 1981) are widely found. Recently, an increasing amount of attention has been paid to the role played in stimulating or blocking innovation of *organizational strategy, climate and culture* (West and Farr, 1989; Handy, 1985; Cooper, 1984), though empirical work in these areas has been in short supply.

Extra-organizational factors are the third set of variables which appear in organizational level research. These include *community/city size, competition* and *environmental turbulence and complexity*. Up to now, frequent references to the importance of these variables have not been matched by extensive empirical investigation.

Process research

Numerous models exist in the literature proposing the stages of sequences of events comprising the innovation process. Given the strong similarities between most of them, the present review described one representative example in detail (Rogers, 1983), and then compared it and five others in the way key aspects of the innovation process were represented. In particular, similarities and differences between models were examined in their *initiation–implementation* balance (i.e. relative emphasis on pre- and post-adoption stages), and depiction of the *start* and *end of the process*. Schroeder *et al*. (1986) criticized all the conventional stage-based models for their lack of grounding in observations of actual innovations, and questioned whether discrete stages in the process can in fact be identified. They proposed an alternative, more fluid model, based on common features of a set of seven widely varied innovations. Extensive testing of this approach and the conventional type of model is urgently required.

Types of innovation

A large number of innovation types have been identified in the literature. These include: *technical and administrative* innovations (Daft, 1978), *product* innovation (Normann, 1971), and the three dimensions proposed by Zaltman *et al.* (1973)—*programmed–non-programmed*, *instrumental–ultimate*, and *radicalness*. On the whole, little empirical work on how and why types differ can be found, with the exception of the technical–administrative distinction (e.g. Kimberly, 1981; Damanpour and Evan, 1984).

Future research directions

Six recommendations for future organizational level research emerged from the review. More clarity and sophistication is needed in the *operationalization* of some variables, such as resources and organizational age. *Diffusion bias*— the assumption that all innovations are imported rather than internally generated—should not be allowed to influence research design. More work is required on *organizational climate and culture* and *extra-organizational factors*, avoiding any tendency to reduce these to well-tested organizational factors like structure. There should be a shift of emphasis away from antecedent factors and towards *process* research. In particular, process models need testing in the field. The *individual blame bias* should be challenged, by designing studies to take account of a multiplicity of perspectives, rather than just that of management. Finally, more empirical *comparisons of innovation types* are required.

Correspondence address:
Centre for Primary Care Research, Department of General Practice, University of Manchester, Rusholme Health Centre, Walmer Street, Manchester M14 5NP, UK.

REFERENCES

Ackerman, C. and Harrop, J. (1985). The management of technological innovation in the machine tool industry: a cross-national regional survey of Britain and Switzerland. *R & D Management*, **15**, 207–218.

Aiken, M. and Alford, R. (1970). Community structure and innovation: the case of urban renewal. *American Sociological Review*, **35**, 650–665.

Aiken, M. and Hage, J. (1971). The organic organization and innovation. *Sociology*, **5**, 63–82.

Amabile, T.M. (1983). *The Social Psychology of Creativity*. New York: Springer-Verlag.

Amabile, T.M. (1984). Creativity motivation in research and development. Symposium paper at the American Psychological Association, Toronto, August.

Amabile, T.M. (1986). A model of organizational innovation. Paper presented at the Annual Convention of the American Psychological Association, Washington DC, August.

Asch, S.E. (1956). Studies of independence and conformity: a minority of one against a unanimous majority. *Psychological Monographs*, **70**, 9.

Atkinson, R.C. and Shiffrin, R.M. (1971). The control of short term memory. *Scientific American*, **225**, 82–90.

Baldridge, J.V. and Burnham, R.A. (1975). Organizational innovation: individual, organizational and environmental impacts. *Administrative Science Quarterly*, 20, 165–176.

Basadur, M., Graen, G.B. and Green, G. (1982). Training in creative problem solving: effects on ideation and problem finding and solving in an industrial research organization. *Organizational Behaviour and Human Performance*, 30, 41–70.

Beal, G.M. and Rogers, E.M. (1960). *The Adoption of Two Farm Practices in a Central Iowa Community*, Iowa Agricultural and Home Economics Experiment Station, Special Report 26.

Bedeian, A.G. (1980). *Organizations: Theory and Analysis*. Illinois: Dryden Press.

Beyer, J.M. and H.M. Trice (1978). *Implementing Change*. New York: Free Press.

Bouwen, R. and Fry, R. (1988). An agenda for managing organizational innovation and development in the 1990s. In M. Lambrecht (Ed.), *Corporate Revival*. Leuven, Belgium: Catholic University Press.

Bower, M. (1965). Nurturing innovation in an organization. In G.A. Steiner (Ed.), *The Creative Organization*, Chicago: Chicago University Press.

Brooks-Rooney, A., Rees, A. and Nicholson N. (1987). The development of managers as effective organisational resources: a summary of findings in the wool textiles industry. MRC/ESRC Social and Applied Psychology Unit, University of Sheffield, Memo no. 916.

Burns, T. and Stalker, G.M. (1961). *The Management of Innovation*. London: Tavistock.

Carlson, R.O. (1968). Summary and critique of educational diffusion research. *Research Implications for Educational Diffusion*, Michigan Department of Education.

Carroll, J. (1967). A note on departmental autonomy and innovation in medical schools. *Journal of Business*, 40, 531–534.

Caplow, T. (1964). *Principles of Organization*, New York: Harcourt, Brace and World.

Child, D (1973). *Psychology and the Teacher*. Holt-Rinehart.

Coleman, J. (1966). *Medical Innovation: A Diffusion Study*. New York: Bobbs-Merrill.

Cooper, R.G. (1984). The strategy-performance link in innovation. *R & D Management*, 14, 247–267.

Coopey, J.G. (1987). Creativity in complex organizations. Paper presented at the Annual Occupational Psychology Conference of the British Psychological Society, University of Hull, January.

Daft, R.L. (1978). A dual-core model of organizational innovation. *Academy of Management Journal*, 21, 193–210.

Damanpour, F. and Evan, W.M. (1984). Organizational innovation and performance: the problem of 'organizational lag'. *Administrative Science Quarterly*, 29, 392–409.

Downs, G.W. Jr and Mohr, L.B. (1976). Conceptual issues in the study of innovation. *Administrative Science Quarterly*, 21, 700–714.

Dreistadt, R. (1969). The use of analogies and incubation in obtaining insights in creative problem solving. *Journal of Psychology*, 71, 159–175.

Duncan, R. (1972). Organizational climate and climate for change in three police departments: some preliminary findings. *Urban Affairs Quarterly*, 17, 205–245.

Eindhoven, J.E. and Vinacke, W.E. (1952). Creative processes in painting. *Journal of General Psychology*, 47, 139–164.

Ettlie, J.E. (1983). A note on the relationship between managerial change values, innovative intentions and innovative technology outcomes in food sector firms. *R & D Management*, 13, (4).

Evan, W.M. (1966). Organizational lag. *Human Organization*, 25, 51–53.

Farris, G.F. (1973). The technical supervisor: beyond the Peter principle. *Technical Review*, 75, April.

Festinger, L. (1957). *A Theory of Cognitive Dissonance*. Stanford: Stanford University Press.

Fiedler, F.E., Chelmers, M.M. and Mahar, L. (1976). *Improving Leadership Effectiveness: The Leader Match Concept*. New York: Wiley.

Fischer, W.A. and Farr, C.M. (1985). Dimensions of innovative climate in Chinese R & D units. *R & D Management*, 15, 183–190.

Foster, R. (1986). *Innovation: The Attacker's Advantage*. New York: Macmillan.

Fulgosi, A. and Guilford, J.P. (1968). Short term incubation in divergent production. *American Journal of Psychology*, 81, 241–246.

Geschka, H. (1983). Creativity techniques in product planning and development: a view from West Germany. *R & D Management*, 13, 169–183.

Glassman, E. (1986). Managing for creativity: back to basics in R & D. *R & D Management*, 16, 175–183.

Goldsmith, R. E. (1984). Personality characteristics: association with adaption innovation. *Journal of Psychology*, 117, 159–165.

Goldsmith, R.E. and Matherly, T.A. (1987). Adaption-innovation and creativity: a replication and extension. *British Journal of Social Psychology*, 26, 79–82.

Gross, N., Giacquinta, J.B. and Bernstein, M. (1971). *Implementing Organizational Innovations: A Sociological Analysis of Planned Educational Change*. New York: Basic Books.

Grossman, J.B. (1970). The Supreme Court and social change. *American Behavioural Scientist*, 13.

Guilford, J.P. (1959). Traits of creativity. In H.H. Anderson (Ed.), *Creativity and its Cultivation*. Harper, pp. 142–161.

Hage, J. and Aiken, M. (1967). Program change and organizational properties, a comparative analysis. *American Journal of Sociology*, 72, 503–519.

Hage, J. and Aiken, M. (1970). *Social Change in Complex Organizations*. New York: Random House.

Hage, J. and Dewar, R. (1973). Elite values versus organizational structure in predicting innovation. *Administrative Science Quarterly*, 18, 279–290.

Handy, C. (1985). *Understanding Organizations*. Harmondsworth: Penguin.

Harvey, E. and Mills, R. (1970). Patterns of organizational adaptation: a political perspective. In M.N. Zald (Ed.), *Power in Organizations*. Nashville: Vanderbilt University Press.

Havelock, R.G. (1974). *Educational Innovation in the United States, Vol. II. Five Case Studies at the School District Level*. Research Report, Ann Arbor: University of Michigan, Center for Research on Utilization of Scientific Knowledge.

Hayward, G. and Everett, C. (1983). Adapters and innovators: data from the Kirton Adaption–Innovation Inventory in a local authority setting. *Journal of Occupational Psychology*, 4, 339–342.

Hersey, P. and Blanchard, K. (1982). *Management of Organizational Behaviour: Utilizing Human Resources*, 4th edn. Englewood Cliffs, NJ: Prentice-Hall.

Isen, A.M., Daubman, K.A. and Nowicki, G.P. (1987). Positive affect facilitates creative problem solving. *Journal of Personality and Social Psychology*, 71, 1122–1131.

Jones, L. (1987). Barriers to creativity. Paper presented at a British Psychological Society seminar on Stimulating Creativity at Manchester Business School, 13 June.

Kanter, R.M. (1983). *The Change Masters*. New York: Simon and Schuster.

Kaluzny, A., Veney, J. and Gentry J. (1974). Innovation of health services: a comparative study of hospitals and health departments. *Health and Society*, 15, 22–33.

Kaplan, N. (1963). The relation of creativity to sociological variables in research organizations. In C.W. Taylor and F. Barron (Eds.), *Scientific Creativity: Its Recognition and Development*. New York: Wiley.

Kimberly, J.R. (1978). Organizational size and the structuralist perspective: A review, critique, and proposal. *Administrative Science Quarterly*, 21, 571–597.

Kimberly, J.R. (1981). Managerial innovation. In P.C. Nyström and W.H. Starbuck (Eds.), *Handbook of Organizational Design*. Oxford: Oxford University Press.

Kimberly, J.R. and Evanisko, M.J. (1981). Organizational innovation: the influence of individual, organizational, and contextual factors on hospital adoption of technological and administrative innovations. *Academy of Management Journal*, 24, 689–713.

King, N. (1989). Innovation in elderly care organizations: process and attitude. Unpublished PhD Thesis, University of Sheffield, UK.

King, N. and West, M.A. (1987). Experiences of innovation at work. *Journal of Managerial Psychology*, 2, 6–10.

Kirton, M.J. (1976). Adaptors and innovators: A description and measure. *Journal of Applied Psychology*, 6, 622–629.

Kirton, M.J. (1978). Have adaptors and innovators equal levels of creativity? *Psychological Reports*, 42, 695–698.

Klein, D. (1967). Some notes on the dynamics of resistance to change: The defender role. In G. Watson (Ed.), *Concepts for Social Change*. Washington DC: National Training Laboratories.

Lovelace, R.F. (1986). Stimulating creativity through managerial intervention. *R & D Management*, 16, 161–174.

Maslow, A.H. (1943). A theory of human motivation. *Psychological Review*, 50, 370–396.

MacKinnon, D.W. (1962). The personality correlates of creativity: a study of American architects. *Proceedings of the Fourteenth Congress on Applied Psychology*, Vol. 2. Copenhagen: Munksgaard, pp. 11–39.

McCarrey, M.W. and Edwards, S.A. (1973). Organizational climate conditions for effective research scientist role performance. *Organizational Behaviour and Human Performance*, 9, 439–459.

Meyer, A.D. (1982). Adapting to environmental jolts. *Administrative Science Quarterly*, 27, 515–537.

Michael, R. (1979). How to find—and keep—creative people. *Research Management*, September, 43–45.

Miles, R.E. and Snow, C.C. (1978). *Organizational Strategy, Structure and Process*. New York: McGraw-Hill.

Miller, R.E. (1971). *Innovation, Organization and Environment*. Sherbrooke: Université de Sherbrooke.

Milo, N. (1971). Health care organizations and innovation. *Journal of Health and Social Behaviour*, 12, 163–173.

Mohr, L.B. (1969). Determinants of innovation in organizations. *American Political Science Review*, 63, 111–126.

Morgan, G. (1986). *Images of Organization*. Beverly Hills: Sage.

Mytinger, R.D. (1968). *Innovation in Local Health Services*. Arlington, Virginia: Public Health Service, Division of Medical Care Administration, US Department of Health, Education and Welfare.

Neal, R. and Radnor, M. (1971). The relationship between formal procedures for pursuing OR/MS activities and OR/MS group success. Paper presented at 40th National Conference of the Operations Research Society of America, at Anaheim, California, October.

Nicholls, J.G. (1972). Creativity in the person who will never produce anything original and useful: the concept of creativity as a normally distributed trait. *American Psychologist*, 27, 717–727.

Nicholson, N. and West, M.A. (1988). *Managerial Job Change: Men and Women in Transition*. Cambridge: Cambridge University Press.

Normann, R. (1971). Organizational innovativeness: product variation and reorientation. *Administrative Science Quarterly*, 16, 203–215.

Nystrom, H. (1979). *Creativity and Innovation*. Chichester: Wiley.

Olton, R.M. (1979). Experimental studies of incubations: searching for the elusive. *Journal of Creative Behaviour*, 13, 9–22.

Olton, R.M. and Johnson, D.M. (1976). Mechanisms of incubation in creative problem solving. *American Journal of Psychology*, 89, 617–630.

Patrick, C. (1935). Creative thought in poets. *Archives of Psychology*, 178.

Patrick, C. (1937). Creative thought in artists. *Journal of Psychology*, 4, 35–73.

Patti, R.J. (1974). Organizational resistance and change: the view from below. *Social Service Review*, 48, 367–383.

Pelz, D.C. (1981). 'Staging' effects in adoption of urban innovations. Paper presented at the Evaluation Research Society, Austin.

Pelz, D.C. and Andrews, F.M. (1976). *Productive Climates for Research and Development*. Ann Arbor, Michigan: Institute for Social Research, University of Michigan.

Peters, T.J. and Waterman, R.H. (1982). *In Search of Excellence: Lessons from America's Best Run Companies*. New York: Harper and Row.

Pierce, J.L. and Delbecq, A. (1977). Organizational structure, individual attitude and innovation. *Academy of Management Review*, pp. 27–33.

Poincaré, H. (1924). *The Foundations of Science* (trans. G.B. Halstead). Science Press.

Read, J.D. and Bruce, D. (1982). Longitudinal tracking of difficult memory retrievals. *Cognitive Psychology*, 14, 280–300.

Rogers, E.M. (1983). *Diffusion of Innovations*, 3rd edn. New York: Free Press.

Rogers, E.M. and Agarwala-Rogers, R. (Eds.) (1976). *Communications in Organizations*. New York: Free Press.

Rogers, E.M. *et al.* (1979). *The Innovation Process for Dial-A-Ride*. Research Report, Stanford: Stanford University, Institute for Communication Research.

Sapolsky, H. (1967). Organizational structure and innovation. *Journal of Business*, 40, 497–510.

Schein, E.H. (1969). *Process Consultation: Its Role in Organizational Development*. Englewood Cliffs, New Jersey: Prentice Hall.

Schroeder, R., Van de Ven, A., Scudder, G. and Polley, D. (1986). Observations leading to a process model of innovation. Discussion Paper No. 48, Strategic Management Research Center, University of Minnesota.

Shephard, H.A. (1967). Innovation-resisting and innovation-producing organizations. *Journal of Business*, 40, 470–477.

Smeltz, W. and Cross, B. (1984). Toward a profile of the creative R and D professional. *IEEE Transactions on Engineering Management*, February, 22–25.

Staw, B.M. (1984). Organizational behavior: a review and reformulation of the Field's outcome variables. *Annual Review of Psychology*, 35, 627–666.

Teger, A.I. (1980). *Too Much Invested to Quit*. New York: Pergamon.

Torrance, E.P. and Horng, R.G. (1980). Creativity and style of learning and thinking characteristics of adaptors and innovators. *The Creative Adult and Child Quarterly*, 5, 80–85.

Tushman, M.L. (1977). Special boundary roles in the innovation process. *Administrative Science Quarterly*, **22**, 587–605.

Utterback, J.M. (1975). Innovation in industry and the diffusion of technology. *Science*, **183**, 620–626.

Van de Ven, A. (1986). Central problems in the management of innovation. *Management Science*, **32**, 590–607.

Vernon, P.E. (Ed.) (1970). *Creativity*. Harmondsworth: Penguin.

Wahba, M. and Bridwell, L. (1976). Maslow reconsidered: a review of the research on the need hierarchy theory. *Organizational Behaviour and Human Performance*, **15**, 212–240.

Wallach, M.A. and Kogan, N. (1965). A new look at the creativity–intelligence distinction. *Journal of Personality*, **33**, 348–369.

Wallas, G. (1926). *The Art of Thought*. London: Cape, pp. 79–96.

Walton, R.E. (1987). Innovating to Compete: Lessons for Diffusing and Managing Change in the Workplace. San Francisco: Jossey-Bass.

Watson, G. (1971). Resistance to change. *American Behavioural Scientist*, **14**, 745–766.

Watson, G. (1973). Resistance to change. In G. Zaltman (Ed.), *Processes and Phenomena of Social Change*. New York: Wiley.

Weisberg, R.W. (1986). *Creativity: Genius and other Myths*. New York: Freeman.

West, M.A. (1987). Role innovation in the world of work. *British Journal of Social Psychology*, **26**, 305–315.

West, M.A. (1989). Innovation among health care professionals. *Social Behaviour*, **4**, 173–184.

West, M.A. and Farr, J.L. (1989). Innovation at work: psychological perspectives. *Social Behaviour*, **4**, 15–30.

Wilson, J.Q. (1966). Innovation in organizations: notes towards a theory. In J.D. Thompson (Ed.), *Approaches to Organizational Design*. Pittsburgh: Pittsburgh University Press.

Zaltman, G. and Duncan, R. (1977). *Strategies for Planned Change*. New York: Wiley.

Zaltman, G., Duncan, R. and Holbek J. (1973). *Innovations and Organizations*. New York: Wiley.

Part II

Individual and Group Innovation

3 Individual innovation

James L. Farr and Cameron M. Ford
Pennsylvania State University, USA

In this chapter we focus generally on the work roles of individuals employed in organizational settings. Specifically, we will look at work role innovations introduced in the processes and procedures used by individuals to accomplish certain work role outcomes.

Our definition of work role innovation is consistent with that offered in Chapter 1 of this volume. Thus, we define work role innovation as *the intentional introduction within one's work role of new and useful ideas, processes, products, or procedures.*

This definition presents several subtleties that need to be discussed before continuing. First, the source of an individual's ideas related to a role innovation is not particularly important for our purposes, except that the innovation must be brought about by the role incumbent and not from a mandate from others. Thus, adapting a behavior that was useful in a previous job to a new job would be considered innovative by our definition. Second, the work role should be thought of as a set of imperfectly defined rules and procedures which allows an individual to exercise some degree of discretion rather than as a static set of unbendable rules. Third, the attributes of 'newness' and 'usefulness' can be usefully thought of as continuous rather than dichotomous. In other words, one can refer to one role innovation as being more 'innovative' than another if it rates somewhat higher on these two attributes. Finally, for our purposes, we are using the individual as the frame of reference for evaluations of innovativeness. That is, we are concerned with changes that the individual considers to be innovative in terms of personal use rather than whether the idea or process is new in any objective sense.

Of course, different frames of evaluation could be useful depending on the question one wishes to ask. Therefore, in an effort to consider a broad range of possible work outcomes, we include both work related and personal

Innovation and Creativity at Work   Edited by M.A. West and J.L. Farr
© 1990 John Wiley & Sons Ltd

objectives. We refer to work related outcomes as *role performance*, defined here as *any improvement in either the quantity or quality of an individual's performance as well as improvements in the role relationships with others in the work organization.* Personal outcomes will be described by the term *role adjustment* which will be defined here as *any positive emotional and/or cognitive appraisal related to the self that results from one's job.* These adjustments would include concepts like job satisfaction, commitment, self-efficacy, and self-esteem. By considering both of these sets of outcomes we may explore role innovations which benefit the organization but have little effect on the individual and cases where only the individual benefits as a result of a change in a work role.

Having defined the major concepts to be used in this chapter, we will now focus on our primary objective which is to develop a conceptual model that can serve as a heuristic for organizing research and theorizing about individual role innovation. We do not intend for this to be a 'theory' of role innovation. Rather, it should be considered as an early step in our efforts to better understand the factors influencing the likelihood that an individual would introduce a useful change into the work role. The chapter will, however, offer only limited suggestions for improving innovation at work; it will attempt to be descriptive rather than prescriptive. In addition, since our focus is on individuals, we will only be considering work groups and larger organizational units in terms of their impact on the individuals within them.

TOWARD A MODEL OF INDIVIDUAL INNOVATION

As a means of organizing the research literature that has addressed individual innovation as well as our own thinking about the topic, we have used the model shown in Figure 1. As noted above, we intend this only as a first step in improving our understanding of work role innovation.

It is suggested in Figure 1 that the likelihood of an individual introducing an innovation in the work role is a function of four general factors. These factors are (a) the individual's perception about the need for change to occur in the work role; (b) the individual's perception that change can be successfully implemented in the work role, that is, one's efficacy beliefs concerning the implementation of change; (c) the individual's perception that a positive outcome will result from the introduction of change; and (d) the individual's ability to generate new and useful ideas. This ability may include an awareness of an already existing procedure, process, or object that can be brought into the specific work setting or it may include knowledge that is sufficient to create a procedure, process, or object in those cases in which no appropriate alternative exists.

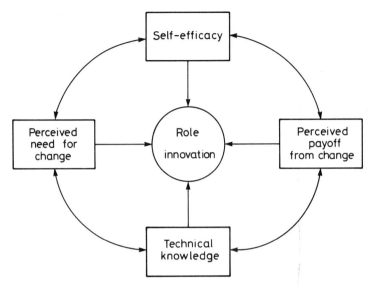

Figure 1 A model of individual motivation

For the sake of an initial discussion of each of these factors in more detail, we will assume that the four factors are independent. However, a consideration of interdependencies among these factors will be undertaken at a later point.

Factors influencing the perceived 'need for change'

One can think about the recognition of a need for change as a recognition of a problem (or performance gap) in one's work. In the creativity and decision-making research literatures, the process of formulating problems to be solved has been referred to as problem finding or problem recognition. Cowan (1986) has recently developed a model of the problem recognition process that details the various processes underlying this activity. The first component process in his model is scanning which involves 'attending to situational stimuli in one's surroundings' (p.767). In other words, by generally 'keeping one's eyes open' an individual will be more likely to discover discrepancies that demand further attention. Managers in particular must monitor a wide variety of events and actively try to make sense of them during their day-to-day activities (Daft and Weick, 1984). When scanning activities point out some discrepancy, problems are then classified or categorized, as was mentioned earlier, so that relevant knowledge can be recalled and utilized (Cowan, 1986).

After a review of the problem finding literature, Dillon (1982) presented an interesting way to think about problems. He suggests that there are three levels of problems: existent, emergent, and potential. *Existent* problems are those which exist as clearly posed, formulated problems, for example, those problems communicated by another person. Since the problem is already articulated, a person need only recognize and comprehend the issue. *Emergent* problems are those which are 'out there' waiting to be discovered during the course of scanning one's environment (this is the type of problem that Cowan's analysis seems most geared toward). On the other hand, *potential* problems are those which are 'invented' by an individual out of elements present in a situation. One might think that an individual facing an existent problem would be much less likely to develop an innovative solution than one who faces an emergent or potential problem since there would be less chance of maintaining a flexible definition of a problem. In fact, the development of a potential problem may be considered as a creative act in and of itself.

Given that scanning activities are necessary for individuals to notice that there is some need for change, what are some of the kinds of information that one might see which could create this perceived need? One category of information could be one's performance on the job. If performance is poor then obviously a person will be more likely to feel a need to change than if things are going well. Another source of information could be the actions of others at work. For example, if one sees a person innovate his or her role by learning a new, more advanced word processing program, then one may feel the need to adopt that program just to keep up. At the organizational level of analysis, the speed with which an organization copies other organizations has been examined in many studies of innovation adoption decisions (Downs and Mohr, 1976).

These sources of information involve more 'pressing' issues which reflect current states of affairs. However, one's expectations about future events could also spur a search for an innovative change. Thus, even if one does not see others pursuing change, one could still feel a need to innovate if he or she anticipates that change is inevitable. These are just a few sources of information that may lead a person to feel pressures to change. While others certainly exist, the problem recognition process described earlier is meant to apply to any situation.

Factors influencing the perceived efficacy for implementing change

Bandura (1977, 1982, 1986) has proposed that *efficacy* has a powerful impact on human behavior, especially behavior related to change. Efficacy can be defined as self-perceptions about one's ability to produce and to regulate events in one's life. 'Objective' efficacy is more than simply having the knowledge of what to do in a particular situation. Competent task or job performance within a work organization requires the integration of many cognitive, social, and behavioral skills into an executable course of action. Efficacy is concerned with self-judgments about how well one can execute those courses of action that are required to deal with a particular problem or challenge (Bandura, 1982, 1986).

Strong perceptions of efficaciousness result in the individual approaching tasks with enthusiasm, expending great amounts of effort toward task accomplishment, and persisting in the face of obstacles (Bandura, 1982). Those with serious self-doubts about their capability to succeed, on the other hand, are more likely to avoid the activity, exert little effort, and give up quickly.

Since change and innovation in a work role may involve both uncertainty about future outcomes as well as possible resistance from others affected by the change, the individual who does not possess a reasonable amount of self-efficacy faces considerable barriers. Given the importance of efficacy in the undertaking of any action, what factors influence efficacy in relation to the implementation of innovations in the work setting?

We suggest that perceptions of efficacy regarding innovation and change at work are affected by past relevant job experiences, formal training and education, personal explanatory style, and support and information systems within the organization that may include peers, superiors, and staff units. We examine each of these in more detail below.

Previous relevant job experiences

Personal experience reduces the uncertainty that may accompany any novel situation or action. Thus, previous job experiences that are related to a specific change or innovation are likely to increase the individual's efficacy beliefs about the implementation of that change. Favorable or successful experiences are, of course, likely to result in more positive impact on efficacy beliefs, but even experiences that were not successful may enhance efficacy if the individual believes that he or she has learned from failure how to be successful in the future.

It should be noted, however, that efficacy beliefs are not simply an isomorphic reflection of past performance (Bandura, 1982; Locke *et al.*, 1984). Indeed, for low performers it is not desirable that efficacy beliefs be entirely based on past performance since these could lead them to avoid certain tasks or exert little effort toward task accomplishment. In most instances, though, a reasonable degree of 'accuracy' of efficacy beliefs is desirable (Bandura, 1986). Work situations that allow the individual to receive feedback about the attainment of reasonable performance goals are likely to yield efficacy beliefs that are of sufficient accuracy. The establishment of measurable subgoals that identify progress toward a larger and more difficult endpoint or final accomplishment may be an effective way to build efficacy beliefs that themselves aid additional progress toward the final goal (Latham, 1988).

Hill *et al.* (1987) found a positive relationship between individuals' previous experience with computers and their efficacy beliefs concerning computers. Structural modeling analysis indicated that previous experience had no *direct* impact on the intention to use computers; rather, experience resulted in more positive efficacy beliefs which, in turn, positively influenced behavioral intentions.

Hill *et al.* (1987) also found that previous experience with computers was positively related to more general efficacy beliefs about the use of other innovative products and services. Thus, generalization from experience with one form of innovation may occur and lead to more positive efficacy beliefs about innovation or change in general.

It should be noted that Bandura (1982, 1986) suggests that individuals can also develop or alter their efficacy beliefs on the basis of *vicarious experience*. Observing others being successful or unsuccessful in the performance of a task can enhance or undermine, respectively, an individual's efficacy beliefs about performing that or related tasks (Bandura *et al.*, 1980; Brown and Inouye, 1978).

Formal training and education

We suggest that efficacy beliefs are, in general, positively influenced by the amount of relevant formal training and education a person has had. Such training and education should enhance the individual's beliefs concerning the possession of those skills and knowledge that permit successful task performance.

Not all instructional and evaluative procedures will equally enhance efficacy beliefs, however, especially for relatively low-achieving individuals. Instructional and evaluative techniques that stress comparisons among the trainees or students may result in more favorable efficacy beliefs among the better performers, but undermine the efficacy of less able individuals (Bandura, 1986).

Instruction in self-management or self-leadership (Manz, 1986) may enhance the perceived self-control that individuals believe they have in the work setting. Also, instructional and evaluative procedures that are more individualized and focus on the relative amount of learning and progress that the individual has demonstrated are likely to enhance the perceptions of efficacy of persons across a wide range of ability levels (Bandura, 1986).

Gist (1986) has noted the importance of active participation by the trainee with the subject matter in order for efficacy to be increased. This suggests that direct experience may be more effective than indirect or vicarious experience in altering efficacy beliefs. In addition, the training content should be meaningful to the trainee so that the links between what is learned in the training program and how it can be applied in the on-the-job situation are clear (Goldstein, 1986).

A distinction should be made between learning situations and the performance of previously learned tasks or skills (Bandura, 1986). While a high level of efficacy is beneficial to the execution of well-learned tasks, it may not always be beneficial in a learning situation. Some uncertainty may lead to more effort expenditure during learning than would occur if an individual was highly confident. If preparatory or learning activities are, in fact, needed for successful performance, then a high degree of efficaciousness may be dysfunctional. The individual needs to be confident that he or she can learn what is required for competent performance, but not overly confident that performance is assured without adequate preparation (e.g. 'I can't do it now, but I'm sure I can learn how!').

Personal explanatory style

Seligman (1987) has recently summarized the results of his research program of the past decade that has been concerned with the types of explanations that people give for the occurrence of 'bad' or negative events. He argues that there are two chronic forms of *explanatory style* which he labels for convenience as *pessimism* and *optimism*. Pessimists believe that bad events are caused by factors that are stable, global, and internal to themselves (e.g. 'I've caused this problem for myself; I always create problems for myself; I make problems for myself with whatever I do.'). Optimists make the opposite sort of attributions for such events, that is, negative events are seen as caused by factors that are unstable (or likely to change), specific (affect only the situation at hand), and external to themselves (It's *not* my fault!'). Many people cannot be neatly categorized into one of these two extreme groups, but we will follow Seligman's lead and use the extremes to illustrate the concept.

Optimists and pessimists differ in a number of ways. In a set of studies involving various methodologies and a wide range of subject samples, Seligman (1987) has shown that pessimists are more likely to become depressed when negative events occur, to achieve less in the classroom and at work, and to have poorer health and immune system functioning than optimists.

Explanatory style and efficacy beliefs appear to be related concepts. The personal explanatory styles identified and measured by Seligman seem to be important *predispositions* that help determine the *state* of an individual's efficacy beliefs. A pessimist would be likely to react to a failure in a way that would result in a low level of efficaciousness for the task or activity.

Furthermore, the pessimist would be likely to generalize from a failure on one type of task to a belief in an enhanced likelihood of failure on a different type of task. The optimist would be more likely to dismiss the past failure as being irrelevant to future performance or, alternatively, view it in a positive way as being informative with regard to factors that the individual could change (e.g. 'I need to work harder the next time.'). The efficacy beliefs of the pessimist may be devastated by a failure, while the optimist's are little changed.

The optimist may be more likely to persevere with the implementation of an innovation. The typical innovation is likely to meet some resistance or encounter various difficulties and short-term inefficiencies that may be sufficient for the pessimist to believe that his or her negative expectations about the change process were justified. The pessimist may then abandon the change process. The optimist with less shaken self-efficacy may be more likely to maintain the innovation and may, indeed, work harder to ensure its success.

Organizational support and information systems

Bandura (1982, 1986) has identified persuasion as a factor influencing efficacy. By persuasion, Bandura is referring to others' verbal attempts to convince the individual of his or her capability of performing a task (Gist, 1987). We label a similar factor as 'organizational support and information systems' in our model. This label can accommodate not only overt persuasion attempts (e.g. 'I know you can do a great job on this project!'), but also feedback from superiors, peers, and others, including quantitative information from organizational control and performance measurement systems.

The importance of feedback in the development and maintenance of efficacy beliefs has been noted previously. Supportive peers and supervisors can enhance an individual's efficacy by reinforcing the individual's role in successful task performance and prevent its drastic decline by lessening the impact of task failures or shortcomings. Supervisors may be able to increase an employee's perceived efficacy by structuring work assignments to permit a greater chance of short-term success while building the long-term capabilities of the individual.

Supportive and constructive feedback from superiors and peers that is specific to the introduction or maintenance of a role innovation will not only build efficacy concerning innovation, but is also likely to encourage role innovation via a more direct reinforcement effect. Such feedback should also be directed toward innovation attempts that may not be implemented (and, therefore, are not 'successful') for various reasons, but which are, nonetheless, viable suggestions for change.

Factors influencing the perceived payoff from change

Even if a person senses a need to change, innovative solutions are unlikely to develop if one feels that the 'payoff' from such actions is too low to offset the potential risks associated with change. We propose that individuals must foresee a 'reasonable' set of positive outcomes from a possible innovation or change before they will attempt to carry out this change (or, alternatively, foresee the avoidance of some set of negative outcomes). We do not attempt to define 'reasonable' in normative terms nor do we specify exactly what outcomes any given individual would value. Thus, we take a *process* rather than a *content* approach (Campbell and Pritchard, 1976) in addressing this issue.

Outcomes that may be positively valued by individuals can be broadly conceived to include financial rewards, organizational advancement, formal and informal recognition by others, increased autonomy, beliefs about self-worth and achievement, greater job security, the reduction or avoidance of boredom, and others. Negative outcomes include the loss or absence of the above as well as sanctions such as demotion, ridicule, etc. We argue that an individual will contrast the likely (as perceived by the individual) outcomes of an innovation with the expected outcomes of keeping the status quo. If the innovation is believed to result in more favorable (or less negative) outcomes for the individual than the status quo, then the individual will be more likely to attempt the innovation, all else being equal. Our thinking here is obviously influenced by expectancy theories of work motivation (e.g. Vroom, 1964; Porter and Lawler, 1968; Naylor *et al.*, 1980).

A number of factors may influence the individual's belief that an attempt to introduce an innovation in the work setting may or may not result in various outcomes, positive and negative. These factors include those more immediate to the individual's work unit such as the managerial and leadership behaviors of one's boss and peer relationships, and more macro level variables such as organizational policies and procedures, resources, and structure. We consider these in more detail below.

Factors in the immediate work unit

Important factors in the immediate work unit include other persons, both peers and superiors. A most critical factor is the degree of support for innovative actions taken by the individual (West and Farr, 1989; West 1989). This support must be demonstrated not only in terms of verbal or written statements, but also in the distribution of unit-level resources and other valued outcomes. Some valued outcomes may not require the explicit expenditure of work unit resources; for example, providing constructive feedback to the role incumbent or being encouraging of innovative attempts.

Others clearly do, such as the provision of discretionary time for working on projects of interest to the individual or the recommendation of bonuses for innovative approaches to work unit concerns. Superiors control many of these resource-based outcomes, but peers also can provide non-resource-based outcomes.

One must not fall into the trap of trying to make all formal organizational rewards strictly contingent on the generation of innovative ideas. Amabile (1988) has found that this type of reward contingency can be actually *inhibiting* of creative behavior. Innovative and creative behaviors cannot be produced on an 'assembly line' basis and a 'piece rate' compensation plan is not likely to be effective here. Kanter (1983) noted that conventional, material rewards were not a major reason for innovative activity in her sample of highly innovative companies.

A participative style of decision-making has been found to encourage innovation (Kanter, 1983; King and West, 1987; Peters and Waterman, 1982). Such decision-making is likely to increase the belief that an innovative idea will be accepted and valued. Seeing one's new ideas become a part of an implementation plan may strengthen the individual's belief that being innovative leads to several desired outcomes, including perceptions of self-worth and the superior's assessment of the competence of the individual.

Organizational factors

Paralleling the factors that are important at the work group level are those that operate at a more macro level. The organization's reward to performance link is important. What aspects of job performance and organizational effectiveness are explicitly rewarded? Are innovative ideas rewarded or does a formula for determining managerial bonuses take into account only last quarter's profitability? The way that performance is operationally measured and rewarded will tend to control the behavior of organizational members. An organizational reward policy that takes a relatively long-term perspective and forecasts improvements that may accrue from innovative practices may facilitate (or at least not *inhibit*) the individual's innovative behavior. It could be argued that organizationally based gainsharing systems (e.g. Scanlon plans; Hammer, 1988) can serve in this manner.

The effective implementation of any reward policy is dependent on the availability of sufficient financial resources so that policy can become reality. Resources also impact the innovativeness of individuals in other ways. There must be adequate 'slack' available in the organization for individuals to have the time to think about the future. If one is stretched or overloaded with tasks to the point that 'fire fighting' is all that is possible, then clearly little innovative, long-term thinking is likely to occur. Excessive levels of stress may produce routinized, well-rehearsed behavior patterns or otherwise interfere with tasks requiring novel responses (Friend, 1982). In addition to material rewards, Amabile (1988) has noted that time pressure has a negative effect on innovative behavior.

Kanter (1983) has noted what she has labeled as a 'culture of pride, climate of success' in highly innovative companies that is not present in less innovative ones. This serves as an incentive for continued innovativeness. Employees view themselves as 'members' and have developed an emotional attachment to the organization and are personally satisfied when the organization succeeds. If the organizational norms favor change, not tradition for its own sake, then its members will seek to initiate changes in order to be culturally appropriate.

The structure of the organization must be compatible with its culture regarding change and innovation. Organizations that are strongly bureaucratic with a rigid and tall hierarchy and with much compartmentalization of function, information, and responsibility will tend to stifle innovation (Kanter, 1983). Organizational structures that permit relative autonomy for lower levels and relative interdependence for various functional groups at the same level in the organization have been found to be associated with high levels of innovativeness (Kanter, 1983).

Incentives for innovation: concluding comment

An important point is that there is not a single or simple answer to the question of how to provide incentive for the encouragement of innovation. Redundant systems (Hackman and Walton, 1986) are needed because innovative actions, like human behavior in general, are usually *overdetermined*, that is, affected by a number of nonindependent factors. Each factor may be only modestly linked to innovativeness, but in concert such factors are much more important than simply the sum of their independent effects.

Another point is that the benefits of any single innovation may take a relatively long time to occur, whereas the short-term costs may be considerable. It is necessary for the support mechanism explicitly to take note of this and be prepared for short-term costs to be put forward as a reason for staying with the status quo. It also argues for the development of a 'climate' for innovation that is not expressly linked to a single innovative program or procedure, but rather is supportive of change and risk-taking in general. The development of such a climate is obviously more time consuming and difficult than the implementation of a single program or policy, but complex issues beget complex answers.

Factors influencing ability to generate new and useful ideas

Usually, innovation process models begin with, or at least include, an idea generation or problem recognition stage (e.g. Marquis, 1969; Zaltman *et al.*,

1973; Utterback 1974; Amabile, 1988; Kanter, 1988). While problem recognition and idea generation activities occur to a greater or lesser extent in virtually all problem solving activities, we propose that one's ability to generate new and useful ideas will be especially important to the development of role innovations. At least two factors will influence this ability: the effectiveness of one's search for ideas and one's creative abilities.

Searching for solutions

March and Simon (1958) wrote about 'problemistic' search processes in which the exploration for alternatives is driven by the perception of a problem. They proposed that once a problem becomes categorized, the search for alternatives will be restricted. In other words, the way a problem is defined and categorized will tend to influence the subsequent search for solutions.

There are, of course, many different sources one could search to discover new ideas. An individual will generally search first through memories of past experiences with similar situations to see if a satisfactory alternative can be found (Mintzberg et al., 1976). Previous training, experience, and expertise will obviously influence the number of ideas one can bring to bear on a given problem (Simon, 1986). However, if exploring alternatives resulting from one's own experiences is ineffective, others may need to be consulted for help in producing additional alternatives as well as for help in evaluating the quality and innovativeness of a solution. For example, managers often use 'sounding boards' to help uncover possible solutions to problems (McCall and Kaplan, 1985). Also, superiors who may possess experience with similar problems occurring within the organizational context could be consulted. In addition to these fairly intimate personal interactions, one may seek help from specialists operating within the organization in different functional areas.

Another source of ideas for innovative solutions that one could explore is one's competitors or others currently facing the same problem. In fact, innovative behavior has frequently been defined in terms of the speed with which an individual adopts a new, existing solution developed elsewhere (e.g. Rogers and Shoemaker, 1971). Finally, innovative solutions for organizational problems may be discovered by talking to an organization's customers or clients. Many of America's most innovative companies try to emphasize customer generated ideas in their product development efforts (Peters and Waterman, 1982). One might expect that more elaborate search processes that explore a variety of potential sources of innovative ideas will improve an individual's ability to innovate.

Creative abilities

Search procedures may be very useful for unearthing existing solutions that could be applied in new and useful ways. However, innovative solutions may need to be created that meet the unique demands of a specific situation. Unfortunately, not everyone possesses the same creative abilities which may be necessary to produce lists of potentially innovative alternative solutions. Amabile (1988) emphasizes the importance of creativity related skills to the innovation process. While a review of the various theories of creativity is beyond the scope of this chapter, several different abilities may be involved in the production of creative alternatives. Among these are the ability to make random associations between ideas, the ability to see divergent uses for a single idea, the ability to access one's subconscious, and the ability to visualize potential solutions (Barron and Harrington, 1981). These creative abilities, coupled with one's use of various sources of existing ideas, will influence the ability to generate new and useful ideas.

Relationships among the factors in the model

In the preceding discussion we, in general, have treated the factors in the model as independent. It can be seen in Figure 1 that we do not consider innovative behavior to be a function of the sum of the four factors. While our current level of development of the model does not permit great precision, we do assume the degree of individual role innovation to follow some multiplicative combination of the four factors. This means that if any one (or more) of the four factors is 'zero' or nonexistent, we would expect the probability of role innovation to be zero or, at least, very small. A combination of the perceived need for change, perceived efficacy for implementing change, and perceived payoff from change factors can be thought of as determining the individual's 'motivation' for change and innovation, while the knowledge of innovative possibilities is more related to one's 'ability' to innovate.

In addition, a careful look at our earlier discussion reveals that the factors may have some common antecedents. Among these are feedback concerning present (and, perhaps, near future) performance, support for risk-taking and change, a reward system that does not demand immediate results, and a job design mechanism that permits 'small wins' and the resulting building of favorable beliefs concerning change.

There are also likely interrelationships among the four factors in our model. Many such relationships may exist, but we will mention just a few here as examples. Those who more readily perceive a 'need for change' are more likely to use self-initiated problem solving and, if individuals do not see a need for change, they will also be less likely to persevere in other-initiated problem solving. Those who have greater knowledge of innovative possibilities should be more likely to have relatively high levels of self-efficacy regarding change than those who do not have such knowledge. Individuals who perceive a great need for change will, no doubt, be more likely to perceive a greater payoff from the implementation of an innovation than those who perceive little or no need for any change.

Having examined the factors that we consider to be important to the understanding of individual role innovation, attention should be given to some broad issues that rarely are discussed in the innovation literature.

SOME QUESTIONS RARELY ASKED

Is individual role innovation always 'good'?

Certainly a consistent (although usually implicit) theme in the published literature on innovation is that innovation is always 'good'. The positive consequences of change are generally cited; for example, flexibility, being abreast of advances, individual growth, capitalizing on opportunities, etc. Are there potentially negative consequences of individual role innovation? We believe that there are.

At the level of individual role innovation a fundamental question can be asked regarding the usefulness or effectiveness of the change that is introduced. Who evaluates the change? Change for change's sake (e.g. the introduction of the latest in computer technology or software whose new features are not really required by the existent application) will not be likely to enhance organizational functioning. Of course, many individual changes will require organizational resources and, thus, may require the (at least minimal) evaluation and approval of other organizational members or units. The trick may be developing a procedure for ensuring the usefulness of innovations that are implemented without stifling all change. There may be a fine line between control and approval mechanisms that save the organization from the introduction of useless or trivial change and mechanisms that forestall all change efforts by their burdensome nature.

Another possible downside to individual role innovation is related to the timing of such innovation. If the organization or work unit is undergoing substantial change, overall organizational or unit effectiveness may be enhanced if individuals do not attempt much self-initiated role innovation at the same time. Although it could be argued that resistance to change may be lower at such points, too much change at one time may lead to chaos and ineffectiveness.

What is the effect of individual innovation on interdependent jobs?

Although this chapter has focused on how individuals initiate innovative changes at work, we also recognize that these changes take place within an organizational context. Therefore, an important consideration regarding an individual role innovation is how these innovations will affect others. For example, one would expect that work role innovations would be easier to implement in roles where the number of people one has to interact with is somewhat limited (Kimberly, 1981). The higher the number of interdependencies in a role, the more complex the issues associated with implementing an innovation.

It may be useful to categorize role activities in terms of their effects on others. Activities that have significant impacts on others should not be changed unless systemic changes are planned, while activities that have relatively little direct impact on others could be changed at the discretion of the person within the role. This highlights the extreme challenge facing an individual who wants to implement a significant innovation which may have a significant effect on others. Not only changes within the job but also changes in other work roles will need to be considered.

Can anyone be an effective innovator?

Because we are arguing that work role innovation begins as an individual process involving a number of perceptual and motivational factors, one may conclude that we believe individual characteristics will determine one's ability to be innovative. However, our focus on work roles, rather than on individual differences among personality traits, is our way of emphasizing that work role innovations arise from configurations of individual, organizational, and situational influences (Amabile, 1983). The factors we have proposed which lead to innovative work behavior involve person/role interactions rather than the sole consideration of an individual's abilities.

We are fairly optimistic that most individuals can be effective work role innovators. Some individuals may be generally more likely to implement changes across a variety of situations (Kirton, 1976). However, in a specific situation those individual differences will be less important than the interactions among situational and personal characteristics.

CONCLUSIONS

This chapter has attempted to identify and organize a number of possible influences on individual innovation. As mentioned earlier, many of the ideas presented are consistent with expectancy theory. We have discussed how self-efficacy beliefs influence a person's decision to put forth the effort to implement changes at work. We have also pointed out how dissatisfaction with the current state of one's situation and perceived payoff from changing that situation can influence the persistence of a person's effort. Because changes in the workplace are likely to encounter a substantial amount of resistance, these motivational influences may be particularly important to the success of individual innovations.

Of course, the actual effectiveness of an individual innovation will be a function not only of effort, but also of ability. In this chapter, we have emphasized an individual's knowledge of innovative possibilities and creativity skills as important dimensions of ability needed for implementing individual innovations. These abilities help guide a person's efforts to productive ends.

Although we are emphasizing the individual as our unit of analysis, we have tried to show how social factors, such as feedback from others, information systems, leadership styles, and organizational reward systems, influence the individual's efforts to innovate. Also, sounding boards, as well as organizational information systems, can be thought of as important contributors to an individual's knowledge of innovative possibilities. In our view, the relative influence of individual and organizational variables is less interesting than the interactions among these phenomena that lead to increased innovation.

Our thinking on this topic is still in its early stages. The variables that we have suggested in this chapter should be thought of as providing a starting point for research that can serve to 'fine tune' our approach. We think that emphasizing the motivational and skill related aspects of individual innovation may provide an impetus for developing more prescriptive statements regarding these processes. However, more research exploring the interaction of individual and social influences on work role innovation is necessary before such statements can be made with any confidence.

Correspondence addresses:
Professor James L. Farr, Department of Psychology, Pennsylvania State University, University Park, Pennsylvania 16802, USA.
Cameron M. Ford, Graduate School of Management, Rutgers University, 92 New Street, Newark, New Jersey 07102, USA.

REFERENCES

Amabile, T.M. (1983). *The Social Psychology of Creativity.* New York: Springer-Verlag.
Amabile, T.M. (1988). A model of creativity and innovation in organizations. *Research in Organizational Behavior,* **10**, 123–167.

Bandura, A. (1977). Self-efficacy: Toward a unifying theory of behavioral change. *Psychological Review*, **84**, 191–215.

Bandura, A. (1982). Self-efficacy mechanism in human agency. *American Psychologist*, **37**, 122–147.

Bandura, A. (1986). *Social Foundations of Thought and Action*. Englewood Cliffs, NJ: Prentice-Hall.

Bandura, A., Adams, N.E., Hardy, A.B. and Howells, G.N. (1980). Tests of the generality of self-efficacy theory. *Cognitive Theory and Research*, **4**, 39–66.

Barron, F. and Harrington, D.M. (1981). Creativity, intelligence, and personality. *Annual Review of Psychology*, **32**, 439–476.

Brown, I., Jr. and Inouye, D.K. (1978). Learned helplessness through modeling: The role of perceived similarity in competence. *Journal of Personality and Social Psychology*, **36**, 900–908.

Campbell, J.P. and Pritchard, R.D. (1976). Motivation theory in industrial and organizational psychology. In M.D. Dunnette (Ed.), *Handbook of Industrial and Organizational Psychology*. Chicago: Rand McNally.

Cowan, D.A. (1986). Developing a process model of problem recognition. *Academy of Management Review*, **11**, 763–776.

Daft, R.L. and Weick, K.E. (1984). Toward a model of organizations as interpretative systems. *Academy of Management Review*, **9**, 284–295.

Dillon, J.T. (1982). Problem solving and finding. *Journal of Creative Behavior*, **16**, 97–111.

Downs, G.W. Jr and Mohr, L.B. (1976). Conceptual issues in the study of innovation. *Administrative Science Quarterly*, **21**, 700–714.

Friend, K.E. (1982). Stress and performance: Effects of subjective work load and time urgency. *Personnel Psychology*, **35**, 623–633.

Gist, M.E. (1986). The effects of self-efficacy training on training task performance. *Academy of Management Best Papers Proceedings*, **46**, 250–254.

Gist, M.E. (1987). Self-efficacy: Implications for organizational behavior and human resource management. *Academy of Management Review*, **12**, 472–485.

Goldstein, I.L. (1986). *Training in Organizations: Needs Assessment, Development, and Evaluation*, 2nd edn. Monterey, CA: Brooks/Cole.

Hackman, J.R. and Walton, R.E. (1986). Leading groups in organizations. In Goodman, P.S. and associates, *Designing Effective Work Groups*. San Francisco: Jossey-Bass.

Hammer, T.H. (1988). New developments in profit sharing, gainsharing, and employee ownership. In J.P. Campbell and R.J. Campbell (Eds.), *Productivity in Organizations*. San Francisco: Jossey-Bass.

Hill, T., Smith, N.D. and Mann, M.F. (1987). Role of efficacy expectations in predicting the decision to use advanced technologies: The case of computers. *Journal of Applied Psychology*, **72**, 307–313.

Kanter, R.M. (1983). *The Change Masters*. New York: Simon and Schuster.

Kanter, R.M. (1988). When a thousand flowers bloom: Structural, collective, and social conditions for innovation in organizations. *Research in Organizational Behavior*, **10**, 169–211.

Kimberly, J.R. (1981). Managerial innovations. In W.H. Starbuck (Ed.), *Handbook of Organizational Design*. New York: Oxford University Press, pp. 84–104.

King, N. and West, M.A. (1987). Reactions to innovation in elderly care institutions. (Abstract.) *Bulletin of the British Psychological Society*, **40**, A31.

Kirton, M.J. (1976). Adaptors and innovators: A description and measure. *Journal of Applied Psychology*, **61**, 622–629.

Latham, G.P. (1988). Human resource training and development. *Annual Review of Psychology*, **39**, 545–582.

Locke, E.A., Frederick, E., Lee, C. and Bobko, P. (1984). Effect of self-efficacy, goals, and task strategies on task performance. *Journal of Applied Psychology*, **69**, 241–251.

Manz, C.C. (1986). Self leadership: Toward an expanded theory of self influence processes in organizations. *Academy of Management Review*, **11**, 585–600.

March, J. and Simon, H. (1958). *Organizations*. New York: Wiley.

Marquis, D.G. (1969). The anatomy of successful innovations. *Innovation*, **1**, 35–48.

McCall, M.W. and Kaplan, R.E. (1985). *Whatever it Takes: Decision Makers at Work*. Englewood Cliffs, NJ: Prentice-Hall.

Mintzberg, H., Raisinghani, D. and Theoret, A. (1976). The structure of 'unstructured' decision processes. *Administrative Science Quarterly*, **21**, 246–275.

Naylor, J.C., Pritchard, R.D. and Ilgen, D.R. (1980). *A Theory of Behavior in Organizations*. New York: Academic Press.

Peters, T.J. and Waterman, R.H. (1982). *In Search of Excellence: Lessons from America's Best Run Companies*. New York: Harper and Row.

Porter, L.W. and Lawler, E.E. (1968). *Managerial Attitudes and Performance*. Homewood, IL: Dorsey-Irwin.

Rogers, E.M. and Shoemaker, F.F. (1971). *Communication of Innovations: A Cross-cultural Approach*. New York: The Free Press.

Seligman, M.E.P. (1987). *Predicting Depression, Poor Health and Presidential Elections*. Washington, DC: Federation of Behavioral, Psychological and Cognitive Sciences.

Simon, H.A. (1986). How managers express their creativity. *Across the Board*, March, 11–16.

Utterback, J.M. (1974). Innovation in industry and the diffusion of technology. *Science*, **183**, 620–626.

Vroom, V.H. (1964). *Work and Motivation*. New York: Wiley.

West, M.A. (1989). Innovation among health care professionals. *Social Behaviour*, **4**, 173–184.

West, M.A. and Farr, J.L. (1989). Innovation at work: Psychological perspectives. *Social Behavior*, **4**, 15–30.

Zaltman, G., Duncan, R. and Holbek, J. (1973). *Innovations and Organizations*. Chichester: Wiley.

4 *Innovation in working groups*

Nigel King[1] and Neil Anderson[2]

Universities of [1]*Manchester and* [2]*Sheffield, UK*

INTRODUCTION

Groups play a crucial role in the innovation process within organizations; an innovation may be invented by an R & D team, adopted by a management group or board of directors, and modified and utilized by a work group such as a primary health care team or a sales group. Despite this, innovation at the level of the working group has received much less attention than at the individual and organizational levels.

The current chapter aims to help redress the balance. The first section summarizes and presents a critique of the existing literature on group level innovation. The second section goes on to present findings from an empirical study (King, 1989) of status group differences in perceptions of the innovation process. The final section suggests strategies for future group level innovation research, concluding with five specific recommendations.

SECTION I: THE LITERATURE ON GROUP LEVEL INNOVATION

Previous research into work group innovation may be categorized into two distinct approaches, as the individual and organizational level literature was in the second chapter of this volume: namely *antecedent factors* and *process* research. Antecedent studies are concerned with factors facilitating or inhibiting the occurrence of innovation while process studies focus on the sequence of events and decisions by which an innovation is introduced. Following the review, a critique of the literature will be presented.

Innovation and Creativity at Work   Edited by M.A. West and J.L. Farr
© 1990 John Wiley & Sons Ltd

A definition of work group innovation

Prior to reviewing the literature, it is useful to consider the following definition of innovation at the level of the work group:

> Group innovation is the emergence, import, or imposition of new ideas which are pursued towards implementation by the group through inter-personal discussions and successive re-mouldings of the original proposal over time. (Anderson, 1989; p.4)

Two points in particular need to be emphasized in relation to this definition. First, ideas new to the group may be *emergent* (i.e. developed entirely by the group), *imported* (i.e. adopted and/or adapted by the group from established practices elsewhere), or *imposed* (i.e. imposed upon the group by senior management). Antecedents to, and processes of, the three types of innovation are likely to differ fundamentally. For instance, an emergent group innovation will commence with some form of ideation or creativity (Glassman, 1986) and proceed through group discussions towards implementation and routinization. An imposed innovation, in contrast, precludes proactive ideation on the part of group members, but may demand reactive modification by the group as well as the development of plans to implement the innovation. An imported innovation is likely to allow the group more discretion than an imposed one over how it is implemented and used, and the option to reject it is more likely to be available. Clearly, emergent, imported and imposed innovations generate different empirical questions, and this typology therefore seems a valuable categorization system.

The second key feature of the definition is its *process orientation*. That is, innovation is asserted to be *the process* of intra-group negotiations and re-mouldings of the original proposal. In common with process-based definitions of organizational innovation (Rickards, 1985; West and Farr, 1989), this definition emphasizes that innovation is the process by which a new proposal is initiated, implemented and absorbed into the group, rather than simply the product of these negotiations.

Antecedent factors approaches

Five main antecedents of group level innovation are found in the literature; of these, the most frequently discussed are *leadership* and *group cohesiveness*.

1. Leadership

Many writers have concluded that a democratic collaborative leadership style encourages group innovation (Nyström, 1979; Coopey, 1987). Coopey points to a study by Farris (1973), which showed that in research laboratories, the more innovative groups 'collaborated more highly with their supervisors and with each other than did the less innovative groups'. Similarly, West and Wallace (1988) found that 'peer leadership' (Taylor and Bowers, 1971) discriminated significantly between highly innovative and less innovative teams in primary health care practices, as reliably rated by independent experts. The highly innovative teams exhibited a higher degree of leadership support, goal emphasis, team building and work facilitation.

Although at all levels of analysis, innovation is held to be encouraged by high levels of discretion (Amabile, 1983; Nicholson and West, 1988), there is evidence from work on scientific research teams that the highest levels of innovation are elicited by leaders who exerted moderate control over the group (Farris, 1973; Pelz and Andrews, 1976).

. . . complete freedom of choice of how to spend one's time is not as effective as moderate freedom involving supportive consultations with supervisors or managers. (Glassman, 1986; p.176)

One major problem with such research into leadership is that group factors have been neglected and research has generally not gone beyond applying individual level concepts directly to groups. Managers are encouraged to create and maintain a favourable environment for innovation by such activities as identifying and removing blocks to creativity (Glassman, 1986; Jones, 1987), and allowing the individual to be motivated intrinsically (Amabile, 1983, 1984; Lovelace, 1986). But there has been a lack of concern with how to manage intra-group processes such as conformity or norm-formation. Until more is known about the kind of group environment that encourages innovation, it is premature to make recommendations about how leaders may influence groups to be innovative.

2. Cohesiveness

The one specifically group level factor which is commonly mentioned as an antecedent to innovation is *cohesiveness*. However, on the basis of current knowledge of the effects of cohesiveness on group performance, contradictory influences are evident. On the one hand, it is argued that cohesiveness facilitates innovation because it increases feelings of self-actualization and psychological safety, as Nyström (1979) points out:

> *When cohesiveness is high the individual evidently identifies more directly with what the group does and achieves greater satisfaction from group action. At the same time he is not alone responsible for possible failures, which is reassuring. (Nyström, 1979; p.45)*

On the other hand, an important factor in producing high cohesiveness is group homogeneity (Crosby, 1968), which is likely to be an inhibitor of innovation because it leads to unwillingness to question group decisions, and a focus on relationships rather than tasks—in the extreme leading to the 'Group Think' phenomenon (Janis, 1982).

Not surprisingly then, the empirical evidence is ambiguous. Wallace (1988) found that cohesiveness discriminated significantly between health care teams previously identified as high or low in innovativeness by independent expert raters, but that across all the practices there was no significant correlation. Further research is necessary to determine whether a simple linear or some form of curvilinear relationship exists between innovation and cohesiveness. Also, the possibility that the type of relationship varies according to the content and context of the innovation should be investigated.

Nyström (1979) attempts to resolve the contradiction by stating the need to alter group characteristics according to the current stage of the innovation process. Early on loosely joined, heterogeneous groups are required to facilitate the production of innovative ideas, while later groups should be cohesive and homogeneous to facilitate implementation. The problem, of course, is how such a structural transition could be achieved in practice, especially as any given group may be involved in the introduction of several innovations at the same time, all at different phases in the process.

3. Group longevity

Another variable which has been discussed as a possible influence on innovation is *group longevity*. Lovelace (1986) suggests that research scientists will be more creative if not assigned to permanent groups, and Nyström (1979) too argues for the advantages of relatively short-lived groups, at least as far as the early stages of the innovation process are concerned. A study by Katz (1982) found longevity to be negatively related to performance in R & D teams; however, this represents only indirect support for Nyström's argument as it cannot be assumed that the general level of performance and the level of innovation will always be equivalent. To further complicate matters, it might be expected that group longevity will contribute towards cohesiveness. Again, more research is needed before a clear understanding emerges of how the longevity of a work group affects its innovativeness.

4. Group composition

As well as longevity, *group composition* is an important question. Geschka (1983) proposes that specially trained innovation planning teams be constituted within organizations, comprising six to eight members drawn from differing fields or functions. Teams should include one or two 'opinion leaders' who can aid in dissemination of innovation. The need for 'stimulating colleagues' has also been stressed (Parmeter and Gaber, 1971) but more precise knowledge of how composition of the group can affect innovation is required. Social psychological research on minority influence in groups may offer pointers here, suggesting that a minority of dissenting members in group decision-making can lead to more possibilities being examined and potentially to better quality decisions (Nemeth and Wachtler, 1983; Maass and Clark 1983). This is in line with Janis' (1982) recommendations for avoiding 'Group Think', which include the presence of an individual who will play a 'devil's advocate' role, ensuring all decisions made are thoroughly questioned. In any case, even at this early stage in our understanding, it would be naive to presume that the best way to ensure that a group is innovative is simply to ensure that it is composed of highly creative individuals.

5. Group structure

Finally, it has been proposed that *group structure* influences innovation. Meadows (1980) has attempted to apply Burns and Stalker's (1961) concept of 'organic' organizational structure to small working groups. (A highly 'organic' group has characteristics such as an integrative, team-based approach to tasks, blurred boundaries of authority and influence, professional commitment, etc.). In a study involving R & D and technical departments in the chemical and telecommunications industries, he found a significant positive relationship between their measure of *organicity* and the perceived innovativeness of group tasks. However, the relationship between these factors and actual innovative performance remains to be tested.

To summarize, although existing research has addressed the influence of (1) leadership, (2) cohesiveness, (3) longevity, (4) composition and (5) structure upon work group innovation, it has mostly done so indirectly, and considerable further research is required. In particular, it is surprising how atheoretical is most of the work taking an antecedent approach to group level innovation, given the extensive social psychological literature on groups which could offer much to the development of a theoretical foundation. This is an issue we will return to in the critique.

Process approaches

If the body of literature in the area of group level innovation is small, studies which adopt a process approach are virtually non-existent. There have been a few attempts to apply models from the study of individual creativity; for instance Amabile (1986) states that her social psychological model of individual creativity (1983) is applicable to small groups as well, while Nyström (1979) extends the use of Wallas' (1926) model of the creative process to small, informal working groups. In neither case does the author clearly explain how the models can be applied to groups. In Amabile's model we are not given any indication of how the levels of the three 'components' of motivation, task-skills and creative thinking skills may be determined for groups—is it simply a matter of aggregating those of all the individual members? Nyström's use of Wallas' model is even more problematic; Amabile's is at least a social model, but Wallas' is concerned purely with thought processes: preparation, incubation, illumination and verification. It is, for instance, very difficult to imagine how a group could 'incubate' an innovative idea.

Rather than converting individual level models to groups, we might look outside the innovation literature for work upon which a truly group level model could be based. One potential source is the literature on group decision-making; decisions about the innovation process are likely to be mostly 'non-programmed' (Simon, 1984)—that is, novel and unstructured, and as Ivancevich and Matteson (1987) point out, this type of decision within organizations is commonly taken by a group rather than an individual. However, it would be wrong just to apply a decision-making model such as Ivancevich and Matteson's (1987) directly to the innovation process, as decision-making is only one of the processes of relevance; others include conformity, resistance, attitude change, and so on. Also, the kinds of decision groups have to make about innovation may not be typical of the decisions they have to make about more routine matters.

As work group innovation is a process, it is essential that empirically validated process models are produced; without them, knowledge of the subject will remain severely limited. Existing models of individual, and perhaps even organizational, level innovation processes, and research in areas such as group decision-making, may be usefully drawn upon, but care must be taken to ensure that the distinct characteristics of group level innovation are not disregarded.

SECTION II: A BRIEF CRITIQUE OF WORK GROUP INNOVATION RESEARCH

The preceding review of work group innovation research highlights central weaknesses in the coverage of the existing literature, and hence our understanding of the innovation process (see also West and Farr, 1989).

Certainly, group level innovation research is at an embryonic stage, and in particular sheds little light upon fundamental questions regarding the influence of group dynamics and development over time upon innovation.

More fundamental than this criticism of restricted coverage, however, are a number of inherent methodological and conceptual shortcomings in most of the work reviewed earlier in this chapter. Firstly, existing research at the group level has tended to adopt what may be termed a *univariate design* by attempting to evaluate the impact of one particular group characteristic, or at best a few selected characteristics, upon group innovativeness. Although, for instance, a participative leadership style has been found to correlate with innovation, pertinent doubts remain that a host of other, unmeasured independent variables could have influenced group innovativeness. A *multivariate design* approach is therefore called for to examine the impact of the numerous group characteristics which may impinge upon innovation.

A second major criticism concerns the assumption implicit in many studies that innovation is desirable and represents an appropriate social process for managers to attempt to initiate and/or control. Dealing with pro-innovation bias first, Kimberly (1981) makes the following recommendation, with which we strongly concur:

> *The most useful prescription for managerial innovation is to avoid the assumption that innovation is good and more innovation is better. (p.81)*

The assumption that innovation is universally beneficial is also prevalent in popular prescriptive texts (cf. Kanter, 1983; Peters and Waterman, 1982), but clearly this assumption runs counter to situations where organizational contingencies would dictate low levels of innovation as being more appropriate (cf. Child, 1975, 1983; Lupton, 1975; Galbraith, 1973).

Further doubts arise over the 'manageability' of group innovation processes. The extent to which management can instigate, encourage or control the process is certainly moderated by the disruptive nature of innovation and its implicit challenge to the status quo (Bouwen, 1988, 1989; Anderson, 1989).

These doubts highlight a third major criticism against the existing group innovation literature, concerning its managerialist and apolitical orientation. Few studies have focused on the effects of innovations as perceived by individual employees within work groups, and this has led to a predominantly 'top-down' view of innovation. Research designs seeking a *plurality of perceptions* on specific cases of innovation are therefore needed to illustrate differing perceptions of the same innovation process, and an example of this is provided in section III of this chapter.

Finally, perhaps the most critical weakness in innovation research is its myopic isolation from existing themes in the social psychological literature. Several relevant areas of research can be identified, all of which offer pointers for future empirical and theoretical work. This is particularly true for research into *group decision-making*. 'Group think' (Janis, 1982) has already been referred to as a possible consequence of high cohesiveness and homogeneity; we might expect it to lead to a failure to be sufficiently critical of proposed innovations and to consider alternatives, leading to a deterioration in quality, rather than quantity, of innovation. The 'risky shift' (Stoner, 1968) phenomenon—the observation that groups tend to take riskier decisions than individuals—may also have an effect on innovation, with the implication that where innovation is being inhibited by too much caution, decisions should be made by groups rather than individuals. Social psychological studies of escalation in decision-making is a third relevant area; Teger (1980) studied experimentally the escalation process and showed that both individuals and groups will continue with behaviour which is ineffective, costly and unlikely to succeed because they are unwilling to 'lose' what they have already invested. This may help to explain why practices which have proved unsuccessful, or are outdated, may be retained rather than terminated in favour of new, innovative ideas.

Another potentially valuable source is the research into *creative problem solving* (Bell, 1982; Mabry, 1975) and *idea development* (Poole, 1981; Scheidel and Crowell, 1964) which contains useful process models which may be applicable to the group innovation process. Groups are constantly evolving, and so studies into *group development* over time (Gersick, 1988; Moreland and Levine, 1988) and *individual socialization* into the group (Wanous *et al.*, 1984) hold promise for guiding longitudinal studies of group innovation. Similarly, process models of group decision-making such as Ivancevich and Matteson's (1987), mentioned earlier, may be drawn upon for the development of group level innovation process models. Finally, work on *inter-group processes* may be applied to innovation. Our knowledge of inter-group conflict (Sherif and Sherif, 1969) and identification with the group (Tajfel, 1974) suggests that there may be circumstances in which competition between groups would facilitate innovation, even though at the individual level research has tended to find that extrinsic factors such as competition inhibit innovation (Amabile, 1983).

Thus, to summarize, several themes of existing social psychological research seem relevant to the study of work group innovation but have been overlooked by research to date. This theoretical shortcoming, together with the methodological and conceptual weaknesses outlined earlier in this section, casts doubt upon the contribution of the restricted body of literature to any real understanding of the antecedents to, and processes of, work group innovation.

SECTION III: PERCEPTIONS OF THE INNOVATION PROCESS: AN EMPIRICAL STUDY

This section examines the findings from a study which was carried out in response to some of the issues which we have raised in the first part of the chapter.

Introduction

The study sought to examine historically cases of innovation in two Homes for the Elderly. A broad range of issues was addressed, but the present account confines itself to inter-group differences in perceptions of the innovation process (for full details of the study see King, 1989). The research question was stated as follows:

Are there differences between staff groups in participants' reports of (i) where influences on the innovation process originated from (influence source), and (ii) whether the influences were helps or hindrances to the process (influence direction)?

Additionally, differences between staff groups in their relative emphasis on *initiation* and *implementation phases* of the process were examined.

A brief description of the two Homes will help the reader put the subsequent discussion into context. Both were local authority run Homes, in the same administrative area. The head of a Home is the principal, who has a managerial team of 'senior staff' (a deputy and three or four assistants). Care of the residents and upkeep of the Homes are the responsibilities of the care and domestic staffs respectively. To preserve their anonymity, the Homes are referred to by pseudonyms.

Beech Court is a 12-bedded purpose built unit, which opened in January, 1983. It is a single floor building with a total staff of 22: five senior staff and 17 care and domestic staff.

Watersmeet is a 49-bedded purpose built unit, which at the time the interviews were carried out had been open for approximately 18 years. It is built on three levels, and has 25 care and domestic, and five senior staff.

Procedure

One innovation was selected from each Home, from lists of significant changes provided by participants on a preliminary questionnaire. These formed the foci for 'case history' interviews with members of staff. They were chosen on the basis of compatibility of examples across Homes, both in terms of content and time-scale. Brief descriptions of the innovations are given below.

Beech Court: 'flexi-respite care'

This innovation concerned the way beds were used in the Home. Instead of being occupied by permanent residents, who would usually stay there for the rest of their lives, the Home chose to admit only 'short stay' residents; either on a regular basis ('respite') of two weeks in every eight, or for other irregular periods to meet specific needs.

Watersmeet: 'short stay wing'

This involved the same kind of change in the use of beds as Beech Court's introduction of flexi-respite care. The only major difference was that at Watersmeet, the innovation was just introduced on one of the three floors, instead of throughout the Home, though because of the larger size of Watersmeet, the actual number of beds involved was about the same.

Method

The main data collection took place between March and May, 1986, and consisted of interviews with members of staff, carried out at the Homes. At Beech Court, 20 out of 22 members of staff were interviewed; at Watersmeet the figure was 15 out of 30, making a total of 35 interviews. However, at both Homes some interviewees were unable to give full accounts of the selected innovation—often because they had not been at the Home long enough to have seen the earlier stages of the process. These interviews were therefore not included in the present analysis, leaving the total numbers of valid cases as 15 at Beech Court and 10 at Watersmeet.

In keeping with the exploratory nature of the study, the interviews were semi-structured, whereby the researcher allowed interviewees to describe the histories of the innovations, but raised certain key issues with them if they did not bring them up themselves. These were:

- What was the situation before the innovation was introduced?
- Who introduced the innovation?
- How was the innovation introduced?—gradually or suddenly, with or without a trial period?
- How is the innovation working now? (for continuing innovations)
- How did the innovation come to be abandoned? (for discontinued innovations)

Analysis

The form of content analysis used on the interview transcripts drew upon phenomenological approaches, in particular the guidelines suggested by Hycner (1985). The aim was to allow the classification of sources of influence to emerge from the data, instead of deriving categories from existing theory. This was felt to be appropriate to the exploratory nature of the study, and necessary given the lack of theoretical work on groups and small organizations, already discussed in this chapter.

The first stage was to divide each text into units of analysis. Following Hycner (1985), the unit used was the 'unit of general meeting', which is defined as a segment of text containing a discrete meaning separate from preceding and subsequent meanings. Once this had been carried out on all transcripts, the next task was to identify which units were relevant to the research area—in this case, influences on the innovation process. Hycner (1985) calls these 'units of relevant meaning'.

In the next stage of the analysis, statements identified as units of relevant meaning were classified by *source of influence*. For each innovation, a list of influences mentioned was compiled and these were then clustered according to whose actions, demands or needs were primarily responsible for them. As a result, five categories of influence source were produced:

(1) *Clients*, including residents, their relatives, and elderly people in the community.
(2) *Home management*, including the principals and senior staff of the Homes.
(3) *Non-management staff*, including care assistants and domestic/kitchen staff.
(4) *Higher management and other outside agencies* including social workers, principals of other Homes, general practitioners etc.
(5) *Influence source not determinable.*

As well as source of influence, each statement was classified on two further dimensions. The first of these was according to the *direction of the influence*—whether it was positive (a '*help*'), negative (a '*hindrance*') or of no clear direction ('*indefinite*').

The final dimension was *process phase*, that is, the stage of the innovation process a particular statement referred to. Here there were three possible categories:

(1) *Initiation*—all the actions, events and conditions leading up to the point at which the organization starts to implement the innovation.
(2) *Implementation–absorption*—everything happening to the innovation

from its first implementation to the point at which it is routinized into
the organization's life.

(3) *Non-specifiable*—cases where the interviewee is referring to the process
as a whole or where it is impossible to determine which phase she/he
is referring to.

All stages of the coding were guided by written criteria, and inter-rater
reliability was tested for on selected transcripts. The kappa coefficients of
agreement—between four raters for units of relevant meaning, and three
raters for the other stages—were all above the minimum acceptable level of
0.4, cited by Fleiss (1981): kappas = 0.62 (units of relevant meaning), 0.57
(influence source), 0.45 (influence direction), and 0.69 (phase). The coefficient
for influence direction is rather lower than the other dimensions, but it should
be pointed out that there were hardly any cases of diametrically opposed
codings (i.e. positive against negative)—only four such disagreements were
found out of 76 units of relevant meaning coded.

The percentage of statements falling into each category of each coding
dimension was calculated for every participant. These percentage scores were
used as measures of the relative emphasis placed by each interviewee on the
different categories.

Findings

(i) Comparisons between the Homes

Comparisons between the Homes of scores on all coding dimension categories
were carried out, using the full sets of data from each Home. A significant
difference was found on one of the categories from the 'influence source'
dimension; 'non-management staff' were mentioned more frequently at Beech
Court than at Watersmeet. There were no significant differences on any of
the other 'influence source' categories nor on any of the 'influence direction'
or 'innovation process phase' categories. Given this near complete absence
of significant differences between the Homes, it may be concluded that the
two innovations were similar enough in content and context to enable valid
comparisons of staff groups across Homes to be carried out.

(ii) Defining staff groups

The simplest division of participants was into managerial (i.e. principals and
senior staff: $n = 6$) and non-managerial ($n = 19$) groups. A finer level of
division distinguished five groups by post: principals ($n = 2$), senior staff
($n = 4$), day care assistants ($n = 12$), night care assistants ($n = 4$), and
domestic/kitchen staff ($n = 3$). This latter method, with day and night care

staff combined, also represented a rank ordering by status. There are problems with both ways of grouping staff. Division by post results in some very small groups, but amalgamating these into managerial and non-managerial staff obscures some quite large differences between constituent groups. It was decided to rely chiefly on the two-way division, on practical grounds, but to look also at differences between 'post' groups where preliminary examination of the data suggested this was appropriate. The comparisons between staff groups were carried out on all three coding dimensions; influence source, influence direction, and innovation process phase. Because of the small size of the whole sample, the uneven group sizes, and the unknown characteristics of the distributions, non-parametric statistics were employed throughout the analysis.

(iii) Differences in perceptions of influence source

Preliminary examination of the data indicated that in several of the influence source categories, differences between the sub-groups of the managerial and non-managerial staff groupings were larger than those between the main groups themselves. Comparisons were therefore carried out between all five staff post groups, using the Kruskal–Wallis 1-Way Analysis of Variance. There were no significant differences, except on the *source not determinable* category, where the percentage scores were lower for night care staff and the principals than other groups.

(iv) Differences in perceptions of influence direction

No significant differences were found between managerial and non-managerial staff on any of the influence direction categories. When staff were divided by post, however, examination of group medians for *positive influences* suggested that scores on this category might be related to staff status (where domestics are ranked lowest and principals highest, with day and night care assistants counted as a single group). This can be seen in Table 1.

Table 1 Median scores on the 'positive' influence direction category for staff groups

Staff group	Status ranking	Positive influence: median score
Principals	4	67.5
Senior staff	3	54.5
Care staff	2	51.0
Domestics	1	31.0

Spearman's rank order correlation coefficient was calculated between status ranks and scores on the positive influence category for all participants (continuing innovations only). The relationship was significant ($\rho = 0.41$, $p \leq 0.05$), indicating that the higher an individual's status, the more references to positive influences on the innovation process she or he tended to make. Interestingly, there was no significant relationship found between group status and scores for *negative influences*.

(v) Differences in perceptions of innovation process phase

Managerial and non-managerial staff groups were compared on percentage scores for the three process phase categories. Mann–Whitney U tests revealed significant differences between the groups on both the initiation and implementation–absorption phases ($p \leq 0.05$). Managerial staff referred more frequently than non-managerial staff to the *initiation phase*, and less frequently than them to the *implementation–absorption phase*, as can be seen in Table 2. There were no differences on the *phase not specified* category.

Table 2 Differences in median scores for innovation process phases; managerial vs non-managerial staff

	Median percentage score	
	Initiation phase	Implementation–absorption phase
Managerial staff	55	31
Non-managerial staff	39	45

Discussion

For two of the three coding dimensions ('innovation process phase' and 'influence direction') there was evidence of important relationships between participants' accounts and their group membership.

On the 'influence direction' dimension, the correlation between positive influences and group status can be interpreted as a reflection of the stake in the innovations held by each group. Thus the principals, as the people ultimately responsible for the decision to implement an innovation and for its consequences, referred most frequently to positive influences. The domestics, who were least involved in and affected by the innovation, mentioned positive influences the least often, while the other two groups (senior staff and care assistants) fell between these extremes. It is important to note that the higher status groups did not evade discussion of problems faced by the innovations, as is shown by the non-significant correlation between status and scores on the negative influence category.

Turning to the innovation process phase, we have seen that managerial staff referred more frequently in their interviews to the initiation phase than did the non-managerial staff, while the reverse was true for the implementation–absorption phase. This difference may reflect the fact that management were more directly involved in the innovations during initiation, as planners and decision-makers, than during implementation–absorption. The initiation phase was therefore more salient to them when it came to discussing the innovations' histories. In contrast, the staff's major involvement came after implementation, when the innovation began to have a direct impact on the nature of their work, and they consequently dwelt for longer on the implementation–absorption phase.

Finally, staff group membership did not appear to affect accounts of influence sources. These shared perceptions across groups of what facilitated or inhibited progress of the innovations suggest good communications between groups and a strong sense of identity within the Homes. There are features of the two Homes and their histories which might explain why this should be the case. At both Homes, the principals encouraged an informal atmosphere, with relationships on a first-name basis. Also at both Homes turnover was low; many staff had worked together for a considerable length of time and knew each other very well. At Beech Court, a third relevant factor was that the principal made a conscious effort from the start to recruit staff who shared her philosophy towards the care of the elderly.

Conclusions

The findings of this study highlight a number of possible determinants of work group perceptions of the innovation process. Firstly, *role in the innovation process* is likely to be important. This was apparent in the difference between managerial and non-managerial staff in frequency of references to the initiation and implementation–absorption phases. Secondly, the correlation between emphasis placed on positive influences and staff group status suggests that the group's *stake in the innovation* will affect its perceptions of the process. Thirdly, the agreement between groups over sources of influence indicates that good *inter-group communications* and a sense of *identity with the organization* (rather than just with the group) may serve to maximize shared perceptions of the innovation process across groups.

Clearly these conclusions must be treated as speculative, based as they are upon the findings of one small-scale exploratory study. Nevertheless, they do point to useful directions for future research to take. In particular, intervention-based research strategies may be useful. Researchers could, for instance, intervene to increase a work group's stake in an innovation attempt, and observe the effect on members' perceptions of the innovation. Studies of this nature could also address the issue of how perceptions of the innovation process affect its outcome.

SECTION IV: STRATEGIES FOR FUTURE GROUP LEVEL INNOVATION RESEARCH

As noted earlier in this chapter, the lack of studies into innovation at the level of the work group presents a wide range of possible directions for future research. However, initially two parallel and inter-dependent research strategies are called for:

(1) the *'antecedent factors'* approach;
(2) the *'longitudinal process'* approach.

Figure 1 summarizes the methodological characteristics and likely contributions of each approach. Multivariate *antecedent factors* studies examining the influence of a range of group characteristics would offer the promise of identifying important independent variables associated with work group innovation. In particular, this requires the development of validated questionnaire measures of both independent variables (group characteristics and dynamics, member attitudes, etc.) and the dependent variable (quantity *and* quality of work group innovation). The publication of these measures is essential and will contribute towards establishing a generally accessible item-bank of validated work group innovation measures.

Longitudinal process studies can help to bring about a much greater understanding of the conceptualization, initiation, negotiation and implementation of group innovations. A case study methodology is appropriate, using observational, ethnographic techniques to follow innovations as they develop over time. In addition, retrospective reconstructions of innovation histories can make an important contribution by revealing inter- and intra-group differences in perceptions of how innovations produced particular outcomes.

A complementary relationship should exist between the two research orientations; thus antecedent factors studies can reveal important determinants of the development of the innovation process, while longitudinal and retrospective case studies can identify likely antecedents of innovation which had previously been overlooked. Both strands of research need to make more extensive use of relevant existing theory, particularly in the areas of social

	Antecedent factors study designs	Process study designs
Research objectives	To quantify the relative influence of different group characteristics upon innovativeness	To delineate phases in the innovation process, and identify patterns of influence upon it
Predominant methodologies	Administration of validated attitude scale measures and open-response reports of innovation	In-depth case studies using participant/non-participant observation, and semi-structured interviewing.
Sample characteristics	Sufficient numbers of participants to ensure external validity and generality	Small numbers of cases to ensure internal validity and depth of coverage
Contributions to innovation research	Development of validated work group innovation measures Development and testing of new theoretical models of antecedents to group innovativeness	Development of empirically grounded models of phases in the innovation process Identification of previously neglected influences on innovation process

Figure 1 Approaches to group level innovation research

psychology detailed in section II, as the bases for constructing new theoretical frameworks.

Concluding recommendations

To conclude this chapter on work group innovation, it seems appropriate in the light of the limitations of existing research at this level to offer recommendations for the focus of future studies. Five principal recommendations are proposed:

(1) That, in the short term, both multivariate antecedent factors studies, and longitudinal (and retrospective) process case studies should be conducted.
(2) That, in the medium term, models of the stages in the group innovation process should be developed from real-life observational and historical data. Such models will need validation across multiple case studies.
(3) That research studies should seek to examine the innovation process from all relevant perspectives, not only from that of management.
(4) That research studies should be sensitive to possible differences in antecedents and processes between emergent, imported and imposed innovations.

(5) That, in the longer term, intervention strategies are developed, grounded in empirically tested theory. The aims of such interventions should not be simply to maximize group innovativeness, but rather to match the level of innovation to the requirements of the group's environment.

Correspondence addresses:
Dr Nigel King, Centre for Primary Care Research, The Department of General Practice, University of Manchester, Rusholme Health Centre, Walmer Street, Manchester M14 5NP, UK.
Dr Neil Anderson, MRC/ESRC Social and Applied Psychology Unit, Department of Psychology, University of Sheffield, Sheffield S10 2TN, UK.

REFERENCES

Amabile, T. (1983). *The Social Psychology of Creativity*. New York: Springer-Verlag.

Amabile, T. (1984). Creativity motivation in research and development. Symposium paper at the American Psychological Association, Toronto, August.

Amabile, T. (1986). A model of organizational innovation. Paper presented at the Annual Convention of the American Psychological Association, Washington DC, August.

Anderson, N.R. (1989). Work group innovation: current research concerns and future directions. Paper presented as part of a symposium at the Fourth West European Congress on the Psychology of Work and Organization, Cambridge, UK, April.

Bell, M.A. (1982). Phases in group problem solving. *Small Group Behaviour*, **13**, 475–495.

Bouwen, R. (1988). Management of innovation. Paper presented as part of symposium 'Interpretive Approaches to Occupational Psychology' at the Annual Occupational Psychology Conference of the British Psychological Society, University of Manchester, January 1988.

Bouwen, R. (1989). Innovation projects in organizations: Complementing the dominant logic by organizational learning. Paper presented at the Fourth West European Congress on the Psychology of Work and Organization, Cambridge, UK, April.

Burns, T. and Stalker, G.M. (1961). *The Management of Innovation*. London: Tavistock.

Child, J. (1975). Managerial and organizational factors associated with company performance—part II, a contingency analysis. *Journal of Management Studies*, **12**, 12–27.

Child, J. (1983). *Organization: A Guide to Problems and Practice*. London: Harper and Row.

Coopey, (1987). Creativity in complex organizations. Paper presented at the Annual Occupational Psychology Conference of the British Psychological Society, University of Hull, January.

Farris, G.F. (1973). The technical supervisor: Beyond the Peter principle. *Technical Review*, **75**, April.

Fleiss, J.L. (1981). *Statistical Methods for Rates and Proportions*. New York: Wiley.

Galbraith, J. (1973). *Designing Complex Organizations*. Reading, Mass.: Addison-Wesley.

Gersick, C.J.G. (1988). Time and transition in work teams: toward a new model of group development. *Academy of Management Journal*, **31**, 9–41.

Geschka, H. (1983). Creativity techniques in product planning and development: a view from West Germany. *R & D Management*, **13**, 169–183.

Glassman, E. (1986). Managing for creativity: back to basics in R & D. *R & D Management*, **16**, 175–183.

Hycner, R.H. (1985). Some guidelines for the phenomenological analysis of interview data. *Human Studies*, **8**, 279–303.

Ivancevich, J.M. and Matteson, M.T. (1987). *Organizational Behaviour and Management*, Plamo, Texas: Business Publications Inc.

Janis, I.L. (1982). *Groupthink*, 2nd edn. Boston: Houghton Mifflin.

Jones, L. (1987). Barriers to creativity. Paper presented at a British Psychological Society seminar on stimulating creativity at Manchester Business School, 13 June.

Kanter, R.M. (1983). *The Change Masters: Corporate Entrepreneurs at Work*. London: Allen and Unwin.

Katz, R. (1982). The effects of group longevity on project communication and performance. *Administrative Science Quarterly*, **27**, 81–104.

Kimberly, J.R. (1981). Managerial innovation. In P.C. Nyström and W.H. Starbuck (Eds.), *Handbook of Organizational Design*, Vol. 1. Oxford: OUP.

King, N. (1989). Innovation in elderly care organizations: process and attitudes. Unpublished PhD Thesis, MRC/ESRC Social and Applied Psychology Unit, University of Sheffield, UK.

Lovelace, R.F. (1986). Stimulating creativity through managerial intervention. *R & D Management*, **16**, 161–174.

Lupton, T. (1975). 'Best Fit' in the design of organizations. *Personnel Review*, **4**, 15–30.

Maass, A. and Clark, R.D. (1983). Internalization versus compliance: differential processes underlying minority influence and conformity. *European Journal of Social Psychology*, **13**, 197–215.

Mabry, E.A. (1975). Exploratory analysis of a developmental model for task-oriented small groups. *Human Communication Research*, **2**, 66–74.

Meadows, I.S.G. (1980). Organic structure and innovation in small work groups. *Human Relations*, **33**, 369–382.

Moreland, R.L. and Levine, J.M. (1988). Group dynamics over time: development and socialization in small groups. In J.E. McGrath (Ed.), *The Social Psychology of Time*. London: Sage.

Nemeth, C.J. and Wachtler, J. (1983). Creative problem solving as a result of majority vs. minority influence. *European Journal of Social Psychology*, **13**, 45–55.

Nicholson, N. and West, M.A. (1988). *Managerial Job Change: Men and Women in Transition*. Cambridge: Cambridge University Press.

Nyström, H. (1979). *Creativity and Innovation*. New York: Wiley.

Parmeter, S.M. and Gaber, J.D. (1971). Creative scientists rate creativity factors. *Research Management*, November, 65–70.

Pelz, D.C. and Andrews, F.M. (1976). *Productive Climates for Research and Development*. Ann Arbor, Michigan: Institute for Social Research, University of Michigan.

Peters, T.J. and Waterman, R.H. (1982). *In Search of Excellence: Lessons from America's Best-Run Companies*. New York: Warner.

Poole, M.S. (1981). Decision development in small groups I: a comparison of two models. *Communication Monographs*, **48**, 1–24.

Rickards, T. (1985). *Stimulating Innovation*.

Scheidel, T. and Crowell, L. (1964). Idea development in small discussion groups. *Quarterly Journal of Speech*, 50, 140–145.

Simon, H.A. (1984). Decision making and organizational design. In D.S. Pugh (Ed.), *Organisation Theory*. Harmondsworth: Penguin.

Stoner, J.A.F. (1968). Risky and cautious shifts in group decisions: the influence of widely held values. *Journal of Experimental Social Psychology*, 4, 442–459.

Wallace, M. and West, M.A. (1987). Innovation in primary health care teams: the effects of roles and climate. Paper presented at the Annual Occupational Psychology Conference of the British Psychological Society, University of Manchester, January. Abstract in *The Psychologist*, 1, 2.

Wallas, G. (1926). *The Art of Thought*. London: Cape, pp. 79–96.

Wanous, J.P., Reichers, A.E. and Malik, S.D. (1984). Organizational socialization and group development: toward an integrative perspective. *Academy of Management Review*, 9, 670–683.

West, M.A. and Farr, J.L. (1989). Innovation at work: psychological perspectives. *Social Behaviour*, 4, 15–30.

West, M.A. and Wallace, M. (1988). Innovation in primary health care teams: the effects of roles and climates. Paper presented at the British Psychological Society Occupational Psychology Annual Conference, University of Manchester. Abstract in *Bulletin of the British Psychological Society*, Abstracts, p. 23.

5 The effectiveness of research teams: a review

Roy Payne

Manchester Business School, UK

Whilst major breakthroughs in science tend to be attributed to single individuals, the scale and complexity of 'normal science' (Kuhn, 1962) is such that most scientific work gets done in specialist institutions such as universities, government or industrial laboratories. Science, and the innovations in thinking and practice it produces is, therefore, done in teams, and these teams are managed. Understanding how to manage them effectively is, therefore, vital if innovation is to be a sustained activity.

The empirical work available on this topic derives from two different, but overlapping groups. They are project groups and research teams. The focus of this chapter is on research teams. The major reason for this is that there is a larger body of research about them, particularly a large study sponsored by UNESCO based on 1222 research teams (Andrews, 1979a). Whilst there is empirical research on project management, much of the literature on it is actually prescriptive (e.g. Bergen, 1986; Randolph and Posner, 1988). There is a social psychological/organizational difference between these two sorts of groups, even though the managerial prescriptions deriving from the literature on them contain considerable similarities.

Having noted the distinction between project groups and research teams, the chapter discusses recent findings about the effects of matrix structures on performance in both groups. The matrix has been an enduring fashion in the management of R & D (research and development) and some assessment of its current status as a determinant of success is necessary. The next consideration is how to measure success or performance itself. This turns out to be a complex issue and it colours the interpretation of much of the data that follows. The different kinds of performance measures are derived from the UNESCO studies (recognition, number of papers, patents, etc.), as is the

Innovation and Creativity at Work Edited by M.A. West and J.L. Farr
© 1990 John Wiley & Sons Ltd

bulk of the evidence relating socio-psychological factors to team performance.

The reason for concentrating on the UNESCO study is that no other studies provide anything like its comprehensibility, quality and size. Thus the findings it contains can be regarded as more reliable than those in smaller and less well designed studies. The following factors are considered as correlates of team performance: leadership style, communications, size of team, diversity of team membership, and motivation. The chapter ends by listing the factors that need to be considered in managing research teams, and emphasizing their role in creativity and innovation.

PROJECT GROUPS VERSUS RESEARCH TEAMS

An obvious difference between research teams and project groups is that a project is mounted to meet a specific problem, and usually it will have time limits in which to solve the problem, carry out the work etc. Relevant personnel and resources are allocated and assembled with the assumption that these will be dispersed once the project is finished. In universities and research laboratories which are ongoing, the research teams are relatively more permanent, and have a broad brief to produce research in a given area. The scientist's career is based within the research team rather than the project team, so there are ongoing management problems which differ. Pinto and Prescott (1987) claim that the literature on project management *per se* is largely descriptive and/or prescriptive. Part of this descriptive focus concerns the stages through which projects pass. They report an empirical study consisting of reports about 418 projects. Their main hypothesis is that different phases of the project will be successes or failures according to the presence or absence of critical success factors (CSFs).

Table 1 presents their findings. The projects studied are from a whole range of industries and are not necessarily carried out by scientists or engineers, but the study is of interest because (1) it illustrates the nature of projects, (2) it identifies the role of different success factors at different times throughout the life cycle of a project, and (3) it indicates the percentage of variance the different success factors account for.

The results in Table 1 show that having a clearly stated mission is important to success throughout the life-span of a project. This level of mission clarity is likely to be much more difficult to obtain in ongoing research teams, for it will likely be much broader and fuzzier or even renegotiated over the life-span of the team. The second theme that runs throughout the different stages of projects is the involvement of the client. Again, in many ongoing research teams the client is more diffuse (e.g. the organization or the scientific community). The existence of technical skills and expertise only appears to be crucial during the execution phase and the termination phase of projects.

Table 1 Key factors for each stage of the project life cycle from stepwise regression analysis

Stage of project life cycle	Number of projects	Factors	Adjusted R^2
Conceptual	35	Missions	0.57**
		Client consultation	0.64
Planning	72	Mission	0.55
		Top management support	0.61
		Client acceptance	0.63
Execution	198	Mission	0.50
		Trouble-shooting	0.55
		Schedule/plan	0.57
		Technical tasks	0.59
		Client consultation	0.60
Termination	103	Technical tasks	0.59
		Mission	0.57
		Client consultation	0.60

**All = $p < 0.01$ R^2 = % of predictable variance
Source: Pinto and Prescott (1987) reproduced by permission of Academy of Management.

It is, perhaps, worth reflecting that in ongoing research teams expertise is usually the main criterion for recruitment. This might imply that the mission definition, client consultation, and resource acquisition skills of such teams may be less focused than they are in project groups, creating a considerable managerial challenge for the research team leader.

It is no great surprise that the execution phase of a project involves critical skills to do with trouble-shooting, scheduling/planning (i.e. solving problems by their wits). These seem to be the very skills for which researchers are recruited in the first place.

It is important to note that other CSFs were identified in this study, but they were not included in the regressions because the measures were found not to be sufficiently reliable. They were monitoring, communication and feedback and since most studies of skilled managers have shown these are important to managerial effectiveness it can be concluded they are also important to managing scientists and engineers (see also Miller, 1986, on managing R & D professionals).

A second study of projects makes an interesting contrast because it is (a) concerned with projects carried out in academic settings, (b) particularly concerned with projects that are interdisciplinary in nature, and (c) longitudinal in design. Birnbaum's study (1983) differs from the previous study in that it is concerned with predicting ultimate outcomes rather than achievements throughout the project. Data collected in 1975 were used to predict performance in 1977. There were a range of performance criteria: quality of articles, log of quantity of articles, log of quantity of books, log of quantity of technical reports, log of quantity of published papers, log of quantity of patents. A mixture of group structural variables and group process variables were used to predict these. The structural variables were: horizontal and vertical differentiation (variety of different roles). The process variables were concerned with group integration, open discussion of disagreements, and perceived group effectiveness, whilst turnover of staff was also used as an indirect measure of group relationships. One variable did not fall into these two categories and that was a measure of scientific recognition.

Whilst the detailed results are interesting they can be summarized as follows: the predictor variables accounted for between 4% and 83% of the variance. The 4% was for published papers and the 83% for technical reports. Birnbaum's conclusions, however, are the most important, for they are echoed by the results of the other studies cited throughout this chapter.

These results indicate that scientific activities tend to be product specific. Clearly defined division of labour facilitates article quality and quantity. A loosely defined horizontal division of labour and participation by many people in decisions facilitates technical report production. Thus, attempting to achieve the tight integration of activities, usually associated with interdisciplinary research, is negatively associated with article production ... Thus, research managers who sail blindly ahead on the assumption that clearly defined tasks, integrated effort, reduced turnover, open discussions of disagreements, and self evaluations of successful performance are universally desirable are likely to experience problems. (p.57)

In a nutshell, different project groups have different goals, and the achievement of those goals demands different organizational forms and different leadership styles: context counts!

Birnbaum does not refer to the structural issues of having project groups in university settings, but these are dealt with extensively by Lambert and Teich (1981). They certainly raise the problems of turning collections of project groups into enduring research institutions or teams. They note how this problem has grown in universities with the increasing dependence on grants which are awarded for carrying out specific, often interdisciplinary, projects. The need to obtain the clarity of mission and specific control inherent in a project, whilst maintaining the integrity of the wider research organization as a team led, of course, to the development of matrix structures. Since they are so widely used in modern research organizations it is desirable to consider current views on their strengths and weaknesses.

MATRIX STRUCTURES AND MANAGEMENT OF R & D ORGANIZATIONS

Since the matrix sprang to prominence as a major structural tool in the US National Aeronautics and Space Administration's efforts to get man to the moon a series of books have been published both in the UK and the US extolling its virtues and reporting research (e.g. Kingdon, 1973; Davis and Lawrence, 1977; Knight, 1978; Cleland, 1984).

The 'pure matrix' structure involves a series of functional departments (e.g. physics, mathematics, biology, pharmacology, etc.) having a more or less conventional hierarchical structure, and a series of project groups each of which is managed by a project manager. The project manager recruits the people from the functional departments according to the special needs of the project. The functional boss is responsible for building organizational commitment and identity and looks after career decisions, technical development and training, corporate resources, technical quality, technical equipment and efficiency. The project manager has to build project identity in order to satisfy client needs. This requires task scheduling and budgeting, resource acquisition and delivery to time and quality (Jerkovsky 1983). Whilst this describes the idealized view of a matrix structure there is evidence from a study of 40 organizations employing the matrix that it rarely exists in this idealized form (Gunz and Pearson, 1977).

Despite its popularity as a creative structural solution the matrix has always had its critics. Denis (1986) hypothesized that the matrix has been abandoned, but to her surprise a survey of 300 engineers in five Quebec engineering organizations showed that 45% of them had worked in matrix structures for 10 years or more. Similarly Katz and Allen (1985) surveyed 201 project teams and found 86 of them employed scientists and engineers in matrix dual-reporting relationships. The matrix does appear to be alive. The question is, how well is it?

Consistent with the fundamental problems of organizing (Mintzberg, 1979) the matrix creates differentiation by separating responsibility and power into the function and the project. The problem this creates is how to integrate the people who have been given these different responsibilities and powers.

A traditional answer to this question has been that it is best to provide a balance of power/influence for the two managers. This hypothesis was tested by Katz and Allen (1985) who examined their respective influence over three areas: technical matters, rewards and career influences, and personnel assignments to projects. Over the 86 projects they studied the influence of the functional versus project managers differed considerably across these issues. Relating influence to performance, however, they found little support for the balance hypothesis. Instead they found that specialization of roles was most highly associated with project performance. Performance was highest when project managers attended to external relations and they were helped to do this by acquiring, or being given, influence within the wider organization. Functional managers were then able to attend to technical excellence and employee development and this combination of roles produced better performance. The one area where both managers seem to have important roles is in the area of organizational rewards, and good co-operation between functional and project managers is associated with higher project performance.

Jerkovsky (1983) is also concerned with the balance of roles of the two managers in the matrix. His prime concern is with the functional manager because he believes their role has been much less well studied. He compared the perceived time spent by matrix functional managers in six roles: knowledge updater, technical consultant, task manager (technical), technical administrator, employee developer and organization developer. Project managers were also asked their perceptions of how the functional managers spent their time in each of these roles. Table 2 shows the percentage of time spent in the six role areas. The table shows variation by organizational level with level 4 being the most senior level. There was good agreement between functional and project managers and their views are combined in the table. The change from an emphasis on technical, through administrative to people management with a change in level of responsibility is evident from the table. Both the functional and the project managers agreed that it was important to get the balance of power between the two roles right. A major practical solution Jerkovsky offers is regular job rotation between the two roles to sensitize managers to the different demands and responsibilities in each, but particularly to the importance of collaboration on rewards and staff development.

There is no empirical evidence on performance in this paper though Jerkovsky indicates the benefits and disadvantages of the matrix. However, a more systematic study of these is reported by Denis (1986). She investigated

Table 2 % Time spent in functional manager roles

Roles	Functional manager level		
	2	3	4
Knowledge updater	14	9	4
Technical consultant	43	22	13
Task manager	25	28	21
Technical administrator	7	22	38
Employee developer	6	9	9
Organization developer	5	10	16

Reprinted with permission from Jerkovsky (1983). Functional management in matrix organizations. *IEEE Transactions on Engineering Management*, EM-30(2), 89–97. © 1983, IEEE.

the ability of the matrix to provide a good 'Quality of Working Life': i.e. a complete task, responsibility, challenge, opportunity to develop and job autonomy (Davis and Cherns, 1975). She found considerable differences amongst the engineers in the three firms she studied. Thus in firm A 92% of respondents thought the matrix was more motivating than the normal pyramidal structure, but the figure drops to 56% and 50% for firms B and C. Overall 74% reported they got more satisfaction from matrix working. These generally positive findings about quality of life, however, must be tempered by the finding that 49% of the engineers did not attribute these desirable characteristics to the matrix *per se*, but to management style and general policies. The matrix was accorded benefits in terms of both individual (63%) and group productivity (80%). The matrix was believed to provide the best compomise between high quality and lower costs in a project, given two conditions: first, that it was managed well (otherwise it becomes too costly in time and personnel), and second, that it is applied to the right type of project. In this case that meant medium sized projects, because it is too costly for small ones, and large ones are better managed in a traditional pyramidal structure.

In sum, despite the potential for conflict built into the matrix, the challenge it offers, and the autonomy it provides tend to lead to a good group climate and a better quality of working life. But its success depends ultimately on how well it is managed, and at the heart of that is the problem of managing projects and managing ongoing teams at the same time.

Having started out with the distinction between projects and teams let us now turn to the evidence for what makes a successful scientific team. As a precursor to this it is necessary to explore how we measure the performance of such teams.

MEASURING THE PERFORMANCE OF RESEARCH TEAMS

The largest body of empirical information on this topic, of which I am aware, is published in Andrews (1979a). This book presents the results of the UNESCO funded study of 1222 scientific research groups which were located in six different countries. Over 11 000 people completed questionnaires. Apart from the amount of data collected the study included an extremely thorough analysis of the performance measures. Surprisingly, despite its merits, the study has not been widely quoted in the recent literature on R & D performance. Table 3 shows the citations to the book as recorded in the Social Science and Science Citations Indexes since 1980. If the citations made by Pelz, a past collaborator of Andrews (Pelz and Andrews, 1966) and Cheng, a doctoral student of Andrews, are removed then the frequencies in Table 3 would be reduced by about a third. I wish to draw attention to this because the quantity and quality of other studies is quite poor. Given this paucity it is interesting that social science and management writers have paid little attention to this empirical goldmine.

The findings on the nature and measurement of scientific performance deserve attention because they remind us of some fundamental difficulties in trying to summarize what we know about managing scientific research groups.

The international collaborators on the UNESCO project collected information about two broad classes of performance indicators: numbers of products and ratings of quality indicators.

The subjective ratings were collected from three sources: unit heads, a sample of staff scientists, and external evaluators. The quantitative data on the number and types of products were collected from unit heads and related to the previous three years. Many of these measures produced skewed

Table 3 Frequency of citations of Andrews's book since its publication in 1979

	Year of citations							
	1987	1986	1985	1984	1983	1982	1981	1980
SSCI	10	0	5	10	8	4	9	5
SCI	3	0	2	8	2	1	0	3

SSCI = Social Science Citation Index.
SCI = Science Citation Index.
NB   These citations would be reduced by about 35% if the ones made by Pelz (a collaborator of Andrews) and Cheng (a PhD student of his) are excluded.

distributions and a bracketing procedure (Andrews, 1979b; p.36) was used to reduce the problems this created. Various clustering techniques were applied to these quantitative data and they revealed three clusters:

(1) Published written outputs.
(2) Patents and prototypes.
(3) Reports (internal to organization) and algorithms.

Within each category different items were weighted according to their importance. Since they have been shown to be empirically separate clusters it is obvious that research teams may be high on some of them and low on others, with all possible combinations being feasible.

A similar procedure was applied to the qualitative ratings. Thirty-nine of 41 measures were shown to be usable meeting the following criteria: (1) at least modest agreement amongst raters in different roles (i.e. unit heads, staff scientists and external evaluators; (2) greater agreement amongst ratings of the same unit than amongst ratings of different units. The items were again clustered/factored producing seven clusters which were shown to be reasonably stable across the three different groups of raters. This enabled the researchers to combine information from the three sources to increase the reliability of the ratings.

The seven clusters appear below:

(1) General contribution of the unit to science and technology.
(2) Recognition and international reputation.
(3) Social effectiveness of the unit's work.
(4) Training effectiveness of the unit.
(5) Administrative effectiveness (meeting times and budgets).
(6) R & D effectiveness (productiveness, innovativeness).
(7) Applications effectiveness.

As Andrews indicates, relying on the judgments of people about their own performance is not a perfect way of evaluating their activities, but as he acknowledges, 'no more useful approach has been identified' (p.41). It is interesting that the external evaluators actually rated the research units higher on the criteria than the unit heads or unit scientists, and that the addition of the external evaluators' ratings added nothing to the validity of the effectiveness ratings of the heads and the scientists, though each of those added unique variance (Andrews, 1979c; pp. 413–415).

An additional strength of the UNESCO study is that it included research groups from academic and industrial organizations. It is immediately apparent that the performance criteria listed above will differ in importance for the different types of research groups: academic groups, not surprisingly, produce more external publications, but fewer patents. Five different types of group were identified by the UNESCO researchers and a procedure was developed so that performance measures were adjusted according to the type of unit. Variations in the patterns of relationships for the different groups appear later.

As already indicated the three clusters of the output measures and the seven clusters of the ratings were derived from cluster analyses so it is no great surprise that the different clusters within each group do not correlate very strongly with each other. This illustrates the complexity of the construct of team performance itself. It is perhaps less obvious that there are only low correlations between the three quantitative output measures and the qualitative/subjective ratings. The highest correlations are all with published output and the two 'significant' correlations, adjusted for type of unit, are for Recognition ($r = 0.45$), and General Contribution ($r = 0.29$) which correlate 0.56 with each other.

Before considering the factors which predict these performance measures Andrews deserves further acknowledgement for his careful assessment of the validity of the performance measures. In a separate chapter on this (Andrews, 1979c; pp. 414–422) Andrews decomposes the variance into three components: (1) true variance, (2) correlated error variance, and (3) random error variance. Apart from showing that the external evaluators produced higher levels of both correlated error variance and random error variance than the unit heads and scientists Andrews also estimates the amounts of true variance in performance that one is able to predict. To quote the man himself:

They (the performance measures) have moderately high reliabilities (.72 to .82) but a significant part of the reliability is traceable to correlated measurement error rather than to true variance. We have estimated that only slightly more than half the total variance in a typical composite performance measure is valid variance. Although this is not very high, it nevertheless seems substantial enough to make possible an in-depth analysis of factors that relate to research unit effectiveness. Given the subtlety of this concept, one should perhaps be pleased that it has been captured at all, and that the performance measures seem as sensitive to it as we estimate them to be. (p.418)

This point is emphasized in another chapter on the performance ratings where Bonmariage *et al.* (1979) conclude, 'The instability of measurements and of relationships observed in our research seems to indicate that appropriate performance measures can only be built for subsets of units belonging to a similar environment' (p.330). Further empirical support for this view is added by Cole's chapter in which he shows striking differences in performance and patterns of influence according to whether the units are located in academic, government or industrial settings (Cole, 1979). Within the academic institutions there are even considerable differences between pure science, medical and social sciences and the applied/technological sciences.

Apart from wishing to extol the virtues of this particular study my purpose has been to emphasize the subtlety of the problem of measuring, judging, understanding what determines the performance of scientific teams. There are many indicators, they are not particularly strongly related to each other whether they are objective or subjectively assessed, they apply to some groups better than others and no doubt the practices that encourage/facilitate one form of effectiveness do nothing to facilitate another, nay may even inhibit its achievement. This should serve as a precaution in interpreting any generalizations that follow, and as an explanation for the apparently low variances accounted for in most studies of scientific performance. This low correlation amongst performance indicators also applies to business organizations (Friedlander and Pickle, 1968).

With these precautionary remarks in mind, my aim is to give some idea of the percentage of variance in team performance that is currently accountable. In attempting to be reasonably thorough I conducted two on-line searches. These produced very few studies based on the keywords, group, team, scientists and engineers. Out of over 7000 items only 22 produced combinations of these keywords. Of these only one was carried out in such a way as to allow calculation of effect sizes. This was by Thamhain and Wilemon (1987) and scrutiny of its 40 references failed to produce any other studies to add to this list.

Thamhain and Wilemon studied engineers in 30 companies collecting information from over 500 engineering professionals and including 37 managers. Their studies show that high performing engineering teams not only produce technical results on time and to budget but do so, by implication at least, because they demonstrate specific task and people related qualities. These are:

Task related Oriented to technical success; results oriented; innovative and creative; concern for quality; willing to change plans; ability to predict trends; on budget performance.

People related High involvement, work interest and energy; capacity to solve conflict; good communication; good team spirit; mutual trust; self-development of team members; effective organizational interfacing; high need for achievement.

An average rank-order correlation of 0.37 was found between these characteristics and team performance. Thamhain and Wilemon went on to investigate factors in the environment which are seen by their engineers to help or hinder the development of these qualities. They labelled these *drivers* and *barriers* and they are obviously similar in concept to the notion of team support and constraint proposed by Payne (1981), and to work facilitation factors as defined and operationalized by Schoorman and Schneider (1988).

Thamhain and Wilemon correlated 60 potential drivers or barriers to the team performance characteristics and found 12 reached the 5% confidence level. Six barriers had negative relationships to the characteristics identified above. They are listed below and the correlations with technical team performance appear in brackets:

Barriers to team performance Unclear objectives (0.31), insufficient resources (0.26), conflict (0.26), uninvolved management (0.23), poor job security (0.23), and shifting goals and priorities (0.22).

The average correlation was 0.25 indicating that these accounted for about 6.25% of the variance in team performance.

The average correlation for the drivers was slightly higher; the drivers were:

Drivers to team performance Interesting work (0.32), recognition/accomplishment (0.27), experienced engineering management (0.26), good direction and leadership (0.25), qualified team personnel (0.24) and potential for professional growth (0.14).

No multivariate procedures were used and no doubt a combination of the drivers and the barriers would improve the prediction of team performance, but it is impossible to judge by how much and 10% is likely to be an underestimate. However, the number of teams studied is not given in the paper, though it may be that each of the 37 managers were responsible for a team. In any event the size of N is relatively small and the results are therefore less likely to be reliable.

This is even more true in Jabri's (1985) study of team performance. As part of a study of the performance and satisfaction of scientists from three companies he was able to study 18 teams. Jabri's main interest was in the effect of team climate on team performance. His climate questionnaire was also modelled on the idea of climates as supporting or constraining performance. Jabri found that the key climate factors facilitating team performance were team autonomy and leader supportiveness.

Since there are so few comparative studies of the performance of scientific teams it is worth mentioning these, but the small Ns involved do make their results questionable. This merely highlights the power of the UNESCO studies. In a penetrating review of the theoretical and empirical achievements of industrial and organizational psychology, Webster and Starbuck (1988) castigate the practitioners in the discipline for failing to learn from the best studies, and making the mistake of preferring to aggregate numerous small studies many of which will contain unreliable results.

With 1222 research teams the results of even the smallest grouping of teams in the UNESCO studies are based on an N of 103. This group constitutes the academic medical and social sciences group. The other four groups are:

Academic exact and natural sciences $(N = 437)$;
Academic applied sciences and technology $(N = 208)$;
Government/cooperative research units $(N = 254)$;
Private enterprise research units $(N = 220)$.

These figures are from Cole (1979, p.386). With Ns of this size we should be able to reliably detect 'true' relationships between variables as small as $r = 0.20$ for a 2-tailed test with $p = 0.5$ and power set at 0.80 (Cohen, 1977). For these reasons it seems reasonable to assume that the UNESCO studies provide the most reliable and the most comprehensive set of data on the performance of scientific *teams*. There are, of course, other studies of factors that influence the performance of individual scientists (e.g. Roe, 1952; Pelz and Andrews, 1966; Jaunch and Gluech, 1975; Keller and Holland, 1978; Abbey and Dickson, 1983; Jabri, 1985; Payne *et al.*, 1988). What then are the main findings of the UNESCO studies?

THE UNESCO FINDINGS ON THE EFFECTIVENESS OF RESEARCH GROUPS

I have already indicated two of the 'background' findings that need to be considered in this literature. One is that team performance is multidimensional and the other is that the performance criteria apply differentially to different kinds of research (university vs. industrial etc.). The UNESCO study was also international and included countries from different economic systems (e.g. Hungary). Despite this there was much similarity in the pattern of results across the six countries: 'Although significant differences appeared in the survey data between the participating countries as regards R & D Management practices, organizational settings, and climate of work, the relations that emerged from between these factors and performance of research units tend to show the same directional patterns' (de Hemptinne and Andrews, 1979; p.9).

Resource availability and team performance

One important finding that needs to be highlighted, yet removed from our consideration, is that of the importance of economic and physical resources.

There was no evidence from these studies that more resources and better facilities led necessarily to better scientific performance. Once there was sufficient to employ good people in reasonable facilities there was little additional effect of throwing more money at the research problem (at least on average!). As de Hemptinne and Andrews point out, the ratio of benefits to costs for some scientific inventions is so large that conventional cost–benefit analysis becomes difficult to apply to discoveries which emerge from serendipity and intuition as much as rationality and good management practice. Nevertheless, leaders responsible for the management of knowledge generation will no doubt wish to optimize the conditions which might encourage discovery and invention however it might occur.

Leadership and team performance

As indicated earlier the UNESCO study developed measures of performance based on numbers of articles and books, and other performance measures based on perceptions. The former are more quantitative and the latter more qualitative, and the two types of measures are not highly related. In a fascinating analysis of the predictors of the quantitative measures in academic settings Knorr et al. (1979) show the large effect of the leader's contribution to the prediction of group output. In academic natural science groups the correlation between the unit heads' productivity and group productivity (articles and books) is 0.62 compared with 0.29 for unit members. The correlations are 0.68 vs. 0.34, and 0.68 vs. 0.38 for the academic technological scientists and the industrial technological scientists, respectively.

The authors suggest these correlations reflect the leader's personal scientific excellence but supplemented by the resources that accrue to him/her as a result or promotion. This argument is partly reinforced by further analyses which explored the role of other factors in predicting group performance. Group size, group age and scientific exchanges correlated positively with group output, though they did not add a great deal of variance once unit heads' and staff scientists' publications had been included. Between 44% and 59% of the variance was accounted for by these variables. However, when a per capita measure of group productivity was calculated a negative relationship was found with group size. The authors conclude that the effect of group size on group performance will vary according to the specific tasks and institutions. Some problems require a greater diversity of skills etc., but that all other things being equal larger size tends to lead to lower per capita performance. As the authors themselves indicate most of these relationships are not surprising, and they throw little light on the processes involved in increasing group performance. To tackle this issue they turn their attention to the more qualitative performance measures.

The qualitative performance measures included productivity, innovativeness and usefulness as assessed by heads, staff and external experts. The leadership variables related to adequacy of the supervisor in terms of:

- Planning and co-ordinating.
- Degree of integration created in the team.
- Career promoting quality of the supervisor.
- The overall status of the supervisor.

Figure 1 presents the basic 'model' of the processes that result in improved effectiveness. The model was tested by LISREL techniques and analyses carried out with and without the effects of response bias included. With response bias effects included the model explained 18% of the variance in team performance for the academic natural science units. For the academic technological science units the model explained 51% of the variance in R & D effectiveness. The large difference is explained by the fact that group climate accounts for almost twice as much of the variance in the technological groups, which may indicate the greater importance of teamwork in these more integrated technologies, where the reduced levels of uncertainty allow groupworking to work effectively.

What can be concluded from these results is that the supervisor in academic settings has a direct effect on the group through the papers he or she produces personally, but a major indirect effect in getting the planning and group climate right to encourage other members of staff to innovate and produce.

This finding is reiterated by Stolte-Heiskanen (1979) in a chapter which concentrates on the role of external resources in predicting group performance.

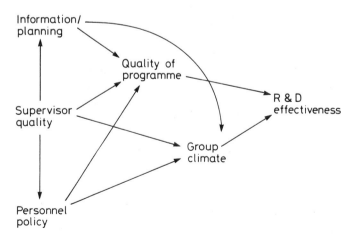

Figure 1 Leadership and group performance

As already indicated actual level of resources plays little part in predicting group performance, though members' satisfactions with resources is related to effectiveness. But, '. . . human resources seem to play a more important role in the effectiveness of research units. Of these, the contacts of the unit and the competence of the unit head seem to be the most important objective resources' (p.149).

The effect of group size on performance

One of the factors which affects a leader's ability to influence group members is the size of the group itself. This is explored in some detail by Stankiewicz (1979) whose conclusions are limited to Swedish academic groups, but again there are 172 of them allowing reasonably robust tests of effects to be made. As well as looking at the size of the group Stankiewicz looked at the age of the group and for both variables tested the hypothesis that optimum size and optimum age would enhance group effectiveness. It transpires that the leader's ability to create good group cohesiveness is an important intervening variable. Stankiewicz found the following results:

(1) If cohesiveness is high larger groups tend to perform better than smaller groups (the largest group had 18 people in it).
(2) Groups larger than seven have poor performance unless cohesiveness is high.
(3) The relationship between group size and performance is stronger when the leaders of the groups are experienced.
(4) If the leaders are inexperienced the relationship between performance and group size becomes negative, i.e. young researchers may still be productive researchers, but they are less well positioned to manage teams successfully.

It is not possible to report these results in terms of percentages of variance, but Stankiewicz argues that the effects are strong enough to recommend that groups larger than seven should be avoided. If it is not possible to avoid this then the following guidelines for managing the situation are suggested:

• Ensure the participation of all group members in the management of the group.
• Ensure the leaders can commit more than 33% of their time to the group's work and that they retain a high involvement directly in the research itself.
• Limit the range of projects and have well integrated budgeting.

One of the main reasons for the negative consequences of increasing group size is the difficulties it creates for effective intra-group communication. Visart

(1979) deals with this and with the effect of external communications, within the UNESCO studies.

Communication and group performance

Visart uses a large number of measures combined into quite a complex model to investigate the role of communication in group performance. I have simplified this in Figure 2, and used arrows to indicate the main findings. Those with a serious interest in these findings are recommended to study the original. The major conclusions to be drawn, however, are these:

As far as R & D managers are concerned, they might wish to think of ways to provide research units with those conditions and facilities that enhance both communication between units and within units. Indeed, within the national and the institutional settings, both between-units and within-unit communication proved to have a strong relationship to Recognition of the units, their R & D effectiveness, their Number of published written products, and their Applications effectiveness . . . both between- and within-units communication indices explain as much as 22% of the variance in Recognition, 21% in applications effectiveness, 19% in R & D effectiveness, and 31% in Number of published written products. (Visart, 1979; p.250)

Good scientific and technical communications, as well as good interpersonal communications, seem vital to the effective performance of scientific teams. Of the two broad types of communication, internal and external, internal communications are the more important according to the UNESCO results.

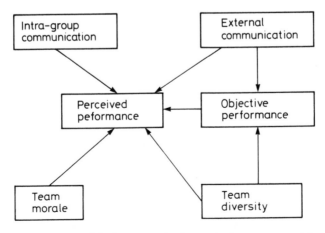

Figure 2 Simplified communications—performance model

As is already evident, the different variables reviewed actually interact with each other, and one obvious effect of communication processes is to influence the motivation of scientists. The effects of motivation on team performance are dealt with by Andrews himself (1979d). In the same chapter Andrews also deals with the motivational effects of the diversity of activities performed by knowledge workers, and the translation of this into better team performance.

Motivation and team performance

The measures of motivation used in the UNESCO study are subjective reports and tap three areas: dedication, voluntary overtime and interest of the work itself. Although there is an effect of hierarchical position on motivation, the higher positions reporting higher motivation, the measures are aggregated to indicate motivation of the team. The resulting motivation index is found to correlate positively with the subjective/qualitative performance measures, but not at all with the objective, quantitative measures. The strongest correlation is with R & D effectiveness where $r = 0.36$, though the median correlation over the seven performance measures is 0.22. As Andrews indicates, although these relationships are not strong they are very general, occurring for units of all types of research groups and across all countries. He also points out that allowing for measurement error etc., the real strength of the relationship between group motivation and group performance, at least on the qualitative measures, is between 10% and 20% of the variance.

In 1979 the journal *R & D Management* published a Special Issue based on the UNESCO studies. Several papers appear there that are not represented in Andrews' book. One was by Alestalo (1979) which was largely concerned with the role of autonomy in group performance. More autonomous groups tended to be more effective ($r = 0.25$), but the paper also includes data on the motivational variables. In an editorial comment Payne and Pearson (1979) noted: 'Only 56% of academics, 44% of people in research institutions, and 26% of industrial scientists are satisfied with the quality and content of their work. This is considerably below the level of satisfaction found in surveys of job satisfaction in other areas and . . . is an issue to which both researchers and managers could pay attention in the future' (p.164). Since motivation accounts for about 10% of the variance in performance, and it appears to be relatively independent as a predictor, it is clearly an area where the skilful leader, and the skilful selector, can make a contribution to team performance.

Diversity and team performance

Victor Frankl, the psychiatrist, is credited with the quotation, 'Variety is not the spice of life, it is the very stuff of it.' There seems to be some truth in this even for researchers, somewhat dissatisfied though some of them are. Andrews (1979d) investigated the influence of diversity on group performance. Over 70 measures of diversity were used, but these were reduced to six main clusters: diversity in projects; interdisciplinary orientation; diversity in specialties; diversity in funding resources; diversity in R & D activities; and diversity in professional functions. All of these had small positive correlations with both qualitative and quantitative performance measures, though they were slightly stronger with the quantitative measures. The major results are that diversity accounts for approximately 10% of the variance in scientific recognition, R & D effectiveness, and number of publications. These results suggest that the flexibility of thought and organization that diverse people bring to a team offer an important and potentially controllable contribution to team performance.

SUMMARY AND CONCLUSION

Whilst there is no attempt to claim this review has captured all of the relevant studies it is unlikely that there are others of the size and scope of the UNESCO studies. Their results can be assumed to provide reasonable estimates of the strengths of relationships amongst the variables they measured. As we have seen these separately, and collectively, account for a good deal of the variance in both the objective and subjective performance measures. The results also indicate that different contexts, and different research or development goals, demand different management strategies. There is a growing list of prescriptive recommendations about managing both research teams (e.g. Badawy, 1982, and the references in Thamhain and Wilemon, 1987) and projects (e.g. Randolph and Posner, 1988). These writers have, of course, been influenced by research findings, but the UNESCO studies are not widely cited and the aim of this chapter has been to try and discover just what good research does exist. Much less than most people think, I suspect. Some of the questions scientific leaders might be asking themselves, however, are:

(1) What kind of organization is the team in? University science or technology, industrial or governmental science or technology? Basic research, applied research, development or creation?
(2) What is the major aim for the team? Papers, books, technical reports, patents?
(3) Can the team be kept below seven in number, but preferably larger than two?
(4) How long has the team been together?
(5) Have they adequate, rather than generous, resources?

(6) Can they spend enough years together to become an effective team (about three to seven years)?

(7) Is the team keeping in touch with its external worlds (i.e. the scientific community, the client, the wider organization, the political world)?

(8) Are the team's goals and missions clear and effectively communicated to them?

(9) Is the team leader skilful in managing his scientific team and sufficiently experienced at communicating and motivating to build a climate that is cooperative yet able to use conflict creatively?

(10) Is the work itself interesting and challenging to the team members, and does the organization offer reasonable chances of promotion and development to offer scientific as well as managerial careers?

(11) If a matrix is in operation, are the roles of the function and the project clear and sensibly specialized?

These seem the major contextual factors which affect the success of different managerial styles and strategies, and as the findings show the variance they account for is large enough not to be ignored. As Stolte-Heiskanen (1987) says '. . . research groups have become the fundamental social and cognitive entities wherein research takes place' (p.255), so R & D managers need to know how to manage them most effectively, and managerial tactics would appear to be just as important as managerial strategies.

Much of this volume is about the psychology of creativity and innovation. Apart from the pure psychology of the creative act itself much creativity takes place in social contexts. And the application of creative acts in the world itself (innovation) almost always involves social collaboration and influence. Understanding how to manage people so that they continuously achieve creative thinking and turn it into innovations is fundamental to the continued progress of science and society itself. The underlying processes revealed by the research reviewed in this chapter have applications well beyond the small scientific teams on which it was developed.

Correspondence address:
Manchester Business School, Booth Street West, Manchester M15 6PB, UK.

REFERENCES

Abbey, A. and Dickson, J.W. (1983). R & D work climate and innovation in semi-conductors. *Academy of Management Journal*, 26, 362–368.

Alestalo, M. (1979). Patterns of influence in research work: the problems of autonomy and democracy, *R & D Management (Special Issue on the Management of Research Groups)*, 9, 221–230.

Andrews, F.M. (Ed.), (1979a). *Scientific Productivity*, Cambridge: Cambridge University Press.

Andrews, F.M. (1979b). The international study: its data sources and measurement procedures. In F.M. Andrews (Ed.), *Scientific Productivity*. Cambridge: Cambridge University Press, pp. 16–52.

Andrews, F.M. (1979c). Estimating the construct validity and correlated error components of the rated-effectiveness measures. In F.M. Andrews (Ed.), *Scientific Productivity*. Cambridge: Cambridge University Press, pp. 401–421.

Andrews, F.M. (1979d). Motivation, diversity, and the performance of research units. In F.M. Andrews (Ed.), *Scientific Productivity*. Cambridge: Cambridge University Press, pp. 252–287.

Badaway, M.K. (1982). *Developing Managerial Skills in Engineers and Scientists*. Princeton, NJ: Van Nostrand.

Bergen, S.A. (1986). *Project Management: an Introduction to Issues in Industrial Research and Development*. Oxford, Blackwell.

Birnbaum, P.H. (1983). Predictors of long-term research performance. In S.R. Epton, R.L. Payne, A.W. Pearson (Eds.), *Managing Interdisciplinary Research*. Chichester: J. Wiley & Sons, pp. 47–58.

Bonmariage, J., Legros, E., and Vessiere, M. (1979). Ratings of research-unit performance. In F.M. Andrews (Ed.), *Scientific Productivity*. Cambridge: Cambridge University Press, pp. 293–331.

Cleland, D.I. (Ed.) (1984). *Matrix Management Systems Handbook*. New York: Van Nostrand Reinhold Co.

Cohen, J. (1977). *Statistical Power Analysis for the Behavioural Sciences*, 2nd edn. New York: Wiley.

Cole, G.A. (1979). Classifying research units by patterns of performance and influence: a typology of the Round 1 data. In F.M. Andrews (Ed.), *Scientific Productivity*. Cambridge: Cambridge University Press, pp. 353–400.

Davis, L.E. and Cherns, A.B. (1975). *The Quality of Working Life*, Vols. 1 & 2. New York: Free Press.

Davis, S.M. and Lawrence, P.R. (1977). In collaboration with H. Kolodny and N. Beer, *Matrix*, Reading, Mass: Addison-Wesley, pp. 52–58.

Denis, H. (1986). Matrix structures, quality of working life and engineering productivity. *IEEE Transactions on Engineering Management*, EM-33 (3), 148–156.

de Hemptinne, Y. and Andrews, F.M. (1979). The international comparative study on the organization and performance of research units: an overview. In F.M. Andrews (Ed.), *Scientific Productivity*. Cambridge: Cambridge University Press, pp. 3–15.

Friedlander, F. and Pickle, H. (1968). Components of effectiveness in small organizations. *Administrative Science Quarterly*, 13(2), 289–304.

Gunz, H.P. and Pearson, A.W. (1977). Matrix organisation in research and development. In K. Knight (Ed.), *Matrix Management*. London: Gower Press.

Jabri, M. (1985). Job-team: its dimensionality and importance in the management of R & D teams. PhD Thesis, Manchester Business School.

Jaunch, L. and Gluech, W.F. (1975). Evaluation of university professors' research performance. *Management of Science*, 22, 66.

Jerkovsky, W. (1983). Functional management in matrix organizations. *IEEE Transactions on Engineering Management*, EM-30(2), 89–97.

Katz, R. and Allen, T.J. (1985). Project performance and the locus of influence in the R & D matrix. *Academy of Management Journal*, 28(1), 67–87.

Keller, R.T. and Holland, W.E. (1978). Individual characteristics of innovativeness and communication in R & D organisations. *Journal of Applied Psychology*, 63, 759.

Kingdon, O.R. (1973). *Matrix Organization: Managing Information Technologies.* London: Tavistock.

Knight, K. (Ed.) (1978). *Matrix Management.* London: Gower Press.

Knorr, K.D., Mittermeir, R., Aichholzer, G. and Waller, G. (1979). Leadership and group performance: a positive relationship in academic research units. In F.M. Andrews (Ed.), *Scientific Productivity.* Cambridge: Cambridge University Press, pp. 95–117.

Kuhn, T.S. (1962). *The Structure of Scientific Revolutions.* Chicago: University of Chicago Press.

Lambert, W.H. and Teich, A.H. (1981). The organizational context of scientific research. In P.C. Nyström and W.H. Starbuck (Eds.), *Handbook of Organizational Design*, Vol. 2. Oxford: Oxford University Press, pp. 305–319.

Miller, D.B. (1986). *Managing Professionals in Research and Development.* San Francisco: Jossey-Bass.

Mintzberg, H. (1979). *The Structuring of Organizations.* Englewood Cliffs, NJ: Prentice-Hall.

Payne, R.L. (1981). Stress in task-focussed groups. *Small Group Behaviour*, **12**(3), 253–268.

Payne, R.L., Jabri, M.M. and Pearson, A.W. (1988). On the importance of knowing the affective meaning of job demands. *Journal of Organizational Behaviour*, **9**, 149–158.

Payne, R.L. and Pearson, A.W. (1979). The management of research groups: Editorial Comment, *Special Issue of R & D Management*, **9**, 161–165.

Pelz, D.C. and Andrews, F.M. (1966). *Scientists in Organisations: Productive Climates for Research and Development.* New York: Wiley.

Pinto, J.K. and Prescott, J.E. (1987). Changes in critical success factor importance over the life of a project. *Academy of Management Proceedings*, New Orleans, pp. 328–332.

Randolph, W.A. and Posner, B.Z. (1988), *Effective Project Planning & Management: Getting the Job Done.* Englewood Cliffs, NJ: Prentice-Hall.

Roe, A. (1952). *The Making of a Scientist.* Nashville: Dodd-Mead.

Sayles, L.R. and Chandler, M.K. (1971). *Managing Large Systems: Organizations for the Future.* New York: Harper & Row.

Schoorman, F.D. and Schneider, B. (Eds.) (1988). *Facilitating Work Effectiveness.* Lexington: D.C. Heath.

Stankiewicz, R. (1979). The size and age of Swedish academic research groups and their scientific performance. In F.M. Andrews (Ed.), *Scientific Productivity.* Cambridge: Cambridge University Press, pp. 191–221.

Stolte-Heiskanen, V. (1979). Externally determined resources and the effectiveness of research units. In F.M. Andrews (Ed.), *Scientific Productivity.* Cambridge: Cambridge University Press, pp. 121–151.

Stolte-Heiskanen, V. (1987). Comparative perspectives on research dynamics and performance: A view from the periphery. *R & D Management*, **17**(4), 253–262.

Thamhain, H.J. and Wilemon, D.L. (1987). Building high performing engineering project teams. *IEEE Transactions on Engineering Management*, EM-**34**(3), 130–137.

Visart, N. (1979). Communication between and within research units. In F.M. Andrews (Ed.), *Scientific Productivity.* Cambridge: Cambridge University Press, pp. 223–251.

Webster, J. and Starbuck, W.H. (1988). Theory building in industrial and organizational psychology. In C.L. Cooper and I.T. Robertson (Eds.), *International Review of Industrial and Organizational Psychology.* Chichester: Wiley.

Part III

Organizational Innovation

6 Innovation effectiveness, adoption and organizational performance

Fariborz Damanpour

Rutgers University, Newark, USA

The influence of attributes of innovations on the adoption and diffusion of innovations in a variety of social systems has been widely probed (for a review and synthesis, see Rogers, 1983; Tornatzky and Klein, 1982). Also investigated, but not as extensively, are individual, organizational, and contextual properties that affect the adoption of innovations in organizations (Baldridge and Burnham, 1975; Daft and Becker, 1978; Keller and Holland, 1978; Kimberly and Evanisko, 1981; Kirton, 1980; Miller *et al.*, 1982; Moch, 1976). However, empirical studies of the consequences of innovations in organizations, particularly studies that focus on the impact of the adoption of innovations on the effectiveness or performance of the adopting organizations, are scarce. This inadequacy exists despite continuous assertions that innovativeness is the main hope for organizations to maintain their high performance levels (Kanter, 1984), and that the low rate of adoption of innovations is a cause of organizational and economic decline (Hayes and Abernathy, 1980).

This chapter focuses on the consequences of the adoption of innovations in organizations. The relationships between the rate of adoption of innovations, effectiveness of innovations as perceived by the organization's top management (hereafter referred to as 'innovation effectiveness'), and organizational performance or effectiveness will be explored. The distinction between innovation effectiveness and organizational performance could be helpful in examining the notion of the 'pro-innovation bias', i.e. the prevailing assumption that the adoption of innovations positively influences organizational performance (Kimberly, 1981; Rogers, 1983), in studies of innovations.

In describing the relationships between the rate of adoption, innovation effectiveness, and organizational performance, a distinction will be made

Innovation and Creativity at Work   Edited by M.A. West and J.L. Farr
© 1990 John Wiley & Sons Ltd

between different types of innovations. The importance of distinguishing between types of innovations is well established in the organizational innovation literature (Evan, 1966; Knight, 1967; Rowe and Boise, 1974). Different types of innovations do not have identical attributes (Downs and Mohr, 1976), their process of adoption is not the same (Daft, 1978), and their predictors are different (Aiken *et al.*, 1980; Damanpour, 1987; Evan and Black, 1967; Moch and Morse, 1977). Our major point is that the perceived effectiveness of different types of innovations is not the same, and the impact of different types of innovations on organizational performance is not necessarily compatible with their perceived effectiveness. An analysis of the data from a sample of 85 public libraries will be used to illustrate the relationships.

ORGANIZATIONAL INNOVATION

Innovation is defined as the adoption of an idea or behavior that is new to the adopting organization (Aiken and Hage, 1971; Daft, 1982). This view, rather than the newness to a population of organizations, is taken because the impact of the adoption of innovations on the performance of the adopting organization is being explored. The innovation can be a new system, device, policy, process, program, product, or service (Damanpour and Evan, 1984). That is, innovations pertaining to all parts of the organization and all aspects of its operation are to be considered. The inclusion of all innovations of different types is necessary when the aggregate effect of innovation adoption on the overall performance of the organization is explored. Moreover, to study the adoption of a large number of innovations provides a more valid profile of innovation adoption behavior, which is preferable to cases in which a less general pattern is studied by selecting a limited number of innovations (Daft and Becker, 1978).

The differential impact of various types of innovations on the rate of adoption and on organizational performance will be probed by distinguishing among three types of innovations—technological, administrative, and ancillary (Damanpour, 1987). *Technological innovations* are defined as those that bring change to the organization by introducing changes in the technology (Dalton *et al.*, 1968). They occur as a result of the use of a new tool, technique, device, or system, and produce changes in products or services, or in the way products or services are produced. *Administrative innovations* produce changes in the organization's structure or its administrative processes. They are only indirectly related to the basic work activity of the organization and are more immediately related to its management (Kimberly and Evanisko, 1981). An administrative innovation is 'the implementation of an idea for a new policy pertaining to the recruitment of personnel, the allocation of resources, the structuring of tasks, of authority, of rewards' (Evan, 1966; p.51). *Ancillary innovations*, as defined in the present study, are organization–environment boundary innovations that pertain to programs and services that go beyond the primary functional activities of the organization. For instance, in public libraries, ancillary innovations are those that go beyond traditional functions of collecting, maintaining, and providing information, and include services to the community such as career development programs, tutorial services, and adult continuing education programs (Damanpour, 1987). After-school supplementary education programs and customer-active programs for product-idea generation (von Hipple, 1978) are, respectively, examples of ancillary innovations in education and marketing.

EFFECTIVENESS OF TYPES OF INNOVATIONS

Is the effectiveness of various types of innovations as perceived by executives (the decision makers in the innovation adoption process) the same? Will the innovations that are perceived to be more effective contribute to organizational performance more than the other innovations? Despite the criticisms of the pro-innovation bias, and the evidence of the importance of studying the consequences of adoption of innovations, these questions have not thus far been examined empirically.

Among the three types of innovations defined above, technological innovations are discussed more in almost all social science fields, presumably because their adoption is perceived to be more essential to organizational effectiveness. One reason is what Nelkin (1973) has called 'technological fix', an over-dependence on technological innovations to solve organizational problems (Rogers, 1983). Also, more visible innovations are expected to be adopted more readily because of the professional and social status associated with their adoption (Rogers, 1983). In this regard, both technological and ancillary innovations (as mainly output-oriented innovations) are more visible than administrative innovations, and thus could be perceived to be more effective. On the other hand, administrative innovations are considered less effective because they are less observable, more complex to implement, and relatively less advantageous (Damanpour and Evan, 1984). Therefore, it is proposed that *technological innovations are perceived to be more effective than administrative and ancillary innovations*.

Are innovations that are perceived to be more effective adopted more frequently? In other words, is the rate of adoption of technological innovations greater than administrative or ancillary innovations? When the adoption of innovations is conceived as a means of obtaining or improving the effectiveness of the adopting organization, and if executives of the adopting unit have a choice in adopting or rejecting the innovation (i.e. when innovations are not enforced from outside due to regulations or decisions of higher level executives in a parent company or a supervisory agency), innovations that are perceived to be more effective are expected to have a higher rate of adoption, and those that are perceived to be less effective have a lower rate of adoption. Thus, *perceived effectiveness of innovation by executives is positively related to the rate of adoption of innovations.*

CONSEQUENCES OF INNOVATIONS

In nearly all studies of organizational innovations, the rate of adoption of innovations or innovativeness is considered as the dependent variable. But, in reality, organizations adopt innovations to maintain or improve their performance levels; thus, innovation is a means toward an end: the overall effectiveness or performance of the organization. The rate of adoption of innovations, therefore, is a predictor of a more ultimate dependent variable, consequences of innovations.

Consequences are the changes that occur to an organization as a result of the adoption (or non-adoption) of innovations (Rogers, 1983). Consequences are difficult to measure in a precise manner because they are not always 'direct' or 'anticipated', but may be 'indirect' and 'unanticipated' (Goss, 1979; Rogers, 1983). A (direct) change introduced in a part of an organization as a result of the adoption of an innovation may produce (indirect) changes in the other parts of the organization. The consequence of the innovation would be desirable if the organization as a whole can cope with and benefit from these changes. Moreover, not all consequences of an innovation are anticipated by the adopters; instead, there are often unanticipated consequences, i.e. changes that are neither intended nor recognized (Rogers, 1983). Unanticipated consequences are due to a lack of understanding of the internal and external forces at work on the adopting unit, and its relationship with the larger social system (Goss, 1979).

Perceived innovation effectiveness most likely represents direct, desirable, and anticipated consequences, because information on these categories of consequences is more readily available to the decision makers (Rogers, 1983). On the other hand, the impact of innovation adoption on the organizational performance would be a result of both desirable and undesirable, direct and indirect, and anticipated and unanticipated consequences.

INNOVATION ADOPTION AND ORGANIZATIONAL PERFORMANCE

Empirical investigations of the relationship between the rate of adoption of innovations and individual or organizational performance are scarce. Among studies that have measured the association between these two variables, some have reported a negative or an insignificant relationship (Becker and Stafford, 1967; Bean *et al.*, 1975), some have indicated a positive relationship (Armour and Teece, 1978; Mansfield, 1968; Mason and Halter, 1968), while others have reported mixed results, depending on the measure of performance used (Hage and Aiken, 1967) or the type of organization (Kaluzny *et al.*, 1974). It is even argued that the objective of determining the economic effects of innovations is generally unattainable (Gold, 1976). Therefore, a proposed relationship between the two variables can only be established conceptually. The performance gap theory of innovation provides such a conceptual underpinning.

Performance gap is the discrepancy between what the organization is actually doing and what its executives believe it can potentially do (Downs, 1966, cited in Zaltman *et al.*, 1973; p. 55). It is the difference between the executives' criteria of satisfaction and the actual performance of the organization. Perceived performance gap creates a need for a change in the organization which would, in turn, stimulate the adoption of innovations in order to reduce or remove the performance gap (Zaltman *et al.*, 1973). Performance gap can be created by both internal and external changes. Whether it is externally or internally produced, the organization would try to remove it by adopting innovations.

The performance gap concept, therefore, suggests that (1) innovative organizations respond to perceived performance gap by adopting innovations, and (2) the adoption of innovations would remove the gap and contribute to the performance of the organization. Considering organizational performance as a function of an organization's ability to reach and maintain equilibrium with its environment (Lawrence and Lorsch, 1967), the adoption of innovation can be conceived as a way of changing the organization to adapt to changes in its internal and external environment to maintain or enhance its performance level. Hence, *the rate of adoption of innovation would be positively related to organizational performance.*

How would different types of innovations affect the relationship between the rate of adoption and organizational performance? Are technological innovations, which are perceived to be more effective than the other types, more highly associated with performance? There is no empirical research on the differential impacts of types of innovations on performance. Conceptually, however, the following arguments can be made. First, innovations that are perceived more effective may not necessarily influence organizational performance more than those perceived less effective, because innovations are perceived to be effective not only for their potential contribution to performance, but also for social status, visibility, the immediacy of rewards, compatibility, and so on (Rogers, 1983). Second, the primacy of one type of innovation versus other types in influencing organizational performance depends on the relative rate of change in a specific subenvironment of the organization (Daft, 1982). For instance, when the administrative subenvironment—which pertains to the administrative component of the organization, including the community context, resource granting agencies, political and social factors, and government organizations—changes more rapidly than the technical subenvironment, the dominant innovation issue is administrative; and the role of administrative innovations in affecting organizational performance would be more crucial than technological innovations (Daft, 1982; Damanpour *et al.*, 1989). On the other hand, when the technical subenvironment—which pertains to the technical system, and is composed of clients, suppliers, technical groups, and competitors—changes more rapidly than the administrative subenvironment, technological innovations would influence performance more than administrative innovations (Daft, 1982; Damanpour *et al.*, 1989). In sum, no one particular type of innovation can be assumed to influence organizational performance more than other types in all environmental conditions. Thus, *technological innovations do not necessarily contribute to organizational performance more than administrative or ancillary innovations.*

Is the relationship between the adoption of innovation and organizational performance affected by innovation effectiveness? Perceived innovation effectiveness primarily portrays the consequences of the adoption of individual innovations. When the consequences of individual innovations are highly positive, the aggregate impact of the adoption of innovations at the level of the organization might also be positive. On the other hand, when individual innovations are not very effective, the overall contribution of their adoption to the organization's performance would also be less effective. Therefore, *innovation effectiveness is expected to moderate the relationship between innovation adoption and organizational performance.*

ANALYSIS

The data

The data from a 1982 study of public libraries in the United States (Damanpour and Evan, 1984) were used to illustrate the propositions. Information on innovation adoption and effectiveness was collected from the directors of libraries. A total of 158 questionnaires were mailed to libraries that served a population of 50 000 or more; smaller libraries were not included, on the assumption that many innovations listed on the questionnaire do not apply to them. A total of 99 questionnaires were returned, of which 85 were usable. A comparison of respondent and nonrespondent libraries showed that the difference between the means of total expenditure, total income, and the number of professional librarians in the two groups were not significantly different from each other at the 0.05 level.

The list of library innovations was developed through a literature search and then was refined through a series of individual interviews and group meetings with librarians, library executives, and educators in several sites. A questionnaire was then prepared and pretested in five locations. The questionnaire embodied four time intervals; libraries were asked to identify the period in which each innovation was implemented. After a preliminary analysis, to preserve the integrity of the innovation scores for early adopters, those innovations that were adopted by more than 50% of libraries prior to 1970 were excluded (Damanpour and Evan, 1984). The remaining innovations, for the purpose of this study, were categorized into three types: 26 technological, 22 administrative, and 13 ancillary innovations. The scores for technological, administrative, and ancillary innovations for each library were determined by the number of innovations of each type implemented in that library.

Effectiveness of each implemented innovation was rated on a five-point scale by the library director. *Innovation effectiveness* was defined as the extent to which the innovation contributes to the library's ability to fulfill its mission and to meet its objectives. The innovation effectiveness score for each time period was identified by a weighted average of effectiveness of innovations adopted in that period (five points on the scale were given weights of 1 to 5 for low to high effectiveness, respectively). Separate scores were computed for the three types of innovations in each time period. However, only the last two periods—1975–1979 (period 1) and 1980–1982 (period 2)—were included in the analysis to avoid the probable errors in rating the effectiveness of innovations adopted in earlier periods. Since the great majority of library directors either have long tenure or are promoted from inside, it was assumed that their rating of innovation effectiveness in the two most recent periods would be accurate.

Two indicators of organizational performance are used in the analysis. The subjective measure of performance was based on the library director's rating of the overall performance of his/her library against that of other libraries of the same type and size (similar to an approach used by Lawrence and Lorsch, 1967, p. 261). This measure was only applied in period 2. The objective performance measure, computed in periods 1 and 2, is a composite measure of the mean of three performance indicators—circulation per holdings, circulation per total expenditure, and circulation per number of employees—obtained from library statistics published by the states. The mean was used because the three indicators were highly intercorrelated—pairwise zero-order correlations were 0.64 or higher, significant at 0.001. This objective performance measure was selected over three other objective measures because analysis showed that it is the most consistent measure over time (Damanpour and Evan, 1984). The measure is, in fact, an efficiency measure of performance (an output–input ratio) used as a surrogate for overall organizational performance, on the assumption that well-managed libraries are more efficiently run than poorly managed ones.

Results

It was proposed that technological innovations are perceived to be more effective than administrative and ancillary innovations. The results shown in Table 1 are in the proposed direction in both periods 1 and 2; however, the differences between the means are not statistically significant. Technological innovations, on average, were rated only slightly more effective than administrative and ancillary innovations. Also, it was found that the rate of adoption of technological innovations is higher than administrative innovations, but not always higher than ancillary innovations (Table 2). As programs and services offered to the community, ancillary innovations are quite visible to library constituents. Their adoption, therefore, tends to be higher than less observable administrative innovations. On the other hand, ancillary innovations are perceived to be less effective than technological innovations because they are auxiliary to the library's primary function, while

Table 1 Descriptive statistics of effectiveness of innovations

Type of innovation	Period 1			Period 2		
	Cases	Mean	Standard deviation	Cases	Mean	Standard deviation
Technological	66	3.93	0.65	76	3.98	0.83
Administrative	55	3.57	0.70	54	3.43	0.90
Ancillary	56	3.65	0.89	42	3.38	1.03
All innovations	80	3.72	0.63	83	3.79	0.76

Table 2 Rate of adoption of technological, administrative, and ancillary innovations $(N = 85)$[a]

Type of innovation	Period 1	Period 2
Technological	11.27	16.14
Administrative	9.44	9.82
Ancillary	16.01	14.02
All innovations	11.78	13.56

[a] Based on a relative measure of innovation—the percentage of innovations adopted from the total innovations available for adoption by the organization in each period.

technological innovations pertain to products, services, and systems that are primary to the library's main functions.

Innovation effectiveness was proposed to be positively related to innovation adoption, but the data did not support this relationship (Table 3). The degree of association between innovation effectiveness and innovation adoption, for all types of innovations and in both time periods, was low and nonsignificant. Two likely explanations are as follows. First, the adoption of innovations in public libraries, which are non-profit-making state- or city-financed organizations, is more influenced by the external organizational forces than the internal managerial choices. That is, decisions for innovations are strongly influenced by the parent or funding institution. The second explanation deals with the way that innovation is operationalized in the library study with respect to the stages of the innovation adoption process. Based on a two-stage conceptualization—initiation and implementation (Duncan, 1976; Rogers, 1983; Zaltman *et al.*, 1973)—innovation can be defined such that it pertains to the initiation or implementation of a new program. The initiation stage consists of all activities leading to the decision to adopt the innovation, while the implementation stage includes all activities leading to the continued use of the innovation (Damanpour, 1988). Perceived effectiveness would most likely be a stronger correlate of initiation of innovations because it can influence the decision to adopt. In the library study, the innovation was defined in relation to the implementation stage.

To explore the effect of innovation adoption on organizational performance, the correlations with both subjective and objective measures of performance

Table 3 Zero-order correlations between innovation effectiveness and adoption of innovations ($N = 42$–83)

Innovation effectiveness	Adoption of innovations			
	Technological	Administrative	Ancillary	All innovations
Period 1				
Technological	*0.014*	0.194*	0.079	0.143
Administrative	0.071	*−0.003*	−0.100	−0.009
Ancillary	−0.105	−0.175*	*0.048*	−0.126
All innovations	0.067	−0.061	0.034	*0.018*
Period 2				
Technological	*0.087*	−0.060	0.015	0.022
Administrative	0.126	*0.078*	0.107	0.146
Ancillary	−0.021	0.136	*0.160*	0.118
All innovations	0.040	−0.135	−0.041	*−0.056*

*$*p < 0.10$.

are reported (Table 4). When all innovations were considered, the data showed an insignificant relationship between adoption and performance within a period (for both periods 1 and 2), but a significant relationship between adoption in period 1 and both subjective and objective measures of performance in period 2. This would indicate a time lag in the effect of adoption on performance. The lag effect was also observed for administrative and ancillary innovations, but not for technological innovations.

The association between technological innovations and the subjective measure of performance increased from 0.027, across periods 1 and 2, to 0.195, in period 2, which is in the opposite direction of administrative, ancillary, and all innovations. The within-period relationship might portray the anticipated effect of technological innovation on performance, while the cross-period relationship could represent the actual effect. Higher correlations between technological innovations and subjective measure of performance in period 2 may reflect library directors' higher expectations of the contribution of technological innovations to performance in that period. It should be noted that the rate of adoption of technological innovations increased markedly from period 1 to period 2 (Table 2).

As was suggested, the association between technological innovation and performance is not necessarily stronger than the association between performance and other types of innovations (Table 4). In fact, administrative

Table 4 Zero-order correlations between adoption of innovations and organizational performance ($N = 85$)

	Organizational performance		
	Period 1	Period 2	
Adoption of innovations	Objective	Subjective	Objective
Period 1			
Technological	−0.012	0.027	0.033
Administrative	0.137	0.168*	0.189**
Ancillary	0.027	0.248**	0.110
All innovations	0.072	0.199**	0.155*
Period 2			
Technological		0.195**	−0.001
Administrative		−0.137	0.096
Ancillary		0.037	0.014
All innovations		0.055	0.048

*$p < 0.10$.
**$p < 0.05$.

innovation is the only innovation type that shows significant correlations with both subjective and objective measures of performance. The greater influence of administrative innovations may be due to the primacy of the administrative subenvironment in library organizations.

The moderating effect of innovation effectiveness on the relationship between innovation adoption and performance was examined by a 'median split sample approach', using simple correlations, because the degree of relationship between two variables, rather than the pattern or form of a relationship, was of interest (Howell *et al.*, 1986). A comparison of high innovation effectiveness libraries with low innovation effectiveness libraries reveals stronger associations in the high effectiveness category for the subjective performance measures (Table 5). This may suggest that aggregate consequences of innovations at the level of the organization are not unrelated to the average perceived effectiveness of individual innovations. However, the results are mixed, and the objective performance measure does not differ significantly between the low and high effectiveness groups.

According to Table 5, the correlation between ancillary innovations and objective performance measure, for both low and high innovation effectiveness groups, is negative and significant. When the sample is not divided into low and high innovation effectiveness, however, the same correlation is near zero and insignificant ($r = 0.014$, Table 4). This apparent inconsistency could be a result of the missing cases. In period 2, only 42 libraries rated the effectiveness of ancillary innovations (Table 1). Correlations for ancillary innovation in Table 5 are based on a total of 42 cases, while those in Table 4 are based on all cases ($N = 85$).

Table 5 Zero-order correlation between adoption of innovations and organizational performance by innovation effectiveness[a]

	Low innovation effectiveness			High innovation effectiveness		
		Performance			Performance	
Adoption of innovations	Cases	Subjective	Objective	Cases	Subjective	Objective
Technological	27	−0.234	−0.018	49	0.347***	0.095
Administrative	26	−0.244	0.021	28	−0.280*	0.176
Ancillary	19	0.072	−0.343*	23	0.155	−0.391**
All innovations	41	−0.188	−0.031	42	0.292**	0.134

[a] Based on the data in period 2.
*$p < 0.10$.
**$p < 0.05$.
***$p < 0.01$.

CONCLUDING REMARKS

The consequences of adoption of innovations at the level of the organization have not been explored widely, perhaps partly because of the pro-innovation bias and partly due to the complexity of both innovation and performance concepts. Although similar difficulties are alluded to in the diffusion research (Goss, 1979; Rogers, 1983), the need for studies of consequences of organizational adoption of innovation is inevitable—especially when innovation is regarded as a focal point of an organization's strategy and a crucial element of its long-term strength and survival (Tushman and Moore, 1982). In fact, future research should establish the study of consequences of adoption of innovations as an important part of the organizational evaluation process.

The present study has been an exploratory analysis and the results do not portray high degrees of association between variables; however, they provide some important insights for more elaborate future investigations.

The variation in organizational effectiveness, as the result of the adoption of innovations, is attributable to both the efficiency of an innovation and the manager's expectations for the effectiveness of the innovation (King, 1974). The results of the present study suggest that the average perceived effectiveness of innovations adopted within a specific period is not a significant correlate of the rate of adoption of innovations. Innovation effectiveness, as perceived by managers, may influence the decision to adopt, but it may not necessarily result in the successful implementation of innovations. Managers' expectations should be communicated to organizational members whose acceptance and cooperation is necessary for making the innovation effective for the organization.

Managers' ability to communicate their own expectations of an innovation to organizational members creates mutual expectancy of high performance and greatly stimulates productivity (King, 1974). The combined effects of innovation effectiveness as perceived by managers, innovation effectiveness as perceived by organizational members, the efficiency of the innovation itself, and managers' expectations of the innovation and their ability to communicate their expectations to workers, on the rate of adoption and consequences of innovations, are among the interesting topics for future investigations.

Past research has shown that communication—both internal (among members or units within the organization) and external (between the organization and its environment) facilitates the adoption of innovation in organizations (Aiken *et al.*, 1980; Jervis, 1975; Kim, 1980; Kimberly and Evanisko, 1981). Internal and external communication resembles, respectively, Ross' (1974) 'sustaining' and 'initiating' mechanisms required for organizational innovativeness. According to Ross (1974, pp. 31–32), the successful adoption of innovations in organizations is a function of the presence of three mechanisms: (1) an initiating mechanism, which carries new ideas to the organization; (2) a sustaining mechanism, which creates a favorable internal climate for innovation adoption; and (3) a feedback mechanism, which evaluates outcomes (consequences) of the innovation and provides information for retention, modification, or abandonment of the innovation. Organizational performance depends on these processes because the organization's current practices are a function of its innovation adoption and the retention of innovation adopted in the past (Ross, 1974).

The results of this study showed that the rate of adoption of innovations has a lagged effect on organizational performance. That is, the combined effects of the adoption of various innovations on performance would not be felt immediately; rather, it would become evident at a later time. The reason is probably that the adoption of an innovation creates changes in one part of the organization which, in turn, would initiate changes in other parts. The consequences of adoption of innovations on the entire organization are due to both direct and indirect, as well as anticipated and unanticipated, consequences (Goss, 1979; Rogers, 1983), which would most likely take some time to fully affect organizational performance.

The differential role of three types of innovations was also considered in exploring the relationship between adoption and performance. Contrary to conventional wisdom, administrative innovations were found to be a stronger correlate of organizational performance than technological innovations. This finding, however, could be due to the nature of the sample organizations. According to Daft's (1982) conception of administrative and technical subenvironments, the subenvironments of an organization do not change at equal rates; hence, they may not stimulate different types of innovations equally. When subenvironments change at unequal rates, the requirement for the adoption of different types of innovations differs; for instance, when the administrative subenvironment changes more rapidly, organizations would need to adopt administrative innovations to adapt to environmental changes. The adoption of appropriate types of innovations, in accordance with the organization's dominant subenvironment, would enhance organizational performance (Damanpour *et al.*, 1989). Thus, the stronger effect of administrative innovations on performance in the present study could be due to the primacy of the administrative subenvironment in public libraries. Future research can focus on other types of organizations, i.e. those for which the technical subenvironment is more dynamic than the administrative subenvironment.

Types of innovations were analyzed separately in the present study, and their interactive effects were not considered. A recent study, however, showed that organizational performance is more a function of a 'fit' between types of innovations than each type alone (Damanpour and Evan, 1984). The value and impact of innovations become apparent if they are viewed in terms of related sets, when each innovation's contribution is enhanced by the adoption of other innovations (Rosenberg, 1982, cited in Butler, 1988). Certain innovations may be linked in such a way that the adoption of one innovation facilitates the adoption of another (Kaluzny and Hernandez, 1988).

Various concepts of 'fit' (Drazin and Van de Ven, 1985) may underlie the interaction among different kinds of innovations. For instance, according to one concept of fit, a certain combination of administrative and technological innovations, adopted in a given context, would be associated with a higher organizational performance, while the lack of such a combination would result in a lower performance (Damanpour, 1988). Another approach may suggest that not one but various combinations of different types of innovations could result in high performance in a given context. Both approaches, however, agree that organizational performance would be a function of 'innovating', not adopting technological or any other kind of innovation alone. Longitudinal studies of a large number of various types of innovations adopted over time, and their consequences on the adopting organizations, are needed in order to unfold the overall impact of innovations in organizations.

SUMMARY

Focusing on the consequences of adoption of innovations, the relationships between innovation effectiveness as perceived by executives, the rate of adoption of innovations, and organizational effectiveness or performance were examined. The differential effect of types of innovations—technological, administrative, and ancillary—on the above relationships was also examined. The data from a sample of public libraries were used to illustrate the propositions. It was found that (1) technological innovations are perceived to be more effective than the other types, (2) the adoption of innovations is positively related to organizational performance, and (3) innovation effectiveness moderates the relationship between innovation adoption and a subjective measure of organizational performance. More elaborate future studies, which consider the interactive effects of the types of innovations as well as the joint effects of managers' and organizational members' perceived innovation effectiveness, are recommended for unfolding true effects of organizational consequences of the adoption of innovations.

Correspondence address:
Graduate School of Management, Rutgers University, 92 New Street, Newark, NJ 07102, USA.

REFERENCES

Aiken, M., Bacharach, S.B. and French, J.L. (1980). Organizational structure, work process, and proposal making in administrative bureaucracies. *Academy of Management Journal*, 23, 631–652.

Aiken, M. and Hage, J. (1971). The organic organization and innovation. *Sociology*, 5, 63–82.

Armour, H.O. and Teece, D.J. (1978). Organizational structure and economic performance: A test of the multi-divisional hypothesis. *The Bell Journal of Economics and Management Science*, 9, 106–122.

Baldridge, J.V. and Burnham, R. (1975). Organizational innovation: Industrial, organizational, and environmental impact. *Administrative Science Quarterly*, 20, 165–176.

Bean A.S., Neal, R.D., Randor, M., and Tansik, D.A. (1975). Structural and behavioral correlates of implementation in U.S. business organizations. In R.L. Schultz and D.P. Slevin (Eds.), *Implementing Operations Research/Management Science: Research Findings and Implications*. New York: Elsevier, pp. 77–132.

Becker, S.W. and Stafford, F. (1967). Some determinants of organizational success. *Journal of Business*, 40, 511–518.

Butler, J.E. (1988). Theories of technological innovation as useful tools for corporate strategy. *Strategic Management Journal*, 9, 15–29.

Daft, R.L. (1978). A dual-core model of organizational innovation. *Academy of Management Journal*, 21, 193–210.

Daft, R.L. (1982). Bureaucratic versus nonbureaucratic structure and the process of innovation and change. In S.B. Bacharach (Ed.), *Research in the Sociology of Organizations*. Greenwich, CT: JAI Press, pp. 129–166.

Daft, R.L. and Becker, S.W. (1978). *The Innovative Organization*. New York: Elsevier.

Dalton, G.W., Barnes, L.B. and Zaleznick, A. (1968). *The Distribution of Authority in Formal Organizations*. Cambridge, MA: Harvard University Press.

Damanpour, F. (1987). The adoption of technological, administrative, and ancillary innovations: Impact of organizational factors. *Journal of Management*, 13, 675–688.

Damanpour, F. (1988). Innovation type, radicalness, and the adoption process. *Communication Research*, 15, 545–567.

Damanpour, F. and Evan, W.M. (1984). Organizational innovation and performance: The problem of organizational lag. *Administrative Science Quarterly*, 29, 392–409.

Damanpour, F., Szabat, K.A. and Evan, W.M. (1989). The relationship between types of innovation and organizational performance. *Journal of Management Studies*, 26, 587–601.

Downs, A. (1966). *Inside Bureaucracy*. Boston: Little, Brown, and Company.

Downs, G.W. and Mohr, L.B. (1976). Conceptual issues in the study of innovation. *Administrative Science Quarterly*, 21, 700–714.

Drazin, R. and Van de Ven, A.H. (1985). Alternative forms of fit in contingency theory. *Administrative Science Quarterly*, 30, 514–539.

Duncan, R.B. (1976). The ambidextrous organization: Designing dual structures for innovation. In R.H. Kilmann, L.R. Pondy and D.P. Slevin (Eds.), *The Management of Organization: Strategy and Implementation*, Vol 1. New York: North-Holland, pp. 167–188.

Evan, W.M. (1966). Organizational lag. *Human Organizations*, 25, 51–53.

Evan, W.M. and Black, G. (1967). Innovation in business organizations: some factors associated with success or failure. *Journal of Business*, 40, 519–530.

Gold, B. (1976). Tracing gaps between expectations and results of technological innovations: The case of iron and steel. *Journal of Industrial Economics*, 25, 1–28.

Goss, K.F. (1979). Consequences of diffusion of innovations. *Rural Sociology*, 44, 754–772.

Hage, J. and Aiken, M. (1967). Program change and organizational properties: A comparative analysis. *American Journal of Sociology*, 72, 503–519.

Hayes, R.H. and Abernathy, W.J. (1980). Managing our way to economic decline. *Harvard Business Review*, July–August, 67–77.

Howell, J.P., Dorfman, P.W. and Kerr. S. (1986). Moderator variables in leadership research. *Academy of Management Review*, 11, 88–102.

Jervis, P. (1975) Innovation and technology transfer—The roles and characteristics of individuals. *IEEE Transactions on Engineering Management*, EM-22, 19–27.

Kaluzny, A.D. and Hernandez, S.R. (1988). Organizational change and innovation. In S.M. Shortell and A.D. Kaluzny (Eds.), *Health Care Management*. New York: Wiley, pp. 379–417.

Kaluzny, A.D., Veney, J.E. and Gentry, J.T. (1974). Innovation of health services: A comparative study of hospitals and health departments. *Health and Society*, 52, 51–82.

Kanter, R.M. (1984). Innovation—the only hope for times ahead? *Sloan Management Review*, 25, 51–55.

Keller, R.T. and Holland W.E. (1978). Individual characteristics of innovativeness and communication in research and development organizations. *Journal of Applied Psychology*, 63, 759–762.

Kim, L. (1980). Organizational innovation and structure. *Journal of Business Research*, 8, 225–245.

Kimberly, J.R. (1981). Managerial innovation. In P.C. Nyström and W.H. Starbuck (Eds.), *Handbook of Organizational Design*, Vol. 1. New York: Oxford University Press, pp. 84–104.

Kimberly, J.R. and Evanisko, M. (1981). Organizational innovation: The influence of individual, organizational, and contextual factors on hospital adoption of technological and administrative innovations. *Academy of Management Journal*, 24, 689–713.

King., A.S. (1974). Expectation effects in organizational change. *Administrative Science Quarterly*, 19, 221–230.

Kirton, M. (1980). Adaptors and innovators in organizations. *Human Relations*, 33, 213–224.

Knight, K.E. (1967). A descriptive model of the intra-firm innovation process. *Journal of Business*, 40, 478–496.

Lawrence, P.R. and Lorsch, J.W. (1967). *Organization and Environment*. Homewood, IL: Irwin.

Mansfield, E. (1968). *Industrial Research and Technological Innovation: An Econometric Analysis*. New York: Norton.

Mason, R. and Halter, A.N. (1968). The application of a system of simultaneous equations to an innovation diffusion model. *Social Forces*, 47, 182–195.

Miller, D., Kets de Vries, M.F.R. and Toulouse, J. (1982). Top executives, locus of control and its relationship to strategy making, structure, and environment. *Academy of Management Journal*, 25, 237–253.

Moch, M.K. (1976). Structure and organizational resource allocation. *Administrative Science Quarterly*, 21, 661–674.

Moch, M.K. and Morse, E.V. (1977). Size, centralization and organizational adoption of innovations. *American Sociological Review*, 42, 716–725.

Nelkin, D. (1973). *Methodone Maintenance: A Technological Fix.* New York: Braziller.

Rogers, E.M. (1983). *Diffusion of Innovations.* New York: Free Press.

Rosenberg, N. (1982). *Inside the Black Box: Technology and Economics.* New York: Cambridge University Press.

Ross, P.F. (1974). Innovation adoption by organizations. *Personnel Psychology,* **27,** 21–47.

Rowe, L.A. and Boise, W.B. (1974). Organizational innovation: Current research and evolving concepts. *Public Administration Review,* 34, 284–293.

Tornatzky, L.G. and Klein, K.J. (1982). Innovation characteristics and innovation adoption–implementation: A meta-analysis of findings. *IEEE Transactions on Engineering Management,* **EM-29,** 28–45.

Tushman, M.L. and Moore, W.L. (1982). *Readings in the Management of Innovation.* Boston: Pitman.

von Hipple, E. (1978). Successful industrial products from customer ideas. *Journal of Marketing,* **42,** 39–49.

Zaltman, G., Duncan, R. and Holbek J. (1973). *Innovations and Organizations.* New York: Wiley.

7 Organizational innovation

Harry Nyström
Institute for Economics, Uppsala, Sweden

INTRODUCTION

Organizational innovation is viewed in this chapter as a result of the interaction between strategy and structure, with organizational culture and climate as important intervening variables. Structure leads to stability and continuity, while strategy is necessary to achieve innovative direction and radical change. While some organizational cultures and climates are more likely to promote stability others are needed to facilitate creativity and innovation.

Companies emphasizing stability and the status quo are called more positional companies, while companies stressing innovative strategies and the need for radical change are called more innovative companies (Nyström, 1979). In some relatively static environments a strong positional orientation and a focus on short run efficiency are conducive to company success, while in other more dynamic and changing environments a strong innovative orientation is necessary. In this framework structure refers both to more tangible aspects of companies such as production facilities and products and more intangible aspects such as organization status structure.

The goal of this chapter is to present and discuss the above model for organizational innovation in relation to a case study of a leading Swedish Chemical Company, EKA Nobell (Ekvall *et al.*, 1987). Strategy, structure, culture, climate and innovative performance were measured by using personal interviews and a battery of psychological tests and company interviews. Altogether about 50 people were interviewed one or more times, with each interview taking 1–2 hours. Questionnaires and tests were administered to 124 persons and in addition to this group discussions were held to present preliminary results and to get feedback.

Innovation and Creativity at Work   Edited by M.A. West and J.L. Farr
© 1990 John Wiley & Sons Ltd

The study points to the need for considering all these organizational variables in order to understand and successfully influence company innovation. It also points to a gap in the existing literature, since no other studies have been found in our search of the literature which combine a business management and a psychological approach for measuring and evaluating organizational innovation. Within the limitations of our cross-sectional data, our approach makes it possible for us to discuss the possible interactions between strategy, structure and performance in organizational innovation and the ways in which culture and climate may influence this process.

OUR BASIC MODEL FOR ORGANIZATIONAL INNOVATION, DESCRIPTION AND COMPARISON WITH OTHER MODELS IN THE LITERATURE

The basic model of organizational innovation underlying the discussion in this chapter was first developed in the mid 1970s and applied to a large number of studies of innovation in Swedish companies ranging from highly innovative pharmaceutical and electronic companies to highly positional food processing and wood and paper companies (Nyström, 1979, 1983, 1985a, 1985b; Nyström and Edvardsson, 1982).

The first strategic variable in this model (Figure 1) is innovative direction, i.e. what radical changes the company wants to achieve. The second is innovative potential, what the company can do given its structural restraints, i.e. its prevailing material and immaterial resources. In this framework strategic leadership can influence both what the company wants to do and what it can do. By focusing on specific new technologies and markets the company can change its innovative direction and by generating better resources the company can improve its innovative potential, i.e. its possibilities for successful innovation.

In this approach a favorable company culture and climate for achieving successful innovation is viewed as one of the most important resources. This is not explicitly recognized in most of the innovation literature (cf. Zaltman *et al.*, 1973; Baker, 1979; Tushman and Moore, 1982) and in many companies. The purpose of this chapter is to introduce culture and climate as important intervening variables affecting the outcome of innovation strategies and to empirically measure these variables and relate them to our overall model of organizational innovation in a specific empirical context.

Highly positional companies are companies that basically want to continue to do what they have been doing. They do not need much innovative direction or innovative potential. In other words there is no great need for strategic

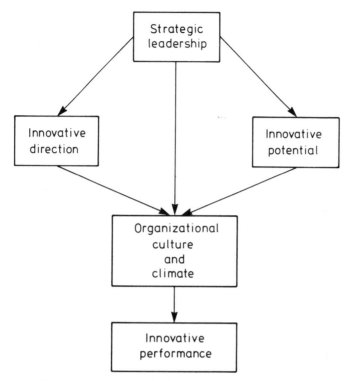

Figure 1   Basic model of organizational innovation

leadership to carry out company goals. Instead structure determines strategy and the direction into the future is given by prevailing tendencies. Highly innovative companies on the other hand are companies who both want to achieve radical change and have the potential to do so. They thus use strategic leadership to achieve both better innovative direction and innovative potential and their long-term success depends on how well they succeed in both these respects.

Since companies may be more or less positional or innovative—and need to be so to succeed, given their internal possibilities and environmental requirements—it is important that we can measure to what extent they are one or the other. Within companies different activities also require different degrees of positional or innovative orientation and different organizational cultures and climates (Weick, 1969; Duncan, 1973). Producing and marketing mature products for established markets, for instance, may be carried out successfully with a highly positional orientation, while developing and marketing new products demands a more innovative orientation. A large part of our research, cited above, has been devoted to defining and measuring how positional or innovative activities are, and relating this to success in product and company development. This, then, has been done without explicitly considering organizational culture and climate. In the case study presented in this chapter, the approach has been extended to measure and evaluate the importance of culture and climate for organizational innovation in both more positional and more innovative situations.

In the static world of classical micro-economic theory all companies by definition are positional, since technologies, products and markets are assumed to be given and well understood. There is therefore no need for creativity and innovation, or for innovative companies. In more dynamic versions of economic theory a certain degree of desirable instability, linked to a need for innovation, is sometimes permitted (Klein, 1977). No discussion of alternative strategies for promoting more or less stability or innovation is, however, usually attempted in these models. Neither economic nor sociological approaches usually recognize that companies may choose different strategies. Instead structure is basically assumed to determine strategy. Also, the need for balancing stability and change—momentarily and over time—is not given much attention.

In the sociological organization literature, for instance, a number of classifications have been presented which to some extent capture what we mean by more positional and more innovative companies. A distinction has, for instance, been drawn between mechanistic and organic organizations, (Burns and Stalker, 1961), static and dynamic organizations (Hage and Aiken, 1970), and segmentalist and integrative organizations (Kanter, 1983).

These alternative classifications, however, are more partial than our classification, since they only consider differences in organization structure and not strategic differences. Hage and Aiken explicitly acknowledge that they only consider structural properties, but at the same time admit that differences in strategic leadership may account for differences which they have ascribed to structural variation.

Strategy in our study has been assessed by interviews with top management in EKA, both at the company and divisional level. Organization structure was measured by a questionnaire containing about 30 statements. The 124 respondents, who were almost all the employees in the divisions, stated their agreement with these statements on a scale of 0–3, with 0 signifying very little agreement and 3 very much. Some of the results of main interest to our present discussion are given in Table 1, and will be discussed in more detail in our case analysis in the next section, as will the other results introduced in this section.

Goal clarity refers to the extent to which members feel they have been informed about the strategy, plans and intentions of their division. Formalization means the extent to which rules and formal procedures govern decision-making. Pre-planning refers to the degree to which decisions are set

Table 1 Some dimensions of organization structure in the various divisions

	Division			
	B	VP	TS	PK
Goal clarity	2.1	1.8	1.6	1.6
Formalization	0.8	0.8	0.9	0.8
Pre-planning	1.8	1.8	1.1	1.0
Role clarity	2.2	2.0	1.4	1.5
Strict routines	1.3	1.5	0.8	0.8

Higher values indicate higher loadings on the factors on a scale from 0 to 3.

ahead of time and followed in practice. Role clarity refers to how precisely employees feel that their functions have been clearly delineated and set out by top management. Strict routines means how closely formal rules and procedures are followed. Since high loadings on all these factors may be assumed to reduce innovative potential by leaving less room for radical change and decentralized initiative, and promote stability by clearly stating in advance what decisions should be taken, we may use them to indicate to what extent organization structure is conducive to innovative or positional development.

Our approach allows structure to primarily determine strategy, in the case of highly positional companies, and strategy to mainly determine structure, in the case of highly innovative companies. Thus we are in agreement with most economic and sociological writers, that structure may influence strategy, and with writers on strategic management (e.g. Chandler, 1962; Ansoff, 1979) that strategic change may lead to structural change. In our approach the relationship between structure and strategy depends on the type of company development, positional or innovative, and therefore either structure or strategy may be the leading factor.

Another difference between the approach used in this chapter and most other economic and sociological approaches to company development is that we explicitly consider and measure organizational culture and climate as factors which may inhibit or promote structural stability and strategic change. When culture and climate (James and Jones, 1984; Frost *et al.*, 1985) are used as explanatory factors in company development this is usually done without directly measuring and relating differences in culture and climate to structural and strategic differences and to performance.

Organizational culture (Deal and Kennedy, 1982; Schein, 1984) is defined as the values, norms, beliefs and assumptions embraced by participants. In our study culture was measured by a content analysis based on an open questionnaire where the 124 respondents were able to use their own words to describe how they perceived this variable. As with the questions on organization structure, almost all EKA employees in the various divisions are included in this sample, both top managers and subordinates.

A number of themes emerged, which were used to classify the cultures prevailing in the different divisions. In this chapter responses to one of the questions, 'What motto would you use to describe the underlying philosophy and striving in your division?', will be used to characterize the cultures, since they seem best to display the aspects we are interested in. The number of times each theme was touched upon in the answers from each divison are given in Table 2.

The themes chosen for the present discussion are factors which may be assumed to either promote or inhibit creativity and change as opposed to stability and the status quo. Risk taking, competitiveness and work enjoyment may be viewed as cultural dimensions which are conducive to innovative performance, while over concern with efficiency, profitability, and survival may be viewed as contributing to more positional behavior.

Organizational climate, on the other hand, may be defined as the feelings, attitudes and behavioral tendencies, which characterize organizational life and may be operationally measured through the perceptions of its members (cf. Payne and Pugh, 1976). While culture is more normative and stable, climate thus is more descriptive and changeable. Climate may thus be seen as the way culture is expressed at each point of time, and by trying to change culture, company leaders may hope to influence climate, which is more directly related to company behavior.

In our study climate has been measured by a previously developed questionnaire (Ekvall *et al.*, 1983; Ekvall and Arvonen, 1984), given to the same people as the organization structure and culture assessments. The

Table 2 Number of times in each division that various themes occurred in response to the question 'What is basic philosophy of the division?'

	Division			
	B	VP	TS	PK
Risk taking	3	6	5	12
Quality	3	2	3	2
Competitiveness	—	3	—	4
Efficiency	2	3	2	—
Profit	9	5	13	—
Survival	7	—	—	7
Work enjoyment	2	7	9	1
Hard work	1	1	1	—
Market and customer orientation	2	2	5	1

respondents were asked to state on a four point scale of 0–3 for 77 questions whether they believed a statement to apply or not. The measuring instrument has proved to possess good reliability and validity in differentiating between more and less innovative organizations. By using factor analysis of the correlations a number of climatic dimensions have been operationally determined, high values for which have been shown to be positively related to creativity and change. These dimensions are challenge, idea support, richness in ideas, liveliness, playfulness, debate, conflicts, trust, freedom to initiate, harmony, achievement motivation, and risk taking (Table 3).

Table 3 Some dimensions of climate in the various divisions

	Division			
	B	VP	TS	PK
Challenge	1.8	2.1	2.2	2.1
Idea support	1.7	2.0	2.1	2.0
Richness of ideas	1.6	1.9	2.2	2.6
Liveliness	1.3	1.7	2.1	1.9
Playfulness	1.3	1.7	2.0	1.8
Debate	0.9	1.0	1.4	1.8
Conflict	0.9	0.3	0.4	1.3
Trust	1.6	1.8	1.8	1.1
Freedom	1.8	2.0	2.3	2.1
Harmony	1.7	1.8	1.8	1.7
Achievement orientation	1.6	2.0	2.0	1.9
Risk taking	0.9	1.4	1.9	2.4

Higher values indicate higher loadings on the factors on a scale from 0 to 3.

CASE DESCRIPTION

Until the beginning of the 1970s EKA Nobell, or EKA Kemi as it was then called, was a highly positional company. Its business consisted in the efficient production and distribution of basic chemicals, and the company had been in this line of business since 1895. During the 1960s profitability in the dominant product line, chlorine/alkali, diminished after being high during the 1950s. The situation was made worse by the greater environmental demands made by the authorities, which threatened a closedown of the established factories.

A necessary reorientation towards new products and markets was difficult to achieve with the existing personnel and organization structure which had little innovative potential. To become a more innovative company a more flexible, market oriented organization and some renewal of personnel was needed.

After top management had decided to change its direction, a number of structural changes were carried out to allow for a more innovative strategy. To begin with a product organization was implemented around 1970. This was followed by divisionalization in the early 1980s to facilitate technological renewal and market adaption. By changing the mix of technologies and markets in the different divisions, a clearer distinction was achieved between them with regard to innovative potential.

This made it possible to increase the technological and marketing development efforts in the more innovative divisions without leading to disturbances in the more positional ones. Since the divisions to a large extent utilized the same basic technologies a problem with divisionalization was how to handle interdependencies from a development point of view. This made necessary formal or informal cross-divisional project groups to integrate joint technology needs.

With regard to culture and climate there were great differences between divisions, which became a major focus of our research. We assumed that these would be related to differences in innovative potential and performance. If so there was a need to promote cultures and climates in the various divisions which would function well in each specific situation. Some types of culture and climate are well suited for achieving stability and efficiency, while others are more likely to lead to creativity and innovative change. A major research question, which we addressed, is to identify these factors and relate them to positional and innovative performance.

After this general description of EKA Nobell we will now describe in more detail the strategies, structures, cultures and climates in the different divisions. It is quite clear that the strategic ambition of top management since the early 1970s had been to make the company more innovative by increasing its innovative potential. At the same time it was easier to achieve this goal in some divisions than in others and this influenced the strategies pursued by divisional leaders.

To find out about these strategies personal interviews were carried out with top management in all divisions. Structure, culture and climate were measured by company interviews at all levels of the organization and by psychological measurements and questionnaires administered to almost all employees. At the same time information on product development was collected as a measure of innovative performance. These data were supplemented by other information such as internal documents and sales material.

We will begin with the most positional division both with regard to structure and strategy, the B-Division. Basically its business is to make caustic soda and chlorine by electrolyzing dissolved salt. This process also leads to hydrogen gas, which is used to make hydrogen peroxide. The chlorine is sold by a company owned by all Swedish producers of this product. It is mainly delivered to the Swedish cellulose industry where it is used for bleaching chemical pulp. The caustic soda is also sold to the same jointly owned company and largely used for bleaching, but also for making soap, water purification and other industrial uses. A large part of the production is sold to the other divisions and further refined by them.

The B-Division thus almost entirely manufactures standard products and virtually no product development to find new products is carried out. Little active marketing to final consumers is pursued. Instead the joint sales company acts as an intermediary between the division and the final market for much of what is produced. The rest of the production sold outside the company is sold on more competitive terms with some active marketing and customer adaptation. In the absence of product development and active marketing rationalization of production to achieve cost reduction and greater efficiency is the main possibility to increase profitability. Most caustic soda is sold in Sweden at profitable prices since transportation costs for importing this commodity are high.

The B-Division thus shows the most positional orientation with regard to products, mainly selling established standard commodities. Its organization structure and sales organization are in line with this orientation. Production processes are large scale and highly specialized and most of its sales go to established sales outlets and customers.

It puts more emphasis on pre-planning than most of the other divisions, and shows greater goal clarity with regard to what it should do. Role clarity also is high, which means that most people know quite well what they are expected to do. Somewhat surprising is that formalization, as in all the other divisions, is fairly low, but the extent to which existing rules are strictly followed is relatively high. The emphasis in this division thus is on stable operations and its leadership largely reflects this need. The head of the division has an authoritarian, production oriented leadership style using distinct orders to achieve planned results.

The culture and climate of the B-Division also reflect its highly positional orientation. The culture, that is the basic values, norms beliefs and assumptions expressed by the people in the B-Division, is dominated by a felt need for profit and survival. This is viewed as much more important than risk taking and enjoying work for its own sake. Efficiency and quality are viewed as important, but competitiveness is not seen as a major requirement to achieve success. This culture reflects positional values such as, security, disciplined work and even complacency, which help to explain why the climate is not very exciting and unlikely to lead to strong innovative efforts.

The climate, that is the psychological mix of feelings and attitudes which affect day to day organizational behaviour, is viewed by subordinates in the

B-Division as low key, with some underlying, unresolved conflicts. It is perceived as less challenging, risk encouraging and playful, than in any other division. It is not seen as very achievement oriented, lively and supportive of new ideas. Debate is not common and the freedom to take initiatives in decision-making is viewed as low. Conflict is fairly high and trust relatively low, compared to most of the other divisions.

Obviously this is not a very creative climate. Instead it is one which promotes stability and faith in the existing way of doing things. As long as the B-Division is seen as a stable backbone in the company and is successful in doing what it has always done, its culture and climate may be quite conducive to achieving its goals. If it is met by demands to become more innovative and creative, as was the case in the 1970s and early 1980s, problems will arise because of its prevailing attitudes and basic values and assumptions.

The VP-Division is the division in EKA which after the B-Division appears to be most positional in its strategy and structure. The main product of this division is hydrogen peroxide. This, as we have noted above, is a very useful chemical produced by using a working solution which is constantly circulated. The basic raw material used is hydrogen, delivered from the B-Division, which is oxidized by using air. Most of this product is sold to the paper industry, where it is used for bleaching chemical and mechanical pulp and return paper. It is also used for purification processes and internally to produce other chemicals for the detergent industry.

Most of the development efforts in the VP-Division are directed towards solving customer problems and technical service is one of its main ways of competing. The division has a high level of competence in bleaching chemistry, which is used to develop new products in cooperation with customers, for instance highly bleached mechanical pulp, raffinated pulp and other high yield types of pulp.

In addition the VP-Division has been able to use its competence to develop new products for different markets. One successful example is Ekarox, which is a derivative of hydrogen peroxide used for chemical purification processes, for instance in the steel and food industry. Most of its development work has been carried out internally in the division in cooperation with customers, and little use has been made of experts from other divisions or outside the company. The reason seems to have been a positional tendency in the division to stay within its basic area of technology, bleaching, and not to try to combine this knowledge in a more innovative fashion with other technologies, for instance mechanical engineering, to find new products. This division thus has tried to become more innovative mainly by finding new applications for existing technology, rather than by developing new technologies.

In line with its relatively positional strategy the VP-Division has developed a structure which, as in the case of the B-Division, is more suited to promoting stability than change. It employs large scale and highly specialized production processes. After the B-Division, it has the second highest goal clarity and a strong emphasis on pre-planning and strict routines. It is also second highest on role clarity.

Divisional leadership in the VP-Division, however, is less authoritarian than in the B-Division. It is divided between three different leaders, each responsible for a clearly defined area. One is responsible for general production and process development, another for technical marketing towards the cellulose industry and the third for technical marketing towards other markets as well as administrative development and control. Both productive and administrative stability are given top priority by all three leaders, although a certain degree of innovative entrepreneurship is permitted.

As may be expected when a fairly positional type of business tries to develop in a somewhat more innovative direction we find fairly strong elements of risk taking and competitiveness in the expressed culture of the VP-Division. Work enjoyment is emphasized quite strongly and the need to be profitable is downplayed somewhat. The need for efficiency, however, is stated more frequently than in any other division. The culture thus seems to be fairly favorable for promoting creativity and change, but the restraints on going too far from the established business are quite strong.

With regard to climate it is high on challenge, idea support, trust and the need for achievement, and fairly high on richness of ideas, risk taking and freedom, all of which are factors which may be viewed as creativity promoting. It is also fairly high on playfulness, but low on debate. It is also very low on conflict and thus seems to stress the need for harmony more than any other division.

The climate in the VP-Division thus seems to be a dual one, in some ways promoting, but in other ways inhibiting creativity and innovation. This may reflect both a dissonance between innovative ambitions and perceived innovative potential and some indecisiveness in strategic leadership, as to how much support should be given to promoting creativity and change. Both culture and climate thus are somewhat contradictory and display a need for more consistency, if either positional or innovative tendencies are to be given priority.

Our third division, the TS-Division, seems to have been more ambitious in trying to become more innovative than the VP-Division, and has also succeeded better in this respect. This is in spite of the fact that it to a large extent produces standard products. Its main business is producing meta silicate and perborate for the detergent and cleaning industry, but it has also developed radically new products based on its silicate technology.

In EKA the TS-Division had been given responsibility for R & D in silicate technology. The division has actively cooperated with other divisions to find new products. Compared to the VP-Division the TS-Division sells most of its products under intense competition, with little customer specific adaptation, technical service and consultation.

Among the new products the TS-Division has developed is Bindzil, a binding medium for carpets. The idea for this new product is related to the idea for Compozil, the paper chemical system which the TS-Division pioneered together with the VP-Division and which subsequently has been spun off to a new division, the PK-Division. Bindzil is technologically and market-wise quite a new product which was developed together with customers and a textile research institute. Another new product developed by the TS-Division, Meta 5, was not as new from a technological standpoint and less unique on the market, but commercially very successful.

The TS-Division thus is relatively innovative in its strategy and performance, and this is reflected in its structure. It has more flexible production facilities and organizational procedures than the VP- and B-Divisions. It has, for instance, used flexible project teams to promote product development. Its organization structure is also characterized by less goal clarity, pre-planning and strict routines, than these other divisions. This is understandable, given its more searching and innovative strategy and greater emphasis on R & D, the results of which are difficult to perceive clearly in advance and use as a basis for detailed planning. There is furthermore less role clarity, that is greater ambiguity in perceived roles in the TS-Division, than in the B- and VP-Divisions, which could both facilitate and be the result of innovative change.

With regard to culture the TS-Division is very strong on work enjoyment and market and customer orientation. It is also characterized by a relatively high preference for risk taking, but surprisingly enough competitiveness is not emphasized, despite the fact that it is working under tougher market conditions than the B- and VP-Division. It also shows a very strong concern for profit, even stronger than the B-Division.

This could be due to its taking a longer run view of profit, consistent with an innovative orientation, but it is not possible to judge this from the data. The fact that its culture is not as strong in emphasizing efficiency suggests such an interpretation. This seems more appropriate for a culture favoring innovation, than a focus of short run profitability. The TS-Division thus, by and large, does not seem to have a very strong culture for facilitating creativity and change. To achieve its relatively ambitious innovative strategy it appears that a somewhat more supportive culture in this respect would have been desirable.

The climate of the TS-Division, on the other hand, seems more creative and favorable to innovation than the culture. It has the highest value of all divisions for challenge, idea support, liveliness, playfulness and freedom to initiate. It has the second highest for richness of ideas, debate, harmony, achievement orientation and risk taking. Together with the VP-Division it is highest in trust and it is second lowest in conflict after the VP-Division.

It would thus appear that the climate of the TS-Division is the most favorable for creativity and innovation in EKA, but looking at its results it is clear that it has not been able to live up to its potential to the same extent as the PK-Division, which we will consider next. Since actually innovating usually leads to substantial debate, conflict, disharmony and even lack of trust, it is not surprising that the PK-Division—whose performance has been most innovative—scores higher in these respects than the TS-Division. This division thus appears to have been less successful in realizing the innovative potential in its climate than in creating it.

The final division in EKA is the PK-Division. Since this, as we have noted above, is a relatively new division, formed to develop a new program of paper chemicals, Compozil, it is not surprising that our data show it to be the most innovative division. Its origin was a joint research project carried out by the VP-Division and the TS-Division with which it still has close ties.

The PK-Division is a good example of how external influences may lead to radical changes in an established line of business. The person who had been division head from the start to the time of our interviews came from the paper industry, where the main potential customers for Compozil were to be found. To begin with he was a consultant to EKA and a member of the joint divisional new product team that started to develop the new concept. Initially this team had been formed to develop a new binding medium together with a customer firm. This effort was not successful and instead the interest turned to the development of new paper chemicals.

A number of coincidences led to Compozil. Shortly after EKA had started a pilot plant for silicic acid and wanted to find more applications for this product, EKA obtained an agency for a chemical which could be used for producing cationic starch to be used in making paper. Together with an expert consultant on silicic acid a number of ideas for using this starch in the paper industry were conceived.

After several failures in the test production of paper by using the new ideas, the project group arrived at an application for filling fine paper, which was patented. By combining cationic starch with silicic acid and other chemicals it proved possible to obtain a superior 'superfilled' fine paper, with a high content of substitutes for wood fibers. These substitutes are cheaper and therefore the process leads to cost reductions, but also to a higher quality paper in many respects, such as retention, dry strength, formation and drainage, compared to other methods for saving fiber.

The resulting paper chemical system, Compozil, thus was quite a new concept in the industry with great potential for improving paper quality and lowering cost. It was, however, broadly marketed too soon, which led to a number of disappointments. The potential market was overestimated as was the willingness of prospective customers to adopt the new process. It was initially not sufficiently adapted to market needs and a number of technical problems remained to be solved.

The PK-Division then changed its marketing strategy for Compozil and began to focus on customer specific applications and selling know-how, rather than on marketing the general process. This was more successful and soon a substantial and growing number of paper mills were using the chemical system. Some customers had even used the process to develop their own new products, such as a low weight bible paper and a better paper for pocket books.

The strategy and structure of the PK-Division are well in line with its highly innovative orientation. It has been highly flexible in responding to customer demand and actively involved in persuading and training them to use its new concept for papermaking. Its organization structure is characterized by low clarity in goals and little pre-planning, which may be viewed as both the result of and facilitating factors for a creative, entrepreneurial style of decision-making, focusing more on action based experimentation and learning than on advance planning. The PK-Division is also low on role clarity, that is the organizational members are often uncertain as to what is expected of them, which is not surprising in a creative organization requiring a lot of self-initiative.

The leadership style of the division head is entrepreneurial. He is highly intuitive, makes rapid decisions, is willing to take great risks and experiment. He is a visionary activist who displays many of the qualities of creative leadership, flexibility, willingness to reconsider and tolerance for ambiguity. This leads to a high innovative potential in the division, but also to uncertainty and anxiety in less creative individuals. At the same time the leader is nonauthoritarian, listens to his staff, supports their ideas and initiatives and delegates responsibility for carrying out major decisions. His leadership thus is highly dynamic and displays both the positive and negative sides of promoting creative change. This is as far as we can get in EKA from administrative stability and positional behavior and in the PK-Division these tendencies are encouraged by the managing director of EKA, who is aware of the need for this type of organized anarchy to achieve radical innovation.

When we look at the culture and climate of the PK-Division we find that the prevailing values and attitudes are also clearly related to a creative, entrepreneurial way of doing business. Risk taking is found as a cultural theme much more often than in the other divisions and together with competitiveness dominates the culture. Efficiency and profit are not stressed, which follows from the innovative focus of the division. Profits are a positional factor related to the present, while innovative organizations are future oriented and need not show immediate profit as long as they can maintain their creditability as the money makers of tomorrow. Surprisingly enough, quality and customer orientation are not stressed either as basic values. Evidently the preoccupation with creativity and change is so strong that it dominates most cultural factors directly linked to performance which are stressed in more positional business organizations.

PK's climate is higher than in any other division on risk taking, richness of ideas, debate and conflict. It is also quite high on challenge, idea support, liveliness, playfulness and freedom. All these climate values are what might be expected in a highly creative and entrepreneurial organization. It is surprising, however, that the climate is fairly low on achievement orientation. The very low value for harmony is, on the other hand, understandable. Creativity and radical change are not very often linked to tranquility. It is more difficult to judge the implications of the low degree of trust displayed. On the one hand dynamic conditions may easily lead to a lack of trust between individuals, but on the other hand creative organizations must learn to fight this tendency to perform well.

Compared to the TS-Division, the PK-Division is somewhat lower on some climatic dimensions, such as challenge, idea support, liveliness, playfulness and freedom. As we have noted the PK-Division is much better, however, on creative performance. This points to the conclusion that the TS-Divison has not been utilizing its creative potential to the same extent that the PK-Division has, nor has it been necessary given its more positional strategy. At the same time it has been able to avoid many of the negative aspects of innovative performance such as conflicts and a certain lack of trust.

COMPARISON BETWEEN DIVISIONS

We may now compare the different divisions along a scale from most positional to most innovative with regard to strategy, structure, culture, climate and performance. As we have seen from our above discussions all the divisions seem to have a relatively good fit between these variables, that is structure, cultures and climates that seem conducive to achieving the type of performance their strategies demand.

B	VP	TS	PK

Most positional   Most innovative

The B-Division has a clearly expressed positional strategy which has been realized in its business activities. Its major objective is to produce basic chemicals in a safe and efficient way and thereby create a basis for more innovative activities in other divisions. It has not been expected to do R & D on its own and has essentially lived up to this expectation. Its production and organization structure are well adapted for this purpose as well as its strategic leadership style stressing stability and predictability. Its culture and climate also show clear stability promoting elements emphasizing efficiency and control. This is a good example of an organizational development situation where structure leads strategy and culture and climate mainly reinforce prevailing structural tendencies, rather than promote strategic change.

The VP-Division has a somewhat more innovative strategy, but essentially concentrates its efforts on a well-defined area of technology—based on hydrogen peroxide—and established markets. Its main marketing efforts are directed towards strengthening its ties to existing customers by helping them to solve their technical problems. Its production and organization structures are well adapted to this purpose. While they display more flexibility than in the B-Division they are still basically geared towards achieving stability in production and sales.

The culture and climate of the VP-Divison seems moderately creativity inducing and it has been able to develop a number of successful new product applications within its established area of technological competence. Although somewhat more change oriented than in the B-Division, it seems more to reflect the need for stability than for change. Its leadership, while less authoritarian than in the B-Division, appears to stress administrative efficiency rather than the need for innovation. From a strategic management point of view this appears to be a rather evolutionary development mode, with strategy stretching structure but not changing its basic configuration.

The TS-Division seems to be more mixed in its basic orientation than the other divisions. It displays relatively strong positional tendencies related to its established products, but also quite strong innovative efforts to develop new products and find new markets. It has been quite active and open in its search for and development of new areas of technology. Its structure has been more flexible and innovation permitting than in the VP-Division and its strategic leadership more aimed at actively promoting innovation.

The culture and climate of the TS-Division seem therefore to have been more favorable for creativity and innovation than its strategy, structure and performance, and its psychological potential for change therefore underutilized. Its organizational atmosphere stresses the positive aspects of creativity and change, such as freedom and playfulness, but there is less awareness of the negative aspects, such as strife and dissension, probably because these factors are more related to actual performance than to potential.

In the TS-Division the interplay between strategy and structure consequently seems to have been more complex and differentiated than in the B- and VP-Divisions. Strategic change has been used to explore possibilities, but there has been less commitment than in the PK-Division to the widespread and far-reaching implementation of new ideas.

The PK-Division, finally, has been most innovative in its orientation and performance, which is not surprising since it is a recently established venture division. It has had no production of its own, which has made it possible for it to concentrate on its development activities. Since its leadership is highly entrepreneurial—focusing on new possibilities and rapid adaptation to action based learning—change has clearly been the name of the game. This is also reflected in its flexible, somewhat ambiguous organization structure and highly challenging and risk willing culture and exciting, but also stress-producing, climate.

In the PK-Division we thus clearly see both the positive and negative aspects of highly innovative performance, and the managing director of EKA has been aware of this and taken a calculated risk in promoting its activities. In this case strategy has clearly been leading structure and led to both the creation and realization of new possibilities. Since the structure has been highly flexible it has been able to accommodate quite radical strategic change, but conscious attempts to eliminate structural restraints have also been successfully carried out by company and divisional leaders.

SUMMARY

Our study shows the need to consider not only strategy and structure if we want to understand and influence organizational creativity and innovation. We also need to explicitly measure and evaluate the effects of culture, climate and leadership styles. We have presented a general framework for looking at and measuring the interaction between these organizational variables and shown how this framework may be applied in studying the strategic development of a Swedish chemical company, EKA Nobell.

We find clear differences between the different divisions in this company both with regard to innovative potential and performance. More positional divisions tend to show greater clarity in goals and behavior, but also less willingness and ability to take risks and explore new possibilities. Their cultures and climates are less challenging, playful and lively. They are also less supportive of, and rich in, ideas. More innovative divisions are more open in their views and behavior, but also show more internal differences in opinion and greater debate as to what action to take to achieve their innovative goals.

The ambition of top management in EKA Nobell initially was to try to make the performance of all divisions more innovative by changing their strategies. Our approach and empirical data indicate that this is not possible without also achieving consistency between structure, culture, climate and strategic leadership, so that they together reinforce and make possible radical change.

By realizing this, and appreciating the fact that radical change is difficult in established organizational units, top management may then choose the more realistic course of letting more positional units basically maintain and strengthen their established activities and orientation. Innovative efforts should instead be concentrated in existing innovative units or in new organizational units with strong innovative potential. If these are built up based on entrepreneurial leadership, creative culture and climate and flexible structures, our data indicate that the likelihood of achieving successful innovation is much greater than if attempts are made to force existing positional units to become more innovative.

There thus is a great need for more balanced and comprehensive views of organizational innovation than the more partial views usually presented in the management literature. Such a view will not permit simple conclusions and generalizations. It must be based on detailed studies of organizational innovation in different types of companies. This research must consider both the need for strategic management to consider technological and market needs and organizational design to allow for flexibility and change. It must also be based on the management of culture and climate to promote creativity and innovation. For this purpose we must combine the thinking and techniques of management theory and practice with psychological theory and measurement to gain a more complete understanding of and basis for influencing organizational innovation.

Correspondence address:
Department of Marketing, Institute for Economics, Box 7013, 750 07, Uppsala, Sweden

REFERENCES

Ansoff, I. (1979). *Strategic Management*. London: Macmillan.
Baker, M. (1979). *Industrial Innovation*. London: Macmillan.
Burns. T. and Stalker, G.M. (1961). *The Management of Innovation*. London: Tavistock.
Chandler, A.D. Jr. (1962). *Strategy and Structure*. Cambridge, Mass. MIT Press.
Deal, T.E. and Kennedy, A.A. (1982). *Corporate Cultures*. Reading, Mass: Addison-Wesley.
Duncan, R. (1973). Multiple decision making structures in adapting to environmental uncertainty: The impact on organizational effectiveness. *Human Relations*, **26**, 273–291.
Ekvall, G. and Arvonen, J. (1984). *Leadership Styles and Organizational Climate for Creativity: Some Findings in One Company*. Stockholm: F.A. Rådet.
Ekvall, G., Arvonen, J. and Nyström, H. (1987). *Organisation och Innovation*. Lund: Studentlitteratur.

Ekvall, G., Arvonen, J. and Waldenström-Lindblad, I. (1983). *Creative Organizational Climate: Construction and Validation of a Measuring Instrument*. Stockholm: F.A. Rådet.

Frost, P.J., Moore, L.F., Louis, M.R., Lundberg, C.C. and Martin, J. (1985). *Organizational Culture*. Beverly Hills: Sage Publications.

Hage, J. and Aiken, M. (1970). *Social Change in Complex Organizations*. New York: Random House.

James, L.R. and Jones, A.D., (1984). Organizational climate: A review of theory and research. *Psychological Bulletin*, 81, 1096–1112.

Kanter, R.M. (1983). *The Change Masters*. New York: Simon & Schuster.

Klein, B.H. (1977). *Dynamic Economics*. Cambridge, Mass: Harvard University Press.

Nyström, H. (1979). *Creativity and Innovation*. New York and London: John Wiley.

Nyström, H. (1983). Positional and innovative elements in product development. *Creativity and Innovation Network*, 1, 21–23.

Nyström, H. (1985a). Company strategies for designing and marketing new products in electrotechnical industry. In P. Langdon and R. Rothwell (Eds.), *Design and Innovation*, pp. 18–26. London: Frances Pinter.

Nyström, H. (1985b). Product development strategy: an intregration of technology and marketing. *Journal of Product Innovation Management*, 2, 25–33.

Nyström, H. and Edvardsson, B. (1982). Product innovation in food processing. *R and D Management*, April, 67–72.

Payne, R.L. and Pugh, D.D. (1976). Organizational structure and climate. In M. Dunnette (Ed.), *Handbook of Industrial and Organizational Psychology*. Chicago: Rand McNally, pp. 1125–1172.

Schein, E.H. (1984). Coming to a new awareness of organizational culture. *Sloan Management Review*, Winter, 3–16.

Tushman, M. and Moore, W. (1982). *Readings in the Management of Innovation*, Boston: Pitman.

Weick, K. (1969). *The Social Psychology of Organizing*. Reading, Mass: Addison-Wesley.

Zaltman, G., Duncan, R. and Holbek, J. (1973). *Innovations and Organizations*, New York: Wiley.

8 Rethinking organizational innovation

John R. Kimberly, Laura R. Renshaw, J. Sanford
Schwartz, Alan L. Hillman, Mark V. Pauly and Jill
D. Teplensky
The Wharton School of the University of Pennsylvania, USA

Two themes link the chapters in this book. First is the theme of innovation, and the questions around this theme have to do with what innovation is, how it can be stimulated, and how particular innovations can become more widely used. The second theme is that of work, the effort expended in organizations in pursuit of given objectives. In this book, work is the setting of, or context for, innovation. Questions having to do with work, therefore, focus either on how the settings or contexts can be designed to enhance innovation or, alternatively, the attributes of settings in which innovation is found most frequently. As we see it, then, the overarching purpose of this book is to explore the *relationship* between innovation and the organizational settings in which it occurs or is desired.

Given that purpose for the book as a whole, the purpose of this chapter is, first, to review how the relationship between organization and innovation has been defined in research on organizational innovation and, second, to outline a somewhat different approach based on our analysis of the diffusion of an innovation in medical technology—magnetic resonance imaging—in the United States. Our approach views the relationship between organization and innovation as complex, dynamic and multi-leveled; our rethinking of organizational innovation urges researchers to reflect this complexity in their efforts to model the relationship.

Innovation and Creativity at Work   Edited by M.A. West and J.L. Farr
© 1990 John Wiley & Sons Ltd

THE RELATIONSHIP BETWEEN ORGANIZATION AND INNOVATION

The relationship between innovation and organization can be viewed in a variety of ways. Kimberly (1986) has distinguished five principal approaches that have been taken in the literature: the organization as user of innovation, the organization as producer of innovation, the organization as both user and producer of innovation, the organization as vehicle for innovation, and the organization *as* innovation. Each of these is described briefly below.

The organization as user of innovation

The organization as *user* of innovation is the relationship most often examined by researchers. The perspective has typically been that of adoption or diffusion. The problem addressed from the perspective of adoption has been why some organizations adopt a given innovation or set of innovations more quickly than others. The question from the diffusion perspective is how to account for patterns in the way in which a given innovation spreads in a population of potential user organizations.

In either case, the implicit assumption seems to be that innovation is good and more innovation is better; the practical concern, then, is how to increase the receptivity of given organizations to a particular innovation or set of innovations (i.e. how to increase the organization's 'adoption potential') or how to speed up the process by which an innovation spreads within a population of potential adopters/users. Both problems are central to the concerns of marketing, where the issue is to increase the frequency or extent of use of certain products throughout a population of organizations or individuals. The latter problem is often encountered by the federal government as it tries to encourage, for example, the widespread use of innovations in medical or educational technology developed with federal funding.

The organization as producer of innovation

In the relationship described above, organizations are the consumers of innovation. This relationship can be contrasted with one in which organizations are the producers of innovations. In this case, the principal research question is how to account for differences in the rates, types, and quality of innovations produced by a sample of organizations or departments. The concern here is with the conditions that spawn innovation initially and the factors that influence the development of subsequent refinements and applications of the innovation. In the research literature, this has generally been referred to as the problem of research creativity. In the more practitioner-oriented literature, it is generally referred to as the problem of the management of research and development or of new product development. Here again, the implicit assumption appears to be that innovation is good and more innovation is better, leading to a search for ways to increase both the volume and quality of innovations produced by a particular department or organizational system.

The organization as producer and user of innovation

Organizations often invent solutions to specific problems that they have. Not every organization has the capacity or the resources to solve problems effectively or frequently, but the normative position seems to be that they should. When organizations develop solutions to their own problems, they are both producing and using innovations.

Researchers have referred to this particular relationship between organization and innovation as 'innovation *in situ*' (e.g. Kanter, 1983). Although not widely researched, the frequency of this type of relationship is undoubtedly high. One example would be the in-house development of software to meet what are believed to be idiosyncratic needs. The innovation is real-time problem solution rather than new product development for an external market. It is not unusual, however, for a company to recognize the market potential of an innovation initially developed for its own use and to move it into the marketplace. General Motors and IBM have done this with robots, for example, as has General Electric with flexible manufacturing systems.

The prevalence of 'user-dominated innovation' (von Hippel, 1976; Shaw, 1985)—the development of new products in response to specific demands from users—would lead one to suppose that organizations are often able to solve particular problems with home-grown remedies. One would predict that the incidence of innovation *in situ* would vary inversely with the capital cost of the solution. One might also believe, therefore, that this type of relationship would be relatively rare when hard technology is involved. A firm would not, for example, be likely to invest heavily in the development of its own advanced manufacturing system (unless it was extremely large, as is the case with GM and robotics or GE and flexible manufacturing systems), but might well find new applications for various components of microelectronic technology. This type of relationship, then, is certainly interesting and worthy of considerably more attention from researchers than it has received.

The organization as vehicle for innovation

In the first three types of relationships discussed, the organization has been directly involved with the innovation in question, whether as a producer, as consumer, or both. In the fourth type of relationship, the organization's relationship to the innovation is that of facilitator or vehicle rather than producer or consumer and is therefore somewhat less direct (although no less central).

Certain kinds of innovations require new organizational forms to facilitate their application. Without these new forms, the innovations would not be available to potential users. Consider, for example, the case of prepayment in medical care in the United States. The innovation here is clearly prepayment, a significant departure from the more usual fee-for-service mode of payment for physicians' services. Prepayment, however, cannot simply be willed into use. It requires that a complex set of relationships be developed between physicians, hospitals, and employer groups—relationships that are themselves somewhat novel. The health maintenance organization, or HMO, is one specific organizational form that was created in order to make it possible for this innovation in mode of payment to become available. The HMO in this example, then, is the vehicle for innovation—prepaid medical care.

What is particularly interesting about this type of relationship between organization and innovation is that frequently the organizational forms that act as facilitators of or vehicles for innovation are themselves new. Joint ventures are good examples. To the usual concerns on the part of potential users about the innovation (Will it work? Is it really better than what I've been doing all along? What do I have to do differently in order to use it?) are added concerns arising from the unfamiliarity (and hence the questionable legitimacy) of the new organizational form. When novelty is as abundant, usual resistances to change are magnified.

The organization as innovation

In some cases, the organization itself is the innovation—that is, a new organizational form is invented to solve a particular problem or set of problems. This type of relationship between organization and innovation differs from the previous one in that the organization that is the vehicle for innovation need not necessarily be innovative itself (although it frequently is).

A particularly interesting example of the organization as innovation is the educational service center in the field of education. Historically, there has been a great deal of tension between state education agencies in the United States, such as the Department of Education, and local school districts. The local school districts tend to guard their autonomy intensely and to regard the state educational bureaucracy with suspicion and mistrust. Initiatives from the state level are generally seen as inimical to local interests, almost by definition, and the amount of cooperation between the state and local authorities is highly variable. Historically, too, there has been relatively little cooperation between local districts. Boundaries tend to be staunchly defended, and each school district generally seeks to maintain its independence by whatever means are necessary.

This situation was tolerable in an era of abundant resources for elementary and secondary education. As resources became scarce, both state and local education officials had to find new ways to fund existing programs and to develop new programs and services. One solution was the creation of a new organization, the educational service center. Located between the state and local levels, the center required the cooperation of several school districts. The objective of these organizations was to provide services to local districts that might be too expensive for any single district to afford (Kimberly *et al.*, 1983). In this case, an innovative organizational form was the response to the problems of the agencies involved. Another example of the organization as innovation is the creation of public or quasi-public organizations to foster linkages between industry and universities in order to generate research funds and develop new technical breakthroughs, organizations such as the Industrial Technology Institute in Michigan whose mission is to promote the adoption of new technologies through a combination of technical assistance and basic and applied research.

We argue in this chapter that the process whereby innovations are developed and subsequently spread in a population is more complex than previous research implies. Using results from a research project designed to test a series of hypotheses derived from classical theory about the adoption and diffusion of innovation, we argue that elements of each of these relationships are present. Furthermore, we indicate where classical theory has proved incapable of accounting for observed phenomena, and suggest some questions that researchers concerned with understanding how and why an innovation spreads in a population of potential users ought to be asking. In so doing, we advocate rethinking organizational innovation.

MAGNETIC RESONANCE IMAGING AND THE DIFFUSION OF INNOVATION

In 1986, a group of researchers at the Leonard Davis Institute of Health Economics at the University of Pennsylvania designed a research project to investigate the diffusion of magnetic resonance imaging (MRI) technology to hospitals throughout the United States.

The initial design of the study was based on classical theory of the diffusion of innovation as summarized in Rogers (1983). Despite some criticisms of the approach (e.g. Downs and Mohr, 1976), we initially oriented the study toward identifying the attributes of hospitals that were early adopters, later adopters, and non-adopters of this innovation in medical technology, and comparing the decision processes that led to these different outcomes. The initial hypotheses, derived from the theory, were that both the structural attributes of and the decision-making processes in those hospitals which were early adopters of this new technology would be significantly different from those that adopted later and from those that did not adopt at all.

Implicit in the research design was an assumption that there was 'a' technology, that there was 'a' set of potential adopters which was easily identifiable, that there was 'a' decision to adopt or not to adopt, and that the research challenge was to capture the attributes of the potential adopters and characterize their decision processes. It was assumed that the explanation for patterns of diffusion of innovation observed would flow from analysis of this information.

Of particular interest in this study was the fact that the 'environment' had recently undergone some dramatic changes, and the research team was interested in trying to assess the effects, if any, of these changes on the decision process at the hospital level, and thus ultimately the impact of these changes on the rate and extent of diffusion.

In its initial conceptualization the study was an example of the type in which the adopting organization was the user of innovation developed in another setting. Following the traditional thinking in innovation research, those hospitals that decided to adopt the new technology early were thought of as the most innovative organizations, while those that decided not to adopt the new technology were thought to be least innovative.

As an innovation in medical technology, MRI had a number of properties which the research team initially found to be particularly interesting. First, it was very expensive; equipment and siting costs were frequently in excess of $2 million. Second, when MRI initially became available commercially and when the study first began, this new technology generated a good deal of public comment and discussion. It was highly visible and there were many questions about its clinical value, particularly given its cost. Finally, it became commercially available at about the same time that the US federal government passed new legislation changing the way in which hospitals were paid for services they rendered to Medicare patients. This change in payment was intended to provide incentives to hospitals to operate more efficiently and thus to help control the escalating costs of health care. We were interested in examining the impact of this legislation on hospital decisions about investment in innovations in medical technology.

Magnetic resonance imaging is a technology which combines the use of magnets, radiofrequency pulsing, and computing to permit pictures of extremely high quality to be taken of various internal parts of the body without the use of radiation. It is used for diagnostic purposes and helps physicians identify and pinpoint a variety of conditions. As the research team became more familiar with this technology, however, it became apparent that our assumption that there was 'a' technology was unfounded, and that there were really a number of ways in which magnets and computing were being applied to achieve the intended results. Furthermore, the technology was evolving and many claims were being made about its potential. This combination of technical advance and exalted potential was creating uncertainty for both producers and users in a variety of areas.

Four areas of uncertainty are particularly noteworthy: clinical efficacy, economic viability, performance characteristics, and obsolescence horizon. With respect to clinical efficacy, there was a great deal of debate when MRI first became available about how it compared to computed tomographic (CT) scanning and other imaging technologies. Did it do new things? Or did it do what existing technologies did, only better? In what situations? Furthermore, while most experts agreed that the quality of the images was high for the central nervous system, there was and is great debate about its relative merits for many other applications. What has been particularly interesting is that expert opinion has been highly divided—no one really knows the answers to these questions. Thus, in sharp contrast to many other technologies, there is considerable disagreement among knowledgeable individuals about its clinical efficacy.

Finally, when MRI first appeared, there was some question about the kinds of side effects that might result from use of the technology. To date, however, no side effects have been observed.

Questions abound regarding the economic viability of MRI. Early in the diffusion process, there was considerable debate about its profitability, the frequency of use of the technology required in order to maintain economic viability, the kinds of margins that an operator of the technology might expect, and its long-run economic future. Questions about the underlying economics of MRI undoubtedly influence investment decisions by potential adopters of the technology. Just how widespread and how profound the impact of uncertainty regarding underlying economics has been on adoption decisions remains to be determined. However, the case of MRI does provide an interesting contrast to technologies where the economics are clearer.

The performance characteristics of the technology have been another source of uncertainty. Here we refer to three characteristics in particular: reliability, durability, and serviceability. It is argued by the advocates of the technology that it is highly reliable, yet there is also debate about the extent to which this is actually the case. No one knows at this point how durable the magnets are, although many argue that they will have long life spans. And finally, there is a great deal of discussion about the maintenance of the equipment over time and just how serviceable defects, when found, may be. From the point of view of the potential adopter, therefore, there is a series of questions about performance over time that at this point cannot be answered.

Another area of uncertainty has to do with obsolescence. As with many technologies, there is some question about the likelihood of MRIs being replaced by a newer, more accurate, more economical, or more powerful diagnostic technology. The producers of the technology have tried to design it in such a way that enhancements can be made incrementally through developing more sophisticated software and ancillary technology (e.g. surface coils) without making any changes in the magnet. This strategy is designed to avoid the problem of early obsolescence, thereby overcoming some of the concerns of potential purchasers. While this strategy may diminish concerns about obsolescence compared to other new technologies, the rapid evolution of incremental changes in individual units does generate concern about potential obsolescence of one MRI unit compared to another. In addition, the magnitude of the initial investment required—somewhere between one and two million dollars—is such that concerns about obsolescence still influence investment decisions in a relatively major way. Furthermore, it is not clear when a replacement technology may appear on the scene.

Thus, not only has the technology been evolving (and continues to evolve), but the level of uncertainty with regard to the investment or adoption decision was, and continues to be, very high. Classical diffusion theory does not take this kind of uncertainty into account in making predictions about rates of adoption and patterns of diffusion.

The adoption decision

Uncertainties about the technology itself were not the only uncertainties confronting managers faced with making investment decisions. Other changes in the contexts in which they were operating influenced their decisions as well. Principal among these were changes in the regulatory environment and changes in the intensity of competition in local markets.

Not only were managers unsure about the degree to which MRI would emerge as a replacement for other established diagnostic technologies, but the regulatory environment, on both the federal and state levels, was of little help in making the wisdom of an investment decision clear. Many states, concerned that MRI was not a proven 'need' to the community, established tight regional limits on the number of MRI units that would be granted a certificate-of-need, a strategy that virtually precluded siting of units outside of major research and teaching hospitals in these areas (Steinberg and Cohen, 1984). As a result, many hospitals desiring MRI could not become involved in the purchase or siting of units. Some states even controlled the installation of MRIs in freestanding imaging facilities, regardless of whether a hospital was or was not involved in the unit's financing and operation. In contrast, other states did not attempt to regulate MRI installation at all.

The prospective payment system (PPS) itself represented an important source of uncertainty since few managers knew in 1983 how this new method of payment for Medicare inpatients would affect hospital profits. Although hospitals in fact achieved record profits during the first two years of PPS, this did not change the fact that prospective payment turned the incentives for patient care upside down, for now *reducing* the cost of tests and procedures performed on many hospitalized patients would increase hospital profits. In this light, MRI was not attractive, since it initially seemed to be merely an 'add on' innovation, rather than a technology which could replace other expensive diagnostic tests.

Aside from the uncertainty generated by the new PPS, there were long delays in determining such key federal policies as support for medical residents and continuing federal support for state health system agencies. In addition, at the time PPS was passed in the US Congress, studies were mandated to explore the possibility of folding payments for capital and equipment into the Diagnostic Related Groups (DRG) payment system, a possibility that struck terror into the fiscal hearts of many hospital administrators, particularly those with aging facilities and equipment. Managers could not anticipate how the resolution of these policies affected their institutions' financial situation, which in turn affected the priorities placed on acquiring new technology versus other hospital objectives.

At about this time the federal law that every state have a certificate-of-need process for capital expansion in hospitals that exceeded a certain threshold was repealed. This had the effect of creating additional uncertainty, as no one knew how individual states would respond.

The federal government added to the complexity of managerial decision-making regarding MRI in the spring of 1986 when Congress proposed several major changes in the tax code for individuals and businesses. Of particular interest were proposals to eliminate the investment tax credit and lengthen the depreciation schedules for capital and equipment, since such measures would significantly reduce the financial attractiveness of MRI to investors. Concern about these financial factors was displayed in managers' investment decisions. There was a burst of investment in MRI prior to the expiration of the investment tax credit and generous depreciation schedules, followed by a marked reduction in the rate of increase in newly operated MRI units in 1986 compared to the two previous years.

PPS, among other factors, was changing the relationship between the hospital administration and staff physicians. DRGs encouraged hospital administrators to become more involved in physicians' practices, since by encouraging doctors' efficiency in patient care, hospitals could increase their own net revenues. Managers were also aware, however, that physicians saw this involvement as a threat both to their autonomy as patients' advocates and to the financially beneficial relationship they enjoyed with hospitals. Technology played an important role in this dynamic, since physicians tend to regard acquiring the most advanced medical technology as an important aspect of maintaining quality patient care.

These issues were reflected in two ways in the case of MRI. First, administrators recognized that the way they dealt with MRI would set a precedent for future hospital–physician interactions, particularly joint ventures. They thus had to weigh the benefits of working with a certain number of physicians through an MRI joint venture with the risk that this would lead other doctors to expect similar cooperation with their requests for new technologies. Many of these future requests, administrators postulated, would include projects that were inconsistent with the financial means or the goals of the hospital. Second, administrators were concerned with the loss of control inherent in a joint venture. Third, although many doctors were 'offering' to finance MRI themselves, either partially or fully, approving such ventures entailed serious unresolved legal and ethical issues regarding the potential for conflict of interest from these units. If physician-financing of MRI came to be defined as inappropriate, it could damage the hospital's image in the community, and create serious (and expensive) legal difficulties as well.

Finally, the MRI manufacturers themselves were creating uncertainty for hospital managers considering purchase of a scanner. By 1984, no fewer than ten separate companies were producing MRI units in the United States. Rumors of potential mergers and bankruptcies among these manufacturers were widespread. Decision-makers had to choose from a wide array of models and several important features, including field strength (ranging from 0.15 tesla to 2.0 tesla magnets), magnet type (superconducting, permanent, or resistive), and alternative computer software systems—each having enormous implications for cost, possibilities for siting, and range of medical applications afforded. In addition, the prior experience many administrators had with having to purchase several generations of CT scanners made them think twice about purchasing a unit that might become 'obsolete' in a year or two. Lastly, the possibility that a unit would be purchased just in time for the manufacturer to go bankrupt or merge with another company (resulting in lost software support and maintenance) loomed large in many managers' minds.

In sum, a host of conditions, many of which did not exist prior to the imposition of PPS or were altered with the new law, increased the financial risks associated with purchase of MRI. Changes in government laws and regulations, hospital–physician dynamics, and characteristics of the technology itself increased uncertainty in a number of areas. Adding to the complexity of the decision-making process, however, was 'the promise' MRI held for hospitals hoping to improve their market position in an increasingly competitive health care environment.

The promise of MRI

Why would managers want to acquire MRI? While many of the above-mentioned factors contributed to delayed acquisiton of MRI, PPS had another important consequence—it intensified competition among health care providers. PPS did this in three ways. First, by making hospitals assume the financial risk of Medicare inpatient care, PPS intensified competition for patients covered by traditional, retrospectively reimbursing private insurance. Second, since Medicare continued to pay for outpatient services on a retrospective, reasonable-cost basis after DRGs were implemented, hospital outpatient treatment became a more financially desirable alternative for Medicare patients who could receive such care. Third, because of inefficiencies in the DRG payment system, it quickly became known to administrators that some DRGs were 'money makers' while others were 'losers' financially. By working to attract Medicare patients who were likely to fall into a 'profitable' DRG, a hospital could improve its financial position. Finally, since many hospital costs are fixed (at least in the short run), high admission rates were important to increase hospital profits. In this way, competition for all patients increased.

In light of these changes brought about by PPS, MRI presented an opportunity for hospitals and private physicians to expand their patient base and remain competitive. By enhancing the image of an institution, technology may attract patients and doctors to that hospital. Indeed, the acquisition of hospital-based and non-hospital-based technology became an important component of many hospitals' strategic plans to achieve a competitive edge in the community (Whitcomb, 1988). Under such circumstances, a highly promising, state-of-the-art, non-invasive diagnostic technology that could be established in an outpatient setting generated a lot of interest. The question posed to potential adopters was how to enjoy the benefits of the technology while minimizing the financial risks.

To complicate the research challenge even further, one effect of the changed federal legislation was to provide incentives to hospitals to do more work on an outpatient basis where services provided did not fall under the new PPS. The effect of this incentive, combined with the uncertainties noted above, led to the creation of a large number of entities to own and operate MRI equipment outside the hospital, sometimes with the financial participation of the hospital and sometimes without any participation whatsoever. In order to understand the diffusion process of this new technology, then, the research had to be expanded from its initial focus exclusively on the hospital as the investor to a variety of other organizational arrangements as well.

Additionally, the study needed to take into account the impact of increasing competition in local market areas. Thus, the design had to include some analyses in which the local market area (however defined) became the unit of analysis instead of the investing organization. Neither of these changes was anticipated by nor encompassed within classical theories of diffusion of innovation.

And, finally, as we began to track the evolution of MRI technology it became apparent that there was considerable feedback between manufacturers and users. The initial study design, predicated as it was on the existence of 'a' technology, did not anticipate the extent and importance of this interaction.

RETHINKING ORGANIZATIONAL INNOVATION

Analysis of the spread of MRI technology in the United States has caused us to rethink how organizational innovation might most productively be analyzed. The relationships between the innovation and the organizations involved in producing, using, regulating it, and facilitating its diffusion are complex and enormously fluid. Decisions about investment in the technology are influenced by vendor strategies, regulatory practices, and initiatives taken by competitors in local markets as well as by perceptions of opportunity, defined broadly, by the potential investor. In following the diffusion of MRI, we have observed the interplay of multiple organizations whose relationship to the innovation covers the entire spectrum outlined at the outset of this chapter, and, in some cases, have seen combinations of relationships operate. Finally, we have observed these relationships evolve over time, in some cases terminating and in others becoming more tightly coupled.

Patterns of diffusion are the aggregation of individual adoption decisions. To understand patterns of diffusion, one needs to understand the mix of factors that affect adoption decisions at the level at which those decisions get made. In our view, there is a set of factors—we call them contextual constraints—which jointly influence the structure of investment incentives operative at any particular point in time for any particular organization. These incentives then influence the timing and content of investment decisions. The outcome of these investment decisions is what researchers typically have called the decision to adopt or not to adopt. The model encompassing these variables is presented in Figure 1.

Our work leads to the conclusion that the decision process is much more complicated than the binary 'adopt' vs. 'not adopt' representation typically found in diffusion research would lead one to believe. In the case of MRI, the high degrees of uncertainty associated with the technology itself, with the regulatory environment, and with competitive initiatives in local markets, led to a variety of decisions enabling organizations to hedge their bets. In some cases, hospitals decided to purchase MRI equipment outright. Other hospitals decided to lease the equipment. In some case, hospitals entered into joint ventures with physicians or others to own and operate the equipment. In some cases, they became members of consortia which jointly purchased the equipment. Still other hospitals accessed the equipment through arrangements with mobile units which would come to the hospital on a regular but limited

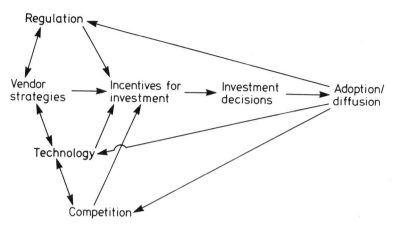

Figure 1 Contextual constraints, investment incentives and adoption of innovation

basis. In still other cases, they permitted units to be built on the hospital grounds but did not participate in any direct way in either the ownership or the operation of the unit itself. And some hospitals decided to defer involvement with the technology. Adding further to the complexity, a hospital's patients could still get access to the technology even if the hospital itself was not involved directly or indirectly as an investor. A nearby unit (no matter who owned it) could provide such access.

Each of these decisions represents a different level of investment by the institution in the technology, and each represents a different level of associated risk and, perhaps, reward. Most significantly, this pattern has convinced us of the need to unpack the 'adoption' decision and to get behind the incentives that drive the outcome. We have no way of judging at this point how typical or atypical the case of MRI may be. But to the extent that it is not an isolated case, then research on diffusion needs to move well beyond binary conceptualizations of the adoption decision.

The aggregation of both the timing and content of these decisions across a population of organizations, then, represents the observed pattern of diffusion of innovation. Under the broad conceptual umbrella of contextual constraints in the case of MRI we would include technological evolution, regulation, competition in local markets, and vendor strategies. The latter, of course, is constrained by technological, regulatory, and competitive factors as well. But from the point of view of the 'adopter' or buyer of innovation, variation in strategies from one vendor to the next will influence the ultimate decision that is made.

The importance of vendor strategies is only now beginning to creep into the literature on diffusion of innovation. Robertson and Gatignon (1987), for example, have proposed that the attributes of the suppliers of innovative technology affect diffusion. In particular, they argue that the competitiveness of the supplier industry, the reputation of supplier firms, the competitive standardization of the technology, the level of vertical coordination, and the allocation of R & D resources to the innovative technology are characteristics which should affect diffusion. Shaw (1985) comes closest to studying the role of adopter/vendor relationships in diffusion. He observes that in the case of medical technology innovations, potential adopters and vendors interact frequently to develop, evaluate, and market the technology. We, too, observed considerable interaction between vendors and adopters in the case of MRI. This relationship between the vendor and a potential adopter typically results in the successful adoption of the technology from the vendor. Our own research on MRI indicates further that different vendors have very different strategies not only with respect to how they want to capitalize on the technology and exploit it commercially, but also on how they choose to segment the market and the way in which they price and market the products (Teplensky *et al.*, 1990).

Taken together, these four sets of contextual constraints influence the incentives that individual organizations have to invest in or adopt a given technology. We take the position that researchers ought to focus more on the influence of contextual constraints on innovation investment decisions. There is a cost to such a focus, however. As research on organizational innovation becomes more tuned to the significance of contextual constraints, generalizability may suffer initially. But as comparisons are made across technologies, the likelihood of general theories developing is increased. At this point in the development of theory it would be preferable to err on the side of overemphasis on the influence of context and the development of an in-depth appreciation of the incentives that influence investment decisions.

CONCLUSIONS

Careful examination of the diffusion of one particular innovation in medical technology, MRI, has led us to draw a number of conclusions about research on organizational innovation:

(1) As noted in the first section of this chapter, research tends to be organized around one of five principal relationships between organization and innovation: the organization as producer of innovation; as user of innovation; as both producer and user of innovation; as vehicle for innovation; and *as* innovation. Our research, however, suggests that these relationships may overlap and that an organization may, for example, be both a user of *and* vehicle for innovation. The picture of

innovation diffusion that emerges from this research is of a complex, dynamic, and fluid set of relationships between organization and innovation, a picture that differs in many important respects from that underlying classical diffusion research.

(2) 'Adoption' of innovation is more complex than the binary 'adopt vs. non-adopt' operational definition used by most researchers implies. We found that, in the face of uncertainty about both the performance characteristics and the profitability of MRI, hospitals used a variety of strategies to access the technology. These strategies ranged from outright purchase (which researchers clearly would define as 'adoption'), to a variety of joint venture, leasing and consortium arrangements, to contracts with mobile units specifying days of the week when the technology would be at the hospital. These different strategies reflect different approaches to risk, and thus different approaches to 'adoption'.

(3) Rather than thinking of adoption of innovation simply as a function of the attributes of potential adopting organizations, the attributes of innovations, and internal decision processes, it appears more reasonable to expand the model to include an appreciation of the evolution of the technology, the strategies that vendors have developed, and changes in other contextual constraints such as regulation and competition. Explicit attention should be paid to how these contextual constraints influence incentives for investment in the technology at the level of individual organizations. Such a focus will lead to a clearer understanding of the timing and outcome of the decision process itself and ultimately to more informed models of organizational innovation.

ACKNOWLEDGEMENTS

Preparation of this chapter was supported, in part, by Grant# 5R01 HS05424 from the National Center for Health Services Research and Development and Health Care Technology Assessment, J. Samford Schwartz, Principal Investigator. An earlier version was presented in the seminar series *Contradictions et Dynamiques des Organisations (CONDOR)* in Paris in November, 1989, by the first author, who would like to thank Michel Berry, Director of the Centre de Recherche en Gestion, Ecole Polytechnique, Paris, for his support and encourgagement.

Correspondence address:
Department of Management, The Wharton School of the University of Pennsylvania, 2000 Steinberg Hall-Dietrich Hall, Philadelphia, Pennsylvania 19104-6370, USA.

REFERENCES

Downs, G. and Mohr, L. (1976). Conceptual issues in the study of innovation. *Administrative Science Quarterly*, **21**, 700–714.

Kanter, R.M. (1983). *The Change Masters: Innovation and Entrepreneurship in the American Corporation*. New York: Simon & Schuster.

Kimberly, J.R. (1986). The organizational context of technological innovation. In D.D. Davis (Ed.), *Managing Technological Innovation*. San Francisco: Jossey-Bass, pp. 23–43.

Kimberly, J.R., Norling, F. and Weiss, J.A. (1983). Pondering the performance puzzle: the politics of effectiveness in interorganizational settings. In R.H. Hall and R.E. Quinn (Eds.) *Organizational Theory and Public Policy*. Beverly Hills: Sage Publications, pp. 249–264.

Robertson, T. and Gatignon, H. (1987). The diffusion of high technology innovations: A marketing perspective: In J. Pennings and A. Buitendam (Eds.), *New Technology as Organizational Innovations*. Cambridge, MA: Ballinger Publishing.

Rogers, E. (1983). *Diffusion of Innovations*, 3rd edn. New York: Free Press.

Shaw, B. (1985). The role of the interaction between the user and the manufacturer in medical equipment innovation. *R & D Management*, **15**(4), 283–292.

Steinberg, E.P. and Cohen, A.B. (1984). Nuclear magnetic resonance imaging technology: a clinical, industrial and policy analysis. Health Technology Case Study 27 for the Office of Technology Assessment's *Assessment of Federal Policies and the Medical Devices Industry*, Washington, DC, September.

Teplensky, J.D., Kimberly J.R., Hillman, A.L. and Schwartz, J. (1990). Scope, timing, and strategic adjustment in emerging markets: manufacturer strategies and the case of MRI. The Wharton School, unpublished manuscript.

Von Hippel, E. (1976). The dominant role of users in the scientific instrument innovation process. *Research Policy*, **5**, 212–239.

Whitcomb, M.E. (1988). Health care technology acquisitions: issues and challenges. *Frontiers of Health Services Management*, **4**(4), 3–25.

9 Organizational innovation in context: culture, interpretation and application

Nigel Nicholson
University of Sheffield, UK

Five people sit round a table in a jazz club. The first, who is making her first foray into music outside the classical repertoire, turns to her neighbour and exclaims that she has never heard such sounds before. It is amazing that performers, without a sheet of notation in sight, can spontaneously create music of this complexity at such length. The second, having led a slighty less sheltered existence, is able to point out that the theme of a well known popular song can be discerned from the underlying chord changes. But although he is acquainted with Dixieland jazz he is also new to this kind of music, and, he adds that he too is mightily impressed at how far the improvisational line departs from the original melody. The third person at the table remarks to his two companions that he has some familiarity and knowledge of the genre, and is pleased to explain to them that these performers are speaking, musically, in a shared vernacular of musical phrases, conventions, and clichés even. But he does concede that the performers do seem to be exhibiting a fair degree of originality in using these elements to construct their solos and ensembles. The fourth member of the group of listeners, overhearing this, snorts cynically and says that she heard the band play at another venue the previous week, and if she wasn't mistaken, they were playing almost identical music on that occasion. The band, she reckons, is overrehearsed and taking no risks. The fifth, nods in agreement, adding that the case is worse than that: he finds the group to be highly derivative, indeed downright plagiarizing much of its material, note for note in some parts. He recognizes passages from a record he owns of a very famous group playing the same number. Indeed, he adds drily, it is his opinion that the bits they play best are where the performers have suffered lapses of memory and been forced to improvise! The first speaker has been listening to these exchanges with a widening smile on her face. 'Who cares?' she says, tapping her feet happily. 'It's all new to me. I like it.'

Innovation and Creativity at Work   Edited by M.A. West and J.L. Farr
© 1990 John Wiley & Sons Ltd

The story illustrates some of the difficulties which may dog our attempts to use the concept of innovation, and its close relatives, in a coherent and consistent fashion. These difficulties may not arise so long as we can use the term generously, in a spirit of constructive agreement. This may often be possible with descriptors which have strong evaluative overtones, but as soon as we disagree then logical and semantic problems are liable to come to the surface.

In the first part of this chapter, I wish to argue that these problems need only inhibit our constructive use of the idea of innovation if we cling to realist assumptions (i.e. that innovation is a verifiable social fact). For all its difficulties, innovation can, if used thoughtfully, still play a valuable role in scholarly and informal social discourse. But whatever value it has depends on its usage, which is shaped by a variety of influences. These are the patterns of meaning and action we call cultures and subcultures.

Following discussion at a general level of the meaning of innovation, the remainder of the chapter is taken up with three different ways it has been applied in the organizational literature. I shall hope to show how cultural interrogation of the concept may lead towards some new thoughts about each of these approaches.*

THE CONCEPT OF INNOVATION

Our story of the five jazz fans illustrates the slipperiness of the concept of innovation. Most of the psychological literature on the topic has overridden rather than explored these potential difficulties. In this chapter it is my aim to bring attention to these issues, by advocating a strategy for conceptual analysis and empirical enquiry, drawing upon ideas from various sources. This involves asking four questions.

They are logically nested, so that the answer to each leads on to the next. Simply expressed these are: (1) What kind of signifier is 'innovation'? (2) What does it mean under current circumstances? (3) Who is using it for what purpose? and (4) What social or personal values are attached to it? These four questions can be linked, respectively, to four related domains of cultural inquiry: semiotics, hermeneutics, epistemology, and ideology. Together they constitute a methodology that is both interdisciplinary and ethnographic.

The first, semiotic, question asks what kind of sign or signifier do we find 'innovation' to be in discourse. The simplest answer is to note its semantic

* In considering these issues, I am indebted to five colleagues who took part with me in a workshop on the topic, as part of a recent conference on 'The Texture of Organizing,' at the University of Exeter, November 1988: Rene Bouwen, John McAuley, Donald McLeod, Susan Read, and Gijs van Rozendal. They supplied case examples from their experience, which we were able to use as a testing ground for elements of the analytical approach described here.

roots as verb or adverb meaning 'to make new'. Metaphorically, it signifies by 'opposition' (Lackoff and Johnson, 1980; Barley, 1983), i.e. relativistically, by making implicit comparison with some assumed or observed reference. When we use the language of innovation, some contrast is being implied with what is already known or has gone before. The innovativeness of the jazz being heard in our imaginary example was an assignment made differently by the five listeners, each one invoking different comparisons to make a judgement. It is evident that people can call upon contrasting referential material to decide whether it would be appropriate to use the concept. This, incidentally, may be the focus of debate about what qualifies for the description: disagreements about innovation may in fact turn out to be about what phenomena are allowable for the comparison, i.e. whether they can be classified as of the same genus. Actual use then depends upon such subsequent questions as whether, under current circumstances, to do so would be consistent with other usage and/or would be meaningfully communicative, i.e. whether the implied contrast would be clear to interlocutors.

It has not been common within the innovation literature for the problems these questions arouse to be recognized. Far too rarely is conscious attention paid to exactly what it is the 'new' is being contrasted with. An exception to this can be found in a paper by Pelz and Munson (1982) who propose an 'originality' dimension running from origination, through adaptation, to borrowing. These distinctions have also been noted by West (1987a, 1987b), who contrasts the different motivations underlying 'converter' and 'developer' role innovations: the former term covering instances where innovation is achieved by transferring familiar elements into unaccustomed settings, the latter being reserved for cases which involve some intentionally creative act.

The second question springs out of the first; the closely related hermeneutic position entails considering how the concept may be analysed as an element lodged within a wider text. To understand the term we must interpret the text. Meaning is to be extracted from a 'thick' description of the context in which usage is embedded (Geertz, 1973). The context is likely to have many layers—semantic, philosophical, historical—sedimented through accumulations of coded experience (Cicourel, 1964). To read the text in our jazz club example, can be taken, at one level, as a relatively simple task; invoked by the observer who noted that the musicians were speaking a 'language', whose utterances should be read in relation to their specific musical/cultural contexts. To call music innovative thus depends upon where and when the attribution is made, and in relation to which contexts, traditions or genres. So we may find in different organizational settings, or indeed within different functions and levels of a single organization, that innovation has very different currency and meaning according to local precept. In one context it may be emblematic of corporate mission and widely used; in another its application may be highly restricted to certain times or particular functions.

This broadens our view further toward the third question of our deconstructive inquiry—what may be termed the epistemological–empirical analysis of how meaning depends on who is using the concept for what purpose (Garfinkel, 1964). Actor–observer differences in how people account for behaviours are well known to be responsible for discrepant understandings and usage (Jones and Nisbett, 1971). In the context of our jazz club example one might speculate what the musicians themselves would have said if invited to express an opinion on the originality of their music, and how one would explain differences between their views and those of their audience.

Their answers would probably highlight how innovativeness may be used differently as a descriptive–explanatory concept by people in different role relationships to the innovation act, event or attribution. In terms of organizational behaviour, the subjectivity of attributions of innovativeness is potentially a source of uncertainty. For example, actor–observer differences may operate as a source or a symptom of controversy about the justice of rewards or other credits ascribed to successful innovations. The fundamental attribution error (Ross, 1977) might thus lead managers to ascribe to an individual an innovation which, from another perspective, could be seen as a happy accident of circumstance. It is not hard to imagine how such sources of bias could result in contested meanings which act as a formidable barrier to the smooth development and implementation of innovation. Indeed, this concern explains why so much importance is attached to consensus as a precondition for innovation in the literature, especially writings on the innovation-diffusion process (Walton, 1987).

This leads us into the fourth realm in which one may interrogate the concept of innovation—its ideological overtones. This category is used broadly to connote the evaluative 'charge' an idea carries. This springs from a combination of the interests of the concept user and the values prevailing in the milieu within which it is used (Beyer, 1981). Evaluative charge can be attached in three ways. The first is *presumptive* or implicit value, where evalution is taken for granted. Value connotations can be so embedded in our usage that some terms, such as innovation, operate as synonyms for 'good', as would be likely to apply in the language of our jazz fans. Indeed, innovation can be seen to hold this presumptive value quite widely within capitalist society, where it is associated with both individualism and performance: the capacity to add value (Salaman, 1979). In this volume, the pro-innovation bias of the literature has been recognized by several writers (cf. King and Anderson (Chapter 4), Kimberly *et al.*, (Chapter 8), and Damanpour (Chapter 6)). The second method is *explicit* value, representing usages containing statements by individuals of their preferences and personal experiences. Here innovations are only ascribed positive or negative value because of their personal significance; as in the last utterance of our illustration, where the first fan asserted her right to appreciate what she found novel.

Contingent process provides a third way in which values are attached to concepts, denoting how connotations depend upon other evaluations being made about attributed intentions and of perceived consequences. In our culture the consequence upon which the value of innovation most clearly attaches is success. This association has become almost indelible enough for the link to become presumptive, such that a failed attempt at innovation may not be dignified with the title by those associated with it. Such contingent evaluations are likely to be highly domain specific. Note, for example, the pejorative connotations that surround 'creative accounting'. Equally, one can find 'innovative' used as a form of sarcastic abuse amongst those organizational actors who accord primary value to efficient, predictable and profitable production.

Attributed intentions will be a more important contingency where innovation is a valued end in itself. The contingent value of intention was demonstrated in our jazz illustration by the fifth speaker, whose approval of innovation was heavily qualified by the claim that it was an enforced departure from script. Indeed in the arts generally in recent decades, it has been commonplace for controversies to hinge on whether the deliberate ̧e of serendipitous or random elements detracts from the value of innovation. In all such debates we find, in effect, presumptive value being converted to contingent value by textual reasoning. Of course, this activity in itself represents part of the process of cultural evolution, for it brings about changes in the contexts, criteria and expressive forms themselves (Martin, 1981).

This last point reveals the interrelatedness of the four dimensions of meaning we have been considering; all are embraced by the notion of culture. Although writers on the subject of culture have attempted in different ways to resolve the complexities of its meaning, it is common to find definitions which identify the contents of culture with the four facets of the present model: symbolic codes, shared contexts of interpretive meanings, patterned and purposive social relations, and systems of values and interests (Pettigrew, 1973; Allaire and Firsirotu, 1984; Schein, 1985). A simple and practical implication of this is that empirical approaches to the topic of innovation could usefully take a reading of the cultural context as their first and most important task. A similar stance is implied by Bouwen (1988) when he defines innovation as the ongoing construction and reconstruction of shared meaning.

This kind of analysis can avoid us becoming trapped by conundrums such as, how does innovation differ from organizational change? Reading the cultural text one can see that, on occasions, it may be used interchangeably with other concepts, but also that this does not revoke its capacity to be used otherwise. It also helps us to circumvent the perennial problem that if there is really nothing new under the sun, how can we use the term innovation meaningfully? The analytical approach advocated here not only is untroubled by the idea that the limits to its signification are indeterminate, but it expects no less. We are free to reserve the term for changes we consider to be truly radical, or equally to endow it with more commonplace connotations. These are situated choices to be made or adopted according to our purposes and circumstances.

This poses difficulties for the would-be researcher of innovation for whom such answers may have an uncomfortably arbitrary ring. There are three options.

First, one can abandon all attempts at empirical research into innovation on the grounds that any kind of structured inquiry will embalm the concept in a lifeless pose, denying us access to its rich complexities.

Second, one can take the pragmatist position of looking for a best available working definition that will legitimize a research strategy, or help to identify a range of phenomena of practical or theoretical interest.

Third, one can follow the ethnographic strategy of qualitatively compiling an inventory of the concept's 'native paradigms' (Gregory, 1983); the varying ways in which the term is socially transacted and deployed within subcultures.

These choices were brought to the surface in our studies of graduate entrants to an oil company (Nicholson and Arnold, 1989a, b), when we tried to find out how innovation figured in their strategies for adjusting to changes in jobs, environments and relationships. Pilot work quickly revealed that asking people about innovation brings the ball smartly back over the net. 'How do you mean?' the respondent is likely to ask. The researcher is then confronted with a problem. To supply example and definitions would defeat the object of finding out about the range of initiating, creative and changeful behaviours to which the term might be applied. The alternative strategy, of asking people in more circumlocutory terms about changes they have helped to bring about, only pushes the analytical problem back one stage; just making it less likely that researcher and respondent will, between them, make explicit what criteria they are using when talking about change. This does not mean one has to abandon all such questioning. It only implies that it is as well to be clear that a primary research task may need to be an exploration of the textual and psychological substrata governing responses. This will help point the researcher, as a next step, toward a critical examination of the relationship between these expressed cognitions and organizational behaviour.

For example, several interviewees in our research were reluctant to make any self-attribution of innovatory behaviours because they held internalized models which decreed that nothing less than wholesale revolutions at the workplace befitted the term, despite our encouragements to the contrary. One young man denied innovating at all in his job, and in the next breath offhandedly described a department reorganization he had initiated! Some restricted their deployment of the concept to cover products and outputs, while others felt able to include such abstractions as changes they had effected in people's attitudes. From this diversity it was apparent that innovation is a concept very apt to take on the colour of its surroundings via the cognitive schema of its users.

In relation to the three options mentioned above, our research certainly did not suggest that questioning about innovation is fruitless, rather that researchers should be clear about what kinds of meanings their methods are likely to elicit. We should not make the mistake of thinking that the valuable and valid collaborative activity of unwinding conceptual threads is the same as collecting objective reports of discrete social phenomena. Can any useful purpose be served by taking the second option of setting up an operational definition? It clearly can be recommended as a device for securing agreement about what we want people to tell us about, but even this is likely to prove unreliable, in the positivist sense, since no definition is going to circumvent the constructive indeterminacies we have been discussing. Perhaps this is why so many writings on the subject are coy about stating definitions. Where writers have had the courage to attempt this, such as the editors of this volume (West and Farr, 1989; see also Damanpour's definition in Chapter 6 of this volume), the potential areas of difficulty are only pushed back into the constitutent terms of the definition. e.g. the terms 'intentional', 'new', and 'benefit' in the West and Farr definition. However, if such attempts do not resolve the conceptual difficulties they do have three useful side-effects. One, they can help us to be clear about where conceptual indeterminacy remains unresolved. Two, they underline how central social values are to the identification of innovation. Three, they show that innovation is a category which embraces a very wide range of phenomena.

In the remainder of this chapter I wish to apply the kind of cultural analysis introduced here, to the three principal ways in which one can find innovation, and related concepts, figuring in discourse about organizations: innovation as product, innovation as climate, and innovation as self-directed change. (Kimberly *et al.*, in Chapter 8 of this volume similarly see value in subcategorizing innovation, in ways partially coterminous with this threefold classification.) But perhaps more important than just viewing these as three different approaches in the literature is to consider the different ways these levels of innovation may be interconnected. This latter theme is perhaps where the concept of culture has its most singular contribution to make to our understanding of innovation.

INNOVATION AS PRODUCT

This domain encompasses the greater part of the traditional literature on innovation, addressing the question: what makes some organizations more willing and able than others to develop and adopt new products, processes or services? Answers have been supplied at three principal levels.

First are arguments about the motivation to innovate. Here we find an implicit analogy between individuals and organizations: the organization is metaphorically endowed with unitary organismic qualities (Morgan, 1986). The conditions known to favour individual creativity and invention, such as a spirit of playfulness, availability of resources, and social approval (Rogers, 1962; Amabile, 1983), are sought at the organizational level. In this manner Steiner (1965) enumerated the organizational preconditions for innovation as direct parallels of the qualities of the creative individual—fluency, flexibility, originality, and complexity. In trying to explain the causes of organizational innovation, Cyert and March (1963) could also be said to be reifying a unitary model of the organization in contrasting two opposing prior conditions for innovation: failures, which motivate the search for novel solutions to problems; and success, which creates the slack that permits the resourcing of attempts to innovate. These contrasting causes—'distress' and 'slack' innovation, as they have been termed (Zaltman *et al.*, 1973), can be seen as intrinsically psychological. It is striking to note the parallel theorizing to be found in the literature on the psychology of human emotions, showing how both positive and negative emotional states are capable of energizing cognitive change in individuals (Isen, 1984). The 'performance-gap' explanation of innovation discussed by Damanpour (Chapter 6, this volume) offers similar arguments about the preconditions for innovation.

Second are writings which focus on the activities through which innovations emerge, such as Poincaré's oft quoted description of the process as following the sequence: preparation–incubation–illumination–verification (Wallas, 1926). Much of this literature is written in a popular vein, in a how-to-do-it cookbook style (see Perkins, 1981, for one of the best in this genre). Few examples of this kind are to be found in the organizational literature, though concern with the causal flow of emergent innovation is widespread, and indeed embodies some of the best that has been written on the subject. Notable examples are Bouwen's (Bouwen, 1988; Bouwen and Fry, 1988) analysis of the processes of search, development, implementation, and integration; and Van de Ven's discussion (1986) of the perceptual processes, transactional dynamics, and leadership activities which favour innovation.

Closely related is a third body of literature on the contextual factors that influence the emergence of innovation. The work of West and colleagues has, in this manner, identified the norms, supports, and structures that help or hinder innovative processes (West and Farr, 1989). Writings on innovation diffusion also fall under this heading, probably best known through the writings of E.M. Rogers (Rogers and Shoemaker, 1971; Rogers, 1981) which analyse the agencies and pressures steering the innovation process. A recent major contribution to this tradition has come from Walton (1987), who points out that the process is more complex than a two-step innovation–diffusion model would suggest; he argues that the diffusion process itself often involves the modification or reinvention of the product. Kimberly *et al.* (Chapter 8, this volume) draw attention to a related, but neglected, question: the importance of vendor strategies and the response of organizations in adopting their innovations.

Under the heading of innovation as product, mention should also be made of a large body of much more focused, applied, atheoretical writing on entrepreneurship, concerned with how organizations orient themselves to their market and other environments. This literature has been dominated by quasi-economic analyses of uncertainty and risk bearing (Knight, 1921; Kirzner, 1973). More recent writings from the behavioural literature have recast the problem in terms of cognitive processes (Burch, 1986), personality (Stanworth and Curran, 1973; Kets de Vries, 1977) or strategy (Miles and Snow, 1978). There is also a large literature on R & D management which deals with similar issues (Pelz and Andrews, 1976; Martin, 1984).

Applying the deconstructive model proposed at the outset of this chapter would draw our attention to several issues that are typically passed over by the writings we have been considering. First, it is clear that a strong culture bias is detectable across most of this literature, a theme we shall return to in the following sections of this chapter. Briefly, this takes the form of an unquestioning affirmation of consensual, liberal and individualistic values. Implicit is the assumption that individual and collective self-interests can be mutually satisfied through innovations—everyone can be a winner. This is particularly evident in the so-called 'excellence' literature (Peters and Waterman, 1982; Kanter, 1983; Hickman and Silva, 1984) where it is alleged that the most successful companies harness individual inventiveness for the common good.

Alternative views do not get much airing in the organizational literature, though some writings from a Marxian or critical theoretical standpoint (Clegg and Dunkerley, 1977; Burrell and Morgan, 1979; Salaman, 1979) do point the way toward more dialectical appreciations of the origins of innovation. From a less ideologically committed standpoint, Bouwen (Bouwen, 1988; Bouwen and De Visch, 1989) has been more explicit about what these dialectics demand in practice; how innovation may depend upon the interaction of contrasting logics of change, competing interests in decision-making, and the inevitability of its causing disruptions to the flow of organizational action. However, the endstate of Bouwen's analysis is also consensual: innovation as the reconciliation of these tensions through shared meanings. Our cultural perspective might lead us to be more sceptical and less sanguine about how radical and innovatory such resolutions are likely to be, an argument advanced by Schon (1966) to which we shall return later.

Now turning to the substantive empirical relationships described in the writings we have reviewed, cultural analysis does draw our attention toward the process discussed by Bouwen: the dependence of innovation on systems of meaning, whether shared or conflicting. Little needs to be added to Bouwen's thorough review of what these processes look like, but our four-dimensional deconstruction of innovation can point to how some fine-grained texture might be added to such analyses.

It shows first, for example, how organizational units and subunits may be analysed as language communities in which people share and use rich or impoverished networks of meanings about innovation and change. These communities will have the effect of sensitizing awareness, which, empirically, as most theories agree, is a critical first step in innovatory action sequences. Second, we should not assume that because signing systems are in a philosophical sense, arbitrary, this means they are easily manipulable in our social world. They are rooted in the context of shared histories and the interpretive schemata that have evolved from them. Careful ethnography is needed to demonstrate how the predominant themes of shared cultures constrain or reinforce innovation as a sub-theme.

Third, our attention is drawn to how such themes are transactable elements in the political economy of organizations. One is led to ask who are the stakeholders in the production and diffusion of change (Mitroff, 1984) and how do they then seek to control the process by which it is defined and evaluated. This leads inexorably to the fourth theme of our analysis, which is how values are attached to elements of the system by the association of reward and communication media. These produce ideologies—cognitive schemata or belief systems—that contain and construe innovatory behaviours. It is, of course, also possible for innovation, like other behaviours, to be framed by conflicting ideologies. This may signify the existence of a contested frontier between one ideology and another, or that a counter-culture is mounting an active challenge to the hegemony of a dominant culture in some sphere. Under such circumstances, it is a sure bet that there will be low agreement among disputants about what behaviours deserve to be called innovations and how they are to be evaluated. An example of this was provided in our workshop on innovation (see footnote on page 180), where one case described the challenge mounted by a 'progressive' group to the assessment methods of the dominant 'traditionalist' experts in a personnel function. This was acted out, at one level, in the form of debates about how necessary, i.e. new, were the proposed changes. Indeed, in some highly ideological organizational cultures, factional conflicts may be fought almost entirely at the symbolic level, as my colleagues and I found in debates over definitions of 'democracy' in trade union politics (Nicholson *et al.*, 1981).

Case analysis is likely to reveal how the four analytical dimensions we have considered operate together. The operation of 'total quality systems' in Japanese industry, for example, illustrates the way these elements can be tightly woven into the fabric of the organizational culture. A sloganizing language is promoted, evoking deeper associations of a shared cultural fate, by means of which power holders define, encourage, reward and control changes in order to reinforce current practice and cement the dispositions of interests.

The degree of synchrony we may often find among these processes suggests it may be possible to characterize organizations as a whole in how they manage innovation. This represents our second domain of application.

INNOVATION AS CLIMATE

Under this heading one can group writings which characterize organizations in terms of how innovative they are in their *modus vivendi*. The underlying theme detectable here is a humanistic concern for self-actualization through work experience, rather than an interest in identifying the innovative qualities of products. Here we find a presumed identity between the organizational culture and its outputs. Creative organizations generate innovative products.

It is in this vein that Burns and Stalker (1961) described organizations as 'interpretive systems', meaning that their procedures, functions and structural arrangements manage environmental pressures and challenges in distinctive and characteristic ways. Their case studies of electronics companies identified mechanistic vs. organic organizational systems as suited to, respectively, stable and unstable conditions: a classic and influential formulation of contingency theory. Organic systems can be considered analogous to the 'creative' or 'innovative' organization (Steiner, 1965; Nyström 1979; see also Nyström, Chapter 7, this volume), for what Burns and Stalker are describing are essentially fluid and spontaneous ways of organizing inventiveness. Within the behavioural literature on strategy, a similar identity of type with function can be found in Miles and Snow's (1978) 'Prospector' ideal type of organization. Choices are portrayed as characteristically made through informal processes of mutual adjustment in decentralized decision systems, permitting a high rate of market flexibility and creativity.

In all of these writings one can detect a sense of approbation of the organic values over the mechanistic, even though, ostensibly, contingency formulations are committed to the more impartial view that different organizational forms are appropriate to differing circumstances. Indeed, across the innovation literature generally one detects a strong anti-bureaucratic theme.

The contingency assumption seems to have been openly jettisoned in recent writings on organizational performance. Explicitly and unequivocally normative stances are taken by the new wave of 'excellence' writings (Peters and Waterman, 1982; Kanter, 1983; Hickman and Silva, 1984). However, these could be seen as covert contingency theories to the degree that what they are recommending is a best way of organizing to equip Western capitalism to meet a particular set of contemporary challenges, arising from the heightened uncertainties of employee interests and market conditions. They, and a growing body of similar writings, have two features relevant to the concerns of this chapter: they make strong and explicit reference to organizational culture, and, within that, accord innovation a position of central and emblematic importance.

Innovation here seems to relate to the way decisions are made and how effort is coordinated: the differentiation and integration problems as they are known in the contingency literature (Lawrence and Lorsch, 1967; Child, 1984). The differentiation problem can be analysed as questioning how discretion is distributed across organizational space. One of the most complete statements of this logic is to be found in Jaques (1976), for whom non-hierarchical and decentralized forms, allowing a wide span of decision latitude in individual roles, are assumed to yield benefits in terms of individual creativity. The integration problem relates to the existence of horizontal divisions, boundary spanning mechanisms, intraorganizational mobility, and methods of coordinating decisions and actions. Kanter (1983) is primarily concerned with these when she distinguishes between 'innovative' and 'segmentalist' organizational forms.

The thrust of these writings is a presumed identity between structure and culture, as observed by Nyström (Chapter 7, this volume) in his investigation of intraorganizational divisional climate differences. However, some writers have extended this reasoning to the questionable point of suggesting that cultures can be manipulated by management processes (Kilmann *et al.*, 1985). However, more critical stances can be found amongst scholars who have inquired into the nature of culture.

One tenable view is that any social collective capable of sharing definitions of their situation can operate as a microculture (Fine, 1979), an idea which also implies that within most organizations there exists considerable scope for subcultural conflict and evolution (Van Maanen and Barley, 1985). A second position is that organizations do not contain cultures—they are cultures (Smircich, 1983). Their self-defining symbolic operations operate as expressive and instantive manifestations of collective consciousness. A third argument runs that organizations mostly do not have distinctive cultures, because they operate under broadly similar conditions and with comparable human capital (Wilkins and Ouchi, 1983). Their common character is attributable to their suffusion in the values of wider cultural systems— associated with technologies, national identity, and regional sub-cultures. There are persuasive data on international differences which support this latter position (Hofstede, 1980), but these do not deny either of the former arguments, and nor, of course, are they capable of resolving the underlying philosophical differences between the three positions.

Given our purpose of establishing whether it is meaningful to talk of organizations or their major sub-units as 'innovative' in character, and if so to explain how they come to be so, the interpretive approach presented here offers a way of reconciling all three of these perspectives on culture. A first step is to establish how people talk about what they do, noting if this suggests consistencies in how they think about the qualities of their working lives. This may be achieved from more than one methodological paradigm; measuring whether there is internal consistency in a population's perception of climate (Payne and Pugh, 1976; Glick, 1985) could bring one to similar conclusions as might be obtained from ethnographic inquiries about shared perceptions of the work setting. Either way. these inquiries are capable of revealing whether we are looking at the wrong level of aggregation to make sense of innovation. More macroscopic cultural frameworks may be needed if it is concluded that there is nothing to distinguish local usage from wider practice in a social system. Conversely, more individualistic perspectives will be appropriate where individuals communicate little and hold idiosyncratic beliefs about their context and their experience of it.

Second, having established that shared perceptions are held, then this should not be taken as a social fact, but as one strand of the culture's capacity for self-regard. Elsewhere, in the role of discussant to a paper on organizational culture (Nicholson, 1984), I noted how ideology may be mistakenly identified with culture, when on closer examination their contents may turn out to be logically contradictory. For example, one can imagine an organizational culture where members conform to an ideology of non-conformity, a phenomenon frequently noted about the idealistic collectives of the 1960s. Such contradictions often only become visible when seen over distances in time and space, i.e. in retrospect or from an 'outside-in' perspective. This argument, in effect, is an extension of Smircich's point about organizations *being* rather than *having* cultures. It is ideologies that organizations can 'have'; an idea which has wider implications for organization culture change, as we shall discuss in the next section.

The point at issue here is that when people in an organization talk about it as a creative or innovative environment, we need to question what kind of discourse they are engaged upon. Is it the spontaneous shared expression of their cognitions and interest? Or is it the vocalization of some local interpretive rhetoric (Gowler and Legge, 1984)? In either event these expressive activities could be said to be creating the phenomena they claim only to be reflecting.

External affirmation and validation can be critical to this process. The importation of meanings has become big business for consulting behavioural scientists whose mission is to help move organizational members toward shared positive self-perceptions. Such symbolic activity can have material consequences, altering perceptions of possibilities, probabilities, rights and obligations (Silverman, 1970; Schein, 1985). Adopting this perspective, one can see how the concept of innovation is 'under construction' in the popular media of human resources management, corporate strategy and the like. This culture-work is not a neutral task, but amounts to a search for new ways of defining self-interest, in order to deal with the currently perceived threats and opportunities in the social and economic relationships that enmesh businesses. This reasoning implies that it is misguided to debate the merits or otherwise of the 'excellence' scholars by arguing about how good are their methods of picking winners (Aupperle *et al.*, 1986), for, after all, who deserves the accolade of 'excellence' will change, as surely as fashion. The key question is *whether this ideal imagery corresponds to what we want*. Do the proposed models implicitly make the kinds of choices we consider congenial and morally acceptable? What sort of society do we want to live in?

This carries a warning about how we appraise cultures defined as innovative, and the dangers of becoming so beguiled by the attractions of the notion that we are moved to give carte blanche to any who ride under its banner. We should be reminded that in cultures that extol the virtues of innovation it is also possible to find little value being placed on the security of the weak, or a frightening carelessness about the unaccountability of the powerful or the gifted. One may say, therefore, that cultural analysis should lead us head on into the thick of the ethical and ideological undergrowth. If it has not, as seems to be the case in much current American writing on the topic seems not to, then we have probably lost our way.

INNOVATION AS SELF-DIRECTED CHANGE

In turning to look at our third area of application, we move on to the point at which organizations have a presumption about where they are now and where they want to get to. Or, at least, it is now time to engage the thorny issue of how they know that they need to change, and how this knowledge can be converted into effective self-directed action. Innovation here means internal reform or transformation. There is a huge and scattered literature on this topic, discussing the question from diverse standpoints, such as how organizations adapt to changing environmental demands, the internal politics of organizational change, transformational leadership, and the role of the change agent (Hedberg, 1981; Bass, 1985). All of these writings are, in one way or another, taking the structure, contents and process of the organization itself as the object of innovation attempts, with new organizational forms and practices as the 'product'. Nyström (1979) in this manner defines innovation as 'radical, discontinuous change' which results in company development. He then goes on to dichotomize organizations' capacity for such development by contrasting 'innovative' with 'positional' companies (see also Nyström, Chapter 7 in this volume), a distinction analogous to Hage and Aiken's (1970) division of static vs. dynamic organizations and several other classifications we have considered earlier (Burns and Stalker, 1961; Kanter, 1983).

Indeed, one can see this third domain of application as a direct extension of the second. The creative organization is not merely an environment in which self-actualization is rife, but also one where creative energies effect lasting changes in organizational arrangements. Within the innovation literature, this line of reasoning finds expression in the writings of scholars who distinguish 'administrative' and 'technical' innovation (Daft, 1978; Damanpour and Evan, 1984), to which the third class of 'ancillary' innovation is additionally discussed by Damanpour in Chapter 6 of this volume. The main thrust of this research is to examine their causal interdependence. The emerging consensus is that there is a time-lagged causal flow between the domains of innovation. Technical innovations require administrative innovations to create the conditions for their emergence, and in order to consolidate them into organizational forms afterwards. Not only are administrative innovations logically and empirically prior to technical changes, but they are also more infrequent, unpredictable and difficult to engineer (Kimberly and Evanisko, 1981). Thus one administrative innovation can spawn several technical ones.

The analytical approach we have been considering in this essay, however, would suggest that we should not take for granted these sub-divisions of organizational space. For self-directed change to have a major or lasting impact, these categories may need to be jettisoned in favour of more holistic or alternative ways of seeing. For example it may be more helpful not to think in terms of domain-specific innovation, and instead simply acknowledge that it is generally more difficult to change the way people think and interact with one another than it is to alter the methods they use in working. Indeed, it is one of the seductive dangers of introducing new technology that it creates the illusion of radical innovation. Changing from traditional to electronic instruments in our jazz band might fool some listeners that the music is new, but under the surface the culture and process may be untouched.

Yet the alternative constructionist view of self-directed change might be thought to invite the opposite danger of over-emphasizing the symbolic and the cognitive aspects of organization, and thereby exaggerating the fluidity and indeterminacy of organization. The interpretive paradigm, that organizational structures are a manifestation of 'negotiated order' (Silverman, 1970; Strauss, 1978), may prompt us to ask why we should not simply tear up these implicit agreements about organizing and starting afresh. We would do well to remind ourselves how deeply rooted are forms of consciousness in institutional praxis (Brown, 1978), and how resistant to revision they become with time. Symbols and rituals undoubtedly deserve attention as the surface expression of deeper process (Trice and Beyer, 1984) but you cannot effect fundamental change just by altering them, any more than new instruments in themselves will make the band play better.

Our method of inquiry should help to reveal where supposed re-directions of organizational life turn out to be transient or heavily disguised superficial changes (Blackler and Brown, 1980). One may find such sleight-of-hand born of what Schon (1966) calls a fundamental 'fear of innovation'; organizations want new ideas and products 'but fight hard to prevent anything new from ever happening' (p. 290). Organizational rationality, he argues, can cope with risk because it is calculable, but not with uncertainty, because it is not. Consequently, organizational agents spare no pains in trying to convert uncertainty into risk. Innovations increase uncertainty, and therefore are compartmentalized or neutered so as not to disturb the stable state.

Schon's work with Argyris extends this theme by showing how this leads to discrepancies between how managers talk about what they do—espoused theory—and what they actually do—theory-in-use (Argyris and Schon, 1974; 1978). In order to bring about genuine, radical and lasting changes, organizational members need to be able to step outside and challenge their accustomed assumptions and rationalities. This Agyris and Schon term 'double-loop learning', borrowing Ashby's cybernetic concept to denote evaluative processes that are capable of revealing errors in the error detection system itself. Real and radical self-directed change may be almost impossible without some means of cultural introspection from an exterior vantage point. Argyris and Schon's work is concerned with how to confront this apparent paradox (see also Watzlawick *et al.*, 1974, for an analysis of directly analogous challenges in individual psychotherapy).

Such questions are implicit in the way Brunsson (1985) has reasoned how organizations' cognitive schemata (which he calls 'ideologies') affect the kinds of changes they are capable of. Strong ideologies—i.e. elaborated and consistent schemata—are quick to note inconsistent elements, such as unmet environmental pressures, and, if they are important and unmanipulable, implement the necessary change responses. The ambiguous, unarticulated and inconsistent nature of what Brunsson calls weak ideologies makes it easy for them to assimilate change demands without making such real substantive changes. This theory has the interesting implication that organizations differ in kind and degree as 'interpretive systems'. Some will be much more adept than others at making symbolic rather than substantive adjustments to pressures, whether internal or external. How this might come to be so deserves further elaboration. Our analysis suggests one crucial element is likely to be the kinds of reflexive discourse that are customary within organizational systems, and in which ways these allow organizations to contain and represent themselves as elements in their symbolic and decisional activity. This is likely to be especially evident in the ways senior managers engage in strategic planning and environmental scanning (Pettigrew, 1985; Morgan, 1988).

This argument finds a parallel in neo-Piagetian theorizing about personality development, in which progressively more sophisticated disembedded states of self-consciousness mediate adjustment and self-control (Kegan, 1982). The theory states that psychological growth and development is achieved by successive cognitive revolutions, in which the person becomes, in effect, less self-centred and more self-aware. The personal system becomes increasingly capable of complex reflexive appraisal, moving from undifferentiated conceptions of self and environment toward more indeterminate and thereby free constructions of identity. It may be reasoned that this idea has some generality for all kinds of sentient systems—that forms of self-awareness are some of the most potent determinants of the range and type of actions they are capable of.

Self-awareness is not an absolute or final condition, but a method of inquiry, and, of necessity, symbolically mediated. The strategy discussed in this chapter, therefore, of exploring the meanings of innovation and change in organizations, can help to reveal and create opportunities for their enactment.

INTERCONNECTIONS

Finally, let us turn to the issue of relationships between innovation at the three conceptual levels reviewed: innovation as product, climate and self-directed change. Many of the writings we have considered contain fairly clear statements about what connections they presume. In most cases these are conceived as simple positive correlations between the three domains. So we have seen that the connection between innovation as climate and innovation as product is assumed or argued by several writers on the naive reasoning that the creative organization engenders creative products. Such thoughts, dangerously close to tautology, remind one of similar reasoning in individual psychology about behaviours being caused by corresponding traits: aggression by aggressiveness, sociability by gregariousness, invention by creativity, etc. To avoid such tautology one needs to take care to use independent means of assessing innovation at different system levels. Some writers, considering this issue, have come to an almost completely opposite position, implying that innovations at these levels are often mutually exclusive (Wilson, 1966; Zaltman *et al.*, 1973). They reason that the organizational conditions conducive to the generation of innovative energy (innovation as climate) are unconducive to the development and implementation of innovation (innovation as product); as well as vice versa.

As contingency theory would predict, when one examines these relationships empirically, the data neither support assumptions of isomorphism nor of opposition between the first two levels we have discussed: product and climate. In a recent study of eight wool textile companies (Nicholson *et al.*, in press), we found that expressed degrees of role innovation (changes people are able to effect to their work objectives and methods)—which may be taken as an indication of innovative climate—can be unrelated to the rated innovativeness of companies in their product development and marketing. Rather, one should say that no *single* relationship is to be expected. In fact we found innovations at these levels were connected in a number of ways.

The most successful company in our study was so largely by virtue of its ability to harness individual innovative energies and collectivize them, a positive connection between climate and product much as we have seen described in the innovation diffusion literature. However, in other cases we observed various combinations of innovativeness at different system levels: some with a high degree of local non-radical innovativeness coupled with market conservatism; others with fluid and creative climates but a high degree of failed innovations, and yet others exhibiting buttoned-down internal climates combined with innovative market orientations. These different relationships are types of causal flow which can be observed in corporate cultures and sub-cultures; the product of strategic orientation, leadership climate, and ways of organizing (Hosking and Morley, 1987; Nyström, Chapter 7, this volume).

Yet if the relationship between product and climate is less straightforward than might be assumed, the picture becomes more complicated when one also considers self-directed change. Again there is a presumption, though generally less clearly articulated, in the excellence literature that the best companies are as effective in working on themselves as, allegedly, they are in the innovativeness of their climates and products. We have already spelled out the challenge to this thinking mounted by Schon and Argyris, and the emerging consensus in the literature on organizational culture that fundamental change is slow, difficult, and elusive. To paraphrase the arguments of both Schein (1985) and, much earlier, Cyert and March (1963), it takes the shock of trauma or failure to bring many organizations to the brink of new ways of thinking about themselves; or, alternatively, it requires a considerable cushioning of slack coupled with vision and willpower about the desirability of altered future states.

In our wool textile study, we did find most of the eight organizations thinking about self-directed change in one way or another. For half the sample we coined the new strategic type of 'Transformer' to denote those cases where major orientational changes were currently under way, in every one from more mechanistic/positional types toward more organic/innovative types. In all cases this took the form of one set of interests trying to pull other more inertial or opposing interests in new directions. In some it was the dominant coalition who were trying to mobilize their staff, in others it was the leaders who were the resistant anchors around which the tides of change were swirling. What success would mean in each of these cases would differ, and have quite contrasting implications in terms of their innovativeness in products or climate.

Indeed, one could depict these interconnections as causal flows between the three triangulated domains we have discussed: product, climate and identity. Our constructionist analysis, however, demands that they be seen as inseparable, though differently configured in any particular case. These differences can be understood by attending to how the meanings of innovation change across contexts and over time. Cultures, as shared systems of meaning, contain implicit models of the linkages between different forms of innovation, with the interpretive processes discussed earlier acting to keep these models stable and self-replicating. These relationships are in the engine room of capitalist development.

The way we have suggested that innovation may be culturally deconstructed offers a view of these processes which is fundamentally interdisciplinary in thought and method. In terms of our four dimensions, these are respectively the linguistic/literary work of symbolic analysis; the historical/sociological interpretation of context and culture; psychological and philosophical attention to the intersubjectivity of thought and action; and political/ anthropological consideration of ideologies in social systems.

SUMMARY AND CONCLUSION

In this chapter I have sought to raise some generally unasked questions about the nature of organizational innovation, by reviewing how the topic has been treated in the literature of work and organizational psychology. As a body of knowledge, this literature is diverse and voluminous, underlining the economic and social importance of understanding the nature of change and renewal. The artifacts, social processes and states of identity on which this work has focused are of the utmost material importance in people's lives. Yet there is little coherence and integration between the approaches and levels of analysis we have identified, namely those that try to explain how innovative products come into being, why some collectives have more creative climates than others, and how organizations differ in their ability to change themselves.

The questions raised under these headings have sought to indicate some neglected areas for exploration, and possible bridgeheads for building between them. This involves questioning assumptions that lie at the root of theory, research and practice, and extracting new themes and methods. In one way or another, these amount to trying to understand innovation in its cultural context. This is especially important for innovation, a concept which has more broad and shifting boundaries than many others in work and organizational psychology. My thesis is that, rather than viewing this indeterminacy as a problem to be circumvented, it is fruitful to let the social construction of innovation occupy the centre of our attention.

The fourfold method proposed is not an invitation for abstract philosophizing, but a highly grounded system of inquiry. It would take case analysis beyond the scope of this chapter to illustrate this, as was shown in our recent workshop on the subject (see footnote on p. 180). However, some examples of practical implications can be given, in relation to each of the areas discussed in this chapter.

First, as a way of understanding the birth and diffusion of new products and processes, the present approach recommends attention to more than a single level of analysis. One would need to see how decisions and discriminations are made by individuals, groups and organizational systems via the filters which frame them (Goffman, 1974). At what point and how is an act or a product defined as new? Who or what is principally responsible for this discrimination? What characteristic social processes debate or legitimize this? What local importance is accorded to elements so defined? What actions or rewards typically follow? The goal of such questioning is to disclose the subcultural value and practice of innovation in organizations. This would reveal when innovation is compartmentalized, as the defended province of some elite or specialized sub-group, such as R & D, senior management, or functional areas (e.g. sales and marketing). It would show when individuals regard innovation as their right, their survival strategy, or their expression of identity with intent to challenge the boundaries of managerial control. It would identify the contradictory logics of organizations which elevate innovation as a central mission, whilst seeking to avoid risk, disruption or failure.

Second, in looking at organizational climates our approach recommends that one looks beneath the surface of people's reports of the perceived local environment and the more objective indicators of how people work, interact and make decisions. This entails questioning about the imagery contained in these descriptions, and how it arises. Mission statements, job descriptions, training goals, informal systems of socialization, and other vehicles for the transmission of individual and corporate identity, need to come under scrutiny. These can reveal how overtly or covertly ideological is organizational self-imagery, and how meanings are transacted between levels. So we may find, as in one of the cases discussed in our workshop, that there exist unresolved contradictions between the view from the upper and lower levels of the organization, and between the kinds of influence attempts and resistance behaviours these give rise to.

Third, our method would view organizational change in dialectical terms; akin to systems of argument between agents and interest groups, for whom the language of innovation is an instrument of their various purposes. To do this one would seek to uncover their causal logics and value assumptions, by exploring the scenarios of change each party envisages, and by observing how these are (or are not) debated when people interact. By these means, one may find innovation operating as a rallying point for generating consensus about what is safe and desirable, whilst enabling people to appear bold and imaginative. Or it might reveal how people try to contest each other's claims to be the standard bearers of change.

Fourth, it will be apparent that similar insights may be gained about the different ways these three areas of application are interconnected. In each we have been considering how the meanings of novelty and change are central to the capacity of organizations and their members to achieve their objectives. The linkages between levels/forms of innovation are mediated by the core values of the culture, which hold in place the way action is structured. The study of organizations as cultures—including inquiry into systems of language use, cognition, social praxis, and ideology—should seek to reveal why, *inter alia*, in some organizations one can find antagonism between different levels and domains of innovation while in others there is a smoother, more sympathetic reciprocation.

A corollary of these four arguments is that the analytical approach we have been considering can be an important first step towards achieving actual innovation, by clarifying what might and what might not be at stake in the attempt. By helping individuals and organizations toward a deeper understanding of what innovation means to them, what it assumes, and on what it depends, the way may become cleared for complex, subtle or powerful actions. Conceptual unclarity, cross-purposes usages, misunderstood value positions, and inconsistent beliefs may be removed, and opportunities created for new forms of interaction and decision-making to be put in their place.

Last, the arguments of this chapter contain critical implications for the viability of theory-building and empirical hypothesis testing in the area. They suggest that there are severely limited prospects for monolithic theorizing about innovation as if it were a unitary phenomenon around which universalistic cause–effect relationships are waiting to be uncovered. First, we need to be clear about what it means, and, as has been illustrated here, this is not an easy or even perhaps a soluble problem. Attempting to operationally define our way out of the problem, it has been argued, only relegates the ambiguities temporarily into the background. This is not to deny the reality or the importance of innovation. Indeed, the motivation for this essay is the author's conviction that innovation undoubtedly is 'real', in the sense that awareness of and striving toward change is a fundamental theme of human psychology. But this means, first, that innovation is a process not a thing, and second, that it comes in as many forms as there are ways of discerning it, i.e. as there are actors and contexts to which it may apply.

This in turn implies that there are two available paths for theory building about innovation. First, we should locate some specific phenomena, which might normally be included under the broad genus of innovation and restrict our attempts to advancing knowledge within the domain so defined. For example, product development, scientific invention, or strategic reorientation would likely prove more tractable than a concept conceived to embrace all of these and more besides. The second path is not to study innovation at all, but to focus on some domain of human action in which innovation is one of many alternative processes governing events. Accepting the premise that innovation is endemic to human functioning, this then could be said to apply to almost any sphere where behaviour may be systematically studied, such as group dynamics, negotiating behaviour, human–computer interaction, stress-coping and such like—all bounded areas of human action in which there is a need for theoretical understandings that show how acts of renewal and change are interwoven with acts of stabilization and replication. Indeed, one could conclude that perhaps the greatest service scholars of innovation could render to knowledge is to scatter their insights into the many fields where inventiveness, change, renewal and analogous notions are undervalued. In overviewing the field, the analogy comes to mind of the organization that feels no need to be aware of the role of innovation across the entire range of its divisions because it has defined this function as the province of the R & D department. Perhaps we court the same danger of overspecifying the general in organizational science by the way in which we isolate innovation as an object of study.

Correspondence address:
MRC/ESRC Social and Applied Psychology Unit, Department of Psychology, University of Sheffield, Sheffield S10 2TN, UK.

REFERENCES

Allaire, Y. and Firsirotu, M.E (1984). Theories of organizational culture. *Organization Studies*, 5, 192–226.

Amabile, T.M. (1983). The social psychology of creativity: a componential conceptualization. *Journal of Personality and Social Psychology*, 45, 357–376.

Argyris, C. and Schon, D. (1974). *Theory in Practice*. San Francisco: Jossey-Bass.

Argyris, C. and Schon, D. (1978). *Organizational Learning*. Reading, MA: Addison-Wesley.

Aupperle, K.E., Acar, W. and Booth, D.E. (1986). An empirical critique of *In Search of Excellence*. How excellent are the excellent companies? *Journal of Management*, 12, 499–512.

Barley, S.R. (1983). Semiotics and the study of occupational and organizational cultures. *Administrative Science Quarterly*, 28, 393–413.

Bass, B.M. (1985). *Leadership and Performance Beyond Expectations*. New York: Free Press.

Beyer, J.M. (1981). Ideologies, values and decision-making in organizations. In P.C. Nyström and W.H. Starbuck (Eds.), *Handbook of Organizational Design*, Vol. 2. New York: Oxford University Press.

Blackler, F. and Brown, C. (1980). *Whatever Happened to Shell's New Philosophy of Management.* London: Saxon House.

Bouwen, R. (1988). The management of innovation. Paper presented to Annual Occupational Psychology Conference of the British Psychological Society, University of Manchester.

Bouwen, R. and De Visch, J. (1989). Innovation projects in organizations: Complementing the dominant logic by organizational learning. Paper presented to the 4th West European Congress of Work and Organizational Psychology, Cambridge, England.

Bouwen, R. and Fry, D. (1988). An agenda for managing organizational innovation and development in the 1990's. In M. Lambrecht (Ed.), *Corporate Revival.* Leuven, Belgium: Catholic University Press.

Brown, R.H. (1978). Bureaucracy as praxis: towards a political phenomenology of formal organizations. *Administrative Science Quarterly,* 23, 365–382.

Brunsson, N. (1985). *The Irrational Organization.* Chichester: Wiley.

Burch, J. (1986). *Entrepreneurship.* New York: Wiley.

Burns, T. and Stalker, G.M. (1961). *The Management of Innovation.* London: Tavistock.

Burrell, G. and Morgan, G. (1979). *Sociological Paradigms and Organisational Analysis.* London: Heinemann.

Child, J. (1984). *Organization: A Guide to Problems and Practice,* 2nd edn. London: Harper & Row.

Cicourel, A.V. (1974). *Cognitive Sociology.* New York: The Free Press.

Clegg, S. and Dunkerley, D. (1979). *Critical Issues in Organisations.* London: Routledge and Kegan Paul.

Cyert, R.M. and March, J.G. (1963). *A Behavioral Theory of the Firm.* Englewood Cliffs, NJ: Prentice-Hall.

Daft, R.L. (1978). A dual-core model of organizational innovation. *Academy of Management Journal,* 21, 193–210.

Damanpour, F. and Evan, W.M. (1984). Organizational innovation and performance: the problem of 'organizational lag'. *Administrative Science Quarterly,* 29, 392–409.

Fine, G.A. (1979). Rethinking subculture: an interactionist analysis. *American Journal of Sociology,* 85, 1–20.

Garfinkel, H. (1964). *Studies in Ethnomethodology.* Englewood Cliffs, NJ: Prentice-Hall.

Geertz, C. (1973). *The Interpretation of Cultures.* New York: Basic Books.

Gergen, K.J. (1973). Social psychology as history. *Journal of Personality and Social Psychology,* 26, 309–320.

Glick, W.H. (1985). Conceptualizing and measuring organizational and psychological climate: pitfalls in multilevel research. *Academy of Management Review,* 10, 601–616.

Goffman, E. (1974). *Frame Analysis.* New York: Harper & Row.

Gowler, D. and Legge, K. (1984). The meaning of management and the management of meaning: A view from social anthropology. In M.J. Earl (Ed.), *Perspectives on Management: a Multidisciplinary Analysis.* London: Oxford University Press.

Gregory, K.L. (1983). Native-view paradigms: Multiple cultures and culture conflicts in organizations. *Administrative Science Quarterly,* 28, 359–376.

Hage, J. and Aiken, M. (1970). *Social Change in Complex Organizations.* New York: Random House.

Hedberg, B.L.T. (1981). How organizations learn and unlearn. In P.C. Nyström and W.H. Starbuck (Eds.), *Handbook of Organizational Design,* Vol. 1. New York: Oxford University Press.

Hickman, C.R and Silva, M.A. (1984). *Creating Excellence: Merging Corporate Culture, Strategy and Change in the New Age*. London: Allen & Unwin.

Hofstede, G. (1980). *Culture's Consequences: International Differences in Work-Related Values*. Beverly Hills, CA: Sage.

Hosking, D.M. and Morley, I. (1988). The skills of leadership. In J.G. Hunt, B.R. Baliga, H.P. Dachler, and C.A. Schriesheim (Eds.), *Emerging Leadership Vistas*. Boston, MA: Lexington.

Isen, A.M. (1984). Towards understanding the role of affect in cognition. In R.S. Wyer and T.K Snell. (Eds.), *Handbook of Social Cognition*. Vol. 3. Hillsdale, NJ: Erlbaum.

Jaques, E. (1976). *A General Theory of Bureaucracy*. London: Heinemann.

Jones, E.E. and Nisbett, R.E. (1971). *The Actor and the Observer: Divergent Perceptions of the Causes of Behavior*. Morristown, NJ: General Learning Press.

Kanter, R.M. (1983). *The Change Masters*. London: Allen & Unwin.

Kegan, R. (1982). *The Evolving Self*. Cambridge, MA: Harvard University Press.

Kets de Vries, M.F.R. (1977). The entrepreneurial personality: a person at the crossroads. *Journal of Management Studies*, 14, 34–57.

Kilmann, R.H., Saxton, J.M. and Serpa, R. (Eds.). (1985). *Gaining Control of the Corporate Culture*. San Francisco: Jossey-Bass.

Kimberly, J.R and Evanisko, M.J. (1981). Organizational innovation: the influence of contextual factors on hospital adoption of technological and administrative innovations. *Academy of Management Journal*, 24, 689–713.

Kirzner, I.M. (1973). *Competition and Entrepreneurship*. Chicago: University of Chicago Press.

Knight, F. (1921). *Risk, Uncertainty and Profit*. Chicago: University of Chicago Press.

Lackoff, G. and Johnson, M. (1980). *Metaphors We Live By*. Chicago: University of Chicago Press.

Lawrence, P.R. and Lorsch, J.W. (1967): *Organization and Environment*. Cambridge, MA: Harvard University Graduate School of Business Administration.

Litwin, G.H. and Stringer, R.A. (1968). *Motivation and Organizational Climate*. Cambridge, MA: Harvard University Press.

Martin, B. (1981). *A Sociology of Contemporary Cultural Change*. Oxford: Blackwell.

Martin, M.J.C. (1984). *Managing Technological Innovation and Entrepreneurship*. Reston, VA: Reston Publishing Co.

Miles, R.E. and Snow, C.C. (1978). *Organizational Strategy, Structure and Process*. New York: McGraw-Hill.

Mintzberg, H. (1979). *The Structuring of Organizations*. Englewood Cliffs, NJ: Prentice-Hall.

Mitroff, I.I. (1984). *Stakeholders of the Mind*. San Francisco: Jossey-Bass.

Morgan, G. (1986). *Images of Organization*. Beverly Hills, CA: Sage.

Morgan, G. (1988). *Riding the Waves of Change*. San Francisco: Jossey-Bass.

Nicholson, N. (1984). Organizational culture, ideology, and management. In J.G. Hunt, D.M. Hosking, C.A. Schriesheim and R. Stewart (Eds.), *Leaders and Managers: International Perspectives on Managerial Behavior and Leadership*. Oxford: Pergamon Press.

Nicholson, N. and Arnold, J. (1989a). Graduate entry and adjustment to corporate life. *Personnel Review*, 18(3), 23–25.

Nicholson, N. and Arnold, J. (1989b) Graduate early experience in a multinational corporation. *Personnel Review*, 18(4), 3–14.

Nicholson, N., Rees, A. and Brooks-Rooney, A. (1991). Strategy, innovation, and performance. *Journal of Management Studies*, in press.

Nicholson, N. Ursell, G. and Blyton, P. (1981). *The Dynamics of White Collar Unionism*. London: Academic Press.
Nyström, H. (1979). *Creativity and Innovation*. New York: Wiley.
Payne, R.L. and Pugh, D.S. (1976). Organizational structure and climate. In M.D. Dunnette (Ed.), *Handbook of Industrial and Organizational Psychology*. Chicago: Rand McNally.
Pelz, D.C. and Andrews, F.M. (1976). *Scientists in Organizations*. Ann Arbor, MI: University of Michigan Press.
Pelz, D.C. and Munson, F.C. (1982). Originality level and the innovating process in organizations. *Human Systems Management*. 3, 173–187.
Perkins, D.N. (1981). *The Mind's Best Work*. Cambridge, MA: Harvard University Press.
Peters, T.J. and Waterman, R.H. (1982). *In Search Of Excellence*. New York: Harper & Row.
Pettigrew, A.M. (1979). On studying organizational cultures. *Administrative Science Quarterly*, 24, 570–581.
Pettigrew, A.M. (1985). *The Awakening Giant: Continuity and Change at Imperial Chemicals Industries*. Oxford: Blackwell.
Rogers, C. (1962). Towards a theory of creativity. In S.J. Parnes and H.F. Harding (Eds.), *A Source Book for Creative Thinking*. New York: Charles Scribner.
Rogers, E.M. (1981). *Diffusion of Innovations*. 3rd edn. New York: Free Press.
Rogers, E.M. and Shoemaker, F.F. (1971). *Communication of Innovations*. New York: Free Press.
Ross, L. (1977). The intuitive psychologist and his shortcomings: Distortions in the attribution process. In L. Berkowitz (Ed.), *Advances in Experimental Social Psychology*, Vol. 10. New York: Academic Press.
Salaman, G. (1979). *Work Organisations: Resistance and Control*. London: Longman.
Schein, E.H. (1985). *Organizational Culture and Leadership*. San Francisco: Jossey-Bass.
Schon, D. (1966). The fear of innovation. In R.M Hainer, S. Kingsbury and D.B. Gleicher (Eds.), *Uncertainty in Research, Management and New Product Development*. New York: Conover-Mast.
Silverman, D. (1970). *The Theory of Organisations*. London: Heinemann.
Smircich, L. (1983). Concepts of culture and organizational analysis. *Administrative Science Quarterly*, 28, 339–358.
Smith, P.B. and Peterson, M.F. (1988). *Leadership, Organizations and Culture*. London: Sage.
Stanworth, M.J.K. and Curran, J. (1973). *Management Motivation in the Smaller Business*. Epping: Gower.
Steiner, G.A. (1965). *The Creative Organization*. Chicago: University of Chicago Press.
Strauss, A. (1978). *Negotiations: Varieties, Contexts, Processes, and Social Order*. San Francisco: Jossey-Bass.
Trice, H.M. and Beyer, J.M. (1984). Studying organizational cultures through rites and ceremonials. *Academy of Management Review*, 9, 653–669.
Van de Ven, A. (1986). Central problems in the management of innovation. *Management Science*, 32, 590–607.
Van Maanen, J. and Barley, S.R. (1985). Cultural organization: fragments of a theory. In P.J. Frost, L.F. Moore, M.R. Louis, C.C. Lundberg and J. Martin (Eds.), *Organizational Culture*. Beverly Hills, CA: Sage.
Wallas, G. (1926). *The Art of Thought*. London: Cape.

Walton, R.E. (1987). *Innovating to Compete: Lessons for Diffusing and Managing Change in the Workplace*. San Francisco: Jossey-Bass.

Watzlawick, P., Weakland, J.H. and Fisch, R. (1974). *Change: Principles of Problem Formation and Problem Resolution*. New York: Norton.

West, M.A. (1987a). A measure of role innovation. *British Journal of Social Psychology*, **26**, 83–85.

West, M.A. (1987b). Role innovation in the world of work. *British Journal of Social Psychology*. **26**, 305–315.

West, M.A. and Farr, J.L. (1989). Innovation at work: psychological perspectives. *Social Behavior*, **4**, 15–30.

Wilkins, A.L. and Ouchi, W.G. (1983). Efficient cultures: exploring the relationship between culture and organizational performance. *Administrative Science Quarterly*, **28**, 468–481.

Wilson, J.Q. (1966). Innovation in organization: notes towards a theory. In J.D. Thompson (Ed.), *Approaches to Organizational Design*. Pittsburgh: Pittsburgh University Press.

Zaltman, G., Duncan, R. and Holbeck, J. (1973). *Innovations and Organizations*. New York: Wiley.

Part IV

Interventions

10 Facilitating individual role innovation

James L. Farr

Pennsylvania State University, USA

This chapter focuses on methods for facilitating innovation at the level of the individual work role. While the extent to which the individual introduces change into his or her job is the outcome measure of primary interest, some of the interventions discussed are applicable to work groups or even larger organizational units. Indeed, some of the procedures were initially developed for use in group settings.

An underlying assumption of the discussion is that most, if not all, individuals are capable of being innovative in their work roles. Similar views have been expressed by a number of authors, including Amabile (1983), Farr and Ford (Chapter 3, this volume), Simon (1988), and Weisberg (1986). Further, it is assumed that most individuals are capable of increasing the level of innovation that they introduce into their jobs.

The possible interventions that are discussed include traditional 'creativity enhancement' techniques, such as brainstorming and synectics, as well as techniques that are derived from theory and research in such areas as social psychology, work motivation, job design, and organizational development. In addition, implications of the model of antecedents of individual innovation described in Chapter 3 of this volume (Farr and Ford) are briefly discussed with regard to the enhancement of innovation.

A basic goal of the chapter is the expansion of the set of possible interventions beyond those associated with the long-standing, creativity-associated approaches. The use of these approaches is often limited to specific attempts to solve particular problems, rather than to increase innovative behavior on an ongoing basis. The enhancement of work role innovation is likely to require the existence of many programs and policies within a supportive climate. Recent research and thinking in several areas of social

Innovation and Creativity at Work   Edited by M.A. West and J.L. Farr
© 1990 John Wiley & Sons Ltd

and organizational psychology offer suggestions for innovation enhancement that should be explored. Before these more recent interventions are discussed, however, it is appropriate to review the more traditional procedures.

CREATIVITY ENHANCEMENT TECHNIQUES

A variety of techniques have been suggested for increasing the degree of creativity in solutions to existing problems facing organizations or individuals at work. Rickards (1987) has indicated that perhaps *hundreds* of such techniques exist if one counts all the variations of broader categories. However, following Rickards (1987), the techniques are clustered into three major groupings for purposes of this discussion. These groupings are composed of techniques that are both widely used and for which a theoretical basis supporting their use has been proposed. The three groupings are *brainstorming*, *morphological analysis*, and *lateral or divergent thinking*.

Brainstorming

The first of the techniques designed to promote more creative solutions to problems was brainstorming (Osborn, 1963). While the term 'brainstorming' has come to be applied to many forms of group discussion directed toward some problem or issue, here it will be used in the technical sense meant by Osborn.

Brainstorming is based on several assumptions (Osborn, 1963). First, creative solutions are often blocked by premature self-judgments that a potential approach is incorrect; premature judgments of others' ideas in a group setting can also censor creative solutions. Second, in initial stages of problem solving the emphasis should be on the *quantity* of ideas produced, not the quality of individual ideas. Finally, potential approaches to a problem that are extreme and 'wild' should be encouraged in order to lessen inhibitions about varied and innovative solutions.

A brainstorming session based on the assumptions noted above is governed by the following rules (Weisberg, 1986).

(1) Judgments about ideas are withheld until all ideas have been generated; in particular, criticism is not allowed during the idea generation stage.
(2) 'Freewheeling' is encouraged; that is, members of the group are told that the more the idea deviates from existing practice, the better.
(3) Quantity of possible solutions is stated as the goal of the idea generation stage.
(4) Combination of ideas already expressed is encouraged as well as the extension or modification of others' solutions.

Participants in a session are trained in these rules and typically practice them on some 'warm up' problems before commencing on the actual task.

Other forms of brainstorming

There are variations and extensions of brainstorming that have been used. *Negative* or *reverse brainstorming* focuses on what is wrong with the existing process, outcome, or product. After all problems are listed, possible ways to overcome, improve, or correct each one are considered. This may be used as a first step before more typical brainstorming procedures are followed.

Synectics employs fantasy and analogy to create solutions to existing problems (Gordon, 1961), while adhering to the basic underlying principles of brainstorming. However, the synectics group has a 'client' who has a specific concern. The solution must be acceptable to this client who usually is involved in the group process. The other group members are selected for the variety of expertise that they have related to the problem. The process includes a series of steps such as formulating a definition of the problem, a restatement of the problem by each group member using 'wishful' goals, 'excursions' that use imagery and knowledge about other subjects as a source of innovative ideas about the problem at hand, and then 'force fitting' the results of these excursions to the problem. If the fit appears to be a good one, then this is viewed as a possible solution. A number of possible solutions are typically generated by the group.

Research on brainstorming

Almost all of the rigorous, empirical research has been conducted on the brainstorming technique as originally conceived by Osborn (1963). Much of the psychological research on brainstorming has focused on the issue of whether brainstorming by groups leads to larger numbers of unique ideas or solutions to problems than other possible approaches to idea generation. Osborn hypothesized that the use of brainstorming in groups would be beneficial because of the varied backgrounds of the individuals comprising the groups. The most frequent comparison has been between brainstorming groups and 'nominal' groups. A nominal group is the aggregation of the unique ideas independently produced by a set of individuals, equal in size to the brainstorming group, who have also been trained in the brainstorming rules. Typically, ideas must be generated within a relatively brief time period (10–20 minutes).

Laboratory experiments conducted by Taylor *et al.* (1958) and Dunnette *et al.* (1963) found that nominal groups produced more ideas on average than the brainstorming groups. Bouchard and Hare (1970) replicated this finding and also found that nominal groups had a larger advantage over the brainstorming groups as group size increased. These research findings, along with those of other laboratory investigations, have led to the general conclusion (e.g. Weisberg, 1986; Rickards and Freedman, 1978) that participation in interactive group brainstorming produces fewer ideas per individual than in nominal groups. It should be noted that this research does not often compare brainstorming with other problem solving procedures, but contrasts two ways that brainstorming can be implemented since the individuals who comprise the nominal groups have been trained in brainstorming techniques.

The issue of quality of solutions must also be addressed. Dunnette *et al.* (1963) found that their subjects in the nominal group condition produced solutions that were equal to or better in quality than those produced in the group brainstorming condition. However, Necka (1984) found that brainstorming resulted in higher quality (greater originality) solutions than did a control condition in which subjects were merely instructed to produce as many creative solutions as they could.

Weisberg (1986) has reviewed research that has examined the effects of postponing judgment on the quality of alternative solutions. Osborn (1963) had suggested that good quality solutions were often discarded prematurely by quick judgments that they were incorrect. Thus, brainstorming with its explicit instructions to group members to suspend judgment during idea generation could lead to solutions of higher quality than those resulting from group procedures in which participants were instructed to evaluate ideas, using criteria of what would constitute a good solution, as they were suggested. The research reviewed by Weisberg, however, indicated that higher quality solutions were produced in the condition in which explicit solution criteria had been specified prior to the generation of possible solutions than in the brainstorming condition.

The question of individual differences among participants in brainstorming has been considered. While expertise related to the problem at hand is an obvious individual difference variable, several studies have found that personality characteristics are also important. Comadena (1984) found that individuals who were tolerant of ambiguity and low in communication apprehension produced more ideas in brainstorming groups. Hyams and Graham (1984) reported that level of initiative was positively related to the number of ideas produced in individual brainstorming.

Issues and unanswered questions

Rickards and Freedman (1978) have questioned whether postponement of judgment actually occurs in brainstorming. They suggest that, despite instructions and practice, the participants in an interactive group are likely to be evaluative during the idea generation stage. Thus, a truly 'fair' test of this underlying principle of brainstorming may not be possible. Since interactive groups may inhibit the postponement of judgment, Rickards and Freedman suggest that nominal groups be used in the idea generation stage. Dunnette *et al.* (1963), whose findings would support the conclusion reached by Rickards and Freedman, did note that group brainstorming may be useful as a way of allowing practice of the technique, focusing on problems not related to the real problem of concern.

Bouchard (1971) has indicated that groups may still be preferred in two situations: when the problem calls for expertise that is distributed across persons and when it is important for the solution to be 'sold' to others. For the latter situation Bouchard notes that a proposed solution coming from a group may be more convincing to decision makers in the organization than one coming from an individual. It could be better, however, to use individual brainstorming for idea generation and a group to evaluate the possible solutions and to make the final recommendation.

Morphological analysis

As its name implies, *morphological analysis* is concerned with attacking a complex problem by looking at its structural components (Allen, 1962). In particular, the problem or issue for which a creative solution is desired is first broken down into its independent components. Then for each component all possible solutions are listed (these lists could be obtained via brainstorming techniques, for example). Next, all combinations of possible solutions for the various components are created; thus, if there are three components and three possible solutions for each component, then there are $3^3 = 27$ possible combinations. Each of these combinations would be evaluated in regard to the original problem or issue. Some can usually be eliminated quickly at this point as obviously unworkable. The viable solutions are further analyzed for the feasibility of intermediate steps required to meet the initial needs (Mohan, 1987). A disadvantage is the potentially large number of combinations that may be generated by a very complex problem. However, there is a tradeoff in that no possibility goes unexamined so all creative solutions should be given attention. This is not likely to happen in a stand-alone brainstorming session. Although morphological analysis has been used for over 25 years, it has not generated much empirical research interest among psychologists or others interested in innovation at work. Case studies exist that purport to demonstrate its effectiveness, but these are difficult to evaluate since adequate controls are lacking.

Lateral or divergent thinking

It has been argued (e.g. DeBono, 1968, 1971) that creative solutions to problems are often blocked by an approach to problem solving that is too logical and based exclusively on existing information and ways of doing things. A different form of thinking is advocated in order to arrive at creative solutions, that of *lateral* or *divergent thinking*.

The case for divergent thinking (this term is used as it is more common in the general psychological literature) is based largely on Guilford's (1967) theory of human intelligence that hypothesized a distinction between convergent and divergent thinking. Convergent thinking takes existing input information and derives an answer based on that information. DeBono would argue that this rarely leads to a creative solution to a problem. Divergent thinking, on the other hand, is more concerned with the fluency and flexibility of thinking, that is, with the flow of ideas and the readiness to change direction or modify information (Guilford, 1967). DeBono indicates that divergent thinking should result in more creative ideas.

The relationship of divergent thinking to creative outcomes has been questioned (Weisberg, 1986). Weisberg has argued that many innovations do not represent radically different ideas or approaches to problems, but rather are better characterized as incremental advancements over existing solutions. In addition, Barron and Harrington (1981) have raised the issue of whether divergent and convergent thinking are really separable or whether they go hand-in-hand in any problem solving situation. These authors also note several methodological issues that make it difficult to determine the degree to which divergent thinking is correlated with creative behavior.

Despite the questions raised above, there are many advocates of divergent or lateral thinking as a facilitator of creative outcomes. DeBono (1968, 1971) and others (e.g. Adams, 1979) have suggested ways to break away from convergent thinking in favor of a more divergent approach to problems. These are essentially a number of techniques that an individual can use to approach a problem from different vantage points to see what results. They can be used in groups, but they are not typically predicated on any assumption that a group context would make them more effective. These techniques include the introduction of random elements to the thought process; the use of reversals of logic concerning the situation or problem; the deliberate instruction to problem solvers to derive 'impossible' solutions, i.e. the stretching of ideas beyond what is commonly thought to be possible, etc. (Rickards, 1987).

Evaluation of creativity enhancement procedures

The brief review of creativity enhancement techniques suggests that they are not *the* pancrea for low levels of innovation that their advocates might claim. At the same time they do not appear to be completely lacking in value as some critics might conclude. Their most important value may be in focusing the attention of organizational members on certain important problems or concerns and on the organization's interest in innovative ideas. A common situation seems to be that a 'principle of least effort' often operates at the individual (as well as group and organizational) level in work organizations.

Most people are too busy to do more than repeat what has been done in the past or to recognize that a problem has outgrown old solutions. The use of creativity enhancement procedures may raise the salience of these problems and also provide justification for new answers and approaches. Such justification may be important to those who fear that innovation may be seen as rocking the organizational boat. Thus, brainstorming and synectics sessions and other related techniques may provide visible signals to organizational members that the organization values innovative thinking and is not opposed to change.

It is important to note that creativity enhancement procedures are best used as a part of larger mechanisms concerned with innovation throughout the organization. They are not extremely useful as stand-alone devices. For example, these approaches rarely discuss in detail how one pares down the list of suggested alternatives to something that may be manageable. Jones and Sims (1985) and Rickards (1987) have recently discussed approaches to 'closing down' (Rickards, 1987) problem solving sessions, such as mapping or clustering, voting, hurdles, etc. The goal of all of these procedures is to select high quality alternative solutions from the often large set of potential ones that can be further explored in trial implementations, detailed cost analyses, etc. They suggest that no one approach is likely to be best for this but that the choice will be dependent on situational factors. The reader is referred to these articles for more detailed discussions of such techniques.

Having concluded that traditional creativity enhancement techniques are not the sole answer to the individual's or organization's need for increased innovation, attention is now directed to interventions based on research and theory drawn from social and organizational psychology. In the space available there cannot be an exhaustive listing of possible ways of increasing individual work role innovation. Rather it is hoped that the selected examples will direct the interested reader to the relevant research literatures.

INNOVATION INTERVENTIONS DERIVED FROM SOCIAL COGNITION AND ATTITUDE RESEARCH

The literature concerned with *social cognition* addresses how social information is stored, organized, and retrieved from memory; how does that information affect subsequent information processing and decision making; and how is such stored information altered by new information and reflection or reappraisal of existing information (Sherman *et al.*, 1989). Since innovation in work settings is likely to be affected by social information, social cognition research and theory seem good choices to examine for suggestions of how to enhance innovation.

Creating change in beliefs and expectancies

It is clear that prior social information influences the perception, storage, and other processing of new information (Sherman *et al.*, 1989; Higgins and Bargh, 1987). The typical processes of assimilation and accommodation suggest that beliefs and expectancies based on previous experience will usually not be changed drastically by a small amount of new information. Thus, successful attempts to change work role incumbents' beliefs about one's ability to implement change or about the likely payoffs to be received from innovative work behavior (as examples) will not be easy to develop. There are findings in the social cognition literature, however, that can guide such efforts. Since information that is 'similar' to what has been previously experienced is likely to invoke current beliefs and expectations (Higgins, *et al.*, 1982; Lord *et al.*, 1984), the presentation of a problem or issue to organizational members should emphasize how this *differs* from previous situations rather than highlight similarities. It is likely that it will be useful also to force the explicit 'disconfirmation' of existing beliefs about acceptable solutions to the problem (Higgins and Bargh, 1987), although the realization of the inadequacy of past solutions would be ideally 'discovered' by work role incumbents, not forced on them by organizational superiors or others.

An organization may want to communicate to its members information about successful innovations that have been implemented within its various units. It has been found that *vivid* information is more likely to impact our beliefs and judgments than pallid information (Nisbett and Ross, 1980). By vivid, Nisbett and Ross mean that the information is emotionally interesting, concrete and imagery provoking, and personally more meaningful to the individual. For our purposes this would mean that it would be better to promote innovation within the organization by the use of very specific *examples* of successful innovation, rather than present a report of statistical tables detailing, for example, the number of suggestions, the number of accepted suggestions, etc. The use of photographs and other graphics, direct quotes from those involved in the innovation, and indications of how the change improved specific aspects of work could also enhance the promotion of innovative behavior.

Furthermore, the more tailored the innovation examples can be to the target audience(s) in terms of geographical location, job type and level, etc., the more likely that they will have a positive impact. This is a special case of the *self-reference effect* (Rogers, *et al.*, 1977) in which information is better recalled and available for use when it was encoded with reference to the self. Thus, broad band attempts to use generic procedures and materials to promote innovation across a large organization are not likely to be as effective as those aimed at specific individuals or work groups within the organization.

Influencing the salience of alternative beliefs

Some research has found a tendency for individuals to seek information that is likely to *confirm* existing beliefs (such as 'The decision I made last year about this issue was a good one') rather than look for possibly disconfirming information (Higgins and Bargh, 1987). However, Higgins and Bargh suggest that people will prefer (and seek) information that will allow a choice between two (or more) alternatives *if* such alternatives are clearly available to them. In the case of whether an existing or an innovative approach to a problem is better, this means that the idea of 'doing things differently' must be as salient to the individual as following existing procedures. Since 'standard operating procedures' will, in general, have a saliency advantage due to their concrete existence, campaigns to encourage innovation start with a disadvantage.

Some suggestions can be made in regard to increasing the salience of innovative approaches. Vividness in communicating successful innovations has been mentioned previously. In addition, research has shown that having individuals imagine particular future situations or outcomes and explain how such events could occur can make more positive their judgments about the likelihood of the events or outcomes (e.g. Campbell and Fairey, 1985; Hirt and Sherman, 1985; Sherman *et al.*, 1985). Thus, it might be possible to improve the perceived likelihood of being able to be more innovative, to make organizational changes, or to implement a suggested innovation through guided sessions. For example, the participants in the sessions could be those employees who would be involved in a change. They would be asked to imagine the change in place and to explain how it was successfully implemented and the positive benefits that were derived from its use.

Attitude change and persuasive communications

Research in social psychology concerned with *attitude change and persuasion* can also be applied to the question of increasing work role innovation. The impact of *depth of processing* of persuasive messages has received much recent interest (e.g. Chaiken, 1987; Eagly and Chaiken, 1984; Petty and Cacioppo, 1986). Depth of processing refers to the extent to which the semantic content of the message is processed in contrast to nonsemantic factors related to the message such as the expertise of the source, the number of arguments, etc. When a message is not processed in depth, the individual uses *heuristic processing* (Chaiken, 1980) or relatively simple rules to react to the communication. In most instances related to innovation in organizations, it would be advantageous for deep processing of relevant information to occur. Such processing is more likely to occur when the message recipient is highly motivated (Chaiken and Stangor, 1987) due to involvement with the issue; when persuasive messages come from multiple sources (Harkins and Petty, 1987); and when the recipient has had direct contact with the object of the message (Wu and Shaffer, 1987). This suggests, as did the previously discussed work regarding the vividness of information, the targeting of persuasive messages toward small groups for whom a particular problem or concern is most important to the daily conduct of their jobs.

Fazio and his colleagues (e.g. Fazio, 1986; Fazio *et al.*, 1982, 1986) have found that *attitude accessibility* influences the evaluation of the attitude object and the attitude–behavior relationship. Accessibility refers to the ease and spontaneity with which an attitude can be retrieved from memory. Easily accessed attitudes are more likely to result in strong object-evaluation associations. Strong object-evaluation associations lead to more consistent attitude–behavior relationships (Fazio, 1986). Attitude accessibility can be strengthened by repeated, direct exposure to the attitude object and by expression of the attitude (e.g. public statements expressing one's positive attitude about innovation) (Fazio *et al.*, 1982).

Implications of the attitude accessibility research for enhancing work role innovation include the likely positive impact on an individual's innovativeness by the active involvement of the individual in change processes and in the implementation of innovations suggested by others. Having individuals make presentations about their innovative activities may also strengthen their attitudes about innovation through exposure effects and through the effect that behavior can have on subsequent internalizations of attitudes consistent with the behavior (Chaiken and Stangor, 1987). This type of involvement and expression would be expected to produce more positive attitudes concerning innovation as well as enhance the link between such attitudes and work role behavior.

Minority group influence

Of considerable interest to European social psychologists has been the influence of minority group attitudes on those of the majority (e.g. Maass and Clark, 1984; Moscovici *et al.*, 1985; Nemeth, 1985). (*Minority* and *majority* in this context refer to the relative number of members of a group who share an attitude or belief.) This research has shown that a *consistent* minority within a group can have an important effect on the perceptions, attitudes, and behavior of the majority members of the group. Consistent here refers to stable, systematic, or patterned responses of the minority group members over time.

It has been argued that change induced by a minority may be more likely to be internalized and long lasting than change induced by a majority (Moscovici *et al.*, 1985). Majority-induced change may be simply compliance with the larger group on a public level without any underlying change at the latent level. One could even speculate that the reaction to a large (and vociferous) majority might be public compliance with the majority opinion and private reactance in the direction *opposite* to that advocated by the majority (cf. reactance theory, Brehm, 1966). This would suggest that attempts to influence 'innovation reluctant' groups should not be based on a strategy of overwhelming the opposition with sheer numbers if commitment to innovation, rather than just compliance, is desired.

Of particular importance to the topic of innovation is the finding by Nemeth and her associates (e.g. Nemeth, 1985; Nemeth and Kwan, 1985; Nemeth and Wachtler, 1983) that minority sources lead to more *thinking* about their positions on a topic and that this thinking is more divergent than that produced by majority sources. Solutions produced by groups exposed to consistent minority viewpoints were more likely to be novel (but still correct) ones than those produced with a comparable viewpoint expressed by a majority. When majorities express their opinion or favor a solution, the remaining group members may uncritically accept 'majority rule' and not examine closely the opinion or solution for flaws or ways that it could be improved. An implication of this research finding is that innovation may be improved if groups addressing a problem or issue are intentionally composed of several 'minority' groups, each likely to champion initially different approaches or solutions. There is the danger of the group being unable to reach common ground, but the increase in critical thinking may easily be worth that risk.

Having examined the implications for enhancing individual work role innovation of some recent research from the domain of social psychology, the focus will shift to topics typically of primary interest to organizational psychologists.

INNOVATION INTERVENTIONS DERIVED FROM WORK MOTIVATION AND JOB DESIGN RESEARCH AND THEORY

There are many theories of work motivation and job design (cf. Pinder, 1984; Steers and Porter, 1987). Rather than attempt a comprehensive review of these, some implications for the enhancement of work role innovation are drawn from a few selected topics within this large literature.

Job scope and challenge

A consistent finding is that *job scope* is posititively related to job satisfaction (Loher *et al.*, 1985) and intrinsic work motivation (Hackman and Oldham,

1980), among other outcome variables. Job scope is the degree of enrichment associated with a job (Stone, 1976), that is, the degree to which the job is high on autonomy, variety, task identity and significance, and feedback (cf. Hackman and Oldham, 1980).

Enriched jobs are likely to be associated with increased levels of work role innovation for several reasons. First, the increased amount of autonomy that the role incumbent has in such a job legitimizes discretionary behavior (such as developing new ways of dealing with task demands), that is, the received role definition is consistent with being innovative. Second, since enriched jobs are inherently more challenging due their increased levels of autonomy, variety, and task identity, they require more knowledges, skills, abilities, and decision making. In short, enriched jobs require more *thinking* than simplified ones. Thinking should foster innovation. Third, a high level of task significance (the degree to which a job has impact on other people's lives or work) helps to increase the meaningfulness and perceived importance of the work that a person does. This should motivate the individual toward improvement of the quality of one's performance and doing things differently (i.e. innovating) is a likely improvement strategy.

Not every job can be made high on every dimension of job scope. However, some general principles can be followed. Some examples are given here. See Hackman (1987) for additional approaches. Push the authority (and responsibility) for making decisions that directly affect a job down to the level of the job whenever possible. Organizational management may not like to give up this authority, but it is important for employees to gain autonomy. If there exists a pool of related tasks that are individually low in enrichment but which cannot be combined at the level of a single job, create an *autonomous* or *self-managing* work team (composed of some number of employees) that is collectively responsible for the tasks and give the team the additional tasks of making specific work assignments, evaluating performance, changing work procedures, etc. (Goodman *et al.*, 1988).

Feedback, goals, and efficacy

Motivation can be conceptualized as the allocation of one's personal resources of time and effort to various possible activities so that the probability that the individual receives valued outcomes increases (Naylor *et al.*, 1980). From this perspective an individual's motivation toward work role innovation is the amount of time and/or effort devoted by the individual to innovative activities and, furthermore, increasing such motivation will increase the time and effort so devoted.

Two factors that affect work motivation are performance feedback (Ilgen *et al.*, 1979) and goals (Locke *et al.*, 1981). Both of these factors can direct the efforts of the work performer toward particular outcomes and influence the amount of effort expended toward such outcomes. Specific applications of these two determinants of individual motivation to the case of work role innovation can be made.

Feedback and goals are not independent of each other. Feedback serves to provide information to the individual concerning the extent to which goals are being achieved. Feedback can also help determine the nature of goals, both qualitatively and quantitatively. The present concern is how can a goal related to work role innovation be established and how should feedback concerning such a goal be provided to the individual. One approach to this concern is suggested by recent research in *goal orientations* (Dweck, 1986; Dweck and Leggett, 1988).

Dweck (1986) describes two goal orientations that individuals may have: a *performance goal* or a *learning goal* orientation. The individual with a performance goal orientation is concerned with *achieving positive evaluations* (and avoiding negative evaluations) of performance and competence, tends to attribute success or failure to one's ability level, and is likely to choose tasks which can currently be performed well and to avoid challenging tasks. An individual with a learning goal orientation, on the other hand, is concerned with *increasing competence* or performance, tends to attribute success or failure to one's effort level, and is likely to choose challenging tasks that foster learning and competence growth.

Clearly, from the perspective of work role innovation, the preferred goal orientation is the learning one. How can this orientation be encouraged? Feedback may be one mechanism for achieving this. The value of learning goals for an individual may be increased if a manager through formal and informal feedback positively notes work activities that demonstrate new or enhanced competencies, stresses the importance of becoming more skilled and knowledgeable, indicates that most learning occurs during the performance of difficult and new tasks, and does not punish errors that occur in the performance of such tasks. The manager should also suggest that any failure is primarily due to insufficient effort and indicate that additional time spent on difficult tasks is likely to improve one's abilities related to such performance. It is necessary for the manager to communicate a developmental perspective to the role incumbent that downplays immediate performance and stresses the importance of becoming more competent over a longer time span.

While a learning goal orientation provides a general motivation that should encourage work role innovation, the allocation of effort and time to specific activities may also require more specific influences on motivation. One such influence is *self-efficacy beliefs* (Bandura, 1986).

Self-efficacy beliefs are people's judgments of their capacity to organize and execute courses of action necessary for the successful performance of designated tasks (Bandura, 1986). Such beliefs are especially important for our purposes because they influence the kinds of goals that individuals may strive for and the kinds of outcomes (e.g. rewards and punishments) that are anticipated (Bandura and Cervone, 1983; Locke *et al.*, 1984). Thus, efficacy beliefs concerning developing new competencies would seem necessary before an individual embraces a learning goal orientation.

Some discussion of factors that influence one's level of efficacy has been provided in Farr and Ford (Chapter 3, this volume). These factors are examined here with the specific purpose of highlighting how efficacy beliefs concerning work role innovation may be enhanced.

Bandura (1986) notes that efficacy can be influenced by enactive attainment, vicarious experience, and verbal persuasion. Enactive attainment refers to the individual's own past successes and failures. Vicarious experience concerns the individual's observation or visualization of another person performing a task successfully or unsuccessfully. Verbal persuasion can be directed toward convincing the individual that he or she is capable of performing the task or achieving the goal (e.g. being innovative). Each of these three influences can be used to improve innovation efficacy beliefs.

Past success only enhances efficacy if one's attention is drawn to the success (Bandura, 1986). An important function that superiors and peers can play in increasing the incidence of work role innovation is to 'remind' the individual of past innovations that have been successful. Instances in which the innovation led to the successful performance of a difficult task or the attainment of a challenging goal will be especially useful in boosting the individual's efficacy toward innovative behavior.

Vicarious experience may be an important positive influence on innovative efficacy because some individuals may have few, if any, previous successful innovations to their credit. For these individuals direct personal experience will only reinforce inefficacious beliefs. Individuals in work settings do monitor the work environment for information related to performance and its evaluation (Ashford and Cummings, 1983; Farr, in press). Thus, they are likely to have some awareness of others' innovative successes and failures. What is desired from the perspective of the enhancement of innovation efficacy is to increase the salience of others' successful innovative activity. This can be done through the explicit communication throughout the organization of new ways of meeting work requirements (which may also stimulate the specific use of the innovative procedures so communicated).

Observers are more likely to be influenced by others who are similar to themselves (Bandura, 1986) and by multiple others performing successfully, rather than only one other person successfully performing several times (Kazdin, 1976). Thus, it is important to communicate about the innovative activities of many people in the organization who are employed in various organizational units if the intent is to increase innovation throughout the organization. If a more specific group is the target, then the communication effort should also be more targeted in order to increase similarity.

The observation of another person failing at a task or activity can be very devastating to an individual's self-efficacy beliefs (Brown and Inouye, 1978). A manager can lessen the negative impact of a failure (e.g. an unsuccessful innovation implemented within the organization) by attributing the failure to factors that can be improved in future instances, such as the amount of effort expended.

In work settings individuals are likely to have some difficulty evaluating their own degree of innovativeness because of an inadequate information base. In such instances verbal persuasion is likely to be effective in altering efficacy beliefs. Verbal persuasion can have an impact on self-efficacy when the source of the message is perceived to be credible and knowledgeable by the recipient. In addition, while the persuasive message should 'stretch' the person's efficacy by suggesting that the individual can be more innovative than he or she is at present, highly inflated appraisals of efficacy are likely to lower the credibility of the source (Bandura, 1986).

It appears that similar mechanisms can be used to encourage a learning goal orientation and to increase the self-efficacy of work role incumbents regarding innovation. Feedback that stresses becoming competent rather than evaluating the outcomes of current performance and that specifically does not punish errors associated with new and innovative activities is likely to facilitate the development of both of these important cognitive factors. Vicarious learning processes, while considered in detail for developing self-efficacy, should work with the facilitation of learning goals as well. The direct encouragement of work role innovation and learning goals by superiors and peers by appealing to the individual's capacity for related behavior is also likely to be of value.

At a more macro level, organizational development techniques may provide some suggestions for enhancing individual work role innovation.

IMPLICATIONS OF ORGANIZATIONAL DEVELOPMENT FOR THE FACILITATION OF WORK ROLE INNOVATION

Organizational development techniques are directed toward the improvement of organizational functioning through more effective and collaborative management of the organization's culture (the way people within the organization behave toward each other, the way they think and feel, and their values) (French and Bell, 1978). Some selected applications of organizational development to the enhancement of work role innovation are discussed below.

Espoused theories versus theories in use

A major contribution that organizational development can make in regard to innovation is the emphasis given to examining one's assumptions about people and their roles within the organization. This examination of assumptions can take place in several different modes, but a common feature is that individuals are taught to identify and evaluate these assumptions, to understand better how these assumptions influence behavior, and to alter assumptions and behavior if they are damaging to personal and organizational functioning.

For example, Argyris (1985) argues that a major barrier to change and innovation is that individuals do not distinguish between their *espoused theories* and their *theories in use*. The espoused theory is a set of beliefs and values expressed (or espoused) when an individual is asked about how he or she would act in a given situation. Theories in use are the actual behaviors of the individual in the situation (or one similar to it). Often the espoused theories are conducive to change and innovation (e.g. take risks), but the theories in use are not (e.g. punish all failures). Argyris notes that this contradiction is rarely brought out into the open and, thus, no or little real change is possible. He suggests that the individual must be confronted with the inconsistency and forced to resolve it. Such confrontation would be guided by a change agent, starting with individuals at the top of the organization.

It may be useful for top organizational management to examine its espoused theories and theories in use with regard to the issue of individual work role innovation. It is likely that most top executives would espouse favorable statements regarding such innovation within their organization and about allowing individuals to make decisions that affect their own work. It is also likely that often these same individuals will behave in ways that indicate that conformity to existing patterns of behavior and deference to higher management are paths to 'success' in the organization. These inconsistencies should be addressed to remove such barriers to innovation.

Role analysis

Another approach that could be used to increase individual innovation is *role analysis* (French and Bell, 1978). Individuals may not introduce as much change into their work roles as may be desired because they simply do not view this as part of the expected behavior for their role within the organization. The role analysis process involves the role incumbent as well as others who are part of the role set (role senders and role receivers). It is a consensual process that defines the role of the incumbent in terms of behaviors to which all members of the role set agree. Change agents who may facilitate the role analysis process can be used to insure that the introduction of change is discussed as a possible role behavior for all role incumbents if role set members do not address it. Increased levels of individual discretion and autonomy could also be negotiated with this type of process. The introduction of *boundary spanning* behaviors into the work role may also enhance innovation (Rubenstein and Woodman, 1984; Tushman and Katz, 1980). Boundary spanning refers to interactions with individuals outside of the organization or with those in other functional units of the same organization.

Self-fulfilling prophecies

Organizational development has long noted the important impact that managerial expectations play in affecting the behavior of others within the organization (Beer and Walton, 1987; Eden, 1988). Eden (1988) has noted that expectations can become self-fulfilling prophecies (King, 1971) and has reviewed research indicating that randomly assigned subordinates whose managers were told that they were expected to be high performing employees actually outperformed other randomly assigned individuals whose managers were not given positive expectations about their performance. On the basis of this research, Eden has argued for active interventions that raise the performance expectations of organizational members. While Eden has focused on current job performance and training performance as primary outcome measures for expectation interventions, the extension to individual work role innovation appears to be relatively straightforward.

The active interventions that Eden has suggested include raising the expectations that managers have about their subordinates, eradicating already existing low expectations about subordinates, and raising the self-expectations that organizational members have about their own performance levels (akin to the self-efficacy enhancement discussed earlier in this chapter).

Changing the expectations that managers have about current employees would be difficult in most cases (Eden, 1988). Therefore, raising expectations may be best done when a manager has no prior history with a work group (e.g. newly assigned to the group; a special group or task force convened to deal with a particular problem; or a group of new employees or trainees). Managerial expectations can be raised, for example, by an organizational development consultant or someone from the human resources department of the organization discussing with the manager the quality of the work group members, noting especially positive points from personnel files or past performance records, and generally advocating high goals for unit performance (for the purposes of this discussion emphasis would be given to work role innovation).

Eradicating low expectations can be difficult, especially when these expectations have been established over a long period of time. One novel approach suggested by Eden (1988) is to immunize potential victims against the negative effects of low managerial expectations. Training individuals to recognize behavioral signs of low expectations, encouraging them not to succumb to such expectations, and indicating how they can alter their managers' expectations through effective job behavior are the major elements in such a process. Again, emphasizing work role innovation in the immunization process would address the primary concern of this chapter.

Enhancing the individual's expectations should be an ongoing process. While earlier discussion in this chapter focused on managerial feedback that could raise self-efficacy beliefs regarding work role innovation, Eden (1988) stresses 'piggy-backing' expectation enhancement onto any and all organizational changes that may occur. Active attempts to bolster role innovation expectations could be made part of training and development programs, orientation sessions following the introduction of new technologies or organizational structures, and as part of promotion, transfer, or reassignment procedures.

Weick's (1984) concept of *small wins* can be applied to expectation enhancement. This refers to breaking down a large project into a series of smaller stages, the successful completion of which can be 'celebrated' as a win with concomitant bolstering of the expectations of the project participants. To the extent that innovative procedures were used in the successful attainment of these small wins, future innovation expectations can be enhanced as part of the celebratory review of that stage of the project. A myriad of opportunities exist in any organization for such expectation enhancement and advantage should be taken of them.

INNOVATION INTERVENTIONS AND THE FARR AND FORD MODEL OF INDIVIDUAL INNOVATION

The various ways that individual work role innovation could be increased that have been discussed in this chapter are consistent with the model of individual innovation described by Farr and Ford (Chapter 3, this volume). This section provides a brief discussion of how these interventions fit into the Farr and Ford model.

The Farr and Ford model contains four general factors that influence individual work role innovation: perceived efficacy for implementing change; perceived need for change; perceived payoff from change; and capacity to generate new and useful ideas.

Perceived efficacy for implementing change

The present chapter's discussion of efficacy beliefs and goal orientations with its emphasis on feedback from superiors, peers, and others in the work setting has an obvious link with the efficacy component of the Farr and Ford model, as does the section on the enhancement of expectations. The discussion of social cognition and attitude change is not as obviously related, but points raised in that discussion offer ideas about how to increase efficacy beliefs concerning innovation. Attempts to change an individual's goal orientation, efficacy, or expectations are more likely to be successful if the information or message used to create the change is vivid, personally relevant to the individual, and focuses on differences from previous situations or problems. Procedures that encourage deep processing of persuasive messages and the active expression of innovation favorable statements are also likely to change such beliefs and expectations.

Perceived need for change

The social cognition and attitude change literature is also directly relevant to the issue of perceived need for change. Information that stresses how a problem differs from past concerns is likely to aid in the recognition of existent and emergent problems that require change. Again, vivid and personally relevant messages are more likely to be persuasive. Role analysis with an emphasis on boundary spanning behaviors may enhance the individual's ability to detect emergent and potential problems that require innovative solutions.

Perceived payoff from change

Several of the techniques for enhancing individual innovation increase the perceived payoff from change. Feedback from superiors and peers that reinforces past innovation should be a positive payoff for the individual. Personal growth and development that result from the performance of enriched and challenging jobs have been found to be satisfying in a large number of research studies. Similarly, increased self-efficacy regarding innovation can be rewarding. Role analysis can reduce uncertainty about the acceptability of innovative role behavior and increase the favorability of reward expectations concerning innovation.

Capacity to generate new and useful ideas

The creativity enhancement techniques can increase one's capacity to generate ideas by giving the individual both training and practice in divergent and creative thinking. The license to be free and unbounded in one's thinking that these techniques promote may be a worthwhile aid for idea generation. Performing a challenging and enriched job that requires thinking and decision making on a daily basis may also strengthen one's capacity for generating more solution alternatives.

This brief look at how the selected techniques for innovation facilitation presented in this chapter are related to the components of the Farr and Ford model of individual innovation demonstrates that several techniques relate to each model component and some techniques are linked to more than one component. This suggests that the enhancement of individual work role innovation is best served by an integrated system of programs and procedures, each addressing some part of the total process.

SUMMARY AND CONCLUSIONS

It seems clear that psychological theory and research can identify a number of techniques and procedures for facilitating individual work role innovation. This chapter has not attempted to present a comprehensive list of these, but rather to suggest to the reader some of the relevant research literatures that can be explored for possibilities. Illustrative examples have been provided.

A prescriptive set of innovation enhancement techniques will not be attempted. It is highly doubtful that such prescriptions would have generalizable value across organizations and individuals. Rather, it seems reasonable to stress that any attempt to facilitate individual work role innovation should use several techniques that address each of the four components of the Farr and Ford model. This is in keeping with Hackman and Walton's (1986) observation that there usually exist multiple and at least partially redundant determinants of individual and group effectiveness in work organizations. Each one in isolation is much less likely to have the desired effect, that is, the system effect is more than the simple aggregation of the singular effects.

Efforts to facilitate individual role innovation should be directed by research and theory. Innovative work behaviors are not qualitatively different from other effective behaviors related to successful job performance. Techniques and procedures that have been shown to lead to more effective work performance are likely candidates for also improving innovative behavior. The application of concepts and procedures derived from 'mainstream' research and theory in social psychology, industrial/organizational psychology, and organizational development to work role innovation in this chapter has yielded promising results. It is hoped that the reader can be innovative in the derivation of additional applications and that the present discussion has facilitated that innovation.

Correspondence address:
Department of Psychology, Pennsylvania State University, University Park, Pennsylvania 16802, USA.

REFERENCES

Adams, J.L. (1979). *Conceptual Blockbusting*, 2nd edn. New York: Norton.
Allen, M.S. (1962). *Morphological Creativity*. Englewood Cliffs, NJ: Prentice-Hall.
Amabile, T.M. (1983). *The Social Psychology of Creativity*. New York: Springer-Verlag.
Argyris, C. (1985). *Strategic Change and Defensive Routines*. Boston: Pitman.
Ashford, S.J. and Cummings, L.L. (1983). Feedback as an individual resource: Personal Strategies of creating information. *Organizational Behavior and Human Performance*, 32, 370–398.
Baffon, F. and Harrington, D.M. (1981). Creativity, intelligence, and personality. *Annual Review of Psychology*, 32, 439–476.
Bandura, A. (1986). *Social Foundations of Thought and Action*. Englewood Cliffs, NJ: Prentice-Hall.
Bandura, A. and Cervone, D. (1983). Self-evaluative and self-efficacy mechanisms governing the motivational effects of goal systems. *Journal of Personality and Social Psychology*, 45, 1017–1028.
Beer, M. and Walton, A.E. (1987). Organization change and development. *Annual Review of Psychology*, 38, 339–367.
Bouchard, T.J. (1971). Whatever happened to brainstorming? *Journal of Creative Behavior*, 5, 182–189.
Bouchard, T.J. and Hare, M. (1970). Size, performance, and potential in brainstorming groups. *Journal of Applied Psychology*, 54, 51–55.
Brehm, J.W. (1966). *A Theory of Psychological Reactance*. New York: Academic Press.
Brown, I., Jr. and Inouye, D.K. (1978). Learned helplessness through modeling: the role of perceived similarity in competence. *Journal of Personality and Social Psychology*, 36, 900–908.
Campbell, J.D. and Fairey, P.J. (1985). Effects of self-esteem, hypothetical explanations, and verbalizations of expectancies on future performance. *Journal of Personality and Social Psychology*, 48, 1097–1111.
Chaiken, S. (1980). Heuristic versus systematic information processing and the use of source versus message cues in persuasion. *Journal of Personality and Social Psychology*, 39, 752–766.
Chaiken, S. (1987). The heuristic model of persuasion. In M.P. Zanna, J.M. Olson and C.P. Herman (Eds.), *Social Influence: The Ontario Symposium*, Vol. 5. Hillsdale, NJ: Erlbaum.
Chaiken, S. and Strangor, C. (1987). Attitudes and attitude change. *Annual Review of Psychology*, 38, 575–630.
Comadena, M.E. (1984). Brainstorming groups: Ambiguity tolerance, communication apprehension, task attraction, and individual productivity. *Small Group Behavior*, 15, 251–264.
DeBono, E. (1968). *New Think*. New York: Basic Books.
DeBono, E. (1971). *Lateral Thinking for Management*. New York: McGraw-Hill.
Dunnette, M.D., Campbell, J. and Jaastad, K. (1963). The effects of group participation on brainstorming effectiveness for two industrial samples. *Journal of Applied Psychology*, 47, 10–37.
Dweck, C.S. (1986). Motivational processes affecting learning. *American Psychologist*, 41, 1040–1048.
Dweck, C.S. and Leggett, E.L. (1988). A social-cognitive approach to motivation and personality. *Psychological Review*, 95, 256–273.

Eagly, A.H. and Chaiken, S. (1984). Cognitive theories of persuasion. *Advances in Experimental Social Psychology*, 17, 268–359.

Eden, D. (1988). Creating expectancy effects in OD: Applying self-fulfilling prophecy. *Research in Organizational Change and Development*, 2, 235–267.

Farr, J.L. (in press). Performance feedback and work behavior. In H. Schuler (Ed.), *Beitrage zur Organisationspsychologie*, Band 4. Stuttgart: Verlag für Angewandte Psychologie.

Fazio, R.H. (1986). How do attitudes guide behavior? In R.M. Sorrentino and E.T. Higgins, (Eds.), *Handbook of Motivation and Cognition: Foundations of Social Behavior*. New York: Guilford.

Fazio, R.H., Chen, J., McDonel, E.C. and Sherman, S.J. (1982). Attitude accessibility, attitude-behavior consistency, and the strength of the object-evaluation association. *Journal of Experimental Social Psychology*, 18, 339–357.

Fazio, R.H., Sanbonmatsu, D.M., Powell, M.C. and Kardes, F.R. (1986). On the automatic activation of attitudes. *Journal of Personality and Social Psychology*, 50, 229–238.

French, W. and Bell, C. (1978). *Organizational Development: Behavioral Science Interventions for Organization Improvement*, 2nd edn. Englewood Cliffs, NJ: Prentice-Hall.

Goodman, P.S., Devedas, R. and Griffith Hughson, T.L. (1988). Groups and productivity: Analyzing the effectiveness of self-managing teams. In J.P. Campbell and R.J. Campbell (Eds.), *Productivity in Organizations*. San Francisco: Jossey-Bass.

Gordon, W.J.J. (1961). *Synectics*. New York: Collier.

Guilford, J.P. (1967). *The Nature of Human Intelligence*. New York: McGraw-Hill.

Hackman, J.R. (1987). Work design. In R.M. Steers and W.L. Porter (Eds.), *Motivation and Work Behavior*, 4th edn. New York: McGraw-Hill.

Hackman, J.R. and Oldham, G.R. (1980). *Work Redesign*. Reading, MA: Addison-Wesley.

Hackman, J.R. and Walton, R.E. (1986). Leading groups in organizations. In P.S. Goodman (Ed.), *Designing Effective Work Groups*. San Francisco: Jossey-Bass.

Harkins, S.G. and Petty, R.E. (1987). Information utility and the multiple source effect. *Journal of Personality and Social Psychology*, 52, 260–268.

Higgins, E.T. and Bargh, J.A. (1987). Social cognition and social perception. *Annual Review of Psychology*, 38, 369–425.

Higgins, E.T., King, G.A. and Mavin, G.H. (1982). Individual construct accessibility and subjective impressions and recall. *Journal of Personality and Social Psychology*, 43, 35–47.

Hirt, E.R. and Sherman, S.J. (1985). The role of prior knowledge in explaining hypothetical events. *Journal of Experimental Social Psychology*, 21, 519–543.

Hyams, N.B. and Graham, W.K. (1984). Effects of goal setting and initiative on individual brainstorming. *Journal of Social Psychology*, 123, 283–284.

Ilgen, D.R., Fisher, C.D. and Taylor, M.S. (1979). Consequences of individual feedback on behavior in organizations. *Journal of Applied Psychology*, 64, 349–371.

Jones, S. and Sims, D. (1985). Mapping as an aid to creativity. *Journal of Management Development*, 4, 47–60.

Kazdin, A.E. (1976). Effects of covert modeling, multiple models, and model reinforcement on assertive behavior. *Behavior Therapy*, 7, 211–222.

King, A. (1971). Self-fulfilling prophecies in training the hardcore: Supervisors' expectations and the underprivileged workers' performance. *Social Science Quarterly*, 52, 369–378.

Locke, E.A., Frederick, E., Lee, C. and Bobko, P. (1984). Effect of self-efficacy, goals, and task strategies on task performance. *Journal of Applied Psychology,* **69**, 241–251.

Locke, E.A., Shaw, K.N., Saari, L.M. and Latham, G.P. (1981). Goal setting and task performance: 1969–1980. *Psychological Bulletin,* **90**, 125–152.

Loher, B.T., Noe, R.A., Moeller, N.L. and Fitzgerald, M.P. (1985). A meta-analysis of the relation of job characteristics to job satisfaction. *Journal of Applied Psychology,* **70**, 280–289.

Lord, C.G., Lepper, M.R. and Mackie, D. (1984). Attitude prototypes as determinants of attitude-behavior consistency. *Journal of Personality and Social Psychology,* **46**, 1254–1266.

Maass, A. and Clark, R.D. III (1984). Hidden impact of minorities: fifteen years of minority influence research. *Psychological Bulletin,* **95**, 428–450.

Mohan, S. (1987). Technology forecasting: An aid to planning, *Management and Labour Studies,* **12**, 145–158.

Moscovici, S., Mugny, G. and Van Avermaet, E. (1985). *Perspectives on Minority Influence.* Cambridge: Cambridge University Press.

Naylor, J.C., Pritchard, R.D. and Ilgen, D.R. (1980). *A Theory of Behavior in Organizations.* New York: Academic Press.

Necka, E. (1984). The effectiveness of synectics and brainstorming as conditioned by socio-emotional climate and type of task. *Polish Psychological Bulletin,* **15**, 41–50.

Nemeth, C.J. (1985). Dissent, group process and creativity: The contributions of minority influence. *Advances in Group Process,* **2**, 57–75.

Nemeth, C.J. and Kwan, J. (1985). Originality of word associations as a function of majority vs. minority influence processes. *Social Psychology Quarterly,* **48**, 277–282.

Nemeth, C.J. and Wachtler, J. (1983). Creative problem solving as a result of majority vs. minority influence. *European Journal of Social Psychology,* **13**, 45–55.

Nisbett, R. and Ross, L. (1980). *Human Inference: Strategies and Shortcomings of Social Judgment.* Englewood Cliffs, NJ: Prentice-Hall.

Osborn, A.F. (1963). *Applied Imagination.* New York: Charles Scribner's Sons.

Petty, R.E. and Cacioppo, J.T. (1986). The elaboration likelihood model of persuasion. *Advances in Experimental Social Psychology,* **19**, 123–205.

Pinder, C.C. (1984). *Work Motivation: Theory, Issues, and Applications.* Glenview, IL: Scott, Foresman.

Rickards, T. (1987). 'Closing down': A classification of creative decision-making aids. *Journal of Managerial Psychology,* **2**, 11–16.

Rickards, T. and Freedman, B.L. (1978). Procedures for managers in idea deficient situations. *Journal of Management Studies,* **15**, 43–55.

Rogers, T.B., Kuiper, N.A. and Kirker, W.S. (1977). Self-reference and the encoding of personal information. *Journal of Personality and Social Psychology,* **35**, 677–688.

Rubenstein, D. and Woodman, R.W. (1984). Spiderman and the Burma raiders: collateral organization theory in action. *Journal of Applied Behavioral Science,* **20**, 1–21.

Sherman, S.J., Cialdini, R.B., Schwartzman, D.F. and Reynolds, K.D. (1985). Imagining can heighten or lower the perceived likelihood of contracting a disease. *Personality and Social Psychology Bulletin,* **11**, 118–127.

Sherman, S.J., Judd, C.M. and Park, B. (1989). Social cognition. *Annual Review of Psychology,* **40**, 281–326.

Simon, H.A. (1988). Understanding creativity and creative management. In R.L. Kuhn (Ed.), *Handbook for Creative and Innovative Managers.* New York: McGraw-Hill.

Steers, R.M. and Porter, L.W. (1987). *Motivation and Work Behavior*, 4th edn. New York: McGraw-Hill.

Stone, E.F. (1976). The moderating effect of work-related values on the job scope–job satisfaction relationship. *Organizational Behavior and Human Performance*, 15, 147–167.

Taylor, D.W., Berry, P.C. and Block, C.H. (1958). Does group participation when using brainstorming facilitate or inhibit creative thinking? *Administrative Science Quarterly*, 3, 23–47.

Tushman, M. and Katz, R. (1980). External communication and project performance: An investigation into the role of gatekeeper. *Management Science*, 26, 1071–1085.

Weick, K. (1984). Small wins: Redefining the scale of social problems. *American Psychologist*, 39, 40–49.

Weisberg, R.W. (1986). *Creativity: Genius and Other Myths*. New York: W. H. Freeman.

Wu, C. and Shaffer, D.R. (1987). Susceptibility to persuasive appeals as a function of source credibility and prior experience with the attitude object. *Journal of Personality and Social Psychology*, 52, 677–688.

11 Innovation and the design of work and learning environments: the concept of exploration in human–computer interaction

Siegfried Greif and Heidi Keller
Universität Osnabrück, West Germany

INTRODUCTION

The progress of technological change and innovation has never been more dramatic in industrial history than today. Computer systems play a central role in these innovation processes, thus, representing environments for innovation and challenges for human mastery and competence. For a better theoretical understanding of the dynamic changes of work roles, work procedures and human learning in innovative human–computer and complex work environments, new conceptual orientations are required. Such theories should also be practically useful for the design of work and learning environments facilitating innovation. Following the comprehensive definition of West and Farr (1989, see Chapter 1 in this volume), innovations can be useful 'new and different ideas, processes, products and procedures'. Therefore not only technological inventions but also new knowledge and practical problem solutions applying to technological systems are relevant for understanding the innovation process. We feel that the concept of *exploration* provides just such a developing and stimulating orientation, contributing both to our theoretical understanding of the acquisition process of new knowledge and individual innovation as well as to the development of useful principles for future systems and work.

In the following we present and discuss the concept of exploration, and conditions supporting the development of new knowledge originally formulated in experimental and developmental psychology but which, in our

Innovation and Creativity at Work Edited by M.A. West and J.L. Farr
© 1990 John Wiley & Sons Ltd

view, have important implications for understanding innovation processes in occupational psychology. Then we deduce principles of training and for the design of environments to facilitate exploratory learning and by extension individual innovation (see also Farr, Chapter 10 in this book). Examples from the field of human–computer interaction and other approaches are used to illustrate the basic concepts and principles. We then describe and evaluate methods designed to enhance exploratory learning and practical design principles which have been applied in the field of computer training and software development. Finally we will summarize the implications for the design of work and learning environments supporting the enhancement of individual innovation in occupational settings.

THE CONCEPT AND PROCESS OF EXPLORATION

Exploration can be described as a behavioural system comprising molar behavioural elements (see below) on different behavioural levels which regulate the relationships between individual and environment (Voss and Keller, 1983). Exploration is a developmental construct since its behavioural expressions vary with the developmental tasks. The first expressions of exploratory activities are perceptual, implying that informational input mostly relies on distal communicational channels, as, for example, hearing and learning. With the development of motor competence, exploration is mostly expressed by means of manipulatory behaviour, i.e. moving around with touching, grasping and manipulating. With developing symbolization, more sophisticated ways of information intake become possible; strategies are applied, hypotheses about functioning are developed and tested; elements of problem solving behaviour become incorporated and language skills allow for novel generations. It is important to notice that earlier behavioural expressions do not disappear with new competencies, but become integrated in more differentiated behavioural patterns (Keller and Boigs, 1990; Voss and Meyer, 1987; McCall, 1979; Ruff, 1982).

Different authors agree, however, that exploration starts at birth as a genetically determined and inborn behavioural system, which has developed because of selection advantages during evolution (e.g. Ellis, 1975). In this chapter we refer to the concept of specific exploration in the sense of Berlyne (1960). The term implies that exploration is instigated by individual encounters with objects or situations which contain a certain degree of novelty, surprise and complexity, i.e. uncertainty.

These degrees of novelty etc., are conceptualized as discrepancies from existing schemata, which have to be located in a medium range (a subjective optimum). If the discrepancies are too big, fear motivated avoidance will block the exploratory tendencies. In the case of small discrepancies, i.e. where the immediate evaluation is one of familiarity, exploration may occur as a consequence of developing feelings of boredom or monotony. The resulting type of exploration is called 'diversive exploration' by Berlyne (1960) since the activities of the individual are directed at changing the environment with the goal of more stimulation. In this respect, person–computer interaction constitutes a situation of specific exploration.

The sequence of behaviour elements

The process of exploration can be analysed as a time dependent sequence of different types of behaviours. Different authors (e.g. Schneider *et al.*, 1983; Voss and Keller, 1987) describe this process as consisting of the following behavioural elements:

(1) Attention to a new object or situation.
(2) Distance exploration.
(3) Manipulatory exploration.
(4) Play.

New objects, for example a new computer game or software system, may at first attract our attention. Then we begin to explore the object visually (distance exploration) and try to gather basic information (many computer games provide the player with a simulation of the game and most professional software firms distribute demonstration disks). The next step consists of manipulatory activities (e.g. using a joy stick or interaction with the program by pressing keys on the keyboard). After phases of (visual and manipulatory) exploration for gathering new information we typically observe a sequence of playful application of the newly acquired knowledge (e.g. the user plays the first easy version of the game or tries to write a letter with a new word processor program) (see also Hutt, 1970; Nunally and Lemond, 1973).

The occurrence of play as part of this sequence demonstrates the close relationship between play and exploration. Psychologists classically try to separate play and exploration on the basis of facial expressions (exploration: neutral, attentional; play: emotional, playful) and neurophysiological parameters (exploration: increased arousal; play: decreased arousal) (Keller *et al.*, 1985). Since both types of behaviours serve the function of competence acquisition (exploration: what can the object or situation do; play: what can I do with the object or situation), we propose to differentiate them by their functions. We differentiate two necessary processes in this respect. First acquiring information, i.e. by means of explorations (distal, manipulative and/or symbolic) (what happens when a button is pressed). Individuals then tend to secure the information they gained by repeating the effect under varying conditions and varying situational parameters. We call this process information securing (see Schölmerich and Keller, 1987; Schölmerich, 1990). These two processes alternate in individual sequences.

We assume that basically the process of individual exploration and invention of new solutions when confronted with new problems at the work place can be described by the same sequence of behaviour elements. However, although in occupational settings we would hesitate to talk about 'play', when at work people repeatedly test their new knowledge and different possible solutions before they are used as definite occupational routines.

Exploration, mental load and pauses

Exploring new situations and processing new information are demanding activities. So the individual needs pauses, intervals of inactivity, or diversions in order to restore capacities or to find relief from a sustained mental load. Often periods of exploration are phased to prevent fatigue due to novelty from becoming so aversive that it leads to the suspension of future exploration of the situation.

A complex new computer game or a software system, for example, is not expected to be explored in one continuous action unit but stepwise with alternating phases of playful application of the newly acquired knowledge and action pauses. Time pressure at the work place therefore may be seen as a critical contextual condition for the development of new knowledge and innovatory problem solving.

Constituting predictable new knowledge: the role of persistence

Inventions may result from unpredictable chance solutions. One goal of fostering innovatory behaviour is, obviously, to make innovation more predictable. Here again, we have to refer to the knowledge constituting function of exploration. Securing information means actively building knowledge structures by repetition and variation. This knowledge then becomes part of the mental structure and is available for individual action guiding.

The whole cycle of acquiring and securing information thus has to be performed repeatedly. The success of the knowledge acquisition process depends on goal oriented persistence to repeat the cycle. Here, obviously, personality and especially motivational factors come into play. From our observations of human–computer interaction, there seem to be large individual differences in the persistence with which people explore computer systems.

Anxiety and exploration

Exploration has been related to basic concepts of motivation, affect, and cognition; the relationship between anxiety and exploration in particular has been discussed extensively (e.g. Voss, 1984). Both theory and research show that excessive levels of anxiety suppress exploratory behaviours, whereas mild levels of anxiety might stimulate exploration.

Before we generalize this widely accepted finding we should differentiate more precisely specific *exploration styles* and observe their antecedents and their consequences for knowledge acquisition. For example, Müller (1989) found *positive* correlations between state anxiety level, an anxious trial and error type of exploratory behaviour and poor performance (in terms of speed and accuracy) on computer training tasks. We therefore should carefully differentiate between inefficient and efficient styles of exploration. These relationships are not always so clear, however, since there appear to be different functions depending on the type of exploration studied and individual differences in functioning associated with moderate and high levels of anxiety.

Novelty and complexity: individual task definition

Since exploration is aimed at acquiring new knowledge, it tends to occur in task situations which cannot be integrated into existing schemata without more information. Berlyne's (1960) original stimulus material, for example, consisted among other things of visual displays constituting ambiguity (e.g. partly airplane, partly flower), heterogeneity of elements, irregularity of arrangement, and varying amounts of information. By means of extended visual study it is possible to restore an incomplete drawing, to develop concepts for different stimuli or to isolate incongruous information. These examples rely on knowledge which can be generated by individual information processing. Other situations provide information which can only indicate means of manipulation, e.g. pressing buttons to elicit feedback mechanisms or to use external expertise in any form. Referring to occupational settings, bureaucratic formalization and standardization or high predictability of work routines should decrease the chances of exploratory activities and innovatory problem solving. However, the degree of novelty which stimulates exploration will also vary very much depending on individual differences in motivation and existing knowledge structures. The optimal discrepancy between individual knowledge and new knowledge required should be sufficiently intrinsically motivating to stimulate active exploratory information seeking. *Exploration, thus, may be seen as an individualized response to new or complex problems which is elicited in order to cope with cognitive conflicts and information deficits.*

It is also evident that not all newly acquired information will be integrated in the cognitive information processing system by the individual. As a necessary precondition, information would first have to be evaluated as relevant and valuable for task performance by the individual. Information selection and processing is therefore preceded by an evaluation process.

Time and self-determination of exploration

There are other important contextual factors facilitating the assimilation and storage of new information and one very important factor is time. As we have argued earlier, the process of exploration occurs in time-based phases. Several developmental studies have demonstrated that the *duration* of the interaction with the new situation influences the *accuracy and amount* of recalled knowledge. For example, children acquire better representations of their spatial surroundings when they can explore them for a sufficiently long period (Acredolo, 1979; Herman and Siegel, 1978).

Exploration thus needs time. But investing valuable time for long-term outcomes is something modern organizations are often loath to do. A typical example is the training of computer novices to use complex multifunctional software systems. Companies often demand that the training time for an introductory course for a complicated multifunctional office system (integrating word processing, database, calculation, graphics and communication subsystems) be compressed into a schedule of a maximum of three days (six to eight hours per day). From practical experience and our first evaluation studies we can infer that such a time schedule is absurd and it is completely worthless (or even produces long-term negative results) to invest time and money in training which is stressful for participants and which offers almost no chances of success.

The second important concept to be discussed here is that of *self-directed exploration*. Assimilating and storing information varies depending on such things as individual learning styles. Some individuals prefer to engage in more self-determined active rather than other-determined passive exploration and such preferences are determined by a variety of environmental and interpersonal factors.

For example, in developmental studies (e.g. Benson and Uzgiris, 1981; Cohen *et al.*, 1980), children who were allowed to explore new surroundings by themselves and at their own pace acquired more information about their spatial settings, and better spatial representations than children who were guided by an adult and who therefore had passively explored their surroundings. This idea is supported by theories which conceptualize cognitive development as being closely related to and dependent on motor acts (Gibson, 1979).

Self-determined exploration has the additional effect of eliciting positive emotional feelings and self-evaluations of competence and efficacy. These emotional qualities might themselves facilitate further exploratory learning, creativity and role innovation (see Farr and Ford, Chapter 3 and Farr, Chapter 10 in this volume).

EXPLORATION AND LEARNING

General principles

The relationship between the concepts of exploration and learning are complex but some links have already been established. For example, the notion of discovery or exploratory learning (see Ausubel, 1968; Bruner, 1966; Neber, 1981) is particularly useful in linking the two conceptual areas. The basic elements of discovery learning are:

(a) learning by solving new and/or complex problems, and
(b) self-determination in the process of learning.

This emphasizes the development of knowledge through a process of information search, active reconstruction and assimilation. The concept therefore excludes learning derived from highly structured learning tasks with complete instruction on how to solve presented problems and learning processes and environments designed to be identical for all who encounter them (e.g. classroom instruction techniques).

Despite its theoretical relevance for facilitating innovation processes, exploratory learning concepts have been seldom applied in industrial training (see below for exceptions in the field of computer training). There are successful applications of the principles of exploratory learning in schools (Neber, 1981). But recent less well known and more advanced applications can be found in the 'Hands on Science Movement' or 'Please Touch Museums', i.e. contemporary approaches for education in museum settings. (e.g. Gregory, 1988; New-science, Ontario Science Museum).

Science museums (e.g. the Exploratorium in San Francisco or the Science Museum in London) and science expositions (e.g. the Phenomena in Zürich) following this approach encourage visitors to actively manipulate the professionally designed exhibits. The visitors, for example, can learn how different sounds form different acoustic waves or how perceptual illusions work. In children's museums and exhibitions (e.g. the Children's Museums in Boston, Brooklyn, Los Angeles) children can learn how the environment works, how the body functions and about history by manipulating exhibits which are designed to maximize learning through exploration.

Evaluations of these exploratory approaches to learning indicate their value (e.g. Kranes, 1987). Visitors not only seem to be more attracted to such museums and exhibitions (as is indicated by the often dramatic increase in visitors) but more important, people start to behave very differently and develop feelings of competence and mastery in the museum setting. This has an effect of raising their levels of interest in the content of the exhibition. Of course for exploration to be motivated in these settings the environment has to be aesthetically pleasing. As we know from environmental research (e.g. Wohlwill, 1976; Kaplan, 1987) people have basic needs for aesthetically pleasing environments and prefer to work and play in environments which better satisfy these needs. Another important aspect of these approaches is that they explicitly attempt to activate different channels of information input (visual, tactile, auditory) for active exploration and knowledge acquisition (see Volpert, 1988, who also advocates a work design stimulating various human senses).

It may be argued that companies are highly unlikely to invest in designing work environments to satisfy both the aesthetic and exploratory needs of their employees. But there are already examples, especially in the architecture of work places for professionals, such as in 'Silicon Valley', which seem to step into just such a new dimension of work environment design.

Exploratory learning in the field of computer training

There is already promising and emerging research on the application of exploratory learning concepts within the field of computer training. Carroll (1985) and his coworkers (Carroll and Mack, 1983) were among the first to develop practical approaches for the design of computer systems and manuals as 'exploratory environments' for supporting active exploratory learning. Similar research has been done by Waern (1986), Frese (1988) and his coworkers, and at our Work and Organizational Psychology Unit in Osnabrück (Greif, 1988; Greif and Janikowski, 1987; Mangel and Lohmann, 1988; Müller, 1989). In the following section we give a summary of the design and training principles beginning with Carroll's approach.

Active exploration of exploratory movements

Carroll and Mack (1983) trained computer novices with word processors. They invited subjects to 'think aloud' and used this data to develop protocols for word processing and problem solving. These protocols are very impressive since they show that trained subjects interacting with the computer very rarely plan in advance or are guided by rational reasoning. Their interaction seems to be chaotic, following a trial and error style (cf. Waern, 1986, for similar results).

Carroll (1985) has shown by empirical evaluation studies that normal computer handbooks, even if they have been designed very carefully following psychological principles, are inadequate for training novices. They give too much information which is also too structured and prevents subjects from self-determined active exploratory learning. 'Minimal Manuals' with short descriptions of basic functions and example tasks are a better alternative for training he argues.

Another theoretically important concept described by Carroll and Mack (1983) is that of 'exploratory environments', i.e. software systems, where the complexity and the risks of errors are artificially lowered for training purposes. Carroll (1985) proposes a 'Minimalist Design' and 'training wheels' where for beginners menu functions are blocked until subjects have learned to master the simpler training versions. The results of evaluation studies of this approach show that the use of Minimal Manuals after exploratory learning increases the speed of performance for typical word processing tasks by about 40%, supports error recovery and promises a substantial reduction of learning time (Carroll, 1985). But these first promising applications of an exploratory learning concept in the field of human–computer interaction still leave important theoretical questions open:

(1) According to Berlyne (1960) it is complexity and novelty that stimulate exploratory activities and not the reduction of complexity as the above-mentioned concept of 'exploratory environments' based on 'Minimalist Design' seems to imply.
(2) Why should an exploratory learning approach take less training time? Exploration theory would suggest the need to spend more time for the acquisition of new knowledge.
(3) How can we enable coping with anxiety, when learners are confronted with novel and complex problems and unavoidable errors?
(4) How can we adapt these principles to take account of individual differences in exploratory learning?

In the following paragraphs we will describe some new design approaches which may give answers to these questions.

The design of exploratory environments: genetic growing systems

Complexity and novelty are basic criteria for the design of 'exploratory environments' which (following theory) are expected to stimulate the acquisition of new knowledge and innovative problem solving through exploratory activities. Only if complexity is too high for the individual adaptation level and knowledge base can a negative influence on exploration be assumed. The 'Minimalist Design' concept seems to be adequate for this special case (e.g. in the training of novices with very low background knowledge and high anxiety). But in general we have to enlarge the complexity and novelty for the design of 'exploratory environments'. Müller (1989) has shown that for students with background computer knowledge and high competencies to cope with complexity a 'Minimalist Design' results in underload, negative emotional feelings and lower exploratory activities in the learning process.

But computer novices obviously profit from the reduction of complexity of software systems (Greif, 1989). These results support the theoretical assumption that for activating exploratory knowledge acquisition we have to design environments with different levels of complexity and novelty depending on the individual knowledge bases and competencies of the subjects to cope with complexity. From a developmental (psychological) view a design solution with differing complexity levels and a stepwise differentiation and integration of complexity in the process of knowledge acquisition should be an ideal solution.

Palme (1983) designed a prototype database system encouraging a stepwise growth of user knowledge. The first level of the system is a simple menu. The higher levels are stepwise enabling the user to reach a good understanding to command language level. Such systems which support a natural stepwise cognitive development and growth of the user may be called 'genetic growing systems' (Greif, 1988). The essential principle of genetic growing systems is the facilitation of the natural development of schemata beginning with simple 'direct manipulatory' systems (see Shneiderman, 1987) and advancing to complex and flexible systems, integrating menu and command language systems, based on complex and abstract knowledge. The system also has to be adaptable to individual learning differences and abilities to cope with the complexity of the system.

Günther Gediga (1989) in our MBQ-Project* has designed a prototype multifunctional office system, which is called the 'individual System (iS)' and which is designed using the following principles:

(1) Task orientation (adapted to the task).
(2) Individualization (adapted to the individual).
(3) Genetic growth.
(4) Application of the exploratory learning-by-errors concept for training and implementation (see below).

On each level of our prototype genetic growing system users are able to do simple but complete tasks. The appropriate level of complexity of the system depends on the occupational task. Complex tasks cannot be managed adequately by software systems with a simple structure and a small number of functions which have very limited possibilities of combination. Complex tasks on the other hand demand knowledge of complex menu systems or knowledge of the syntax of condensed commands (normally the most efficient solution for professionals).

---

*The project 'Multifunktionale Büro-Software und Qualifizierung (MBQ)' (Multifunctional Office-Software and Qualification) is supported by the West German Government, Minister of Research and Technology, 'Humanization of Working Life Program' and conducted by the Work and Organizational Psychology Unit, University of Osnabrück.

Adaptation of complexity levels in the learning process: self-organized learning

A genetic growing and individualized systems design should theoretically help us to solve the problem of individual differences (see Ackermann and Ulich, 1987) in knowledge bases and competencies to cope with complexity if we allow the subjects to determine the level—i.e. individual adaptation of the system. Therefore such a systems design can be an essential tool for individualization and self-organized learning.

In our training courses the subjects determine which tasks they want to try and at what pace they progress using different levels of the system (see below). Self-organized training is not possible in a typical classroom setting with an instructing teacher. Rather the subjects are encouraged to develop their own individual way of learning and to seek the help of the trainers and other trainees when they experience difficulties (Greif, 1989).

Exploratory learning by errors

At the Work and Organizational Psychology Unit, University of Osnabrück, we have conducted several evaluation studies based on Carroll's assumptions and techniques (Greif and Janikowski, 1987; Mangel and Lohmann, 1988; Greif, 1988, 1989; Müller, 1989). Like Carroll we evaluate exploratory learning by developing Minimal Manuals and presenting subjects with tasks which require self-organized problem solving. But before encouraging manipulative explorations of the software system, we instruct the learners to visually explore the system components which are needed for the special task. For example, we show slides of the keyboard and ask the subjects to find specific keys on their own keyboard without depressing them. Later we use 'Orientation Posters', pictographic maps showing the necessary steps for action (see Greif, 1989). By supporting 'distance exploration' (see above) we hope to reduce the anxiety associated with novel and complex tasks.

After each phase of 'distance exploration' the trainer stimulates self-determined manipulative exploration and playful applications of the newly acquired knowledge. This is done by stimulating the subjects to choose between different types of tasks they are working on in the training (routine, exploratory, error detection or self-invented tasks). The role of the trainer is not that of a teacher or instructor. It is basically the role of a counsellor who advises and supports the learners in how to use the prepared task descriptions—Minimal Manuals, Orientation Posters and other learning resources. The trainees determine how much time they will invest on special types of tasks, which learning resources they use and which levels of the genetic growing system they choose.

Applying modern software systems, errors are unavoidable. As a result of errors the level of complexity is often raised substantially and the individual is often confronted with new problems. If in industrial applications the risks and costs of errors are high and standard routines are insufficient the organization is constrained to develop innovative problem solutions.

Innovative modifications of software design and training concepts are necessary if we want to lower the risks of complex error problems in modern software systems for personal computers and work stations. For example, if the user of a typical modern word processor system unintentionally changes a single attribute of the printing format, this may change the page layout completely and the printing can be disturbed (e.g. break down, print page numbers in the middle of the pages, numbers of all lines etc.). Simple errors with even more complex consequences will result from minor changes of numbers and letters in the so-called configuration files of the hard disk of the system. (These files contain basic information for the operating system, e.g. which keyboard is installed. They normally can be edited by any word processor.) Deleting or modifying a single sign in such a file may cause a breakdown of the whole system or radical changes in the functioning of the hard disk system, the keyboard etc. The experience of practitioners in the field is, that these or other complicated error situations occur frequently. It is very difficult for learners and even experienced users to detect the origins of such unintentional errors and they often have to study the handbook for more information or need professional help.

Complex and novel error situations will overload many learners (e.g. typists or students) and even professional users. Our training therefore concentrates on 'exploratory learning by errors' (Greif, 1988) following three basic principles:

(1) Make errors! You can learn from your errors!
(2) Error-tasks: diagnosis and problem solving competencies.
(3) Social support and personal help network.

We make our subjects familiar with the fact that making errors when working with computer systems is unavoidable. This, of course, does not mean that we reinforce error making. The essential principle is to redefine errors as learning situations for which emotional and cognitive coping strategies have to be developed. Cognitive coping strategies are developed by training subjects to use an heuristic schema for systematic error diagnosis and a schema for systematic problem solving. The consequent feelings of self-efficacy and competence as well as practice involving these methods may together contribute to the development of persistence of self-determined exploratory learning and problem solving in their interactions with computers.

Instead of relying on online help systems alone, we prefer to encourage trainees to seek and give personal social support in the training setting. We see this as a basis of a personal help network for trainees when they return to their organizations. The training situation can thus facilitate the establishment of long-term learning partnerships and group meetings of organizational members exchanging knowledge about the efficient and productive use of the computer system. These meetings can be the nucleus of special quality circles. Since such quality circles of software users guided by the former trainer make innovations at work more likely and since the costs of these meetings are comparatively low, any organization can utilize and benefit from the readiness of most trainees to engage in such knowledge exchange.

Compared to traditional tutorial systems exploratory learning by errors does not take more training time (Greif and Janikowski, 1987). While confirming the results of Carroll (1985) this still requires us to explain the unexpected and theoretically inconsistent finding that less time is necessary for exploratory knowledge acquisition. Perhaps exploratory learning is more efficient because other approaches need extra time to overcome inherent problems. In a study by Greif and Janikowski (1987), we observed the behaviour of a group instructed by a WordStar tutorial where the subjects were allowed to repeat the single training lessons as often as they wanted. Some subjects repeated the lessons up to four times. At the end of the training seminar they still felt that they were unable to perform elementary tasks (which was confirmed by subsequent tests). This may explain why the subjects instructed by tutorial or other traditional approaches (see Carroll, 1985) need more training time in comparison to exploratory learning groups.

Several evaluation studies have demonstrated the practical value of our approach (Frese, 1988; Greif and Janikowski, 1987; Mangel and Lohmann, 1988) but we are not proposing that exploratory learning by errors should be seen as the 'one best way' of training. For formalized tasks or tasks with high safety risks other techniques or combinations of techniques will justifiably be preferred. The value of the exploratory learning approach is the acquisition of new knowledge of complex and dynamically changing environments. Since the analysis of the acquisition process of new knowledge is a basic problem of creativity and innovation research, the exploratory learning by errors as applied in the computer field may be relevant also for the design of other innovative learning environments.

The complexity versus simplicity dilemma in organizations

Some brief comments on the organizational implications of genetic growing software design may be useful. Organizations which have to buy a software system for their members face the complexity vs. simplicity dilemma (Greif and Gediga, 1989). To choose the most complex software or most efficient professional system may be not an optimum strategy. Managers with extremely complex jobs who only very seldom use computer systems are likely not to want to be overloaded by complicated software. They will therefore prefer simple, 'low level' systems without any unnecessary or risky functions. It would be inefficient and stressful to train this group for handling complicated and risky technical systems they only seldom need.

But these influential managers should not decide that their assistants or secretaries also have to use their preferred simple versions of the program. Organizational members whose regular tasks can be more efficiently and professionally performed by complex multifunctional software systems should be trained to use 'high level' systems. In organizations it may also be valuable to make use of quality circles and experts who can develop or adapt the programs to special tasks or positions. Since these different program versions will have to meet strict standards of compatibility, an efficient solution for an organization wide software system would be a genetic growing system like the iS which integrates different but compatible versions and operational levels for a large range of tasks or positions.

As the example shows, genetic growing software systems allow for a better adaptation of the software system to different tasks, positions and frequencies of usage in the organization. This should result not only in an overall gain in efficiency for the whole organization but also in fewer conflicts about technological progress in the organization when professionals advocate advances in complexity for their system levels while occasional users resist adapting to a new system. The genetic growing systems design therefore seems to be an approach which solves the complexity vs. simplicity dilemma in organizations.

EXPLORATION AND INNOVATION AT WORK

How do exploration and innovation at work relate? In the following section we will summarize the principles for the design of exploratory environments from our theoretical background, research and application in the field of human–computer interaction and indicate what we see as the major theoretical relations and some important practical implications of our approach for innovation at work.

The design of exploratory work and learning environments

Exploring a new computer or software system can be regarded as applying the principles of an acquisition process of complex new knowledge. We become experts through exploratory experiences. For successful learning acquisition process, however, the learning environment and the learning resources have to be designed carefully according to the following principles:

(1) Opportunities for different exploratory behavioural elements (distance exploration, manipulatory exploration and play) and activation of different senses.

(2) A stepwise 'genetic growing' learning environment.

(3) Self-determined progress to higher complexity levels.

(4) Self-determination of time and pauses.

(5) Aesthetically designed learning tasks and resources (sets of different tasks, Minimal Manuals, Orientation Posters, strategies for error diagnosis and problem solving etc.) which can be used in a self-organized learning process.

(6) Counsellors who are trained to support trainees individually to engage in self-organized learning processes.

(7) Development of a social network of supportive trainees helping each other in the training seminar and back home at the work place.

The design of exploratory work and learning environments that we described is itself an innovation in training and systems design in industry. The majority of our examples come from the field of human–computer interaction—but other examples of exploratory learning were also described, e.g. the advanced 'Hands-on Science' approach of modern museum teaching and the design of work environments. The underlying implication of this work is that the approach may be applied to facilitate the acquisition of new knowledge and innovation at work in general. Psychologists and designers might fruitfully cooperate in developing work and training environments which stimulate individual growth and innovation through self-determined exploratory learning and knowledge acquisition by applying these design principles.

West and Farr (1989) present a comprehensive definition of innovation (see West and Farr, Chapter 1 in this volume). Innovations can be 'new and different ideas, processes, products or procedures'. Following this definition we can see that innovations are not only technological developments but also organizational practices and concrete changes of working procedures. Innovations by definition are new for an individual or a group, but need not be unique, according to a general standard of novelty (a defining element of creative products). As West and Farr also emphasize, innovation involves intentionality of benefit for the individual, group, organization or society.

Intentional innovation is most likely to occur in situations which are mastered and in which the individual feels competent. Thus exploratory learning can be regarded as a first and necessary step in the process of innovation implemented by an individual at work. Furthermore it offers a powerful theoretical approach for describing the dialectical relations between innovation and the environment (see West and Farr, 1989; Chapter 1, and Farr and Ford, Chapter 3 in this volume). Factors which facilitate individual innovation contribute to the innovatory resources of the organization.

Structural versus process models of innovation

There are obvious similarities between some of the subconcepts of the structural model of individual innovation at work of West and Farr (1989) and the theory of exploration. West and Farr describe facilitators like challenge and unpredictability as intrinsic job characteristics. Challenge may result from complexity and novelty of the tasks which, following from our arguments, may be assumed to elicit exploratory processes for the acquisition of new knowledge. The relevance of unpredictability or uncertainty for stimulating exploratory behaviour and creativity has been postulated by Berlyne (1960) and further elaborated in the concept of surprise by Charlesworth (1969). Unpredicted error situations are a special case falling into this category. Errors are stressful but also offer chances of necessary work innovation if they help to reduce future risks of expensive errors for the organization and stimulate the development of new knowledge.

Important individual characteristics like confidence and self-efficacy (West and Farr, 1989; Farr and Ford, Chapter 3 in this book) also have their parallel in the theoretical explanations of exploration. But since the theory of exploration is more concerned with microscopic interaction processes between individual and environment and not so much with the development of general structural models of creativity and innovation, these seemingly obvious similarities at the construct level should be interpreted cautiously. Further and more focused research is necessary to bridge the gap between structural models of innovation and process models of exploration.

Looking at process models of work role innovation we also find striking similarities with our process models of human exploration. Nicholson and West (1988) have studied the impact of job changes on the role innovation of managers. They apply the term 'exploration' synonymously for a combination of personal change and 'role innovation' as an adaptation to job change. As the results of their longitudinal study show, role innovation is a positive long-term outcome of work role transitions (Nicholson, 1984). But the 'transition-cycle', transforming the old to a new role is not without 'pre-transition anxiety' as self-reports of the managers show. The more radical the job change is (in terms of employer, function, status and location moves), the larger the resulting anxiety. Therefore even managers whose roles demand a readiness for change experience anxiety and avoidance tendencies, which could be interpreted as natural psychological reactions in the transition cycle and a psychological barrier to innovative changes.

In comparison to job changes the concept of exploration is applied to study micro-changes but there is an interesting analogy between the 'transition-cycle' of job change and the cyclic sequence of behaviour elements of developmental psychological exploration theory. Both concepts describe dialectic interactions of environmental and individual changes, active individuals at the same time acquiring new knowledge and innovatively changing their environment. Both process models also assume that the novelty and complexity of the situation raises anxiety and avoidance tendencies. But individuals who are self-confident can cope with their anxiety and the changes successfully. Following both approaches the long-term pay-off for the individual is individual growth and the returns for the organization are concrete innovations in work procedures and work roles.

Since there is no research linking processes of individuals coping with macro- and micro-changes, it is merely theoretical speculation to assume an analogy between macro- and micro-transition cycles. But it would be valuable to discover if these assumptions can be validated, since this could help us to develop a broad-range process theory of innovation at work and open a new practical field for the innovative design of work and learning environments.

Correspondence address:
Fachbereich Psychologie, Universität Osnabrück, Postfach 4469, D-4500 Osnabrück, West Germany.

REFERENCES

Ackermann, D. and Ulich, E. (1987). The chances of individualization in human–computer interaction and its consequences. In M. Frese, E. Ulich and W. Dzida (Eds.), *Psychological Issues of Human–Computer Interaction in the Work Place*. Amsterdam: North-Holland, pp. 131–146.
Acredolo, L.P. (1979). Laboratory versus home: the effect of environment on the nine-month-old infants' choice of spatial reference system. *Developmental Psychology*, 15, 666–667.
Ausubel, D.P. (1968). *Educational Psychology*. New York: Holt, Rinehart & Winston.
Benson, J.B. and Uzgiris, I.C. (1981). The role of self-produced movement in spatial understanding. Paper presented at the Biennial Meeting of the Society for Research in Child Development. Boston.
Berlyne, D. (1960). *Conflict, Arousal, and Curiosity*. New York: McGraw-Hill.
Bruner, J.S. (1966). *Toward a Theory of Instruction*. Cambridge: Harvard University Press.
Card, S.K., Moran, T.P. and Newell, A. (1983). *The Psychology of Human–Computer Interaction*. Hillsdale, NJ: Erlbaum.
Carroll, J. (1985). Minimalist Design for the active user. In B. Shackle (Ed.), *Human–Computer Interaction, INTERACT '84*. Amsterdam: North-Holland, pp. 39–44.
Carroll, J.N. and Mack, R.L. (1983). Active learning to use a word processor. In W.E. Cooper (Ed.), *Cognitive Aspects of Skilled Typewriting*. Berlin: Springer, pp. 259–282.
Charlesworth, W.R. (1969). The role of surprise in cognitive development. In D. Elkind and J.H. Flavell (Eds.), *Studies in Cognitive Development*. Oxford: Oxford University Press, pp. 257–314.
Cohen, R., Weatherford, D.L. and Byrd, D. (1980). Distance estimates of children as

a function of acquisition and response activities. *Journal of Experimental Child Psychology*, 30, 464–472.

Ellis, H.D. (1975). Recognizing faces. *British Journal of Psychology*, 66, 409–426.

Frese, M. (1987). A theory of control and complexity: implications for software design and integration of computer systems into the work place. In M. Frese, E. Ulich and W. Dzida (Eds.), *Psychological Issues of Human–Computer Interaction in the Work Place*. Amsterdam: North-Holland, pp. 313–338.

Frese, M. (1988). Training zur Mensch-Computer-Interaktion. Referat, gehalten auf dem 36. Kongress der Deutschen Gesellschaft für Psychologie vom 3.–6. Oktober 1988 an der Technischen Universität Berlin (West).

Gediga, G. (1989). Das Funktionshandbuch zum System iS. Osnabrück, paper published in *Ergebnisse des Projekts MBQ*, No. 15/89 (Special Issue).

Gibson, J.L. (1979). *The Ecological Approach to Visual Perception*. Boston: Houghton Mifflin Comp.

Gregory, (1988). *Hands-on Science*. London: Duckworth.

Greif, S. (1988). Genetic growing systems and self-controlled training. Paper presented at the Swedish-German HdA/MDA-Workshop on the Humanization of Working Life, Stockholm, December 1988. Published in *Ergebnisse des Projekts MBQ*, 9–89 (Special Issue).

Greif, S. (1989). Exploratorisches Lernen durch Fehler und qualifikationsorientiertes Software-Design. In S. Maas and H. Oberquelle (Eds.), *Software-Ergonomie '89. Aufgabenorientierte Systemgestaltung und Funktionalität. Gemeinsame Fachtagung des German Chapter der ACM und Gesellschaft für Information in Hamburg.* Stuttgart: Teubner, S., pp. 204–202.

Greif, S. and Gediga, G. (1989). Individual office-software and organizational change: a project on the development of an adaptable multifunctional program. Contribution for the 4th West European Congress on Psychology of Work and Organisation. Cambridge, 10–12 April 1989.

Greif, S. and Janikowski, A. (1987). Aktives Lernen durch systematische Fehlerexplortation oder programmiertes Lernen durch Tutorials? *Zeitschrift für Arbeits- und Organisationspsychologie*, 31, 94–99.

Herman, J.F. and Siegel, A.W. (1978). The development of cognitive mapping of the large-scale environment. *Journal of Experimental Child Psychology*, 26, 389–406.

Hutt, C. (1970). Specific and diversive exploration. In H.W. Reese and L.P. Lipsitt (Eds.), *Advances in Child Development and Behavior*, Vol. 5. New York: Academic Press, pp. 120–180.

Kaplan, S. (1987). Aesthetics, affect, and cognition: environmental preference from an evolutionary perspective. *Environment and Behavior*, 19 (1), 3–32.

Keller, H. and Boigs, R. (1990). Entwicklung des Explorationsverhaltens. In H. Keller (Ed.), *Handbuch der Kleinkindforschung*. Heidelberg: Springer (in press).

Keller, H., Gauda, G. and Schölmerich, A. (1985). Die Entwicklung des Explorationsverhaltens. Bericht für die Deutsche Forschungsgemeinschaft. Osnabrück.

Kranes, M. (1987). Children's museums: a play-ful development. *Mothers Today*, May–June, 20–23.

Mangel, I. and Lohmann, D. (1988). Alternative Trainingsmethoden für ein Textverarbeitungsprogramm. Unpublished thesis (Diplomarbeit), Department of Psychology, University of Osnabrück.

McCall, R.B. (1979). The development of intellectual functioning in infancy and the prediction of late IQ. In J.D. Oslofsky (Ed.), *Handbook of Infant Development*, 1st edition. New York: Wiley, pp. 707–741.

Müller, M. (1989). Exploratorisches Lernen mit eine gestuften System. Unpublished thesis (Diplomarbeit).

Neber, H. (1981, Ed.). *Entdeckendes Lernen*. Weinheim: Beltz.

Nicholson, N. (1984). A theory of work role transitions. *Administrative Science Quarterly*, **29**, 172–191.

Nicholson, N. and West, M. (1988). *Managerial Job Change. Men and Women in Transition*. Cambridge: Cambridge University Press.

Nunally, J.C. and Lemond, L.C. (1973). Exploratory behavior and human development. In H.W. Reese (Ed.), *Advances in Child Development and Behavior*, Vol. 8. New York: Academic Press, pp. 60–109.

Palme, J. (1983). A human–computer interface encouraging user growth. In M.E. Sieme and M.J. Koombs (Eds.), *Designing for Human–Computer Communication*. London: Academic Press, pp. 139–156.

Ruff, H.A. (1982). Effect of object movement on infants' detection of object structure. *Developmental Psychology*, **18**, 462–472.

Schneider, K., Moch, M., Sandfort, R., Auerwald, M. and Walther-Wckman, K. (1983). Exploring a novel object by preschool children: a sequential analysis of perceptual, manipulating and verbal exploration. *International Journal of Behavioural Development*, **6**, 477–496.

Schölmerich, A. (1990). Informationsaufnahme und -sicherung während des Explorationsprozesses. Osnabrück: Department of Psychology (in preparation).

Schölmerich, A. and Keller, H. (1987). Problemlösen und Exploration. Vortrag, gehalten auf der Tagung für Entwicklungspsychologie, Bern.

Shneiderman, B. (1987). *Designing the User Interface*. Reading, Mass.: Addison-Wesley.

Volpert, W. (1988). What working and learning conditions are conductive to human development? Paper presented at the Swedish-German HdA/MDA-Workshop on the Humanization of Working Life, Stockholm, December 1988.

Voss, H.G. (1984). Curiosity, exploration and anxiety. In H.M. van der Ploeg, R. Schwarzer and C.D. Spielberger (Eds.), *Advances in Anxiety Research, Vol. 3*. Hilldale, NJ: Erlbaum.

Voss, H.G. and Keller, H. (1983). *Curiosity and Exploration. Theories and Results*. New York: Academic Press.

Voss, G. and Keller, H. (1986). Curiosity and exploration. A program of investigation. *German Journal of Psychology*.

Voss, H.G. and Meyer, H.J. (1987). Entwicklung explorativen Verhaltens in der frühen Kindheit (2. bis 4. Lebensjahr) und Genese des Neugiermotivs. Darmstadt: Bericht für die Stiftung Volkswagenwerk (unpublished paper).

Waern, Y. (1986). Learning computerized tasks. In *Human Factors in Information Technology*, No. 8, Series issued by The Cognitive Seminar Department of Psychology, University of Stockholm.

West, M. and Farr, J. (1989). Innovation at work: psychological perspectives. *Social Behaviour*, **4**, 15–30.

Wohlwill, J.F. (1976). Environmental aesthetics: the environment as a source of affect. In I. Altman and J.F. Wohlwill (Eds.), *Human Behavior and Environment*. New York: Plenum Press, pp. 37–86.

12 Facilitating innovation in large organizations

Robert Rosenfeld[1] and Jenny C. Servo[2]

[1]Idea Connection Systems Inc., and [2]Dawnbreaker Inc.,
Rochester, USA

INTRODUCTION

Carl greeted us with a soft-spoken voice. His stature was slight. As he spoke his eyes danced. It was clear that we were about to interview a corporate treasure.

We entered his office in the Research Labs. What a sight! Yellow Post-it notes, glowing with the thoughts of the day, stuck to the shelves of his voluminous bookcase.

'What are all the Post-its, Carl?,' we asked.

'There are no provisions for new ideas, so I keep them posted in my office until I need them,' he said.

Within large organizations innovation faces special problems. As size increases, there is a tendency towards greater depersonalization coupled with a decrease in lateral and vertical communication. Many employees feel like faceless numbers—their position in the structure clearly identified by job descriptions and departmental assignments. In an attempt to protect the growing organizational assets, procedures are put in place. Over time, the organization becomes more rigid and the culture more uniform. Such organizations recognize that within the dynamic world in which we all exist, innovation is essential. Yet, large organizations face a dilemma. They must allow for change while still maintaining a high degree of organizational integrity. In practice, this is extremely difficult to do (Adams, 1976; Andrews, 1975; Shephard, 1967; Van Gundy, 1985).

Innovation and Creativity at Work   Edited by M.A. West and J.L. Farr

The intent of this chapter is to present a model referred to as the 'Office of Innovation', which has been implemented within more than ten Fortune 200 corporations. It is an employee involvement program which draws upon the human resources of the organization. From a financial perspective this model offers a high return on investment; from an administrative perspective it allows one to pace the rate of change; from a humanistic perspective it allows the 'mavericks' a way to contribute more fully to the organization. To understand the model and its adaptation to different environments, attention will initially be given to definitions, roles, and communication gaps.

DIFFERENCES BETWEEN CREATIVITY AND INNOVATION

Many people believe 'creativity' and 'innovation' are synonymous, but they are different. Creativity refers to the generation of novel ideas—innovation to making money with them. Creativity is the starting point for any innovation: in many cases, a solitary process, conjuring up the image of an eccentric scientist buried under mounds of papers, or of an artist surrounded by half-finished canvases and multicolored palettes. Innovation is the hard work that follows idea conceptions and usually involves the labor of many people with varied, yet complementary, skills. The challenge is to transform creative ideas into tangible products or processes that will improve customer services, cut costs and/or generate new earnings for an organization (Levitt, 1963; Rosenfeld and Servo, 1984).

Simply put,

$$\text{Innovation} = \text{Conception} + \text{Invention} + \text{Exploitation}.$$

In this context, the word 'conception' refers to an idea that is novel with respect to some frame of reference (individual, departmental, organizational, or all accumulated knowledge); the word 'invention' applies to any novel idea that is transformed into reality; and the word 'exploitation' refers to getting the most out of an invention. Therefore, 'exploitation' normally implies wide acceptance and/or profitability resulting from the invention. 'Conception, invention, and exploitation' are all necessary ingredients for innovation. The challenge facing large organizations of all types is to reduce the time among these three stages. This can be accomplished by wisely releasing the creative potential of individual employees and empowering them to contribute to the goals of the corporation.

Harnessing an idea and transforming its potential into reality requires turning around the thinking of many people holding claim to resources needed to fuel an idea's growth (financing, information, human resources).

Innovation almost always involves a prolonged battle amongst numerous people and requires tremendous stamina and confidence on the part of a champion (Schon, 1963; Servo, 1988).

INNOVATION PLAYERS

Most large organizations contain individuals who informally promote innovation through their roles as 'ideators', 'inventors', 'technology gatekeepers', 'champions', 'sponsors', and 'entrepreneurs (or intrapreneurs)'. With the exception of inventors and entrepreneurs, these players are frequently not distinguishable to themselves or others. Individuals do not tend to think of themselves as champions, technology gatekeepers, or sponsors. Human Resource departments are also unaccustomed to classifying employees according to these informal roles that are so vital to innovation. Instead, they tend to focus on formal job descriptions, as these are key to performance appraisals. The recognition of these players within an organization is an important first step in facilitating innovation.

An 'ideator' is a prolific idea generator who, by definition, does not like to 'reduce ideas to practice' (i.e. make a prototype), but would rather restrict the ideas to the realm of mental gymnastics. Ideation appears to almost be a form of play. As soon as the ideator's feet hit the floor in the morning, he or she starts to generate countless possibilities. The motivation for the ideator is quite varied: playfulness, fear of failure, and stress reduction are but a few. In many situations, this process is difficult for the ideator to control—ideas just flow.

'Inventors' like to reduce ideas to practice; in fact, they savor it. For them, the challenge is in solving the problem—in putting the solution into a tangible form. More likely than not, their inventions are not initially in a marketable form. There is a *New Yorker* cartoon which depicts various inventions for 'keeping warm': prominent among these are a waterbottle tie and a catnip comforter covered, of course, with cats—practical solutions in the inventor's mind, but would require a master salesman!

Organizations often forget that for an inventor, the joy comes in savoring the solution. Within R & D environments, a project may frequently be stopped or transferred to another department before the inventor has had the opportunity to reap the joy that comes from full explorations of their work. 'It's like a Christmas present' one inventor said. 'If it's for you, you would want to open it yourself. You wouldn't just hand it over to someone else to open. You'd like to delight in its unveiling. Once you've had an opportunity to enjoy it, to see it, you wouldn't mind letting others share it.'

Another important role that is frequently overlooked is that of 'technology gatekeeper'. Often they are viewed by their organizations as technology experts and are used by the organization and individuals for 'reality checks'. For technology gatekeepers, the motivation is to keep on the 'cutting edge'.

A 'champion' has status or clout and advocates on behalf of others. Champions, in fact, help legitimize the idea originator, serving as a bridge, or a translator between the sometimes unconventional idea originator (ideator or inventor) and the more traditional organization.

A 'sponsor' usually has higher status within an organization and a proven track record. By definition, the sponsor also has resources (money, people, equipment) and applies them towards the development of an idea. His or her motivation is usually for strategic gain of their organization, the corporation, or the individual. By connecting with other players in the innovation process, this role ultimately brings great benefit to the corporation in increased earnings and development of personnel.

Finally there is 'the entrepreneur' the individual, calculated risk-taker whose primary drive is to start and develop a new organization, new product, or new process that will profit and thrive.

All of these players are essential for innovation. Yet in American culture, we tend to make folk heroes only of the inventors and entrepreneurs. Perhaps the champions, technology gatekeepers, and sponsors suffer from a lack of press—little glamour or apparent risk attached to their roles. Their roles, however, are essential. Imagine, if you will, a beaver standing at the base of Hoover Dam, saying 'Well, it was my idea'. You can see the absurdity of 'single-handed acceptance' of the responsibility for making anything a commercial success.

INNOVATION AS A RELAY RACE

This cast of players exists without designation in every large organization embedded within a formal structure characterized by bureaucracy, strategic focus, budgetary constraints, and limited time. Innovation players, in their effort to get their idea through the corporate labyrinth, play what can best be likened to a relay race. However, unlike the relay races to which we are accustomed, a player in this team will not, at the outset, know the names of the other players, nor their location within the organization (Rosenfeld, 1984).

The idea itself is analogous to the baton. Each member of the relay race needs to entice others to be on the team. Frequently this is accomplished by changing the baton's form as it is in motion. At times, the relay race may have the appearance of a rugby game, as players move downfield together at the same time, each playing their specific role. However, the goal line may be unclear and the rules of the game are constantly being revised.

The innovation process is complex. If one does not appreciate the complexity of the process, both the ideas and the players will falter. Common places for an idea to be dropped within complex organizations are with (1) the idea originator, (2) middle management, and (3) across organizational boundaries.

COMMUNICATION GAPS

A communication gap occurs at each juncture where an idea may be dropped. The *first communication gap* lies within the idea originator. He or she may fail to take the idea to another for fear of ridicule. This is not without cause. We tend to 'turn each other off' very readily with a casual phrase or sneer. An idea or an invention, however, is like someone's child. The use of a 'killer phrase' such as 'Well, if that's such a great idea, why hasn't someone else done it?' is like telling a parent that their child has no talent.

Fear of the idea's theft, lack of time, or lack of incentives may also be deterrents to the idea originator. We inadvertently tend to reinforce individuals for keeping their ideas to themselves. Often, the risk of sharing is far greater than keeping an idea to oneself. When stepping forth with an idea, an individual may open himself up to personal rejection. 'I don't care how good the idea is, I don't like you and won't give it the time of day.' Such statements are not explicitly stated to the idea originator, but frequently surface behind closed doors.

If an employee overcomes this first hurdle and exercises one of the various informal roles in innovation through the traditional corporate structure, his or her efforts may be poorly received. If an idea originator takes the idea to management prematurely, he or she may get little action. Many managers are chronically overextended and may view a new idea as an annoyance, or at best, a distraction that interferes with assigned objectives.

Additionally, if the idea is extremely complex or tangential to a manager's assigned work, he may simply not know what to do with it. Many organizations fail to disclose the corporate mission, strategy, and business objectives to their employees, fearing that knowledge of this would provide the competition with an advantage. A consequence of this approach is that many managers within one division will not know what is important to another division, as well as the overall corporation. It is, therefore, unreasonable to expect that first-line or even middle management would necessarily have the perspective or information needed to deal effectively with all ideas that are brought to their attention (*second communication gap*).

In actuality, the expertise needed to evaluate complex ideas is housed within different sectors of large, highly bureaucratic, and mature organizations: in research and development, marketing, manufacturing, administration, finance, etc. However, the physical separation, differences in jargon, and differences in mode of operation present yet a *third communication gap*.

Crossing organizational barriers is very difficult. The 'not invented here (NIH)' phenomenon is quite prevalent in many organizations. Many times an idea will be rejected simply because it has come from outside the department. It is viewed as a 'foreign body' invading the department, rather than something which could be of potential value.

IDEA CONNECTIONS

There are numerous opportunities for an idea to be dropped and few occasions for it to be carried through. Many formal and informal approaches have been instituted to prevent ideas from faltering. Heroic efforts have been made by inventors to push their ideas through bureaucratic mazes. Individuals such as Charles Kettering, former Director of R & D for General Motors, have taken it upon themselves to 'buck the system' by developing their own style for dealing with the organizational barriers to innovation. They have bootlegged time (i.e. used discretionary time on the job), found contact people in various sectors of the company, and in general done outlandish things in order to get a hearing for their idea. However, not every idea originator has the know-how, the drive, and the aggressiveness to do so. Many employees and organizations could benefit from a structure that acts as a conduit to help ideas flow more readily through an organization.

THE OFFICE OF INNOVATION

Various structures have been initiated to help facilitate innovation including the 'Office of Innovation' model developed at the Eastman Kodak Company during the late 1970s. This type of model has been implemented by many other large organizations including American Greeting Cards, Amoco Chemical Company, Atomic Energy of Canada, Bell Canada, Electronic Surveillance Command of the United States Air Force, Northwestern Bell, and Union Carbide. This system provides a mechanism for drawing together a cast of informal innovation players around ideas which are often not part of one's assigned work (Rosenfeld and Servo, 1988).

The 'Office of Innovation' is the name of a process that is used to evaluate complex ideas. In other organizations this model may be referred to as 'The New Ideas Process', 'Aviary', 'Discovery', 'The Innovation Network' and the like. The 'Office of Innovation' (OI) transcends the interests of individual departments, thereby allowing for cross-fertilization of ideas among divisions. It operates as a conduit for ideas to flow freely throughout an organization.

This model coexists with other idea systems within the organization that are designed to handle different types of ideas and/or clientele (i.e. suggestion systems and quality circles).

An OI can be a highly decentralized network of individual offices located in various client areas (marketing, sales, manufacturing, R & D). The more decentralized the network, the greater the success. It is in essence a 'point of sale' operation located in various client areas. The office is a physical location that is readily discernible to employees and is staffed by facilitators, referred to as innovation facilitators, connectors, idea facilitators, etc. The idea flow rate is directly proportional to the number of 'Office' sites—the more sites, the greater the idea flow. These staff members have the designated responsibility to seek out and attract individuals who informally play various roles within the innovation process. In this model, people who bring their ideas to the OI (ideators and inventors) are referred to as idea originators; technology gatekeepers serve as consultants; and champions and sponsors are designated in the traditional way.

It takes considerable time and ingenuity to find out who these informal players are, but once discerned, the model performs very well and can be relied upon to enrich, screen, and find sponsorship within the organization for a good number of complex ideas. For example, after several years of operation within the Eastman Kodak Company, the estimated value of ideas harvested in one year alone was approximately $300 million (over the life-time of the idea) while the cost of connecting the ideas through an OI network containing 19 offices was only 0.3% of the potential revenue (Rosenfeld and Servo, 1988).

Very few ideas that are taken to an OI will be adopted (e.g. four out of 100 at Eastman Kodak Company, 1979–88). Yet after 10 years in operation at the Eastman Kodak Company, satisfaction with the process remains high for idea originators, with over 90% of those responding to surveys indicating that they would continue to use OI. This high rate of satisfaction is attributed to the philosophy which guides each OI (see Table 1).

This philosophy serves as the foundation for the model's success. Each facilitator implements the process with regard to his or her cultural area, in a way consistent with the philosophy. The process used (see Figure 1) provides a systematic approach for idea development, autonomy to an idea originator, and weaves in other players at appropriate times. There are five stages to the process:

(1) Idea generation.
(2) Initial screening.
(3) Group review.
(4) Seeking sponsorship.
(5) Sponsorship.

Table 1 The philosophy of the Office of Innovation

1   Ideas are fragile (so are people)
2   Ideas are organic and need to be nurtured (so do people)
3   All ideas have value and should be given a hearing
4   The originator of an idea needs assistance in idea enhancement and in promoting the idea internally
5   The originator is the initial advocate of an idea and should be actively involved in its development
6   Only ideas which have been enhanced and demonstrate potential value will be brought to management
7   Both marketing and technical issues need to be addressed in the development of an idea
8   Differences among people constitute a strength, not a weakness. Individuals can benefit from the opportunity to interact with other professionals from different perspectives
9   A mediator is often necessary to facilitate the communication of people from different cultures and who may possess clashing personalities
10 The most effective way to proceed is not necessarily the most efficient

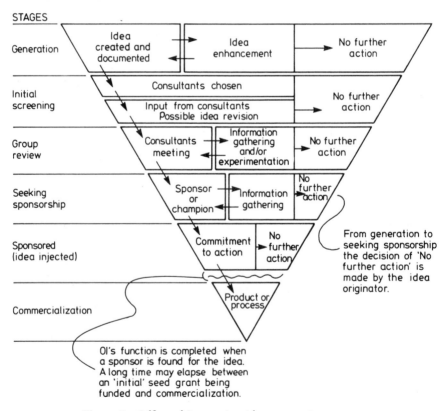

Figure 1   Office of Innovation idea connection process

The process begins with a meeting between the idea originator and a facilitator. The facilitator functions as an advocate of the originator, their guide through the corporate labyrinth, and as their bridge to management. During idea generation, the idea is enriched. The process includes asking the originator to describe the idea, obtaining the reasons for his or her belief of its potential value to the company, and discussing the degree to which technical and marketing concerns have been addressed. If the idea originator wishes to proceed, he or she is then asked to prepare a brief, one or two page description, sometimes referred to as an idea memorandum (IM). Generally, the idea's progress through the process is dependent not only on the quality of the idea and its enhancement, but also upon the amount of drive the originator exerts. If the originator is unable to put in the time and effort required, the OI can only be of limited help (Rosenfeld and Servo, 1985).

If the originator chooses to proceed, he or she enters the next phase referred to as initial screening. Here the facilitator and originator jointly select a group of experts within the organization to review the idea. Many of these are *technology gatekeepers*, and are referred to as consultants. The consultant's involvement is voluntary. Between five and 15 consultants chosen from a large pool of employees, are typically called upon to review any given idea memorandum. This pool of employees is not a fixed stable of designated experts.

The consultants are sent a copy of the idea memorandum along with a brief questionnaire requesting their comments in many areas including: novelty, market needs, and technological feasibility; additions that they would make to improve it; and whether or not they wish to be involved in any further review and/or elaboration of this idea. At the originator's request this stage can proceed as a blind-review, with the originator's name withheld.

The reviews are collected and another meeting scheduled between the facilitator and the idea originator. The goal of this meeting is to review the information provided by the reviewers and to decide jointly how to proceed. The facilitator's role is always similar—responding to the originator's ideas, asking probing questions in a subtle but directive manner, and requiring the individual to make decisions. The decision as to whether or not to proceed is always made by the originator, thus, allowing for his or her growth.

If the decision is made to go ahead, the originator enters the group review stage. This is an individual meeting or series of face-to-face meetings with consultants. The purpose of these meetings is to gather more information and hopefully some assistance and/or resources. If the group review process goes well, the next step may include some experimentation, market research, or prototype development. These tasks may be conducted by the originator or one or more of the consultants who may have expressed a willingness to help. Any time invested by the originator or consultants is on a voluntary or bootleg basis.

As more and more information is gathered and the idea is further enhanced, its value to the organization becomes more apparent. It soon becomes necessary to shift to the fourth stage of the process referred to as seeking sponsorship. Here, the major objective is to find at least a champion, and hopefully an internal sponsor for the idea. The idea has now reached dimensions where it requires some assistance by individuals with stature and/ or money to legitimize its growth. The bootleg efforts have reached their limits. More often than not champions and sponsors have a management position within the formal structure. Thus, this stage marks the beginning of the transition from the informal to formal channels of the organization.

As an idea moves through this process, its progress can be charted. An individual facilitator's performance can be viewed by looking at the percentage of ideas that move successfully from one stage to the next (see Figure 2). Based on Kodak's experience, one should expect that 40% to 60% of ideas should be lost during the first two stages, with the idea originators having screened themselves out of the process as a consequence of the feedback they received through the review process. The last stage, shown in Figure 2, is the 'champion' stage, referring to an idea's advocacy by individuals other than

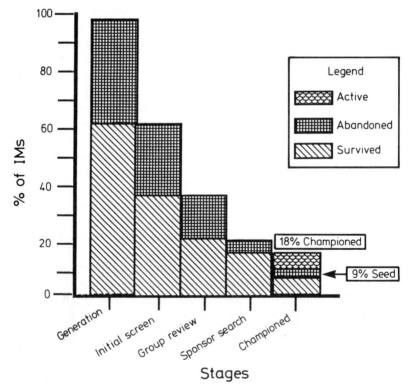

Figure 2 Progression of IMs (idea memoranda) by stage (1985–86) in the Eastman Kodak Company

the idea originator. Eighteen percent of the ideas reached this stage. 'Seed' sponsored (a subset of the champion stage), designates that funding has been provided by a department as a clear budgeted line-item. Nine percent of the ideas reached this stage. At this point it is up to the host organization to nurture further development of the idea. The Office of Innovation's role is completed.

Another benefit of such a system is that it enables one to learn about the human resources of the organization in a different way:

'Until recently,' Carl said 'there were no provisions for new ideas, so I kept them in my files until a need arose. If someone needed something, then I would contribute solutions from my file; but unless there was a need, it was a waste of time to try and peddle them.

Then the emphasis came on innovation. I was really surprised to see that the Innovation System worked. They disseminated my ideas, found interested people, and sponsors for a number of them.'

This idea originator was modest. His ideas were not only prolific, but extremely valuable to the company. Within the space of just three years, he submitted approximately 15 proposals, more than half of which found champions or sponsors, with projected value in the millions of dollars.

Using an Idea-O-Graph, the contributions of individuals can be charted (see Figure 3). The Idea-O-Graph is a plot of different levels of corporate commitment to an idea over a period of time. The level of commitment increases monetary outlay as the corporation commits to higher levels of an idea's growth. The slope of the line indicates how efficiently an organization implements an idea's growth from origination through commercialization. The slope will vary according to the type of idea being implemented. For example, a sales idea will be easier to implement and show a steeper slope (e.g. takes less time from origination to commercialization) than one requiring a new technology involving research and development. By comparing similar projects and their slopes along the graph, one learns how long it takes the organization to transform an idea into a business reality. This graphic representation of idea growth provides information that will assist in the optimization of the stages of the innovation process. This can be extremely valuable knowledge for an organization, making them aware of special skills and how ideas evolve in their company.

Office of Innovation facilitators can act as a guide for those involved with innovation. They make the organizational labyrinth less treacherous, make it easier to find the other team members, help groom the baton before passing it along, assist management by providing them with mature ideas for review and generally increase the odds of getting a hearing for ideas within the organization.

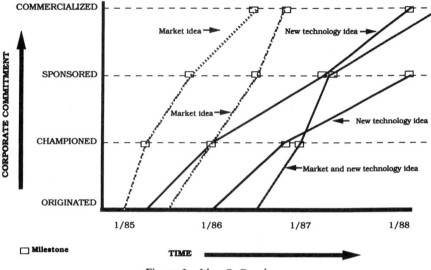

Figure 3   Idea-O-Graph

SUMMARY

The mood in American industry today is highly analytical. There is the tendency to look for quick formulas, for ways to maximize efficiency, and as mentioned at the outset, to view employees in a depersonalized way. Often employees are moved around an organization with the same consideration that one would have for a table or chair. In this climate, it is likely that people may look at the Office of Innovation model through analytical eyes.

However, what makes the innovation process work is a truly personalized interaction between facilitators and the cast of innovation players. Not everyone can play the role of a facilitator, who, like 'the invisible man', helps to make things happen. This personalized process aims at releasing human potential in a way that will benefit the corporation.

In this regard, we can take a lesson from Japanese corporations. It appears that due to the history and cultural values of Japan, it is easier for the Japanese to suppress their 'egos', focusing instead on the greater good. Transforming an idea into reality therefore becomes less of a problem as individuals are less likely to pose barriers. But, they will instead, 'fall in line' to move an innovation ahead. The difficulty for Japanese corporations is the front end of the innovation process. Their devotion to the group makes it less likely that they will think in creative ways that are tangential to, or radically different from, those of the group.

The problems facing American industry are the opposite and are likewise steeped in our culture. Americans have many creative ideas and find it easier to think tangentially. We have a cultural attachment to images of the 'rugged individualist' and the 'sharp shooters of the old west'. Therefore, we find it difficult to 'line up' behind a common cause. The result is that in large American industry, 'egos' and 'politics' frequently get in the way and often are the rate-limiting steps to innovation and growth of new business opportunities.

One of the positive manifestations of the American 'free-spirit' is entrepreneurial behavior. The Japanese demonstrate unified action. The task, therefore, is to merge the Eastern and Western processes into a new paradigm that will unleash the creative potential and 'free-up' innovative activities while focusing on unified goals of the organization.

Correspondence addresses:
Robert Rosenfeld, Idea Connection Systems Inc., 2065 Highland Avenue, Rochester, New York 14620, USA.
Dr Jenny C. Servo, Dawnbreaker Inc., 3999 Buffalo Road, Rochester, New York 14620, USA.

REFERENCES

Adams, J.S. (1976). Structure and dynamics of behavior in organization boundary roles. In M.D. Dunnette (Ed.), *Handbook of Industrial and Organization Psychology*. Chicago: Rand McNally.

Andrews, F.M. (1975). Social and psychological factors which influence the creative process. In I.A. Taylor and J.W. Getzels (Eds.), *Perspectives in Creativity*. Chicago: Aldine.

Levitt, T. (1963). Creativity is not enough. *Harvard Business Review*, May, 72–83.

Rosenfeld, R. (1984). Innovation through investment in people: The consideration of creative styles. *Creativity Week VII: 1984 Proceedings*. Center for Creative Leadership.

Rosenfeld, R. and Servo, J. (1984). Making ideas connect. *The Futurist*, August, 21–26.

Rosenfeld, R. and Servo, J. (1985). The first step to implementing new and better ideas. *Intrapreneurial Excellence*, November, 4, 6–7.

Rosenfeld, R. and Servo, J. (1988). Innovation through investment in people. Unpublished manuscript.

Schon, A. (1963). Champions for radical new inventions. *Harvard Business Review*, March–April, 84.

Servo, J. (1988). Creativity by itself reaps no profits. *Rochester Business Journal*, Nov. 21–27, 7.

Shephard, H.A. (1967). Innovation-resisting and innovation-producing organizations. *Journal of Business*, **48**, 91–102.

Van Gundy, M. (1985). Organizational creativity and innovation: a review and needed future research. In S.G. Isaksen (Ed.), *Frontiers of Creativity Research: Beyond the Basics*. Buffalo: Bearly Limited.

13 Improving corporate climates for creativity

Robert M. Burnside
Center for Creative Leadership, Greensboro, USA

Organizations are today the 'primary crucible for human development' (Bennis, 1969). As such, they have a great influence on humankind's future development, for better or worse. Much has been said and written about organizations from an external, structural point of view: how they should define their business mission, set their strategies for differential advantage, design their structures and objectify their tasks, to assure the efficient and successful attainment of their economic goals. Indeed, this is how we have tended to think of business: as an external structured mechanical approach to attainment of tangible economic goals. Recently, however, questions have been arising about the internal, less tangible side of our organizations: why does the organization have the purpose it does, what values are inherent in its purpose, how are these values manifested in its culture, and how does this culture affect the motivation and contribution of its employees to the company's purpose? This questioning has spurred the scientific inquiry by the behavioral sciences toward a better understanding of this cultural side of organizations.

At the same time as the above trend, the need to increase creativity and innovation in our organizations has emerged. Driven by the globalization of competition, and the increased pace of change in the situation around them, organizations are questioning whether their products or services are sufficiently innovative to meet the needs of the changing environment. On contemplation of the need to increase creativity and innovation, it becomes apparent that faster, smarter technology will not be enough. The creativity of the human being must be enhanced as well. Thus the question is before the organization: how do we increase the creativity of our employees?

Innovation and Creativity at Work   Edited by M.A. West and J.L. Farr
© 1990 John Wiley & Sons Ltd

These two streams of inquiry, how we can understand the contribution of our culture to the achievement of our company purpose, and how we can increase our creativity, come together in the question: how does the culture of an organization affect the creativity of its employees?

This question has been the focus of a research effort by the Center for Creative Leadership (CCL) and Dr Teresa Amabile of Brandeis University. Dr Amabile is well known for her research into the effect of the social environment on the creativity of the individual. Her research has documented a link between the social environment around an individual and the creativity of the individual's work output (Amabile, 1983). The link is the effect the social environment has on the intrinsic motivation of the individual. One does one's most creative work when one is primarily motivated by the enjoyment of the task itself, and not by extrinsic motivators. Thus the basic theory underlying the CCL research is that organizations can increase their employees' creativity by shaping a social environment that encourages the inner motivation of the employee to emerge and engage with the work task.

The CCL research has had two goals: to identify and measure the factors in organizational climates which affect employee creativity, and to provide an organizational intervention methodology which makes this information useful to organizations which desire to improve their climates for creativity. In this research design, Dr Amabile provided the theoretical and empirical expertise, while CCL provided the client interface and the organizational intervention expertise.

RESEARCH BACKGROUND

Basic research was conducted in 120 'critical incident' interviews with R & D scientists. Each scientist told two stories: one of a work event high in creativity and one of an event low in creativity. The interview transcripts were content analyzed for environmental factors, defined as 'any factors outside of the problem-solvers themselves (including other people) that seemed to consistently influence creativity'. Twenty factors were identified, 10 that were stimulants to creativity, and 10 that were obstacles to creativity. For a complete description of this basic research, see Amabile and Gryskiewicz (1987).

Next, a 96-item instrument, named the 'Work Environment Inventory' (WEI), was constructed to measure the factors identified in the basic research. The items were written using words similar to those the managers used in the interviews. For example, two items written for the factor called 'freedom' were: 'I have the freedom to decide how I am going to carry out my projects' and 'In my daily work environment, I feel a sense of control over my own work and my own ideas'. The empirical development of the WEI has focused on building reliable scales that differentiate from each other. The three revisions of the instrument have led to the current version which measures eight stimulant factors, four obstacle factors, and two criterion scales. The number of factors measured was reduced from the original 20 scales to the current 12 by combining scales that were natural opposites (e.g. 'sufficient time' and 'insufficient time' were combined), and by eliminating scales that performed poorly empirically (e.g. the stimulant scale 'pressure'). Factor analysis also guided scale development. Currently, scales have alphas of 0.75 to 0.90. Two criterion scales were developed which have employees give an overall measure of their organization's creativity and productivity, for use as a soft validation measure. Validation research has also been conducted at one site where independent measures of creativity were compared to the WEI measures, and the WEI was compared to a generic work environment instrument to determine if the WEI in fact measured the environment for creativity, and not just the generic work environment. This project gave basic support for the instrument, but left further work to be done. To date, a sample of over 2000 respondents from over 10 organizations has been collected on the WEI. A CCL Technical Report detailing the empirical work on the WEI is expected in autumn, 1990. See Table 1 for a list of the stimulant and obstacle factors which the WEI is currently measuring. Table 1 also includes two sample items from each scale.

CCL combined the instrument and interview methodology into an organizational intervention process named the 'Innovation Assessment Process' (IAP). In the initial contact, CCL and the client set hoped-for outcomes of the process. Next, CCL collects data using the WEI on an evenly weighted randomly distributed sample of the population in the environment being assessed, and using a small number of face-to-face interviews which replicate the basic research interviews. (For an in-depth review of the assessment technique see Burnside, 1988). CCL then analyzes the data, and prepares a feedback report, which is reviewed with the organization. Finally, CCL facilitates action planning based on the feedback.

THE INTERVENTIONS

Given that the WEI is a reasonably reliable and valid climate assessment instrument, then the question is, how can the data provided be made useful for the organization wishing to improve its climate for creativity? At first thought, it would seem to be an easy four-step process: (1) the client identifies the need to improve their climate for creativity; (2) CCL does the assessment; (3) the data are fed back to the client; and (4) the client acts to improve the climate for creativity and monitors the results. Oh, that someday such a clear process could occur! The actual process is much more complex, messy, and

Table 1 Center for Creative Leadership: brief descriptions of the WEI factors with sample items from each scale

STIMULANTS TO CREATIVITY

Coworkers
Teamwork, willingness to help each other, commitment to the work, and trust with fellow workers.
  In my work group, people are willing to help each other.
  The people in my work group are committed to our work.

Resources
Access to appropriate resources, including facilities, equipment, information, funds, and people.
  The facilities I need for my work are readily available to me.
  Generally I can get the resources I need for my work.

Challenge
Challenge due to the importance of the work and the intriguing nature of the task.
  I feel that I am working on important projects.
  The tasks in my work call out the best in me.

Freedom
Freedom in deciding how to accomplish the task. A sense of control over one's work and ideas.
  I have the freedom to decide how I am going to carry out my projects.
  In my daily work environment I feel a sense of control over my own work and my own ideas.

Supervisor
A manager who gives support to subordinates, communicates effectively, and sets clear goals.
  My supervisor clearly sets overall goals for me.
  My supervisor values individual contributions to project(s).

Creativity supports
Encouragement and support for creativity from top management; mechanisms for developing creative ideas in the organization.
  In this organization top management expects that people will do creative work.
  People are encouraged to take risks in this organization.

Recognition
The existence of rewards and recognition for creativity in the organization.
  People are recognized for creative work in this organization.
  People are rewarded for creative work in this organization.

Unity and cooperation
A shared vision within the organization and a cooperative and collaborative atmosphere.
  There is a generally cooperative and collaborative atmosphere in this organization.
  Overall, the people in this organization have a shared 'vision' of what we are trying to do.

Table 1 continued

OBSTACLES TO CREATIVITY
Insufficient time
The lack of time in which to consider alternative ways of doing the work.
   I have too much work to do in too little time.
   We do not have sufficient personnel for the project(s) I am currently doing.

Status quo
The reluctance of managers or coworkers to change their way of doing things, a generally traditional approach.
   There is much emphasis in this organization on doing things the way we have always done them.
   Management avoids controversial ideas in this organization.

Political problems
Lack of cooperation between areas of the organization, and battles over turf issues.
   People in this organization are very concerned about protecting their territory.
   There are many political problems in this organization.

Evaluation pressure
Perceived inappropriate evaluation or feedback systems, or environment focused on criticism and external evaluation.
   People are quite concerned about negative criticism of their work in this organization.
   People in this organization feel pressure to produce anything acceptable, even if quality is lacking.

CRITERION SCALE (OVERALL RATING BY EMPLOYEES)
Creativity
How creative the organization is overall.
   Overall my current work environment is conducive to my own creativity.
   My area of this organization is creative.

Productivity
How productive the organization is overall.
   My area of this organization is effective.
   Overall this organization is productive.

ambiguous. Following will be a review of CCL's experiences in each of these steps in actual interventions. Then, the current recommended step-wise process will be reviewed.

CCL did a number of interventions between January, 1986, and August, 1988, which included the following clients:

Freight, Inc. The 1100-member sales and marketing division of a Fortune 500 freight transportation company.

Health, Inc. The 120-member marketing and clinical testing division of an international pharmaceutical firm.

Health, Inc. Brazil The entire 900 members of the Brazilian subsidiary of Health, Inc.

Chemical, Inc. The 400 members of the R & D division of a chemical company.

STEP 1: THE CLIENT IDENTIFIES THE NEED TO IMPROVE THE CLIMATE FOR CREATIVITY

The first question is, who is the client?

The client ideally should be the responsible senior manager for the environment being assessed, and his or her direct reports should be involved in the decision to do the assessment process.

At Freight, the vice-president of marketing was clear that his group needed quicker and more creative response to customers due to the recent deregulation of the transportation industry. The over 100 years of regulated history for the firm provided a strong status quo inertia that was difficult to change. After some phone discussions, he met with CCL and ordered the assessment process to begin. At the initial meeting at the client's site, it became clear that this person did not have the sole responsibility for the 1100-member department, but shared it with three other vice-presidents at his same level. However, in this initial meeting they seemed willing to follow his lead and to start the process. But they were all very definite that their superior should not be brought in at this stage, to pre-approve the process before it began. Everything seemed to be going fine until about one month before the feedback meeting at the client's site. The vice-president of marketing was suddenly transferred out of the line. With his leadership on the process gone, his former peers lost interest in following up. Since his superior had not been included on the decision, there was no one higher to assure follow through. In the end, there was little direct impact on improving the climate for creativity. What went wrong? The original sponsoring client was lost in the middle of the process, and the true client—the senior manager over the whole environment—had never been brought on board. Finally, there was from the beginning only lukewarm support from the management team.

A second example of the need to determine who is the client occurred with Health-Brazil. Here, a top level executive in headquarters made the decision that Brazil would be a good place to test out the viability of the Innovation

Assessment Process in a foreign country. The lead manager of the Brazil operations was told to participate. Although not opposed to the process, he felt that there were more important issues that needed addressing than creativity. Nonetheless, for reasons other than his desire to improve the environment for creativity, he went along with the corporate directive. Results from this intervention are occurring only at a slow and somewhat dispirited rate. Here was the wrong client again—this time, too high above the environment being studied.

In the other two interventions, the client was just right: he was the senior leader over the environment being assessed, and he involved his management team in the decision to do the assessment. These two interventions to date have had the most impact.

Be sure to probe the need, and clarify that the process assesses the climate

The second part of step 1 is where the client 'sees the need to improve the climate for creativity'. This is difficult at best. There are two factors involved here. To see a need, a client has to have some idea of where he or she is going, and to see a need to improve the climate for creativity, the client has to have some idea of what a climate is. Let us review the latter problem first.

The concepts of culture and climate are fuzzy at best, even among the so-called experts (Schneider, 1985). Out in the busy worlds of organizations, the concepts have little clarity. This is partly due to the point made in the opening paragraphs of this chapter—educational efforts to date to understand business have focused on the external structured approach to achieving economic goals, and have been relatively silent on understanding the interpersonal and human side of the organization. Thus, managers have few skills in talking about and identifying needs in the area of culture and climate. The CCL definitions for these terms are as follows:

Climate Commonly shared, consciously performed, social interaction behaviors, 'what we do'.

Culture Commonly shared, below conscious level, reality-structuring pictures, which form the basis for climate behaviors, 'why we do what we do'.

Of the four clients, only one, the vice-president of R & D at Chemical, was clear from the start that the problem was cultural. He identified such problems as 'lack of receptivity to new ideas, lack of trust between functional areas, and low levels of enthusiasm for the future, which were caused by excessive employee layoffs in the past few years'.

The other clients, however, initially discussed their needs in terms of output, e.g. 'drug development process is too slow, not enough new products in the pipeline'; 'slow responsiveness to customer requests, too many people involved in decisions'. It is important that the client be clear before the decision is made to begin that the process assesses the climate, and is not a structural or strategic analysis of the organization. In contrast to the concepts of culture and climate, clients seemed to have a good grasp of creativity as a concept, though innovation was often used interchangeably. CCL definitions are similar to theirs: *creativity* is the generation of novel associations (new ideas) that are useful; and *innovation* is the implementation of a creative idea.

Ask how improved creativity will contribute to long-range goals

More difficult than clarification of the concepts of climate and creativity is clarification of whether the client knows why the organization needs increased creativity. David Campbell, Senior Fellow at the Center for Creative Leadership, has a saying, 'If you don't know where you're going, you'll end up somewhere else'. In most cases, clients seem to be more clear on the fact that they want an assessment than on why they need one. There are two reasons it is important for clients to know why they want increased creativity: first, this clarifies the relative importance of this issue to them, and builds their commitment to doing something with the assessment results. Second, the only meaningful comparison measure they have for evaluating their assessment results is their identification of where they want to go in the future.

In the four interventions, there was a common fuzziness about the future long-term goals of the organization. Tangible economic goals were the most clear. After thought, a case could generally be made for the role of increased creativity (as one manager said, 'Who could be against it?'), but the role of a better climate, and how it would help achieve organizational goals, was very unclear. Also, there is a tendency for managers to want to make 'increased creativity' a goal in itself, rather than seeing increased creativity in its proper role as a means towards reaching the long-term goals of the organization.

Most of the mission statements of the clients had some words about human values, but did not include concrete goals for climate behaviors. Thus, in all four of these interventions, clients were choosing to go ahead with the process because of their desire for increased creativity, and with little clarity on what climates are, and how they are changed. (As the old saying goes, 'Ready, fire, aim.') The problem with this lack of clarity up front is that the difficulty of changing human social-interaction behaviors is underestimated, and when the reality of the energy needed for the change effort becomes clear at the end of the process, some managers may back away. Although the discussions may be obtuse and frustrating, they are invaluable, because management's commitment to the process must be clear up front. Also, once the assessment has begun, management has intervened in the organization. The act of collecting data from the employees communicates clearly that change is afoot, and raises employee expectations. Over the exit doorway of the meeting room where management decides to go ahead with the assessment process should be the following notice: 'Beware, you have decided to act, and consequences shall surely follow. Whether they are for better or worse remains to be seen, and depends on your follow-up actions.'

STEP 2: THE ASSESSMENT IS CARRIED OUT

The assessment consists of three steps: determine the sample and the data groups; collect the data; analyze the data.

Determine the sample

The best sample is a randomly distributed evenly weighted sample that reflects the actual composition of the environment being assessed. In the different interventions, some groups were excluded. For example, at Freight, the unionized employees were excluded because at that time management was in intense negotiations with them, and there was fear that the assessment would become another negotiation point. As a result of this decision, during the data collection there was some paranoia by the union employees as to why they were not included, and at the end of the process they felt no commitment to the change effort. At Health, of the 120 employees, only the 80 exempt salaried employees were included. Thus, at the end, the 40 nonexempt (hourly) employees were left wondering if they had no role in creativity. The sample distribution itself communicates management's values to employees, and can act to improve or degrade the climate. At Health-Brazil, the client decided to give every employee the questionnaire, in order to make a clear statement that every employee's contribution was valued. This act was not lost on the employees, many of whom noted with pride, 'This was the first time ever in which my opinion was asked for.'

Determine the data groups to be reported out

Part of the sampling decision is to decide which subgroups need to be identified in addition to the overall group. Usually, data breaks by function and by level are desired. However, one must be careful here. Before agreeing to all data breaks requested, two questions must be answered: are the sample sizes by data break large enough to be statistically reliable? Is anyone's confidentiality being compromised? The first question is easier, with a minimum of 30 being the desired size, and as low as 20 if necessary on the smaller groups. The second is more difficult. If data are reported back by functional area, then it is a kind of report card for the functional heads. These are very sensitive data for the organization. It is important to identify before the data are collected exactly who will see the data. Will the senior manager see everyone's data? Will the functional heads see each other's data? The functional heads should be party to these decisions. At Health, the functional heads agreed that the leader should see all their data, but that each of them should see only their own data. This is the traditional situation in most organizations. At Chemical, the understanding was that the leader would not see the divisional data, nor would they see each other's data. At the final feedback session, the functional heads with the best 'report cards' shared their data with the group as a whole. This put pressure on those with poorer functional results to share their data. They did this by talking in generalities, and not sharing their numbers. What was important here was that the functional heads had control of their data. It would have been highly embarrassing and damaging for the researcher to have exposed these data without the functional head's control. Some groups will decide ahead that they are comfortable with common sharing of their department data, but this is more rare.

The reason that these decisions must be more carefully considered in a climate assessment than other assessments is that the climate itself is being shaped in how these decisions are being made. If the climate for creativity needs to improve, then it needs to start with how the assessment process itself is conducted.

Data collection

CCL's Innovation Assessment Process currently uses the Work Environment Questionnaire (WEI) and some personal interviews as its data sources. From an intervention standpoint, the key points are: (1) don't surprise anybody, and (2) assure confidentiality.

Don't surprise anybody

Most large organizations have a sophisticated rumor mill which engages in the most fantastic imaginations possible to explain that which is not clearly explained by management. The announcement of the assessment process should be clearly made by the senior leader down through the ranks to the lowest level. Each questionnaire should be accompanied by a cover letter from a senior manager explaining why the data are being collected and how they will be used. People to be interviewed should receive a letter a week ahead explaining why they are being interviewed, and how their confidentiality will be protected. Without a clear explanation by management, employees will create the most varied imaginings of why the assessment is being done. For example, at Chemical, the common rumor was that it was one more way to determine who was next to be laid off (the organization had been experiencing massive layoffs). Employees easily confuse assessing the environment for creativity with assessing *them* for creativity. The focus on the environment must be made clear.

Assure confidentiality

The questionnaire should request data that cannot be traced to the individual employee. Because CCL is involved in these interventions, the questionnaires are sent directly to CCL after the employee completes them. If an outside vendor is not used, the organization must find a way to assure employees that their answers cannot be traced to them.

Data analysis

Currently, item and scale means are calculated for the overall group. *t*-Tests are calculated for statistically significant differences between subgroups. Open-ended questions on the WEI are content analyzed, as are the interview transcripts. These data sources form the basis for the feedback report to the client. Stimulants and obstacles to creativity in the environment are rank ordered as to their prevalence from most to least prevalent. Meaning is brought to the cold figures by combining the open-ended question responses, the interview content, and the figures into a few main issues for the environment.

STEP 3: DATA ARE FED BACK TO THE CLIENT

Feeding back data about the environment for creativity involves the following: (1) to whom are the data fed back? (2) how are the data internalized? and (3) how is the improvement process furthered and monitored?

Who gets the data?

The data should be fed back in three distinct steps: the senior leader, the senior leader and his or her team, and the greater organization. The senior leader should receive the data first in a private session because it feels like a personal assessment, especially if the leader has been in charge for a long time (Nadler, 1977). At Health, the leader received the data in the same meeting with his subordinates. As his emotions came into play with the noted prevalence of obstacles to creativity, he would look at his subordinates and say, 'Is this really true?' He needed more time to separate out his own feelings from what was actually being reported before he faced his team. At least an overnight or a weekend should be provided for the senior leader to absorb the data and request any clarification before the data are shared with the management team. The meeting with the team should also allow time for the team to absorb the data before they are shared with the organization. Finally, the data should be shared in some form with the entire organization. Since the climate is formed by interpersonal relations, all employees have a part in affecting the climate for creativity, for better or worse. Thus, all need the data to understand what needs to change.

How are the data internalized?

Getting the data from the formal cold report to the minds and hearts of the people in the environment is a difficult task, but is the most critical of all the steps in the entire assessment process. Three steps are important: (1) the feedback report has summarized a few main issues; (2) the feedback is put into the employees' own words; and (3) the focus is on 'what do I want to have happen in the future?'

Summarize the report

Figures in themselves mean little; they are but marks on a page. They are helpful in that they guide the assessment reliably to the highlights of the current climate for creativity—what is helping, and what is hindering. But the analyst fails at the assessment task if he or she leaves the report at the figures. The report must go on to summarize a few main issues. For example, the Freight report noted that over 100 years of regulation in the industry was one issue that underlay a number of the obstacles to creativity. At Health, a summarizing issue was the medical training most employees had experienced with its emphasis on minimizing risk to the patient. At Chemical, it was the distrust caused by the downsizing of the past few years, and at Health-Brazil, it was the uncertain economy and its ravages of inflation. The search for meaning in the figures must be initiated by the analyst, who is the closest to the figures.

Feedback is put into the recipients' own words

For the data analyst, the emphasis on data integrity appropriately leads him or her to stay close to the figures in the interpretation of meaning. The recipients of the data, however, have a different task. They must find a way to make the data useful for changing their behavior. To do this, it is of primary importance that they put the data into their own words. This is the point at which the data are internalized. For example, at Chemical, the management team summarized the feedback report into the following issues: *The Legacy of the Past* (lack of trust and credibility, short-term focus, and political problems); *The Overmanagement Style* (too many constraints, avoiding risks, unclear goals); and *Organizational Barriers* (lack of cross-functional relationships, inadequate communication, and inadequate involvement of technicians). When the management team discussed the feedback with the employees, they were able to talk about the issues in their own words. At Health, when the feedback report was discussed with the management team, it was not put immediately into the team's own words. This slowed down the usefulness and application of the data until a later date, when the data were finally put into the employees' own words at a two day workshop with all employees.

Focus on the future

The data are the least important parts of the process to improve the climate for creativity. They serve only as a reliable starting place for change. An analogy for the role of the data is the starting block against which the Olympic runner places his or her foot. It marks the place at which the change effort starts, and provides a platform against which one can push off towards the goal. As in the Olympics, the starting place should be quickly left behind. In the interventions to date, once employees have put the issues into their own words, they have been asked to identify where it is they want to go, what is the picture of the climate they would like to have? Only with these questions answered is it possible to do action planning. The data provide the picture of 'where we are now', the future goal provides the picture of 'where we want to go' and, by comparing the two pictures, we are able to answer the question 'how do we get there?' Action plans result from the comparison of the present with the future.

This is easier said than done, however. To date, most action plans have concentrated on structural or other tangible issues, reflecting the lack of goals for and awareness of climate behaviors. For example, at Freight, actions identified were to reduce the layers of management, and reduce the involvement of upper management in decision-making. At Health, actions such as reducing the complexity of the yearly business planning process resulted. At Health-Brazil, the need for a more structured career-planning process resulted. These are useful goals which will help increase creativity in the organization. However, the identification of human interpersonal behavioral change has been slower to emerge. At Health-Brazil, the management team did identify the action of an offsite team-building session specifically to improve their interpersonal communication. At Chemical, management identified their desire to reduce 'micro-management', that is, unnecessary involvement in the details with their subordinates. They agreed to monitor each other on how well they were doing in changing this behavior pattern. On the whole, however, identification of changed climate behaviors as goals has been slim. A consultant who has done work helping Scandinavian organizations build their visions of the future, Marjorie Parker of Oslo, Norway, suggests that setting human behavioral goals is very different from traditional goal setting. Traditional goal setting is a logical rational process. Human interpersonal behaviors, by contrast, are a matter of the heart and emotions as well. In her experience, guided imagery has helped managers develop concrete pictures of their desired future behaviors, which acted as strong guides for changing their current behaviors. Development of techniques such as guided imagery will help in the kind of goal setting appropriate for climate improvement.

How is the improvement process furthered and monitored?

The final issue in the feedback step is how the climate improvement process will be carried out and monitored. Two points are important here: involve everybody, and use the human resources department as the monitor.

Involve everybody

All employees in the environment being studied should receive some kind of feedback on the assessment results. This is because on the climate side of the organization, the influence of an individual's personality can be quite different from an individual's position influence, e.g. how much budget an individual controls. Climate is inevitably the result of how individuals treat one another, and its change cannot be as easily dictated from the top as, say, a change in budget allocation. Let us imagine the directive comes down from on high: 'Effective immediately, we will all treat one another with respect.' Despite the worthiness of the goal, it has little meaning. Individuals need to know what are the behaviors now that are getting in the way of creativity. Then, they need to know the future goals that need to be achieved. Finally, they need to be encouraged to find their own behavioral change that will result in attaining the goal. Each employee needs to find the answer to 'How can I change my behavior to improve the climate for creativity?' It is at the individual level only that the climate can begin to change because it is founded on human values, and how those values are reflected in interpersonal behavior. In the four interventions, some form of feedback was given to all employees. At Freight and Health-Brazil, the broad organization received a summarized written report with encouragement to forward ideas about change to management. Needless to say, this stimulated few results. At Health, the entire group of 80 employees attended a two-day offsite session at which they received the data, discussed them in small groups and put them into their own words, then developed action plans for their local areas and the organization overall. There have been a number of actions resulting from these groups. At Chemical, the management team presented the results to all 400 employees, then facilitated smaller group meetings of 20 to 30 people, called 'Vision Action Sessions'. At these sessions, employees created action teams that were committed to work on various improvement plans. There have been many outcomes from these teams.

Use the human resources department as the monitor

The effectiveness of the roll-out of the data assessment to the broader organization, and the outcomes of the assessment process are dependent to a large degree on the internal human resources function and its organizational development skills. The process needs a catalyst to help employee groups internalize the data, put the data into their own words, identify behavioral changes, and follow up on results. In the different interventions, those companies with stronger human resources departments had smoother and more effective results.

STEP 4: THE CHANGE PROCESS IS MONITORED

The goal of doing the assessment process is to increase the creativity of the organization by improving the climate for creativity. There are, therefore, two separate questions indicated: has creativity increased? and has the climate for creativity improved? Although the questions may seem to have the same answer, determining the answer is different for each.

If we seek to know if creativity has increased, then we will collect data at some suitable period after the assessment process is concluded, say one year, and find if employees evidence more creativity in their work. This could be measured directly by the number and quality of new ideas for products and processes that employees create, or indirectly by the number of new products or services introduced by the organization, compared to a previous period. However, this increase in creativity could come from a number of influences, such as increased budgets or new personnel. This measure, then, will not tell us precisely whether the climate has changed for the better.

If we focus on measuring the improvement of the climate for creativity, then we have a more precise idea of whether the assessment process made any difference. Did managers give more freedom to subordinates in deciding how to do their work? Did employees perceive more encouragement to take risks than previously? Here the most likely measure would be to complete the same questionnaire after 18 months to two years, and see if employees report a change in behaviors. This has not yet been achieved in the CCL interventions, but the idea of using a questionnaire to measure the climate for creativity, and to complete it at regular intervals in order to measure change, has been applied in Sweden. Goran Ekvall, at the Swedish Management Institute, has developed a 50-item survey of the climate for creativity (Ekvall *et al.*, 1983). Ekvall's questionnaire has been adopted by a number of institutions as a measure of organizational effectiveness, and is completed at regular intervals as part of the performance assessment process. The idea of regular measurement of the climate for creativity is still a novel one for most organizations. US management is still in the awareness-building stage on the importance of managing climate to achieve innovation by the organization. The use to date of CCL's Innovation Assessment Process has had the quality of a 'onetime fix-it' kind of intervention, rather than being seen as the launch to a longer-term building of skills in climate management. However, the awareness of this need is growing in the management literature, and in the more far-seeing organization leaders.

RECOMMENDED INNOVATION ASSESSMENT PROCESS STEPS

Below is the process for improving the climate for creativity which has evolved from the learning in the interventions to date.

Step 1: clarify the need

At the time the organization is considering whether to do an assessment, the following questions should be discussed in depth:

- Why do we need increased creativity? How will an increase in creativity help us reach our goals?
- Why do we need to work on our climate? How will an improved climate for creativity help us reach our goals? What is our understanding of what climate is?
- How important is increasing our climate for creativity right now? Are there other more important issues we need to be working on?
- We know that to do an assessment is to intervene, and to raise employee expectations for results. Are we ready to commit now to taking action based on the assessment results?
- Who are the major stakeholders in this assessment? Are the proper people involved in the decision to go ahead?

Step 2: collect the data

- Determine the sample, striving for an evenly weighted randomly distributed sample.
- Determine the data subgroups that will be reported out, such as functional breaks and level breaks. Who will see the subgroup data? Is confidentiality protected?
- Announce the process in the organization, clearly noting why it is being done and how the data will be used.
- Protect the confidentiality of all respondents.
- Distribute questionnaires, and conduct any alternative collection of data (such as interviews).
- Analyze the data.
- Prepare the feedback report, including summarizing a few main issues that emerge from the data.

Step 3: feedback and action initiation

- Review the report first with the senior manager, at least 24 hours ahead of the review with the management team. Next, review the report with the management team. Finally, the broader organization should receive some summary of the data.
- Each data recipient should be encouraged to put the data into his or her own words in a summary of a few main issues.
- Next, identify what the future improved climate looks like. How does this new climate help achieve the goals of the organization? What are the implications for the behaviors of the individual employee? What new behaviors can she or he imagine that will help achieve the organization's long-term goals?
- Identify the management team's and the human resources department's role in the feedback and action initiation process.

Step 4: follow-up

- Determine how and when the results of the process will be measured. Will increased creativity be measured, or the improved climate?
- Who will be responsible for the follow-up? What accountability does the human resources department have for the follow-up? What accountability does management have?

SUMMARY

CCL's Innovation Assessment Process assists management in improving the climate for creativity by clarifying for them their motivations and expectations for wanting increased creativity; by clarifying the concepts of climate and creativity; by identifying where and what kind of creativity is needed in the organization; by accurately identifying both the stimulants and obstacles to creativity in their environment; and by focusing them on specific actions to be taken to improve their climate for creativity.

A model for improving organizational climates for creativity is emerging from our studies (see Figure 1). The model focuses on developing the positive aspects of a creative climate.

The focal point of the model is the establishment of both long-term and short-term goal clarity within the organization around the issues of creativity and innovation. Goal clarity is given the central place in the model because goal clarity is what harnesses the creativity of employees, focusing their creativity, and giving it direction. Without goal clarity, employee creativity 'is going nowhere' (remember: 'If you don't know where you're going, you'll end up somewhere else.'). Long-term goal clarity has been achieved by top management when all employees know where the organization is attempting to go in the future, and why increased creativity is important to helping it get there. Short-term goal clarity is achieved when middle and lower level managers set tangible and measurable goals for their subordinates' work which are in alignment with the overall goals of the organization.

Once goal clarity has been established, which provides a form and focus for employee creativity, the other three components of the climate are necessary to bring out their creativity. As I said at the beginning of this chapter, the organization cannot *make* employees have intrinsic motivation, but it can set a climate that will help it emerge and engage with the work task. Challenge is seeing to it that the work task given the employee is meaningful *to him or her*, that it engages the maximum personal interest and enjoyment of the employee. Freedom is giving the employee the maximum operational autonomy in deciding how to do his or her work. The supervisor should set a clear goal, then stay out of the way. The most difficult to attain, because it represents the biggest change from current practice, is encouragement for creativity. The word encouragement comes from the Latin word 'cor' (heart), and means 'to give heart'. This is the establishment of personal bonds between managers and subordinates in which the manager helps build the courage of the employees to take risks and bring forth their new ideas. Mistakes are accepted if the employee learns from them. The manager's motivation in encouraging the development of the subordinate is seeing that only by developing the individual can the organization be developed.

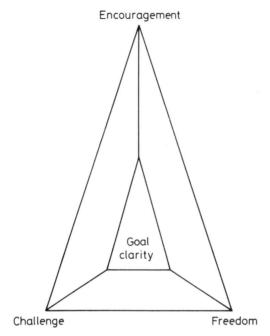

Figure 1 A model for improving the climate for creativity, Center for Creative Leadership, 1989

Improving corporate climates for creativity is an important goal for our times. To achieve it, managers' awareness of the role of climate in organizations must be raised, and their skills for managing climate must be developed. Climate assessment interventions need to develop techniques that can help managers identify their desired improved climate behaviors. Human resources department managers need to develop their understanding of how to facilitate climate change. In the final analysis, managers need to improve their skill at setting clear goals, and they *especially* need to learn how to encourage their employees, how to give them heart. Identifying that it is in the development of the individual that the creativity of organizations will most surely result is the first step in improving corporate climates for creativity. As a result of working towards these goals, managers can create healthier organizations, contributing to the positive development of humankind.

Correspondence address:
Center for Creative Leadership, 5000 Laurinda Drive, PO Box P-1, Greensboro, North Carolina 27402-1660, USA.

REFERENCES

Amabile, T.M. (1983). *The Social Psychology of Creativity.* New York: Springer-Verlag.

Amabile, T.M. and Gryskiewicz, S.S. (1987). *Creativity in the R&D Laboratory (Technical Report No. 30).* Greensboro, NC: Center for Creative Leadership.

Bennis, W.G. (1969). *Organizational Development.* Reading, MA: Addison-Wesley.

Burnside, R.M. (1988). Assessing organizational climates for creativity and innovation: methodological review of large company audits. In Y. Ijiri and R.L. Kuhn (Eds.), *New Directions in Creative and Innovative Management.* Cambridge, MA: Ballinger Publishing Co.

Ekvall, G., Arvonen, J. and Waldenstron-Lendblad, I. (1983). *Creative Organizational Climate (Report Two).* Stockholm, Sweden: The Swedish Council for Management and Organizational Behavior.

Nadler, D.A. (1977). *Feedback and Organization Development: Using Data-based Methods.* Reading, MA: Addison-Wesley.

Schein, E.H. (1985). *Organizational Culture and Leadership.* San Francisco: CA: Jossey-Bass Publishers.

Schneider, B. (1985). Organizational climate and culture. *Annual Review of Psychology,* **36**, 573–611.

Part V

Integrations

14 An evolutionary approach to creativity and innovation*

Barry M. Staw

University of California, Berkeley, USA

This chapter will take the form more of a position paper than a research summary. Rather than reviewing an array of current developments in the creativity and innovation literatures, I will present a broad framework through which individual and organizational innovation can both be viewed. My chief goal will be to help us move closer to a unified theory of innovation, an issue for which scores of models have been developed in fields as disparate as psychology, engineering, and sociology. A secondary objective, and one that is perhaps more realistic given the current balkanization of the social sciences, will be to stimulate some cross-fertilization of research among the disciplinary approaches to innovation. Here, my aim will be to clarify and expand the analogies that can be drawn between innovation at the individual and organizational levels of analysis.

In working toward an integrative and analogous framework I will draw on three principal sources. The intellectual underpinnings of the chapter will be taken from Campbell's (1960) evolutionary model of creativity. Although this model was originally proposed as a counterweight (and a radical alternative) to traditional theories of problem solving, it is both simple and general enough to be extended from individual to organization-level phenomena. Campbell's evolutionary model is devoid of content, however. Thus, I will draw heavily on Amabile's (1983, 1988) recent reviews of the creative problem solving literature to attach more detailed psychological variables to the evolutionary framework. Finally, I will turn to Kanter's (1983, 1988) discussions of what makes organizations innovative to formulate organization-level hypotheses from the evolutionary perspective.

Obviously, three primary sources are insufficient for a full understanding of innovation, be it at the micro or macro level. However, in order to see

*Work on this chapter was supported by a grant from the Institute of Industrial Relations, University of California, Berkeley.

the common threads between the psychological study of creativity and more sociological work on innovation, it is important not to get too absorbed in the intricacies of either approach. Therefore, this essay will start with a rather simplified structure and apply it across levels of analysis. I will briefly describe Campbell's evolutionary framework and then show how it can be used to build analogous theories for both individual and organizational innovation. Toward the end of the essay I will address several unresolved issues in innovation, using the evolutionary perspective to clarify gaps in our understanding of how new ventures grow and perish in organizations.

CAMPBELL'S EVOLUTIONARY MODEL

Nearly thirty years ago Campbell presented what is one of the most important but underutilized models of creativity. He argued against the notion that creativity is a mysterious process performed by the gifted or brilliant mind. He also denied the contingency dictum that by putting the right person to work on the right problem, 'Eureka!', a creative solution will be born. In contrast, Campbell posited that creativity is largely the product of sweaty trial and error, that people must work long and hard to generate multiple solutions to difficult problems. They must, according to Campbell, also bring a wide variety of approaches to the fray. Only by persevering and using a diverse set of alternatives will creative solutions likely be found.

Campbell's evolutionary model relies heavily on variation, but variation alone cannot explain creative problem solving. There also needs to be some mechanism by which the variety of potential solutions can be culled. Campbell argued that such a selective retention function is performed by people applying their background knowledge and skills to decide which alternatives to save and which to discard. To sort the creative insight from the simply bizarre requires factual knowledge, at least moderate intelligence, self-criticism, and high standards—all characteristics commonly associated with creative personalities (Barron and Harrington, 1981).

Campbell's emphasis on blind variation is similar to the Darwinian view of evolving organizational forms now advocated by population ecologists (e.g. Hannan and Freeman, 1977; Carroll, 1984). However, just as many organizational analysts have argued that organizations are not entirely subject to the whims of the environment, but can instead exercise some strategic choices in their adaptation (Child, 1972; Hambrick and Finklestein, 1987), so too can we specify some adjustments to Campbell's evolutionary model. Variation need not always be blind or undirected by individuals. People may consciously alter the creative process. They may intentionally increase the variability of their inputs and also adjust the selective retention process. For example, due to personal preferences, socialization, or perhaps even because of listening to creativity experts, individuals might turn problems on their head, search out exceptions, deviate from established practices, and seek out other points of view—all ways to increase the diversity of their input (e.g. McGuire, 1973). Likewise, individuals can set out to control the selective retention aspect of creative problem solving by guarding against premature criticism of ideas, the preempting of alternatives, or focusing too quickly on a few salient alternatives (e.g. Janis and Mann, 1977). Thus, even though the evolutionary model defines creativity as a product of variation and selective retention processes, this approach need not be one in which the individual has no control over the dynamics of the evolutionary process. In short, variation need not be completely blind nor retention entirely fortuitous.

Campbell's evolutionary model implies that creativity results from the combination of high variation and high selectivity. To have a creative response requires widely varied input to the problem. Yet, the wider the variety of input the more selectivity must be used to decide which of the alternatives to retain. Thus, at the input side of the evolutionary framework we would expect variables such as task motivation, persistence, non-conformity, field independence, cognitive complexity, breadth of experience and knowledge to all serve as determinants of variation. In terms of selective retention, being able to recognize the best of the alternatives would likely be related to personal characteristics such as general intelligence and critical skills, as well as to specific knowledge of the field in which the problem occurs.

Although the absolute levels of variation and selective retention are no doubt important to creativity, so too are the ways these evolutionary processes combine over time. Not only are these two processes often negatively correlated, but the appropriate sequencing of variation and selective retention may determine whether a creative product will be evoked or not. Though I will touch on this problem throughout the discussion of both individual creativity and organizational innovation, suffice to say at this point that maximizing the effects of variation and selective retention will be more complicated than simply increasing their absolute levels. For example, in order to heighten creativity selection should not only be potent; it should also be timed so that potential solutions can be elaborated or developed. Selection that is too quick may in fact be worse than no selection at all, snuffing out alternatives before their merits can be realized.

As one can see from this brief discussion, the evolutionary approach to creativity prompts inquiry into several interesting and unsolved issues. However, before going further into the implications of the evolutionary model, it is necessary to have more information about the creative process itself. For this I now turn to Amabile's componential framework of creative problem solving. Though she did not explicitly intend to use an evolutionary model, Amabile has placed many of the content variables or determinants of creativity into a format that naturally illustrates the evolutionary approach.

Her work will thus help flesh out the mechanisms of both variation and selective retention in individual creativity.

AMABILE'S COMPONENTIAL FRAMEWORK

Amabile (1983, 1988) reviewed many of the personality and environmental determinants of individual creativity and placed them into a sequence of problem solving steps. As shown in Figure 1, the creative process involves five stages. First, a problem presents itself either through some internal or external stimulus. The person can have a burning desire to discover something, be intrinsically motivated to learn about an issue, or simply find himself or herself in a situation where someone demands that a difficult problem be solved. Assuming that the presented problem is motivating enough to capture attention, it should, Amabile argues, lead to a preparation stage. Here the individual builds up or activates a store of information relevant to the problem, including any tricks, shortcuts or algorithms that might be useful for the task. Once this knowledge is activated, the individual begins idea generation. At this third stage in the process, approaches to the problem are attempted, drawing on the person's repertoire of previous experiences, insights and fears. With each idea, or perhaps after a series of them have been formulated, some effort is made to test for their appropriateness and accuracy. Amabile does not delve into the nature of this idea validation stage, but one could make a strong case for a sequential goodness of fit test (e.g. Beach and Mitchell, 1987) rather than the more simultaneous calculation of costs and benefits across multiple solutions. As noted in the figure, regardless of the particular dynamics of validation, each potential solution is eventually tested against the problem. The result of this testing triggers the end of the problem solving effort, if the end-product is a complete attainment of the goal or if no reasonable progress is made on the problem. For outcomes between these extremes, the individual is seen as returning to the first stage in the problem solving sequence, facing the problem once again.

As shown in the top half of Figure 1, Amabile isolates three sets of contributors to creative performance. For the first component she emphasizes that task motivation may provide the initial stimulus for a problem, especially if one is intrinsically motivated to solve the problem or finds it inherently challenging. She notes that extrinsic as opposed to intrinsic motivation may foster functional fixedness and other forms of rigidity in dealing with a difficult problem. Extrinsic rewards, goals, and constraints may all increase motivation to accomplish a task, but with them comes a narrow focusing of attention on the task as originally defined or as might fit a well-learned algorithm (Amabile, 1979, 1985). Intrinsic motivation, Amabile argues, is more conducive to the processing of divergent information, the ability to step away from a problem so as to see non-obvious sides of an issue, and the

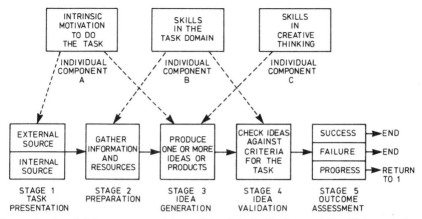

Figure 1 Amabile's componential model of individual creativity (Adapted from Amabile, 1988)

ability to explore alternative solution paths. Thus, whereas extrinsic motivation may be facilitative of performance on well-structured tasks, intrinsic motivation may be better suited to the heuristic nature of creativity endeavors.

The second creativity component that impacts the problem solving sequence is what Amabile calls domain-relevant skills. Here are included knowledge of the problem area, technical skills and talents that may provide the background necessary to solve the problem. Figure 1 shows skills in the task domain as influential in the preparation and idea validation phases of the creativity cycle. Basically what is illustrated is the simple fact that a set of alternatives and their validation do not generally arise from a blank slate. Not only are those with relevant backgrounds likely to generate more potential solutions to a task, but people with domain-relevant skills are also more likely to be able to assess the appropriateness of these ideas as potential solutions, to know when they are on the right track in solving a problem.

Though it is not represented specifically in the figure, creative problem solving may involve a multiplicity of skill domains—a blending together of two approaches so that a problem can be attacked from divergent perspectives. People whose skills are not limited to the most immediately relevant domain would seem to have the advantage in creativity. Because they cast a wider net in terms of experiences, information and heuristics, they may be less likely to fixate on a narrow definition of problems and their potential solutions.

The evolutionary approach

Figure 2 is a restatement of Amabile's problem-solving sequence in terms of the evolutionary approach. Illustrated is the fact that variation not only

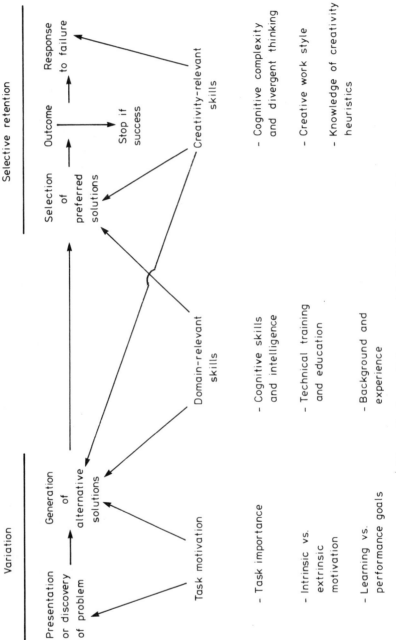

Figure 2 An evolutionary model of individual creativity

occurs when alternatives are generated as potential solutions to a problem, but that variety can be introduced in the very definition of the problem itself. When problems are defined broadly or in ways that do not trigger routine and well-learned responses they are likely to lead to greater creativity. The selective retention process is likewise depicted as a subset of the problem solving steps. Selection of a preferred alternative, be it on the basis of the potential to solve the problem or personal affinity, is obviously a pivotal aspect of selective retention. However, as shown in the figure, the outcome that results from a potential solution is also an important determinant of what gets retained over time. Some problems have 'equifinality', where nearly any solution will work or yield at least a satisfactory result (Connolly, 1988). Other contexts will entail more stringent requirements, thus contributing to a more potent selective retention mechanism. Finally, the figure shows that people's reactions to the outcomes of their solution attempts, be they successes or failures, complete the evolutionary cycle. The individual's response to the situation will determine whether a given solution will be discarded in favor of other alternatives or retained over time.

In the lower portion of the figure, Amabile's three sets of content variables are once again represented. In terms of task motivation I have listed not only the quality of task motivation (whether it is intrinsically or extrinsically based), but also the quantity of motivation as a determinant of creativity. Whether one perceives the problem to be important or trivial will, no doubt, affect how the problem is stated and how many alternatives will be generated. Extreme levels of motivation (at the high and low ends) may function as does extrinsic motivation, narrowing the person's focus to a limited set of options and contributing to functional fixedness (Easterbrook, 1959; Staw *et al.*, 1981). In contrast, having a moderate level of task arousal, preferably derived from an internal desire to learn as opposed to an externally derived performance goal (Dweck and Leggett, 1988), may widen one's definition of the problem and the scope of potential solutions examined.

Figure 2 shows domain-relevant skills as primarily affecting the generation of alternatives and the selection of preferred solutions. Variables such as cognitive skills, technical training and background are all obvious contributors to the reservoir of knowledge from which one can draw alternative solutions. Likewise, having domain-relevant skills (including those in ancillary areas) will no doubt improve one's chances of selecting a useful solution from among the many alternatives. Without substantial task knowledge, the choice of potential solutions would be largely arbitrary, resembling blind trial and error rather than an ordering based on the prospects for success.

Creativity-relevant skills are depicted in Figure 2 as affecting the generation of alternatives, their selection, and one's responses to failure. For example, creative individuals are predicted to generate a greater number of diverse alternatives than those who are less creative, to have the ability to hold back on critical evaluation (or selection) until the full range of possibilities is explored, and to persist on difficult problems (restating them if necessary) rather than giving up or accepting a subpar solution. Thus, creativity skills are shown to be an ever-present factor in the development of creative problem solving over time.

Obviously, it is possible to add any number of variables to the creativity model and to debate the exact demarcations of the various stages of the creativity process. Not only are the elements of the problem solving sequence hard to separate, but so too are its specific determinants. For example, one exception to Figure 2 might be the recognition that people with the highest domain-relevant skills define problems differently from those with less experience (e.g. a chess board configuration does not mean the same thing to the expert and novice). Likewise, it could be noted that the most creative individuals define problems in a more diffuse manner than those lower in cognitive complexity or with a less creative work style. Thus, if stretched to the limit, each of the categories of content variables can be seen as exerting some influence over each of the steps of the problem solving sequence. Hence, represented in Figure 2 are only what might be interpreted as the primary relationships in the evolutionary model, with more secondary influences omitted.

Before leaving this sketch of individual creativity, it should be stressed that many of the content variables in Figure 2 are malleable qualities. They are skills attainable with training and effort, as well as motivations that can be influenced by the task environment. Thus, rather than characterizing creativity strictly as the personality characteristic of a few special individuals or as an immutable cognitive process that applies to all situations, creative problem solving can be seen as a social act that is subject to both environmental and personal influences. Obviously, Amabile's empirical work on intrinsic motivation has taken this social psychological perspective, emphasizing how incentive structures and external pressures can inhibit creative responses. However, it can be argued that Amabile's research has not gone far enough in this direction. To appreciate the context of creativity—what conditions are conducive to or inhibiting of new ideas—we also need to turn to more sociological and managerial treatments of innovation. Kanter's (1983, 1988) description of innovative firms serves this purpose well, providing at least preliminary material for how creativity unfolds in organizational environments.

KANTER'S STRUCTURAL APPROACH

Although Kanter (1983, 1988) describes organizational rather than individual innovation, her conceptual scheme is somewhat parallel to the problem solving sequence used by Amabile. Innovations, as Kanter describes them, move over time from an idea generation stage in which an issue is introduced by internal or external change agents, to a coalition building stage in which power is required to move an idea forward, to an implementation stage in which prototypes are developed and eventually put into full-fledged production. Innovation is therefore much more than the summation of the creativity of individuals making up the organization. Questions of organizational structure, power, communication and external economic conditions are just a few of the situational factors that affect an innovation over time. Yet, like the individual problem solving sequence, there is a basic movement from presentation of the problem to idea generation to application of the solution. And, like individual creativity, it is possible to view organizational innovation as an evolutionary process comprising variation and selective retention processes.

While organizational innovation is no doubt more than the sum of its individual parts, it can still be argued that it begins with the input of individuals. The terms, 'intrapreneurs', 'idea generators', and 'idea champions', are all testimony to the recognition that it is the occasional individual (or set of individuals) that bring forth new approaches to the organization. It is rarely the organization in its collective wisdom that decides that the status quo is unacceptable. Innovation does not, for example, come out of the everyday administration of organizations and the enforcement of its procedures (Scott, 1981). It is something distinct from the natural effort of the system to limit uncertainty and place order on the behavior of its various participants.

It should also be stressed that innovation is something that does not spring naturally from the interaction of individuals in organizational settings. In most organizations the way in which the environment is interpreted, production organized and implemented is subject to consensual agreement (Pfeffer, 1981; Nemeth and Staw, 1989). These conventions may not only form the basis of shared expectations and norms, but may also become codified into rules and regulations of governing. As shown in several normative transmission studies (e.g. Jacobs and Campbell, 1961; Weick and Gilfillan, 1971; Zucker, 1977), common frames of reference can become institutionalized over time. Even when they have little basis in fact, norms for behavior can persist if they have become legitimized and supported by the power structure.

Some recent data illustrate how difficult it is to get people to publicly disagree with existing organizational procedures. Staw and Boettger (1990) asked business students to work on a recruiting brochure that was full of obvious content errors, advertising their school in ways known to be opposed by the students. Two experiments showed that few people were willing to violate role prescriptions in order to improve the faulty task, unless specifically told to do so. This lack of initiative was especially apparent when individuals were placed in a subordinate position, given specific but erroneous goals to achieve, and evaluated on the basis of their actions. Initiative was found to be higher when individuals were placed in a supervisory role and made accountable for the results of the larger social unit. This implies that empowerment of individuals rather than the usual top-down authority system may be needed to get individuals to recognize problems and to initiate steps of innovation.

Variation

Though individuals may have a difficult time recognizing organizational problems and making themselves heard, it should be emphasized that on their shoulders still rests the major source of variation for organizations. Problems may be presented by the organization's environment or its technology, but it is the individual or set of individuals who must interpret the situation—to see shifts as either a threat to the status quo or an opportunity for change. No doubt, individuals are often foiled in their capacity as carriers of ideas and as sources of diversity, yet they do have the inherent capacity to recognize problems and gaps that are not addressed by the existing order of things. A few individuals thrive in this problem-finding role, functioning as devil's advocates to uncover flaws in well-oiled bureaucracies. For others, situational support is probably necessary to reduce the risks of deviation from organizational norms.

If individuals are at least *potential* generators of variation (in the midst of systems generally designed to reduce variability), then organizational innovation and individual creativity have similar starting points. The skills and experiences of organizational participants, their breadth and scope, will affect the innovation process. So too will the set of personality dimensions (e.g. cognitive complexity and flexibility) commonly associated with creativity. Also, like Amabile, one might emphasize that variation (at least in terms of idea generation) is something that can be influenced by the work environment facing the individual. Hence, it is important to specify those aspects of organizational structure and practice that stimulate or inhibit the creative contribution of individuals.

Creative environments

Kanter notes that innovative companies generally hold strong norms for innovation—expectations that they will be technical leaders in their industries. Such norms may serve to legitimize divergent activity and increase the firm's tolerance for failure. To increase innovation further, some firms may also place tangible rewards on creative behavior, attempting to harness extrinsic as well as intrinsic motivation for new products. But, given the experimental results on the interaction of intrinsic and extrinsic motivation, it is not clear whether putting specific rewards on creativity is a practice that is dysfunctional or actually does constitute a double strength incentive.

Less controversial is the way innovative companies structure work roles. Employees may be put into close contact with producers, users or customers so that unmet needs, complaints, and suggestions can be heard loudly as stimuli for change (Marquis, 1969; Von Hippel, 1986). In addition, innovative companies often make use of temporary project teams. As Katz and Allen (1982) have shown, the performance of research groups starts to decline after only about five years' tenure (see also Payne, Chapter 5 in this volume). With stability of membership, research groups start to reduce communication with outsiders, a primary source of variation and vitality. Thus, any procedures (such as job rotation and outside hiring) that increase people's exposure to new ideas (or even the recombination of old ideas) probably contributes to innovation.

As Kanter notes, innovation thrives on the cross-fertilization of ideas. Like the 'bisociation' of two matrices of thought described by Koestler (1964) in the psychology of creativity, the mixing of organizational perspectives can provide the necessary variation to address more complex organizational problems. Thus, whereas traditional organizations try to segment skills and reduce interdependencies, innovative firms tend to use cross-functional teams and shifting project groups to capitalize on multiple perspectives. Instead of simplification and the division of labor, jobs tend to be more broadly defined, crossing functional and line-staff boundaries. And, in terms of supervision, innovative firms often make use of matrix structures where organizational members have multiple sources of responsibility with more than one constituent to please.

Most of the above mechanisms used to increase innovation stand in stark contrast to the usual efforts of organizations to reduce variation. As Schneider (1987) has noted, heterogeneity is commonly reduced through personnel selection, self-selection of individuals into the organization, peer pressure, and socialization. Deviants are seldom promoted and are usually kept on the periphery of organizational power. In addition, most of the organization's efforts to make the system more productive and efficient drive out deviant behavior. Performance evaluation, discipline, and goal-setting can, for example, all be viewed as efforts on behalf of the organization to pull individual behavior in a concerted or prescribed direction. This may reduce waste and increase locomotion toward common goals. Yet, if tasks are ill-structured and the organization's environment not well understood, such control mechanisms may be self-defeating. They can unwittingly decrease the amount of variation available for an organization's adaptation to the environment (Weick, 1976; 1983).

Protection from domain-relevant practices

As both Kanter and other organizational theorists have described them, most organizations are not particularly friendly toward variation. Even if some deviant ideas do get generated, most firms are not supportive of products or courses of action that break with tradition. Basically what happens is that domain-relevant skills used by the organization to keep itself on-track tend to kill off the more innovative ventures. The application of established knowledge, precedent, and expertise are used to find reasons why a new avenue should not be pursued. In a similar manner, control mechanisms such as performance measurement, promotion and advancement policies, goal-setting, budgeting, and the routine exercise of authority also serve as inhibitors of deviant behavior. Together, these domain-relevant practices are the procedural embodiment of what is known and preserved by the organization—the repository of its preferences and well-learned performance programs. For innovations to survive in an organization they therefore require some protection from these domain-relevant practices.

Kanter offers several illustrations of such protection. For example, the high-technology firm, Hewlett-Packard, allows staff members to spend a portion of their time on projects of their own choosing. Even if those in authority are not in favor of a project or it has been officially killed, it may still be followed. On at least one occasion, a persistent staff member who pursued an 'organizationally dead' project reached a breakthrough—and was awarded the 'H-P Order of Defiance'. Such a case illustrates the argument that innovative organizations may not just condone deviant activities; they sometimes provide them with structural protection.

As Kanter describes them, innovative organizations also contain enough slack resources so that new projects need not go through formalized budgetary procedures. Either monies are decentralized so that isolated projects can be independently sponsored, or there is sufficient slack for new ventures to be supported out of corporate-wide 'innovation banks'. In addition, Kanter notes that innovations are often given protection from routine political processes. If a project has the potential to become a major product or new procedure, it will likely challenge existing power structures, resource allocations, or career patterns. Protection from the political opposition that almost inevitably arises to innovation can come in the form of a major stakeholder who runs interference for the project. Protection can also come by altering normal reporting procedures. If project groups are forced to report regularly to others—to defend their every expense and effort—they are not likely to survive. In contrast, many innovative organizations allow new project groups to be 'hidden' in the hierarchy, avoiding the demands for efficiency and accountability that face ongoing units in the system.

In terms of the evolutionary approach to innovation, it can be argued that creative firms are those that promote variation by structuring themselves in ways that include broad jobs, multidisciplinary teams, and cross-fertilization of ideas. Such organizations also contain protections against premature selection processes, so that fledgling projects can be developed to the point that their merits are self-evident. Thus, whereas most organizations snuff out deviations via their application of expertise and financial controls, innovative firms appear to provide some protection against these domain-relevant practices.

Enforcement of domain-relevant practices

If all innovation attempts were given extended protection, many of the least promising projects would no doubt be retained. Consequently, some winnowing of weak prospects needs to take place. Exactly such a natural selection process is captured by Kanter's description of the allocation of resources within innovative firms. As she describes it, selection occurs as innovators struggle to capture slack resources, often 'tin cupping' around the firm to find the capital for their enterprises. Potential donors throughout the organization are typically those who have large ongoing budgets for their established products. They tend to sponsor innovations when they see something that will enhance their own power or the capabilities of their departments. Thus, those innovations with some prospect of growing over time, and especially those that are complementary rather than competitive with existing products, are likely to be supported.

As projects develop over time, it will typically become impossible for them to survive by using other departments' slack resources. But, the requirement of independent funding subjects innovations to more scrutiny. Having to face budget committees and venture capital groups, typical sources of resources for larger projects, necessitates feasibility studies and projections of eventual profitability. Projects that are too uncertain (and especially those without a tangible prototype) are therefore likely to fall by the wayside, unable to meet these increasing accountability requirements.

As projects grow, all of the reporting demands that face ongoing activities are likely to serve as a further selection mechanism. Having to justify their existence, set specific goals, and demonstrate relevance to larger constituencies are exercises that may select out all but the most viable innovations. Whereas relative autonomy allows new ventures to take root, ongoing accountability pressures are thus likely to take their toll on these enterprises. Of course, there is no guarantee that the most promising project will always be the survivor of this selective-retention process. Often the safest or 'most reliable' venture will win out.

For the surviving projects, coalitions will likely grow for and against the innovation. Support for a project will develop in depth and breadth as interdependencies with other organizational units increase over time. However, this support may be coupled with increasing resistance from established product areas or beneficiaries of established practices. New products or procedures can pose a serious challenge to existing patterns of resource

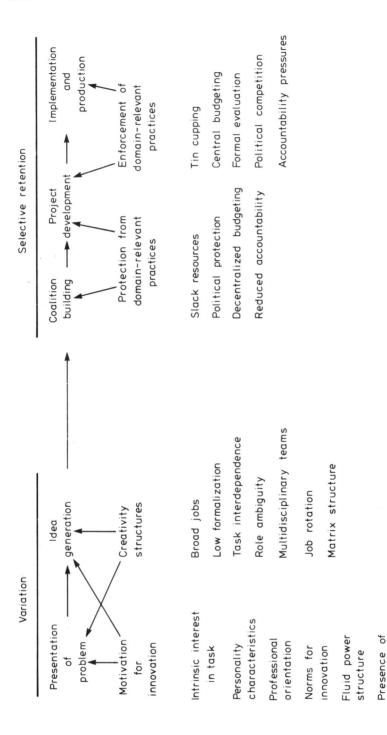

Figure 3 An evolutionary model of organizational innovation

allocation and threaten the very existence of established units. Thus, the greater the potential impact of an innovation (in terms of sales, profits, and practices), the more resistance one might expect to find within the organization.

In some organizations the conflict between established and new ventures is muted and disguised. On the surface discussions may center on merit, but in reality resources may be allocated on the basis of how closely a new activity fits with prior operations and the established political order. In other organizations projects may be subjected to a more overt power struggle. Almost in a Hegelian manner (Mason, 1969), a dialectic may develop in which the weaknesses of competing projects are exposed by administrative rivals. If the organization's political system is relatively permeable (where departments and careers staked to a new project can quickly grow or shrink over time), then new projects are likely to get a thorough hearing. Potentially major innovations are likely to face keen opposition intent on maintaining power, but at the same time, innovations with strong prospects will also gather adherents who see the opportunity for rapid ascent in the organization. If managed properly, this power struggle can provide an effective selection mechanism for sorting the organization's most promising innovations.

VARIATION AND SELECTIVE RETENTION IN INNOVATION

Figure 3 places much of the preceding discussion into an evolutionary model of innovation. In a framework that parallels the process of individual creativity, it is shown how innovations move in stages from presentation of the problem, to idea generation, coalition building, product development, and production. The process is shown, like that of creativity, to be largely a function of variation in the generation of potential solutions and of selective retention in isolating a few of these ideas for further development and implementation. In the lower portion of the figure are four sets of content variables that drive this evolutionary process.

The first grouping of content variables, motivation for innovation, is shown as affecting the perception (or finding) of organizational problems and as influencing the number and quality of ideas generated. Motivation for innovation is, in turn, dependent on both the individual characteristics and task attitudes that Amabile described in her model of individual creativity. Those with intrinsic interest in a task, for example, are more likely to see opportunities for improvement than those who are extrinsically motivated. In a similar manner, one might also predict that those who are more professionally oriented will have a higher motivation for innovation, since they not only have been exposed to outside perspectives but may also seek the professional stature that innovation can bring. In addition to such individual characteristics one might also expect more global aspects of the organization to contribute to motivation for innovation. Here I have included norms for innovation, in which change is expected and rewarded, as well as a fluid power structure, in which it is possible for people to rise extraordinarily fast by developing new products or procedures. As a final determinant of motivation for innovation I have included the presence of 'problem finders'. As Kanter notes, many innovative organizations make specific use of people who float freely in the hierarchy, without a base in a particular department, whose purpose it is to uncover new problems. Because they do not have an intact source of power and must constantly argue for budget and constituency, problem finders could be expected to be the most intensely motivated to seek innovation.

The second category of innovation determinants is labeled creativity structures. These include the many means of cross-fertilization that potentially help organizational participants see more problems and generate a greater array of alternatives. Organizational characteristics such as broad jobs, low formalization, high task interdependence, role ambiguity, job rotation, multidisciplinary teams, and matrix structures are just a few of the ways of creating an environment conducive to problem finding and for what Kanter calls 'kaleidoscopic thinking'.

Figure 3 shows motivation for innovation and creativity structures to be the primary determinants of variation for organizations. As illustrated in the figure, selective retention is determined by the enforcement of and protection from domain-relevant practices. As discussed, projects may be nurtured by some protection from domain-relevant practices, allowing them to gather support in the organization until their potential can be more clearly seen. These protections from premature selection can come in the form of slack resources, political safe-haven, decentralized budgeting and reduced accountability.

As shown in Figure 3, enforcement of domain-relevant practices can occur at both the project development and implementation stages. Listed in the figure are several mechanisms used to separate the least promising from the most effective uses of resources, such as 'tin cupping', central budgeting, project evaluation, political competition, and accountability pressures. Each of these domain-relevant practices can potentially serve as an instigator of selective retention, helping to cull the weakest of the projects and to preserve the fittest. Such domain-relevant practices do not of course *guarantee* that only the best projects will survive. Commitment to losing projects will sometimes interfere with the logic of this selection process.

COMMITMENT TO LOSING PROJECTS

Underlying the evolutionary model is the assumption that projects which are not economically viable will die a timely death, being forced out when they are outdistanced by other candidates for funding. One obvious problem with this assumption is that it ignores project commitment. Projects are rarely dropped voluntarily by their founders and supporters. If they do die, they generally go kicking and screaming to their graves.

The problem of commitment often stems from the project champion. In many instances this is the person who has recognized a problem, developed the resulting project, built a coalition of support, and moved the venture toward implementation. In other cases, the initial idea or innovation has been taken up by another key person in the organization who is more entrepreneurial or hierarchically ambitious than the originator of the idea. In either case, the project champion is generally one who is firmly committed to the success of the venture. He or she is a constant source of optimism and enthusiasm, willing to push the project through the many barriers that inevitably arise over the course of its development.

As we know from experimental studies on commitment (e.g. Brockner and Rubin, 1985; Staw and Ross, 1987), individuals who originate or are responsible for courses of action often become psychologically bound to them. Even in the face of apparent failure, proponents of a project may find it difficult to change direction. Such over-commitment is often a product of both private rationalization and public identification with the course of action. However, as a project progresses over time these sources of individual commitment can also translate themselves into a more collective binding. That is, not only may the career of the project champion become increasingly staked to the continuation of a project, but so too may other individuals and parts of the organization connected to the venture.

An example of collective commitment was recently provided by British Columbia's decision to host the world's fair, Expo 86 (see Ross and Staw, 1986). Although the project, at its inception, promised to bring economic benefits as well as recognition to the Canadian province, its development was marred by increasing losses. Nonetheless, commitment to the fair grew from a small set of officials surrounding the Premier of British Columbia to a broad coalition of business and economic interests. As a result, the fair was completed in the face of forecasted losses of over $300 million. The lesson from Expo 86 is not that administrators will sometimes be foolish; it is that projects can take on a life of their own—a snowball that becomes difficult to stop once sufficient commitment has built up within the organization.

COMMITMENT TO PROBLEMS, NOT PROJECTS

These warnings about commitment to a course of action are not meant to belittle its part in motivating a project staff. Some degree of commitment and enthusiasm is essential to push forward an idea in the organization.

Without it a project will likely die a premature death, having been untested against other uses of funds or likely market consequences.

Yet, it can be argued that innovation is furthered when commitment to problems is stronger than commitment to projects (cf. Campbell, 1969). Just as the creative individual is one who persists in the testing of multiple solutions, so too are innovative organizations flexible in their pursuit of new products or procedures. Such an experimenting organization (Staw, 1977) is one that uses objective and competitive evaluation of a varied set of alternatives. It is also an organization that assumes that it is impossible to predict, *a priori*, which project will be the victor. If a company could effectively analyze all technical and market needs and then correctly design projects to fill those gaps, unswerving commitment would be completely defensible. However, as I have argued from the evolutionary perspective, successful ventures are often the product of trial and error in an uncertain world.

In the same way that creative individuals generate numerous alternatives before subjecting them to criticism, innovative companies appear to pursue multiple prototypes before ruling any of them out. Because it is so difficult to predict project effectiveness, parallel projects are often thinned down only as their probabilities for success and failure become less ambiguous. The winnowing occurs by having each venture meet market tests or standards for performance that are likely predictive of ultimate success. For example, Sony pursued ten different major options in its video-tape recorder program, each with two to three subsystem alternatives (Quinn, 1986). Sony's chairman first set a target of performance that was comparable with Ampex but at one-quarter the cost; shortly thereafter, the target was moved to one-tenth the price (Quinn, 1986; Rosenbloom and Cusumano, 1987).

The number of projects an organization should pursue simultaneously and the point at which selection pressures should optimally be applied are no doubt environmentally driven questions. For uncertain and embryonic fields, where analytical procedures are unlikely to yield accurate prognoses, innovation necessitates a great deal of variation. To capitalize on chance, selection pressures should ideally be deemphasized, perhaps even to the point of letting all projects reach a market test. For example, Richard D. Irwin, a large publisher of business textbooks, is noted for bringing several similar books to market, letting all but the most successful go out of print after the first year or two. Because the sales of particular texts are so unpredictable, this innovation strategy appears to have served the company well. If, on the other hand, market demands were more defined or crystallized, an earlier filtering process, yielding fewer potential products, would likely have been more effective.

SOME FOOTNOTES TO THE EVOLUTIONARY APPROACH

In the most general sense, the evolutionary approach to innovation can be depicted by a funneling process—one in which organizations seek a wide array of input, to be narrowed only after some passage of time and increasingly difficult constraints. As discussed, innovative firms attempt to maintain variation by restraining tests for relevance and efficiency until later stages in project development. Yet, as I have noted, once projects have their own champions and sets of followers, they will not be easy to eliminate. Thus, a conflict in forces frequently develops between the defense of and opposition to particular projects. On the one hand, there will likely be members fiercely loyal to the project team and intent on seeing it survive the selection process. On the other hand, there will be others who will attempt to expose every weakness in the project so as to absorb its resources and power base. Hence, an important challenge for innovative firms is to have accepted standards of performance that can be universally applied to competing project groups. Another is to find ways of integrating members of losing projects into those ventures that will be continued over time. The object, of course, is to achieve an objective and smooth transition in shifting resources from the least to the most promising courses of action.

When the processes of variation and selective retention are working properly, the evolutionary forces facing the organization can be absorbed inward (Burgelman, 1989). Instead of bringing products all the way to market, seeing them fail or succeed depending on the ecology of consumer preferences and the actions of competitors, firms can substitute a more internal competition. If the selection processes inside the organization are isomorphic with those of the environment, then the firm will benefit from these evolutionary forces. Internal competition will likely increase the organization's level of adaptiveness to the outside environment. On the other hand, if the organization's selection mechanisms are non-isomorphic to the environment (e.g. based on political as opposed to economic criteria), then internal competition will likely be maladaptive. In these cases the evolution of innovation will work against the organization's preservation of the best or most profitable alternatives.

CONCLUSION

As I have tried to show in this chapter the process of innovation is parallel for individuals and organizations. For each the game is one of intelligent capitalization on chance. As Campbell has argued in his evolutionary model, the way to improve one's chances is to tinker with the level of variation as well as the severity of the selective retention mechanism. This recommendation obviously becomes more complicated when, as Amabile has shown in her research on individual creativity and Kanter has illustrated with organizational innovation, flesh is put on the bones of this evolutionary model.

Still, some simple lessons can be learned from this exercise. As illustrated by this essay's discussions of both micro and macro aspects of innovation, many of the same evolutionary principles seem to apply across levels of analysis. Therefore, if I now had to assess whether it is possible to have a unified theory of innovation, one that is conceptually analogous between individuals and organizations, I would express some cautious optimism. At the very least, the elaboration of an evolutionary model for both creativity and innovation provides cross-fertilization for these usually disparate research topics. Thus, just as boundary spanning often stimulates new ideas within organizational settings, so might the evolutionary perspective further the study of innovation itself.

SUMMARY

To summarize, this chapter started with Campbell's evolutionary model of creativity, added some qualifications and amplifications from recent psychological research, and applied this framework to thinking about organizational innovation. The movement from micro concepts to macro functions was not entirely smooth, but some overall principles did prevail. Simply put, innovation was found to result from an unfolding of variation and selective-retention processes over time. Factors that determine variation were shown to run the gamut from personality and task orientation to the way work roles are constructed. Likewise, determinants of selective retention were seen as ranging from mechanisms protecting new projects from domain-relevant practices (such as budgetary and accountability pressures) to procedures that speed their enforcement. Thus, innovation was described as a product of conflicting forces. Innovative firms, on the one hand, appear to promote a wide variety of alternatives, yet on the other hand establish procedures to selectively delete many of these same vehicles for change. Obviously the management of this two-edged process is difficult, and as yet no algorithms are available to solve its internal contradictions. This chapter's elaboration of the evolutionary model does however point out where the most serious conflicts lie and suggests some heuristics for managing innovation over time.

Correspondence addresses:
Haas School of Business, University of California, Berkeley, California 94720, USA.

REFERENCES

Amabile, T.M. (1979). Effects of external evaluation on artistic creativity. *Journal of Personality and Social Psychology*, 37, 221–233.

Amabile, T.M. (1983). The social psychology of creativity: A componential conceptualization. *Journal of Personality and Social Psychology*, 45, 357–376.

Amabile, T.M. (1985). Motivation and creativity: Effects of motivational orientation on creative writers. *Journal of Personality and Social Psychology*, 48, 393–399.

Amabile, T.M. (1988). A model of creativity and innovation in organizations. In B. Staw and L.L. Cummings (Eds.), *Research in Organizational Behavior*, Vol. 10. Greenwich, CN: JAI Press, pp. 123–167.

Barron, F. and Harrington, D.M. (1981). Creativity, intelligence and personality. *Annual Review of Psychology*, 32, 439–476.

Beach, L.R. and Mitchell, T.R. (1987). Image theory: Principles, goals, and plans in decision making. *Acta Psychologica*, 66, 201–220.

Brockner, J. and Rubin, J.Z. (1985). *Entrapment in Escalating Conflicts*. New York: Springer-Verlag.

Burgelman, R.A. (1989). Intraorganizational ecology of strategy-making and organizational adaptation. Unpublished manuscript, Graduate School of Business, Stanford University.

Campbell, D.T. (1960). Blind variation and selective retention in creative thought as in other knowledge processes. *Psychological Review*, 67, 380–400.

Campbell, D.T. (1969). Reforms as experiments. *American Psychologist*, 24, 409–429.

Carroll, G.R. (1984). Organizational ecology. *Annual Review of Sociology*, 10, 71–93.

Child, J. (1972). Organizational structure, environment, and performance: The role of strategic choice. *Sociometry*, 6, 2–21.

Connolly, T. (1988). Hedgeclipping, tree selling, and the management of ambiguity. In L.R. Pondy, R.J. Boland and H. Thomas (Eds.), *Managing Ambiguity and Change*. Chichester: Wiley.

Dweck, C.S. and Leggett, E.L. (1988). A social-cognitive approach to motivation and personality. *Psychological Review*, 95, 256–273.

Easterbrook, J.A. (1959). The effect of emotion cue utilization and the organization of behavior. *Psychological Review*, 66, 183–201.

Hambrick, D.C. and Finkelstein, S. (1987). Managerial discretion: A bridge between polar views of organizational outcomes. In L.L. Cummings and B. Staw (Eds.), *Research in Organizational Behavior*, Vol. 9. Greenwich, CT: JAI Press, pp. 369–406.

Hannan, M.T. and Freeman, J. (1977). The population ecology of organizations. *American Journal of Sociology*, 82, 929–964.

Jacobs, R.C. and Campbell, D.T. (1961). The perpetuation of an arbitrary tradition through successive generations of a laboratory microculture. *Journal of Abnormal and Social Psychology*, 62, 649–658.

Janis, I. and Mann, L. (1977). *Decision Making: A Psychological Analysis of Conflict, Choice, and Commitment*. New York: Free Press.

Kanter, R.M. (1983). *The Change Masters*. New York: Simon & Schuster.

Kanter, R.M. (1988). When a thousand flowers bloom: Structural, collective, and social conditions for innovation in organization. In B. Staw and L.L. Cummings (Eds.), *Research in Organizational Behavior*, Vol. 10, Greenwich, CT: JAI Press, pp. 169–211.

Katz, R. and Allen, T.J. (1982). Investigating the not invented here (NIH) syndrome: A look at the performance, tenure, and communication patterns of 50 R & D project groups. *R & D Management*, 12, 7–19.

Koestler, A. (1964). *The Act of Creation.* New York: Dell.

Marquis, D.G. (1969). The anatomy of successful innovations. *Innovation*, 1, 35–48.

Mason, R.O. (1969). A dialectical approach to strategic planning. *Management Science*, 15, 403–414.

McGuire, W. (1973). The yin and yang of progress in social psychology: Seven koan. *Journal of Personality and Social Psychology*, 26, 446–456.

Nemeth, C.J. and Staw, B.M. (1989). The tradeoffs of social control and innovation within groups and organizations. In L. Berkowitz (Ed.), *Advances in Experimental Social Psychology*, Vol. 22. New York: Academic Press, pp. 175–210.

Pfeffer, J. (1981). Management as symbolic action: The creation and maintenance of organizational paradigms. In L.L. Cummings and B.M. Staw (Eds.), *Research in Organizational Behavior*, Vol. 3. Greenwich, CT: JAI Press.

Quinn, J.B. (1986). Innovation and corporate strategy: Management chaos. In M. Horwitch (Ed.), *Technology in the Modern Corporation: A Strategic Perspective.* New York: Pergamon Press.

Rosenbloom, R.S. and Cusumano, M.A. (1987). Technological pioneering and competitive advantage: The birth of the VCR industry. *California Management Review*, 29, 51–76.

Ross, J. and Staw, B.M. (1986). Expo 86: An escalation prototype. *Administrative Science Quarterly*, 31, 274–297.

Schneider, B. (1987). The people make the place. *Personnel Psychology*, 14, 437–453.

Scott, W.R. (1981). *Organizations: Rational, Natural, and Open Systems.* Englewood Cliffs, NJ: Prentice-Hall.

Staw, B.M. (1977). The experimenting organization: Problems and prospects. In B. Staw (Ed.), *Psychological Foundations of Organizational Behavior.* Glenview, Illinois: Scott-Foresman.

Staw, B.M. and Boettger, R.D. (1990). Task revision as a form of work performance. *Academy of Management Journal*, September 1990 (in press).

Staw, B.M. and Ross, J. (1987). Behavior in escalation situations: Antecedents, prototypes, and solutions. In L.L. Cummings and B. Staw (Eds.), *Research in Organizational Behavior*, Vol. 9. Greenwich, CT: JAI Press, pp. 39–78.

Staw, B.M., Sandelands, L.E. and Dutton, J.E. (1981). Threat-rigidity effects in organizational behavior: A multilevel analysis. *Administrative Science Quarterly*, 26, 501–524.

Von Hippel, E. (1986). Lead users: A source of novel product concepts. *Management Science*, 32, 791–805.

Weick, K.E. (1976). Educational organizations as loosely coupled systems. *Administrative Science Quarterly*, 42, 1–19.

Weick, K.E. (1983). Contradictions in a community of scholars: The cohesion–accuracy tradeoff. *The Review of Higher Education*, 6, 253–267.

Weick, K.E. and Gilfillan, D.P. (1971). Fate of arbitrary traditions in a laboratory microculture. *Journal of Personality and Social Psychology*, 17, 179–191.

Zucker, L. (1977). The role of institutionalization in cultural persistence. *American Sociological Review*, 42, 726–743.

15 The social psychology of innovation in groups

Michael A. West

University of Sheffield, UK

INNOVATION IN GROUPS AT WORK

Individuals within organizations frequently attempt to introduce new and improved ways of doing things (West, 1987; Nicholson and West, 1988; West, 1989; West and Farr, 1989) and group factors have considerable influence in facilitating or hindering such innovations (West and Wallace, 1988). Collectively, individual and group innovations within organizations, what I call 'emergent innovations' (cf. Dillon's 1982 distinction between existent, emergent and potential problems), can be a powerful force in the tides of change within organizations. While there is, as we have seen, a very large research literature on organizational innovation, there is little research dealing directly with innovation (as opposed to effectiveness) in working groups.

The widely ranging research on innovation in general does provide important insights and opportunities. Many variables have been shown to influence innovation at the individual, group and organizational levels of analysis and it is likely that some factors which influence individual and organizational innovation will also influence group innovation (West and Farr, 1989; West and Frei, 1989). However, no attempts have been made to systematize the research at the group level and to relate the results to social psychological theories of groups more generally. There is a theoretical vacuum in this area and a need for a framework to draw existing knowledge together in such a way as to promote research and guide practice.

Innovation and Creativity at Work   Edited by M.A. West and J.L. Farr
© 1990 John Wiley & Sons Ltd

The theory of group innovation

Innovation has already been defined in this volume (see Chapter 1) but it is important to clarify the use of the concept in order to develop the theory's propositions. Innovation can be measured in terms of both the quantity of innovations introduced and the quality. Quantity refers to the *number* of new ideas introduced and implemented according to predetermined criteria of significance. Quality can be assessed in three ways—in relation to the *newness* of the idea; to the rated *significance* of the idea; and to the ultimate *effectiveness* of the idea.

Antecedents of innovation

Perhaps the greatest obstacle to an understanding of the psychology of innovation is the sheer diversity of the independent variables used in research in the area. Nevertheless it is possible to discern some pattern in the findings which is proposed as having four major conceptual psychological themes: vision, participative safety, concerns with excellence in quality of task performance, and norms for innovation.

(a) Vision

Vision is an idea of a valued outcome which represents a higher order goal and motivating force at work. Work groups with clearly defined objectives are more likely to be effective and to develop new goal-appropriate methods of working since their efforts have focus and direction. Vision implies in addition a value component to the objective. Thus for a health care work group it might be transferring responsibility for health from professionals back to patients; for a computing organization it might be to spread information technology in order to improve human communication; for the individual researcher it might be to make a practical contribution to improving well-being at work; and for the therapist it might be to enable clients to perceive and make more choices in order to live their lives more freely and fully.

The concept of vision can be better understood by describing its dimensions. Thus it is possible to assess vision in relation to its *clarity* and to argue that the clearer the vision the more effective is it likely to be as a facilitator of innovation since it enables focused development of new ideas which can be assessed more precisely.

If it is to be a facilitator of innovation within a group it is important for vision to be *negotiated* and *shared*. Visions (missions or objectives) of a group imposed by those hierarchically superior are unlikely to be facilitative of innovation. Much research indicates that involvement in goal setting fosters greater commitment to those goals (Wall and Lischeron, 1977). Since groups are in constant flux with some members leaving and joining, and others gradually changing their own values and attitudes in the process of development, then shared visions are likely also by implication to be constantly *evolving*.

It is also suggested that vision will be more facilitative of innovation to the extent that it is *valued* within the group. For example, those working within a voluntary organization concerned with reducing levels of child malnutrition are more likely to have motivating visions about their team's work than those who work within the debt collecting department of a commercial organization. Visions should also be relatively *attainable* if they are to facilitate innovation since if the goal cannot be reached it may either be demotivating, or so abstract that practical steps towards its achievements cannot be realistically envisaged.

What is the evidence for the importance of vision? Peters and Waterman (1982) argue strongly for the importance of *values* in organizations in determining excellence. They report that 'virtually all the better performing companies . . . had a well-defined set of guiding beliefs. The less well performing institutions . . . had no set of coherent beliefs (or) the only ones that they got animated about were theories that could be quantified—the financial objectives, such as earnings per share and growth measures' (p. 281). Pinto and Prescott (1987), in a study of 418 research teams, found that a clearly stated mission was the only factor predictive of success at all stages of the innovation process (conception, planning, execution and termination). Kanter (1983) concluded that innovative organizations tended to have clear organizational goals and visions and that most members of the organization were aligned around the goals or vision.

(b) Participative safety

Participativeness and safety are characterized as a single psychological construct in which the contingencies are such that involvement in decision-making is motivated and reinforced while occurring in an environment which is perceived as interpersonally non-threatening. At the organizational level participative safety might be achieved by encouraging individuals and groups to be involved in the process of organizational development while providing explicit reassurances that such involvement will not jeopardize positions. Within the work group all members of a primary health care team might be encouraged to contribute to discussions and decision-making in important aspects of the team's work. At the same time the team's characteristic interpersonal processes would be non-judgemental and supportive of the individual offering contributions and suggestions, and characterized by socio-emotional cohesiveness.

Research has indicated that high levels of participation in decision-making are associated with less resistance to change and greater likelihood of innovation (Wall and Lischeron, 1977). The more people participate in decision-making through having *influence, interacting* and *information sharing*, the more likely are they to invest in the outcomes of those decisions and also to offer ideas for new and improved ways of working (West and Wallace, 1988).

Wall and Lischeron (1977) describe participation as having these three central components. Interaction involves '. . . two parties attempting to reach agreement through working together rather than through recourse to a balance of power based upon the exercise of sanctions' (p. 37). Information sharing, they say, is also central to participation since '. . . interaction between the two parties undertaken with the ultimate aim of reaching agreement over a decision, requires and results in an exchange of information and increased intercommunication' (p. 38). Finally, they argue, participation may be said to increase 'to the extent that the influence of two or more parties in a decision-making process approaches an equal balance' (p. 37).

Work group participation is sometimes taken to necessarily imply group cohesion but within organizations intergroup conflicts are often played out in situations characterized by both high and low levels of participation. Thus, people may participate very fully in the decision-making process in order to achieve their own political ends, or the political ends of their group ·or department. However, such a situation is unlikely to lead to high levels of innovation since people are often unwilling to take risks in situations which they perceive as unsafe.

Parallels to this latter proposition that risk-taking or innovation is more likely in situations of high psychological safety can be found in both developmental and clinical psychological literatures. In studies of child development, children who are secure in their bondings with parents are more likely to explore new situations sooner and more fully than those children whose bonding seems less secure (Ainsworth and Bell, 1974). Within the therapeutic context, therapeutic alliances which communicate to the patient interpersonal safety, lack of judgement and consistency of support, are those within which patients are more likely to explore the most threatening aspects of their own experience (Rogers, 1961). Similarly, it is argued, in a work group members are more likely to take the risk of proposing new and improved ways of working in a climate which they perceive as personally non-threatening and supportive. Where an individual feels that proposing a new idea will lead to an attack, to him or her being censored, ridiculed or penalized, then the person is less likely to take the risk of proposing that new idea.

In individual as well as organizational level studies, leadership styles appear important in influencing innovation. Kanter (1983) and Peters and Waterman (1982) suggest that innovation is most likely to occur where leadership styles are participative and collaborative. Nyström (1979) and Coopey (1987) argue that democratic and collaborative leadership styles are facilitative of innovation.

At the organizational level most writers concur in concluding that centralization of decision-making (or a low degree of participation in decision-making) inhibits innovation in organizations (Hage and Aiken, 1967; Burns and Stalker, 1961; Shepard, 1967; Griffiths, 1964; Thompson, 1965). These authors argue that where decision-making is devolved from the top levels of the organization there will be more autonomy, more commitment and a freer flow of information. Together these factors will facilitate the initiation and implementation of ideas. However, Zaltman *et al.* (1973) argue that while centralization may impede the initiation of innovations, the clarity and formality it provides will facilitate implementation. There is little empirical evidence to support this hypothesis. For example, in one of the more carefully conducted studies comparing organizations, Kimberly and Evanisko (1981) found a negative relationship between centralization and the adoption of innovation in hospitals.

In European research there are several examples which show how schemes to increase participation have resulted in high levels of innovation amongst industrial workers (e.g. Fricke, 1975; Duell and Frei, 1986a). Furthermore, from an examination of helps and hindrances to innovation (West and Farr, 1989) it seems clear the organization structures and processes which facilitate worker participation are likely to increase overall levels of innovation within the organization (see Duell and Frei, 1986b). Kanter (1983) also found that flat organizational structures characterise the more innovative organizations. Thistlethwaite (1963) and Knapp (1963) describe the climate for innovation amongst scientists as warm, supportive but intellectually demanding. Taylor (1963, 1972) and Andrews (1975) suggest the importance of a climate which encourages independent action, while Pelz (1983) sees supportive climates as those encouraging interaction, autonomy, and the production of knowledge-generated achievement. It is of course questionable whether inferences can be made about group behavior on the basis of organizational level studies, but the group level literature reviewed by King and Anderson (Chapter 4) suggests their initial plausibility.

(c) Climate for excellence

A shared concern with excellence of quality of task performance in relation to shared vision or outcomes, characterized by evaluations, modifications, control systems and critical appraisals, is the third psychological component which may be discerned. Within groups this would be evidenced by emphasis on individual and team accountability; control systems for evaluating and modifying performance, critical approaches to quality of task performance (compatible with socio-emotional cohesiveness); inter-team advice, feedback and cooperation; mutual monitoring; appraisal of performance and ideas; clear outcome criteria; exploration of opposing opinions; and a concern to maximize quality of task performance.

Janis' (1972) work on 'group think' and Steiner's (1972) work on process losses have led to the notion that social interaction can characteristically reduce the effectiveness of decision-making. Similarly, it might be argued that cohesive work groups, characterized by high levels of participative safety, would be more likely to generate potentially damaging innovations than groups characterized by conflict. Indeed the work of Moscovici *et al.* (1985) suggests that minority group influence through conflict processes is the major cause of innovation in group settings. However, research on constructive controversy (Tjosvold, 1982, 1984, 1985; Tjosvold and Johnson, 1977; Tjosvold and Field, 1983; Tjosvold *et al.*, 1986) has indicated the value of social interaction and particularly controversy in decision-making.

Research suggests that constructive controversy occurs where decision-makers believe they are in a cooperative context of emphasizing mutually beneficial goals rather than in a competitive context of trying to win and outdo each other (Tjosvold, 1982; Tjosvold and Deemer, 1980); where decision-makers feel their personal competence is confirmed (Tjosvold *et al.*, 1980, 1981), and where they perceive processes of mutual influence rather than attempted dominance (Tjosvold, 1984). Such controversy is likely to be engendered where there are concerns with quality of task performance. This also implies, as Anderson (1989) has pointed out, that groups with a climate for excellence will demonstrate the kind of tolerance for diversity, which 'groupthink' disallows.

Peters and Waterman's (1982) study of organizational effectiveness also emphasized the pursuit of excellence in quality of task performance as being central to innovation and effectiveness. They report that the dominant beliefs of the excellent companies they studied involved a belief in being 'the best'; a belief in the importance of the details of execution, the nuts and bolts of doing the job well; a belief in superior quality and service; and explicit belief in and recognition of the importance of economic growth and profits. Furthermore, they report 'the excellent companies don't test new waters with both feet. Better yet, when they stuck a toe in new waters and failed, they terminated the experiment quickly.'

Commitment to excellence therefore creates a demanding group environment in which new and existing practices are *appraised* and *challenged* in a constructive way; high standards of performance are encouraged, and a diversity of approaches to achieving excellence is tolerated. In such contexts, group members are also likely to monitor each other's work and performance generally in order to encourage high standards and to exercise control over potential risks and errors. Such controversy facilitates the expression of minority positions which can facilitate innovation (Nemeth and Wachtler, 1983). A group environment in which people feel stimulated to express themselves in an open non-political way is more favourable to innovation than a 'soft' atmosphere with poor standards of performance (e.g. Feldman, 1989).

(d) Norms of and support for innovation

Finally there are the *norms of innovation or the expectation, approval and practical support of attempts to introduce new and improved ways of doing things in the work environment.* At the organizational level such norms may be explicit in the socialization practices for incumbents or implicit in the culture of the organization. Within groups new ideas may be characteristically rejected or ignored, or they may find both verbal and practical support.

Many groups and organizations, as part of their objectives, express support for the development of new and improved ways of working, but often do not practically provide support. It is useful therefore to distinguish between *articulated* and *enacted* support for innovation. The theory proposes that high levels of articulated and enacted support for innovation will lead to more attempts to introduce significant innovations.

This support can take several forms: *verbal support* within and outside group meetings; group and interpersonal *cooperation* in the development and application of new ideas; and the provision of *time* and *resources* by group members to develop and apply the ideas. Some organizations, for example, require members to devote a percentage of their work time to the development of their own new ideas and provide rewards for those who are successful (Daft, 1986). Mumford and Gustafson (1988) and Abbey and Dickson (1983) describe innovative research and development cultures as providing physical support for creative efforts, and recognition and reward for superior performance, particularly with respect to the initial exploratory stages of innovation.

The notion of support for innovation also implies a tolerance of error so that the innovator is not penalized when a risk does not pay off. Among best performing companies, Peters and Waterman (1982) found a shared belief that most members of the organization should be innovative, but importantly, the corollary was enabling safe experimentation.

Those in positions of power often have more influence over norms than subordinates so leaders in groups may well be more influential in supporting group innovation. The research literature suggests that the values and attitudes of the elite in organizations are of importance in determining level of innovation. Schroeder *et al.* (1987) found that innovations are more likely to be pursued when managers two or more levels above the initiation level supported the idea.

Kimberly (1981) concludes that professional administrators committed to innovation and with participative leadership styles are needed to facilitate organizational innovation. Cummings (1965) argues that top management's values for innovation play a crucial role in an organization's level of innovation and that innovations are more likely to be implemented if they are congruent with the goals and values of top management. Hage and Dewar (1973) found that the values of the elite in the organization explained more of the variance in innovation than any single structural dimension. Thus, group norms for innovation may be stronger to the extent that they are congruent with those of group leaders as well as those of top management within organizations.

Finally, a number of writers have drawn attention to the notion of an 'idea champion' whose energy and commitment to a particular idea provides a vital force in securing its implementation. Indeed some organizations institutionalize the role in order to ensure innovations have a better chance of success. They may provide time and resources for the champion to develop the idea to implementation (Daft, 1986). Daft argues that, where the role of the idea champion is formalized and resourced, innovations are more likely to occur.

THE RELATIONSHIP BETWEEN THE PREDICTOR VARIABLES AND INNOVATION OUTCOMES

It is proposed that the four psychological constructs described above can be used to enable prediction of innovation at work. It is further proposed that two of the constructs will relate principally to quantity of innovation and two to quality of innovation. Specifically it is argued that norms for innovation and participative safety are group process variables and are more likely to encourage quantity of attempts to introduce new ideas—the number of innovations—since they influence potential innovators by creating appropriate social reinforcement contingencies. Vision and concern with quality, it is proposed, are more task or product oriented and are therefore more likely to affect the significance and quality of the innovation product—the kind of innovations. Vision provides the specificity of direction which facilitates precise idea generation, while concern with quality is self-evidently more a predictor of quality than quantity of innovation. These relationships are illustrated in Figure 1.

However, it is accepted that all four factors will have some influence on both quality and quantity of group innovation though the magnitude will differ across the factors. The relationships between the antecedents and outcomes are described below. Finally the theory does not consider the complete absence of these psychological factors or the complete absence of innovation as likely in most work environments.

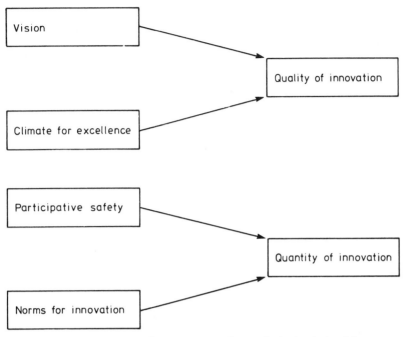

Figure 1 Theory of group innovation: principal relationships

(i) Vision and innovation

It is argued that the primary positive influence of vision will be upon the quality of innovation, but that it will have a secondary positive influence upon quantity.

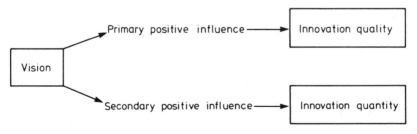

Vision gives group members clear guidelines or criteria for the development of new ideas, i.e. the clearer the vision, the easier will it be to develop effective new and improved ways of working which help to achieve that vision. Thus the effectiveness of ideas will be more easily judged since clarity of vision implies criteria for assessing the suitability and appropriateness of new ways of working. Vision then is considered to exert influence primarily over the content of innovation by enabling its contribution to goal orientation to be judged. It is seen first and foremost as a task-related influence affecting the kind of innovations.

At the same time, the theory proposes that vision has an evaluative and motivational component. To the extent that the vision has intrinsic value for group members (consider the example of reducing child malnutrition), the more likely it is to motivate them to achieve its realization. Vision is therefore likely to have an impact upon the quantity of attempts to introduce new ideas, though it is argued that this effect will be secondary to its effect upon quality of innovations.

It is considered that to achieve high levels of significant, novel and effective innovation within a work group, an implicit or explicit clear shared vision is a necessary, though not sufficient, condition. Without the beacon of such a vision it is argued that groups will be unable to consistently introduce and guide high quality new ways of working.

(ii) Climate of excellence and innovation

The second key variable, climate for excellence, is also seen as primarily influencing quality of innovation primarily, with negligible or even negative impact upon quantity.

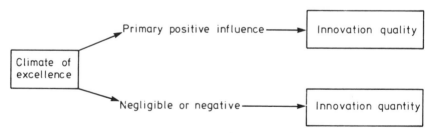

A concern with excellence in task performance directed towards vision will be characterized by evaluations, modifications, control systems, critical appraisals and constructive controversy. It is argued that these processes will affect the quality of innovations and particularly their effectiveness (and by implication their appropriateness). Within such a climate, opposing opinions are explored and the group's concern is to integrate information, opinions and ideas into a high quality solution or decision. By careful appraisal of ideas and their process of application the low quality outcomes observed by Janis (1972) in some highly cohesive groups are more likely to be foreseen and prevented. Climate of excellence is clearly a more task-related variable influencing effectiveness and significance of ideas.

In general it is argued that a climate of excellence will have little positive influence on quantity of ideas and that alone it may well have a negative influence (i.e. in the relative absence of participative safety and norms for innovation). In a group context in which underlying assumptions are challenged, ideas and practices are monitored and appraised, and opposing opinions are encouraged and explored, it is likely that flawed innovative ideas will be rejected prior to their application. Moreover group members may be more likely to privately appraise their own ideas before proposing them and so may reject ideas before presenting them to the group.

This hypothesis differs significantly from that associated with the participative safety construct. Whereas I argue that the relative absence of participative safety will lead to a reluctance by group members to propose any idea, here it is suggested that a climate of excellence will lead members to appraise the value of new ideas before presenting them and will likely lead to the private rejection of only implausible new ideas. I also suggest that the quality of new ideas at initial proposal will be higher since group members will be practised at anticipating and working through quality control issues.

A climate of excellence is seen as a necessary, though not sufficient, condition for sustained high quality group innovation. Without careful appraisal, constructive controversy and a preparedness to explore opposing opinions carefully, groups are likely to be carried along by the momentum of their enthusiasm for an innovative idea, rather than by a clear understanding of its value. Research in social psychology on decision-making (Tversky and Kahneman, 1974; Tjosvold *et al.*, 1986; Janis, 1972; Steiner, 1972) has shown how such unbridled enthusiasm can lead to poor quality decision-making. A climate of excellence is therefore seen as of great importance for the effectiveness of group innovation.

(iii) Participative safety and innovation

Groups characterized by high levels of participative safety are more likely to foster innovation than those with lower levels. Firstly, high levels of interpersonal safety will, as has already been argued, enable risk-taking and a preparedness to suggest new ideas without fear of personal censure. At the same time the high interaction associated with participation will make the cross-fertilization of ideas, considered by Mumford and Gustafson (1988) to be central to creativity and innovation, increasingly likely. Therefore interaction will lead to more new ideas.

Similarly, information sharing will give group members more knowledge upon which to base or develop ideas for new and improved ways of doing things. The element of interpersonal safety, it is argued, will also increase information sharing and interacting as well as fostering quantity of innovation in its own right. Finally the involvement of group members in decision-

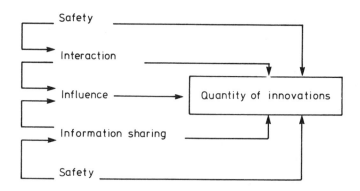

making, it is proposed, will lead to innovation since more people will be contributing ideas from their different perspectives during the decision-making process. Participative safety will therefore have a primary influence upon quantity of innovations.

At the same time, information sharing is likely to produce better quality innovation since, for example, the effectiveness of innovations is likely to be dependent upon knowledge about the domain within which they are being implemented (Amabile, 1983). Moreover, the cross-fertilization of ideas, which is a product of interaction, will affect the significance and novelty of innovations produced by the group. Research indicates that greater involvement of people in the decision-making process is associated with less resistance to change, and therefore is likely to lead to greater effectiveness. Through consultation and interaction, group members are likely to anticipate and prevent potential weaknesses from adversely affecting the outcome of innovation attempts. Safety is also likely to influence quality since group members will be more likely to suggest radical departures (novelty and significance components of quality) from normal practice to the extent that they perceive a climate of interpersonal support and warmth rather than one of competition and aggression. However, this effect of participative safety on quality is seen as secondary to effects on quantity, since it is argued that participative safety is primarily a group process variable influencing interpersonal interactions in general more than task performance in particular.

The theory proposes that groups will only produce sustained high levels of innovation in a climate characterized by participative safety and that participative safety is therefore a necessary, though not sufficient, condition for high innovation. In particular, the element of safety is seen as essential for groups to build a climate of trust within which members will feel free to offer many new ideas without fear of ridicule, censure or loss of political power.

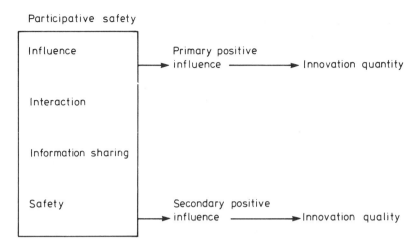

(iv) Norms for innovation

Norms for innovation in the group are proposed to have a primary influence on quantity of new ideas and a negligible positive or negative influence on quality. If articulated support for innovation is characteristic of the group then it is argued that group members, because of the social reinforcement contingencies, will be more likely to propose new ideas regardless of their quality. And where enacted practical support (time, resources, cooperation) is available, more ideas are likely to reach the implementation stage than if it is unavailable. Clearly then norms of innovation are likely to affect quantity of innovation through social support and practical facilitation processes.

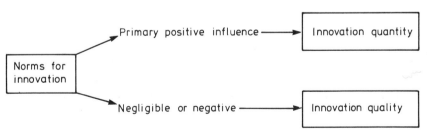

However, since this construct refers to support for new ideas regardless of their content, it may be that high levels of support for innovation, particularly in the absence of clear vision and a climate for excellence, would lead to poor quality. Thus unreserved or uncritical acclaim for new ideas and incautious offers of practical support, might lead to the application of potentially damaging ideas within the group.

Norms for innovation are also considered to be a necessary though insufficient condition for quantity of innovation. When support for innovation is frequently articulated, group members will be alert to the possibility of improving working methods, products, practices or procedures since appropriate social cues will exist. And, if enacted support is high, group members will find it easier to bring their ideas to fruition within the workplace, since support and resources will be generally forthcoming from others in the group. The definition of innovation used in this book requires *application* of new ideas, and the presence of enacted support will therefore clearly increase the level of innovation.

A summary of the hypothesized relationships in the theory of work group innovation is presented in Figure 1. Following this, consideration is given to the effects of different combinations of the antecedent variables upon quality and quantity of innovation.

Interaction of the four factors and their effects on innovation

It has been suggested above that, in any work group, each of the four factors is likely to be present to a greater or lesser degree and that certain factors are necessary but are not alone sufficient for high innovation quantity or quality. Below is presented a set of predictions building on the assumptions described above to predict levels of innovation on the basis of combinations of the antecedent group factors. In order to develop these hypotheses, two levels of each factor are proposed—either relatively high or relatively low. The predictions are as shown in Table 1.

The table shows that a combination of high participative safety and high norms for innovation is considered sufficient for high quantity of innovation.

Table 1 Relationship between combinations of the antecedent factors and innovation outcomes

Level of the four antecedent factors[a]				Innovation outcomes	
Vision	Participative safety	Climate of excellence	Norms of innovation	Quantity	Quality
Low	High	Low	High	High	Low
High	Low	High	Low	Low	High
Low	High	High	High	High	Medium
High	High	High	Low	Medium	High
High	High	High	High	High	High

[a]All other combinations of the antecedent variables are predicted to be associated with both low quantity and quality innovation.

It is thought that participative safety will enable group members to feel sufficiently informed, influential and interpersonally supported in order to offer new ideas, and that norms for innovation will provide the social reinforcement and practical support for ideas to be proposed and implemented. The relative absence of either factor will lead to low levels of innovation.

A combination of clear, shared vision and a persistent climate of excellence is sufficient for high quality of innovation. Clarity of vision will enable precise specifications of the value of innovation so that appropriate ideas will be more easily recognized and therefore implemented. Similarly a climate of excellence will encourage careful exploration of the idea and an intelligent monitoring of the process of its implementation, thereby providing a surer guarantee of effectiveness.

Now I shall briefly consider some of the limitations of the theory. First, it is evident that the theory pays no attention to the extra-group factors which give rise to innovations. The effects of technology, organizational choices, demands and pressures, and economic and social change have been neglected. Innovation is a product of many other variables and the present theory offers little understanding of how these interact with group processes to give rise to innovation. Extension of the framework to include contextual factors would much improve its potential both in the theoretical and practical domains.

Second, the framework does not address the question of the impact of individual differences upon group innovation. It seems reasonable to assume that groups will differ in their innovativeness partly as a function of the collective differences in innovativeness of the people who constitute them. Some research on individual innovation has already been conducted, notably by Kirton and colleagues (Kirton, 1989) but it is unclear how individual differences might affect the relationships between antecedent factors and innovation outcomes described above. At present, it is clear that the theoretical framework currently ignores individual differences which are likely to form part of any comprehensive explanation of the effects of differences between work groups in quality and quantity of innovation.

The value of the theory is that it sets an explicit research agenda and offers testable propositions. It identifies characteristics of groups and how they combine to affect quality and quantity of innovation. In so doing it provides guidelines for research in terms of both content and method. Nevertheless, the theory is far from complete. Justification for its content awaits empirical support, and it does not take into account either organizational or individual difference factors. It is thus a theory which should be refined in the light of new evidence and extended to cover a wider range of variables. It is, however, a theory which provides a much needed and plausible structure to an area of enquiry hitherto neglected and much in need of direction.

THE PROCESS OF INNOVATION

Having considered a variance approach to understanding group innovations, I shall now offer a framework for studying the process of innovation before attempting to integrate the two. This process model is considered to be applicable at the group and organizational levels. It differs fundamentally from previous models in one respect: it considers the innovation process as a cycle. All innovations may be considered to be modifications of existing group or organizational systems whether they be technological, administrative or mixed. Even new systems are never entirely separate from existing systems but rather evolve out of them. The corollary of this assumption is that all systems are a product of and subject to innovation. Thus a human resource management system will likely have developed as a result of repeated introductions of new ways of doing things. The system, and aspects of the system, can therefore be seen as continually going through an innovation cycle, as illustrated in Figure 2.

Four phases of the cycle are proposed. The first is a *recognition* phase in which (a) a performance gap is recognized and ideation occurs in response, or (b) given that innovations may be imported without prior identification of a performance gap, the value of an external innovation may be recognized, or (c) ideation in the absence of a performance gap, or stimulus problem may lead to the recognition of a potentially useful innovation.

The second phase in the process is *initiation* which involves proposing the innovation to others in the work group or organization. This phase is considered to include adjustment and development of the idea in response to reactions from others in the group or organization, and, at the extreme, the adjustment might involve abandonment of the innovation. In most cases it is likely that some anticipatory adjustment will also occur amongst those systems likely to be affected by the proposed innovation, including preparation

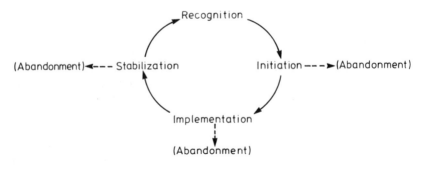

Figure 2   The innovation cycle

to resist. At the initiation phase also, the proposed innovation may spawn other innovations either in addition to or instead of the original idea.

The third phase, *implementation*, is when the innovation is first used by the group or organization and effects are observable in work practices, processes, products or procedures. At this phase again the innovation may undergo development or adjustment as constraints and opportunities become apparent in the innovation process. This phase will also be characterized by processes associated with the introduction of change in organizations such as resistance, cooperation, coercion, conflict and, in some cases, capitulation. Of course the implementation of the innovation may also expose fatal weaknesses or produce resistance such that it is abandoned.

Following implementation is *stabilization* when the innovation becomes a routinized part of the system with associated standardization and control procedures. Again, failure to stabilize is likely to lead to abandonment of the innovation or to further recognition and modification of the innovation, thus beginning the cycle again.

Because of the fundamental premise that all organizational systems and procedures are evolving the innovation process is not deemed to end at stabilization. It is proposed that, at some time, the recognition phase will be reached again, perhaps because of environmental changes (new customer demands), implementation of new ideas of staff (ways of streamlining the production process) or the import of new ideas from similar organizations (introducing autonomous work groups).

The innovation process is seen as cyclical with variations in speed and with interdependence between the different phases. Thus speed of implementation may affect the success of stabilization. Space does not permit a full explication of this process model of innovation (see West and Anderson, 1990, for a fuller account) but I would argue that such a model will prove more useful in practice than traditional stage models of innovation since it more accurately portrays the continuously evolving nature of work practices than those which, I believe, artificially represent innovations as having clearly delineated beginnings and ends.

Group influences on the innovation cycle

Thus far we have focused on the relationship between group level variables and outcomes in terms of quantity and quality of innovation; and on the process of innovation. In Chapter 2 and Chapter 4, King and King and Anderson argued for models which integrated variance and process approaches. In particular, the value of models which proposed relationships between group characteristics and different parts of the process was suggested.

Figure 3 shows the proposed relationship between the four factors of the group innovation theory and the phases of the innovation cycle described

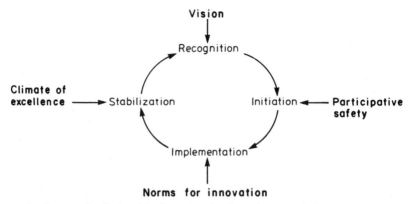

Figure 3 Proposed relationship between the four factors of the group innovation theory and the phases of the innovation cycle

above. If the theory of group innovation is a good representation of reality all four factors should of course have some influence throughout the process. However, what is proposed is that each factor will have primary influence during one phase of the cycle.

First it is suggested that vision will most likely influence the recognition process since clear visions or objectives will heighten sensitivity to performance gaps or to new work practices which will enable achievement of the objectives or vision. Initiation—the proposing of an idea to a group or organization—will be facilitated primarily by a climate of participative safety. The hesitancy of proposing and negotiating change which may represent a threat to the status quo will be moderated by perceptions of psychological safety, cohesiveness, personal influence or empowerment and norms for information sharing and interacting. The actual implementation of the innovation will perhaps be enabled most by articulated and enacted norms for innovation, such that time, cooperation, resources and verbal support are given to the application of the idea and sustained during the initial teething period. Finally, an innovation will only stabilize or be abandoned if critical constructive appraisals of its value are conducted. If an innovation is wanting in terms of its effectiveness but is neither abandoned nor modified, it will continue to be resisted or even sabotaged by those whom it affects. However, in a climate of excellence, the innovation will be subjected to careful scrutiny such that necessary improvements are instituted or, in the absence of improvements, its continuing use within the organization may be sharply questioned.

INFLUENCE PROCESSES AND INNOVATIONS

Nyström, Kimberly *et al.* and Damanpour have argued in this book for representations of innovation processes which reflect the complexity of organizational life. A major unresolved question is how do groups and individuals successfully innovate within organizational settings, particularly when what they propose represents a threat to the status quo?

Much research in organizational psychology has focused on socialization of individuals into organizations (e.g. Van Maanen and Schein, 1979) and how values and norms are communicated to and adopted by people and groups at work. Similarly, until the last 20 years, social psychology was primarily concerned with how majorities bring about compliance, identification and internalization of attitudes in individuals and minorities. The work of Milgram (1974) on obedience to authority and Sherif's (1935) and Asch's (1956) work on conformity have prompted much writing on the processes whereby majority opinion prevails over the viewpoints of individuals.

Within social psychology, however, there has recently been an expansion of research and theorizing into how minorities exert influence over majorities (Moscovici and Faucheux, 1972, referred to also by Farr in Chapter 10). How do groups like the Greens and feminists bring about change in majority opinion when they begin as minorities in conflict with majorities and those in power? A number of researchers have shown that minority consistency of arguments over time is likely to lead to change in majority views (Maass and Clark, 1984). Moreover, the experimental evidence suggests that while majorities bring about attitude change through public compliance prior to attitude change (i.e. that the individual may first publicly conform to the majority view prior to internalizing that view), minority influence works in the opposite direction. People exposed to a confident and consistent minority change their private views prior to expressing public agreement. This process has been labelled by minority influence researchers as 'conversion'.

In an early study by Moscovici et al. (1969) subjects were shown blue and green slides and asked to categorize them accordingly. Subjects in an experimental group were exposed to a minority who consistently categorized some of the blue slides as green. This procedure had no impact on the majority correctly categorizing the blue slides. However, when subjects were subsequently asked to individually rate 'blue-green' slides as either blue or green over half rated the slides in a direction which was consistent with their having been influenced by the minority. A control group showed no such effects. Nemeth and Wachtler (1974) demonstrated similar effects in a study of jury decision-making on compensation claims, showing private shifts towards the minority position in new cases, but public resistance to the minority position on the original case.

The research on minority influence suggests that conversion is most likely to occur where the minority is consistent and confident in the presentation of arguments. Moreover, it is a behavioural style of persistence which is most likely to lead to attitude change and innovation. The prices of minority influences according to Moscovici et al. (1985) are unpopularity and conflict. It is argued that innovation inevitably produces cognitive conflict, and therefore interpersonal conflict, since it represents a challenge to cognitive schema or to the social status quo.

In more recent work Nemeth (Nemeth and Wachtler, 1983; Nemeth, 1986; Nemeth and Kwan, 1987; Nemeth and Chiles, 1988) suggests that minority influences lead to more independence and to divergent and creative thinking. In one study (Nemeth and Chiles, 1988) subjects were exposed to a minority which consistently judged blue stimuli as green. When these subjects were subsequently placed in a majority influence situation where the majority consistently incorrectly rated red stimuli as orange, they showed almost complete independence and did not differ significantly from control subjects who made their judgements of the red stimuli alone. Those not exposed to minority dissent agreed on over 70% of trials with the majority's incorrect judgement of orange.

In a study of originality (Nemeth and Kwan, 1987) subjects were told that a majority or minority saw blue slides as green in previous studies. Each subject was subsequently exposed to a single subject who consistently rated blue slides as green. Finally, each subject was asked to respond seven times in a word association exercise to the words blue or green. Those exposed to a minority judgement gave more word associations and with a higher degree of originality (they were statistically less frequent according to normative data) than those exposed to a majority view. In reviewing this research Nemeth concludes that:

> ... this *york* argues for the importance of minority dissent, even dissent that is wrong. *urther*, we assume that its import lies not in the truth of its position or even in the likelihood that it will prevail. Rather it appears to stimulate divergent thought. Issues and problems are considered from more perspectives and, on balance, [people] detect new solutions and find more correct answers. (Nemeth, 1989; p. 9)

What are the implications of this work for our understanding of innovation in work settings? First, minority influence theory provides one understanding of intra-group processes leading to creativity and innovation. Second, the theory suggests what processes are involved in innovation in organizations— conflict and conversion—while alerting us to the over-simplicity of unitarist views of innovation (all innovation is good and is good for all in the organization). Third, it suggests the importance of dissent within organizations for independence and creativity. Fourth, it implies that individuals and groups can bring about change in organizational settings through consistency, persistence and confidence. This is an area of social psychological research upon which organizational psychology could usefully draw. However, until recently (West and Farr, 1989; Nemeth and Staw, 1989) the link between the two areas has not been made. One task which awaits researchers and writers on innovation is a full and careful analysis of the implications of minority influence research for an understanding of organizational processes and innovation at work.

CONCLUSIONS

At the beginning of this volume it was suggested that the literature on innovation was something of a briar thicket in which the unwary traveller becomes trapped. Implicit in what followed was the idea that the contributors would cut swathes through the thicket so that travellers might find easier ways through or at least see more clearly the road ahead. A brief review of the contents will give some indication of the extent to which this hope has been fulfilled.

In Chapter 2, King described the demography of the thicket in a literature review which goes far beyond anything previously published in its comprehensiveness and carefulness. In Chapter 3, Farr and Ford present the first model of individual level innovation at work and therefore offer a starting point for more precise work in this area. King and Anderson (Chapter 4) critically appraise the literature on groups and offer new methodologies and constructive questions for researchers examining innovation at this level. Payne in Chapter 5 describes and interprets a largely ignored but major research project on group effectiveness and offers clear prescriptions for group level research on innovation. These are important advances for areas where previous research has been limited to theorizing and model building largely borrowed from other areas, often with poor fit.

Chapters 6 to 9 add cogent reasoning and criticism to the literature on organizational innovation. The authors argue for the importance of considering the different types of innovation, the consequences of innovation, and approaches to research which reflect the complexity of the topic. Nicholson, in an iconoclastic essay on writings on innovation, urges researchers and writers to consider fundamental conceptual issues before forging ahead with research, the underlying constructs of which have not been clearly framed. These four chapters taken together offer researchers new starting points and perspectives in an area that has seen much work but limited progress, as King points out in Chapter 2. In Chapters 10 to 13, practical prescriptions for facilitating innovation at work at the individual and organizational levels are offered (for change agents both internal and external to the organization). Finally, in the penultimate chapter, Staw argues for more integrated theory building and interdisciplinary cooperation and illustrates the approach with a new evolutionary model of innovation.

In this final chapter and in the book as a whole it has been repeatedly proposed that an understanding of innovation can be considerably enhanced by psychological analysis and theorizing. The implications of such an understanding for those concerned with the dynamics of human social processes are profound. Some of the most pressing human problems are institutionalized and it is only by bringing about innovative change that many of these problems can be overcome. For example, social systems and structures which institutionalize inequalities in resource and opportunity distribution within communities promote inter-group hostility and alienation (Sherif, 1966; Allport, 1964). Effective responses to these problems require changes not only in individual behaviour, but innovative change in the organizations and institutions which perpetuate them. By developing a more sophisticated understanding of the processes and outcomes of innovation, based on viewing innovation as a social process, we may begin to better understand how organizations can evolve to meet the needs of the people who work within them as well as the communities they serve.

ACKNOWLEDGEMENTS

I wish to thank Toby Wall for very helpful comments on an earlier version of this chapter.

Correspondence address:
MRC/ESRC Social and Applied Psychology Unit, Department of Psychology, University of Sheffield, Sheffield S10 2TN, UK.

REFERENCES

Abbey A. and Dickson, J.W. (1983). R & D work climate and innovation in semi-conductors. _Academy of Management Journal_, **26**, 362–368.

Ainsworth, M.D. and Bell, S.M. (1974). Mother–infant interaction and the development of competence. In K. Connolly and J. Bruner (Eds.), _The Growth of Competence._ New York: Academic Press.

Allport, G.W. (1964). _The Nature of Prejudice._ Cambridge, Mass: Addison-Wesley.

Amabile, T.M. (1983). _The Social Psychology of Creativity._ New York: Springer-Verlag.

Anderson, N. (1989). Work group innovation: Current research concerns and future directions. Paper presented as a symposium contribution at the 4th West European Congress on the Psychology of Work and Organization, Cambridge, England, 10–12 April 1989.

Andrews, F.M. (1975). Social and psychological factors that influence the creative process. In I.A. Taylor and J.W. Getzels (Eds.), _Perspectives in Creativity._ Chicago: Aldine.

Asch, G.E. (1956). Studies of independence and conformity: I. A minority of one against a unanimous majority. *Psychological Monographs*, 70, 9 (whole issue, No. 416).

Burns, T. and Stalker, G. (1961). *The Management of Innovation*. London: Tavistock.

Coopey, J.G. (1987). Creativity in complex organizations. Unpublished MSc dissertation, Department of Occupational Psychology, Birkbeck College, University of London.

Cummings, L. (1965). Organizational climates for creativity. *Academy of Management Journal*, 8, 220–227.

Daft, R.L. (1986). A dual-core model of organizational innovation. *Academy of Management Journal*, 21, 193–210.

Dillon, J.T. (1982). Problem solving and finding. *Journal of Creative Behavior*, 16, 97–111.

Duell, W. and Frei, F. (Eds.) (1986a). *Arbeit Gestalten-Mitarbeiter Beteiligen*. Frankfurt AM Campus: Eine Heuristik Qualifizieren der Arbeitgestaltung.

Duell, W. and Frei, F. (1986b). *Leitfaden fur Qualifizierende Arbeitsgestaltung*. Koln: TUV-Rheinland.

Feldman, S.P. (1989). The broken wheel: The inseparability of autonomy and control in innovation within organizations. *Journal of Management Studies*, 26(2), 22–80.

Fricke, W. (1975). *Arbeitsorganisation und Qualifikation*. Bonn–Bad Godesberg: Neue Gesellschaft.

Griffiths, D.E. (1964). Administrative theory and change in organizations. In M.D. Miles (Ed.), *Innovations in Education*. New York: Teachers College Press.

Hage, J. and Aiken, M. (1967). Program change and organizational properties: a comparative analysis. *American Journal of Sociology*, 72, 503–519.

Hage, J. and Dewar, R. (1973). Elite values versus organizational structure in predicting innovation. *Administrative Science Quarterly*, 18, 279–290.

Janis, I.L. (1972). *Victims of Groupthink: A Psychological Study of Foreign Policy Decisions*. Boston: Houghton Mifflin.

Kanter, R.M. (1983). *The Change Masters*. New York: Simon and Schuster.

Kimberly, J.R. (1981). Managerial innovation. In P.C. Nystrom and W.H. Starbuck (Eds.), *Handbook of Organizational Design*. Oxford: Oxford University Press.

Kimberly, J.R. and Evanisko, M.J. (1981). Organizational innovation: the influence of individual, organizational and contextual factors on hospital adoption of technological and administrative innovations. *Academy of Management Journal*, 24, 689–713.

Kirton, M.J. (Ed.) (1989). *Adaptors and Innovators: Styles of Creativity and Problem Solving*. London: Routledge.

Knapp, R.H. (1963). Demographic, cultural and personality attributes of scientists. In C.W. Taylor and F. Barron (Eds.), *Scientific Creativity: Its Recognition and Development*. New York: John Wiley and Sons.

Maass, A. and Clark, R.D. (1984). Hidden impact of minorities: fifty years of minority influence research. *Psychological Bulletin*, 95(3), 428–450.

Milgram, S. (1974). *Obedience to Authority*. New York: Harper and Row.

Moscovici, S. and Faucheux, C. (1972). Social influence, conforming bias, and the study of active minorities. In L. Berkowitz (Ed.), *Advances in Experimental Social Psychology*, Vol. 6. New York: Academic Press.

Moscovici, S., Lage, E. and Naffrechoux, M. (1969). Influence of a consistent minority on the responses of a majority in a color perception task. *Sociometry*, 32, 365–379.

Moscovici, S., Mugny, G. and Avermaet, E.U. (1985). *Perspectives on Minority Influence*. Cambridge: Cambridge University Press.

Mumford, M.D. and Gustafson, S.B. (1988). Creativity syndrome: integration, application and innovation. *Psychological Bulletin*, **103**, 27–43.

Nemeth, C. (1986). Differential contributions of majority and minority influence. *Psychological Review*, **93**, 23–32.

Nemeth, C. (1989). The stimulating properties of dissent: the case of recall. Paper presented at Third International Symposium on Minority Influence, Perugia, Italy, 22–24 June.

Nemeth, C. and Chiles, C. (1988). Modelling courage: the role of dissent in fostering independence. *European Journal of Social Psychology*, **18**, 275–280.

Nemeth, C. and Kwan, J. (1987). Minority influence, divergent thinking and the detection of correct solutions. *Journal of Applied Social Psychology*, **9**, 788–799.

Nemeth, C. and Staw, B.M. (1989). The trade offs of social control and innovation in groups and organizations. In L. Berkowitz (Ed.), *Advances in Experimental Social Psychology*, Vol. 2. New York: Academic Press.

Nemeth, C.J. and Wachtler, J. (1974). Creating the perceptions of consistency and confidence: a necessary condition for minority influence. *Sociometry*, **37**, 529–540.

Nemeth, C.J. and Wachtler, J. (1983). Creative problem solving as a result of majority vs minority influence. *European Journal of Social Psychology*, **13**, 45–55.

Nicholson, N. and West, M.A. (1988). *Managerial Job Change: Men and Women in Transition*. Cambridge: Cambridge University Press.

Nyström, H. (1979). *Creativity and Innovation*. Chichester: Wiley.

Pelz, D.C. (1983). Use of information channels in urban innovation. *Knowledge*, **5**, 3–25.

Peters, T.J. and Waterman, R.H. (1982). *In Search of Excellence: Lessons from America's Best Run Companies*. New York: Harper and Row.

Pinto, J.K. and Prescott, J.E. (1987). Changes in critical success factor importance over the life of a project. *Academy of Management Proceedings*, New Orleans, 328–332.

Rogers, C.R. (1961). *On Becoming a Person*. Boston: Houghton Mifflin.

Schroeder, R., Van de Ven, A.H., Scudder, G. and Polley, D. (1987). Observations leading to a process model of innovation. *Agribusiness Management Journal*, **2**.

Shepard, H.A. (1967). Innovation-resisting and innovation-producing organizations. *Journal of Business*, **40**, 470–477.

Sherif, M. (1935). A study of some social factors in perception. *Archives of Psychology*, **27**, 187.

Sherif, M. (1966). *Group Conflict and Cooperation: Their Social Psychology*. London: Routledge and Kegan Paul.

Steiner, I.D. (1972). *Group Process and Productivity*. New York: Academic Press.

Taylor, C.W. (1963). Variables related to creativity and productivity among men in two research laboratories. In C.W. Taylor and F. Barron (Eds.), *Scientific Creativity: Its Recognition and Development*. New York: John Wiley and Sons.

Taylor, C.W. (1972). Can organizations be creative too? In C.W. Taylor (Ed.), *Climate for Creativity*. New York: Pergamon Press.

Thompson, V.A. (1965). Bureaucracy and innovation. *Administrative Science Quarterly*, **10**, 1–20.

Thistlethwaite, D.L. (1963). The college environment as a determinant of research potentiality. In C.W. Taylor and F. Barron (Eds.), *Scientific Creativity: Its Recognition and Development*. New York: John Wiley and Sons.

Tjosvold, D. (1982). Effects of approach to controversy on superiors' incorporation of subordinates' information in decision making. *Journal of Applied Psychology*, **67**, 189–193.

Tjosvold, D. (1984). Effects of crisis orientation on managers' approach to controversy in decision making. *Academy of Management Journal*, **27**, 130–138.
Tjosvold, D. (1985). Implications of controversy research for management. *Journal of Management*, **11**, 21–37.
Tjosvold, D. and Deemer, D.K. (1980). Effects of controversy within a cooperative or competitive context on organizational decision-making. *Journal of Applied Psychology*, **65**, 590–595.
Tjosvold, F. and Field, R.H.G. (1983). Effects of social context on consensus and majority vote decision making. *Academy of Management Journal*, **26**, 500–506.
Tjosvold, D. and Johnson, D.W. (1977). The effects of controversy on cognitive perspective-taking. *Journal of Educational Psychology*, **69**, 679–685.
Tjosvold, D., Johnson, D.W. and Fabey, L. (1980). Effects of controversy and defensiveness on cognitive perspective taking. *Psychological Reports*, **4**, 1043–1053.
Tjosvold, D., Johnson, D.W. and Lerner, J. (1981). The effects of affirmation and acceptance on incorporation of an opposing opinion in problem-solving. *Journal of Social Psychology*, **114**, 103–110.
Tjosvold, D., Wedley, W.C. and Field, R.H.G. (1986). Constructive controversy, the Vroom–Yetton Model, and managerial decision-making. *Journal of Occupational Behaviour*, **7**, 125–138.
Tversky, A. and Kahneman, D. (1974). Judgement under uncertainty: heuristics and biases. *Science*, **185**, 1124–1131.
Van Mannen, J. and Schein, E.H. (1979). Toward a theory of organizational socialization. In B.M. Staw (Ed.), *Research in Organizational Behavior*. Vol. 1. Greenwich, CT: JAI Press.
Wall, T.D. and Lischeron, J.H. (1977). *Worker Participation: A Critique of the Literature and Some Fresh Evidence*. Maidenhead, England: McGraw-Hill.
West, M.A. (1987). Role innovation in the world of work. *British Journal of Social Psychology*, **26**, 305–315.
West, M.A. (1989). Innovations amongst health care professionals. *Social Behaviour*, **4**, 173–184.
West, M.A. and Anderson, N. (1990). The process of innovation, in preparation.
West, M.A. and Farr, J.L. (1989). Innovation at work: psychological perspectives. *Social Behaviour*, **4**, 15–30.
West, M.A. and Frei, F. (1989). Innovation. In S. Greif, H. Holling and N. Nicholson (Eds.), *Arbeits- und Organisationspsychologie*. Munich: Psychologie Verlags Union.
West, M.A. and Wallace, M. (1988). Innovation in primary health care teams: the effects of roles and climates. Paper presented at the Royal Psychological Society Occupational Psychology Annual Conference, University of Manchester. Abstract in *Bulletin of the British Psychological Society*, Abstracts, p. 23.
Zaltman, G., Duncan, R. and Holbeck, J. (1973). *Innovations and Organizations*. Chichester: Wiley.

Author index

Subject index